YOU'LL ALWAYS BE WHITE TO ME

D1601230

YOU'LL ALWAYS BE WHITE TO ME

A Memoir

GARON WADE

You'll Always Be White To Me is a work of nonfiction. Some names and identifying details have been changed.

Cover Design by Ebook Launch

Book Layout by Polgarus Studio

For Niki Wade & Steve Wade.
Thank you for giving me a second chance at life.
I am forever grateful.

And to Jamie, Matteo, & Ema.
In some magical way the world brought the four of us
together.
I will never stop loving you.

Contents

PART ONE

1

ABANDONED

I'M NOT SURE WHEN EXACTLY it happened or how I felt. For years I imagined that my biological mother had carried me in the early morning hours, before the town of Kegalle was awake, and left me on the steps of the local hospital. Did she look back at me as she walked away? Did she cry? Did I? I have spent most of my life thinking that she gave me up because of the civil war that engulfed Sri Lanka. Too little money and no opportunity for a young baby boy. But as time has passed, it has occurred to me that perhaps she wasn't the one who left me on those steps in 1985. Could I have been taken from her? Could she still be looking for me?

I'll never know how long I stayed by myself outside that hospital. To this day I am deeply thankful to the stranger who found me and brought me inside. Later, I was taken to a government-run orphanage surrounded by tea plantations an hour away in the former mountain kingdom of Kandy. I was to be cared for. At least, that was the plan. I spent a number of days at the orphanage, but it was soon decided that I was too malnourished to stay. Someone drove me to the only other place that would take in an infant who hadn't eaten well and had trouble staying hydrated: the Jayamani Malnutrition Center in

Colombo on the southwestern coast of Sri Lanka. Jayamani became my home, surrounded by other children struggling to make it back to health. Coincidentally, it was here that I found my way to life.

In February 1986, a white American couple walked into the Jayamani Center with their three-year-old daughter, Ebony, who they had recently adopted when living in the Philippines. New to Colombo, and still high from the addition of Ebony to the family, they decided they wanted to adopt a boy too. As luck would have it, I was the only boy in Jayamani. Her name was Niki Wade: a short, slight blonde with a radiant smile and an eagerness to learn as much as she could about the world. His name was Steve Wade: tall, brown hair, strong, and extremely affable. They had grown up as a darling on the homecoming court and a football player at two rival schools in Louisiana, but their lives took a sharp turn in the 1970s when they traveled across the Atlantic to become Peace Corps volunteers in Botswana. Changed forever by this experience, they vowed to continue traveling the world. Niki had just finished a month living with a remote tribe in the Philippines as she studied to become an anthropologist. Steve had just completed five years as a consultant for Mellon Bank in Manila before accepting a transfer to Sri Lanka.

And so here they were, staring at me. It took months of visits and paperwork and heartache, but in October 1986 I came to know them as *Mom* and *Dad.* I was carried out of the Jayamani Center in my new parents' arms at ten months old and into a world I could never have dreamed of.

Our home in Sri Lanka at 7 De Soysa Avenue in a small part of Colombo called Mt. Lavinia became my playground, especially the lengthy driveway lined with lush grass to run and pedal my tricycle through. Our ever-present housekeeper, Mr. Twan, with his gentle demeanor and flowing sarong, took me under his wing and I enjoyed eating rice and spicy chicken curry with him. Tortoises crept quietly around the back garden. A young cobra occasionally made an appearance. But probably the best thing about my new home was my big sister, Ebony, who became my leader; I followed her around religiously. Doll-faced, with olive skin and jet-black hair, she gallivanted among our sixteen palm trees, played with Barbies, and read her books effortlessly. I tried my best to copy her every move.

We lived in a 1930s Dutch Colonial–style house 400 yards from the Indian Ocean, and the thick humidity that clung to the night air was pushed down our street by the winds off the sea. After struggling to have children naturally, even undergoing in vitro fertilization (IVF) in Singapore years earlier, my parents now sat in their garden on a blanket watching their two brown children play, a world so far from their small-town homes in south Louisiana. Their parents had found the prospect of them living outside of the United States "scary" and "dangerous" and had expressed their hopes that Mom and Dad would have managed to have "their own kids" by now.

Beyond the glossy exterior, our sprawling home doubled as an unassuming place for officers of the Central Intelligence Agency to hold covert meetings, a CIA safe house. The agency had identified our home as an ideal location through my dad's stepbrother, who lived in the United States and worked at headquarters. At 8 p.m. every Wednesday after Ebony and I were fast asleep, the gate would slowly open and a tall American woman would walk in. Dad would set down a tray of tea and biscuits, leaving the clandestine officer by herself. Fifteen minutes later, her Sri Lankan informant would arrive. These meetings went on for five months and then abruptly ended. Nestled in my crib down the hallway, I slept as secrets were exchanged. These meetings were very much a foreshadowing of the political affairs my new family would find themselves entangled in throughout the world.

In late 1988, after investigating new job opportunities around the globe, Dad made a pitch to Mom.

"Hey, Niki, I have a job offer. Would you and the kids like to relocate to Johannesburg?"

She stared quietly at him.

"Steve, you're crazy if you think I'm taking our two brown children into apartheid South Africa."

"C'mon, honey. South Africa is changing. It's moving toward ending apartheid. Our family could be a part of that change."

"There's no way," she told him again. "You remember what happened in Pretoria."

During their time in neighboring Botswana, Mom had needed higher-level medical care so she crossed the border into South Africa. Once in Pretoria, she stopped a taxi and jumped in. The black driver had initially looked at her stone-faced but then began driving. Moments later they were stopped by white police officers, who berated her for riding in a taxi for "blacks only." They forced Mom out and made her get into a taxi for "whites only." She fumed for weeks over the inequity of it all and felt terribly for the black driver whom she had inadvertently put in a precarious situation.

"But, Niki, my work there will be focused on supporting *black* African businesses. Imagine what an education it will be for Garon and Ebony, both raising them in Africa *and* having a front-row seat to the fall of apartheid."

Dad had thoughtfully appealed to Mom's grand sense of

adventure and her strong desire for equality. They had both grown up with the disgraceful lie of "separate but equal" in the American South.

In February 1989, at age three, as the civil war raged on in the northern part of Sri Lanka, I left the island nation that had almost shown me death before it handed me a ticket to life. Whether my biological mother had placed me on those steps in Kegalle or I had been ripped from her embrace, surely she could never have imagined this moment: her little boy boarding a flight that would take me away from her country forever, across the Indian Ocean, and into Africa.

2

FLINT ROAD

I remember when a rock was young
She and Suzie had so much fun
On my hands and skin and stones

THIS WAS PRECISELY WHAT I imagined the lyrics of Elton John's "Crocodile Rock" to be as they came leaping out of my mouth incorrectly and resounded through our home in South Africa. Everyone has those very first fully formed memories of life—and this is mine. We would finish dinner at our home in Parkwood, clear the table, then Mom and Dad would go over to the black stereo in the living room and put on a "hits of the 1970s" CD.

"Garon, come dance with me, honey," Mom said with a giant grin, swaying her hips from side to side and extending her arms out to meet mine. I rushed over to her and locked my fingers in between hers. I felt as though electricity ran through our bodies as we connected. Mom giggled the entire time we danced, and I couldn't help but laugh in excitement along with her. Then we would switch it up. I would rush over to Dad, and Ebony would run over to Mom.

From Elton, they would slow it down to Gladys Knight and

the Pips' "Midnight Train to Georgia." Georgia. All I knew was that it was somewhat close to where my parents were from and that the woman, Gladys, had a stunning voice. Dad twirled me around with his strong hands and flashed his kilowatt smile. It completely lit up our living room. "You're such a great dancer, buddy," he kindly lied as I fumbled about. "You've got much better moves than your old man."

Parkwood was a wealthy white suburb of Johannesburg and I quickly learned my new address, 9 Flint Road, which I rehearsed proudly in the mirror of my yellow-tiled bathroom. The jacaranda trees that anchored Flint bloomed in the full heat of the African sun, blanketing our neighborhood in brilliant purples and blues. Surrounding our expansive home were ten-foot walls with jagged shattered glass aggressively lining the top. Mom and Dad said it was there to "keep bad people from coming in."

I couldn't imagine who in South Africa we were trying to keep out, as the South African I had come to know best was friendly and cared well for me—my Zulu housekeeper, Grace. Grace stood taller than my petite mom, with wide-set hips, hickory-brown skin like mine, and a commanding spirit. One afternoon as Ebony and I gallivanted around the patio, I fell and scraped my knee. Grace picked me up, took me to our kitchen, and sat me on the counter while I wept. I watched her as she walked over to the refrigerator, picked up a carton of butter, and set it down next to me. She washed my knee with soap and water as I winced and pleaded for her to stop. Then she took a knife, dipped it into the creamy butter, and spread the butter across my wound as if I were a piece of toast.

"What are you doing, Grace?" I asked, never having seen

Mom, Dad, or Mr. Twan spread butter on my skin in Sri Lanka. "Trust me, boy. It will make you feel better," Grace promised. I couldn't tell if the butter made me feel better or not, but if Grace had said so, I felt it was probably true. She seemed to know how everything in our house worked.

Bordering the right side of the house was another big lawn, where we kept a badminton net, and a garage, where I could often find Dad completing fix-it projects, a talent he so effortlessly possessed. To the left side of the house was what Ebony and I called Bumble Bee Alley. It was a long, dimly lit alleyway, home to a maze of vines that provided a nectarous wonderland to a colony of dutiful bees. However, Bumble Bee Alley was to be avoided at all costs. If one of us did have to enter it to retrieve a ball, we would run down screaming and swatting. It led to a back garden—a magical garden in our minds—the place of our Easter egg hunts, treehouse, pool, and a sizable jungle gym.

One chilly afternoon in late May (as winter had descended upon Johannesburg), Ebony and I decided we would sneak inside the pool area and throw Ebony's inflatable toy dolphin into the water. Mom was inside and Dad was working in the garage. They had dressed us in long pants and warm sweaters. While we were allowed to play in the backyard by ourselves, we certainly weren't allowed to breach the pool's gate unless Mom or Dad were with us. Ebony and I took turns tossing the dolphin into the pool, screaming with delight each time we heard the splash. Then we would get on our knees, wait for it to float over, outstretch our arms, and pull it toward the side, only to do it all over again.

When it was my turn again, Ebony handed the dolphin to me. With two hands I moved it behind my right shoulder and then threw it as hard as I could toward the surface of the water. As I let go, I felt myself fly forward, my legs sliding out from underneath me, and I plunged into the freezing pool. As I fell to the bottom, I began to inhale water as I gasped for air and kicked my legs in a frenzy, trying desperately to return to the surface. I didn't know how to swim and I felt my body take over, fighting for survival. As I neared the surface, I flung my arms rapidly back and forth and with wide, terrified eyes I watched as my six-year-old sister grabbed the giant pool cleaner, more than double her size, and threw it into the water toward me, net first. I seized the rim of the net and, pulling as hard as she could, she yanked me toward her. Once I reached the side of the pool, she helped drag me out as I pushed my legs against the pool wall and rolled onto the surrounding brick terrace.

"Are you okay?" Ebony yelled in a hushed tone.

I coughed up water and continued gasping for air. It all happened in an instant and I had been so focused on trying to return to the surface that I hadn't noticed how cold I was. With my sweatshirt and pants soaked, the frigid temperature came racing back to my body.

"I'm okay, but I'm freezing," I told her, trying to catch my breath.

"Quick, let's go to the playhouse before Mom and Dad see us."

Ebony and I both knew we would be in big trouble if they found us. Soaking wet and dripping water everywhere, I followed her as she pushed the pool gate open and raced across the grass to our little wooden playhouse. Likely used as a tool shed by the previous owners, it was tall enough for us to stand up in, and Mom and Dad had allowed us to co-opt it as our own while storing a few miscellaneous items in the corner. Once inside, Ebony peeled my waterlogged sweatshirt, T-shirt, and long pants off and tossed them to the side. I sat shivering, trying to warm myself up, wearing only my underwear. She looked around the playhouse and found an empty burlap sack resting in the corner. Ebony shook it out and wrapped it around my body.

"There. Okay, we have to make sure we don't tell Mom or Dad about this or we'll get in big trouble."

I nodded vigorously. I had spent my fair share of time with both my nose in the corner and in timeout and I didn't want Mom and Dad to know that we had broken their pool rule. The burlap sack felt scratchy against my skin and just as I felt my shivering begin to subside we heard footsteps. Dad stepped into the front doorway of the playhouse.

"Oh, hey guys! What are you up to?"

"We're just playing," Ebony said, standing in front of me.

"Why is Garon all wet?"

Ebony and I looked at each other in silence.

"He fell in the pool," Ebony reluctantly admitted.

"He fell in the pool?" Dad said, concerned. "You guys aren't supposed to be in the pool area. Hang on, I'll get you a towel," he said, heading toward the house.

That was Dad. Kind and protective but somewhat unaware of our antics and content to leave the reprimanding to Mom. We knew that not only would Dad return with towels, but he'd return with Mom.

Minutes later, Mom and Dad, I'm sure feeling equally responsible for not keeping an eye on their kids, didn't scold us or send us to a timeout.

"You guys weren't supposed to be in the pool area. But remember, when something serious like this happens, you have to tell us. We're not going to be upset, but we need to know if you're okay. Please, you should have come to us right after it happened. And we should have been watching," Mom said, looking over at Dad.

Ebony and I never tried breaching the pool gate again. Instead, we played tag around the yard, took turns swinging from bar to bar on our orange metal jungle gym, and showed our Barbies how to get in and out of the treehouse. Most of our days were spent hidden behind these ten-foot walls, unaware of the racial revolution that was slowly starting to unfold in South Africa.

Months after we had settled in on Flint Road, one of the very first things Mom started looking for was a place to enroll Ebony and me in gymnastics classes. One afternoon she took us to a nearby recreational center, home to a huge gymnasium with smaller rooms for martial arts classes. With Ebony and me at her side, our small hands clasped in hers, Mom approached the woman sitting at the front desk.

"Can I help you?" asked the white South African woman.

"Yes, I'd like to see about getting my kids into gymnastics classes, please," Mom said.

The lady took a look at the three of us. In 1989 South Africa, a white mother with two brown children was not something often seen.

"I'm sorry. It's not possible," the receptionist said.

"Not possible to enroll them? Are classes full?"

"Your daughter can come in, but your son cannot because he's too dark."

Mom, fighting the fire inside her, took us both by the hand again and marched us out the front door.

Once home, she erupted in frustration.

"Steve! This is exactly the reason I didn't want to bring the kids to South Africa. You see how they are already being treated?"

Dad felt both helpless and saddened over the entire situation.

"If you want to stay here, that's fine," Mom said. "But I want to take the kids to live in Botswana. I will not put up with this."

In the end, we stayed—largely because later that week my mother met with the woman whom we'd bought our house from, a lovely Englishwoman named Sally Bates. Sally, her husband and two sons had just relocated to a nearby neighborhood. Mom told Sally what had happened at the gymnastics center and Sally was dismayed. Sally had arrived in southern Africa from her native England and found the entire system of apartheid repulsive. She also knew journalists at the *Rosebank-Killarney Gazette* who she felt would be interested in the story.

"TODDLER TURNED AWAY FROM REC CENTER" was the headline splashed across the front of the newspaper, followed by:

> The call for a new South Africa made by state President F. W. De Klerk has fallen on deaf ears . . . and all because the Johannesburg City Council is dragging its feet over the desegregation of buses and recreation centers. Garon is a three and a half year old child. His mother, Niki Wade, is American. Yet a staff member at the Parkhurst Recreation Center recently refused to allow Garon to take part in children's activities there. Why? Because Garon was born to Sri Lankan parents and adopted by Niki and her husband Stephen . . . The Wades, who have a positive attitude toward this country's future, will be in South Africa

for at least two years ... but the rejection of her tiny
son—and the possibility of future rejections—fills
Niki with despair and pain.

The story became widely visible. Our resolution came in the form of an apology phone call from the South African government to my parents. The recreation center called and apologized too, making it clear that I could now be enrolled in gymnastics classes. Mom and Dad decided that even though no other children of color had even been permitted into the gymnasium, we'd be the first to kick that door wide open for South African children.

Mom re-entered the building, again holding each of our hands in her grasp. As the doors flung open, the gymnasium, fully in session, came to a complete halt. We walked the perimeter of the room and found a place to sit. For years as Mom recounted the story, she would say, "Everyone stared at us as I walked with the two of you. It was so quiet you could've heard a pin drop." Ebony and I became the first children of color allowed to be at a public recreational center in Johannesburg. I can't remember feeling the difference between us and the white kids.

Many years later I would read Trevor Noah's memoir *Born a Crime,* often shaking my head as he described his black mother walking a few steps behind him at the park during that very same time period. She had to pretend to be his maid, as interracial relationships weren't permitted. I've long said, the only reason our family got any attention was because my parents were American and were *both* white. Had Trevor Noah's family been turned away from the recreation center, there would have been no article, no outrage, and no apology. It was my very first time understanding the importance of the majority speaking out on behalf of minorities.

On weekends we would ride an hour and a half outside of Johannesburg into the bush. The lions, wildebeest, and rhino that surrounded our car thrilled me beyond words. Animals I had only seen in my picture books now foraged through the bush in what seemed like a dream. I watched from the back of our silver Suzuki as herds of colossal mother elephants and their calves rummaged past us, ripping the bark off trees and snapping their branches. One Sunday we had spent much of the day making our way through a game reserve, and as the sun began to set Mom suggested it was time to head to the exit point. Dad, ever the photographer and proud of his new camcorder, was intent on filming the array of African wildlife that surrounded us. As we drove farther into the bush, we came upon a lone mother elephant and her baby. We drove past them and then Dad brought the Suzuki to a stop. He leaned behind his seat to film the African giants, who were delicately framed in our back window.

"Keep moving forward, Steve. We're too close," Mom said.

"I'm just going to reverse a little to get this shot," Dad countered.

As we slowly started to reverse, Ebony and I were glued to the back window, mouths agape at our proximity to the mother elephant.

"Steve, we are too close," Mom stated again.

"We're not *that* close, Niki."

And then suddenly, without warning, the mother elephant, fearing for her calf, began charging our car.

Dad threw the Suzuki into forward gear. Ebony and I remained glued to the window as we screamed, "Go, Dad! Go!"

living for the thrill of it all but also terrified. The image of an elephant coming after you may feel similar to watching a wall of ocean water rushing toward you. There's a feeling of enormous power and an inevitability that you will most certainly lose this race if the elephant chooses a marathon.

The mother elephant chased us for about thirty seconds, which, if you've ever been chased by an elephant, is more than enough to strike fear in your heart. Dad accelerated the Suzuki forward and gradually the space between us and the imposing beast grew wider. The entirety of the situation remains a video for us to watch because even as Dad drove away he held his VHS camcorder behind him. He captured Ebony and me and our excitement at our close call with one of Africa's most marvelous creatures.

With the orange sun brilliantly setting over the bush, we made our way toward the exit of the reserve, passing herds of zebra. Their black-and-white stripes contrasted sharply with the yellowish gold of their surroundings. The light across the savannah gently left, ushering the magnificent landscape into darkness, with only the sounds of the wild echoing through the night air. I was certain we had moved to the most magical of places.

3

ASHOH

ONE EVENING AFTER WE HAD finished dinner, instead of retreating to the living room to dance, Mom and Dad asked Ebony and me to stay seated at the table. They announced that they had a game for us to play. Now five years old, I of course loved games. But the table was left clear with no board games to set up and the two of them sat staring across it at us with sly smiles.

"We have a surprise for you. There is something on this side of the room with us. It's here, but you can't see it," Mom hinted. "What do you think it is?"

Ebony and I looked at each other and giggled. What did we really want?

"A new toothbrush!" I blurted out.

They laughed. "No, no."

Ebony's turn. "A new book?"

"No"

"Is it a parachute?" I asked.

"No" they said, still laughing. "Garon, what do you need a parachute for?"

"Well, then what is it?" we asked, wide-eyed.

"Okay. It's here on this side of the table with Mommy and

18

Daddy. It's going to be a huge part of your life," they said, furthering their little game.

"Wait, it's in the room right now, but we can't see it?" Ebony asked, confused.

"Yes, it's here with us now."

Ebony and I looked at each other again. How was that possible?

"Would you like for us to tell you?" Dad asked.

"Yes!" we said gleefully, bouncing up and down in our chairs.

"It's a baby," Mom said.

My mouth dropped open.

"You're having a baby?" Ebony asked.

"Yes, sweetie. You two are going to have a little brother."

POSSIBLY THE ONLY THING more exciting than the prospect of having a mysterious little brother was the arrival of our grandma, whom we affectionately called Ashoh (pronounced *Awe-Show*). Did *Ashoh* mean *Grandma* in Tagalog, Sinhala, or Zulu? Not at all. When Ebony was younger, she couldn't say *Grandma* and for reasons unknown came up with *Ashoh*. And so my mother's mom forever was renamed Ashoh.

Standing plumply at five-foot-two, with curly light-brown hair and hazel eyes, this southern white woman became the person we loved the most from a country we didn't yet know well but called "The States." Leaving our grandpa at home in Louisiana, she arrived in South Africa to help with our family's newest arrival. Toward the end of summer, our little brother, Yael, came into the world. We now strolled throughout Parkwood together, possibly one of the most conspicuous families around. A white American mother, father, and grandmother, with a Filipina daughter, Sri Lankan son, and a white blond American baby. Our family had changed for the better, and slowly so was South Africa.

"Y'all go get in the car now with your daddy. You're gonna be late to school." Ashoh, who had grown up in Texas but had raised Mom in Louisiana, brought her glaring southern accent all the way to the bottom of Africa. With Mom busy nursing Yael, Ashoh got us ready each morning for our day at the American International School of Johannesburg, or AISJ. Our schoolmates were from Zimbabwe, Greece, Japan, Argentina, and Australia, to name a few.

I loved my kindergarten classroom decorated in bright colors and with a giant white-and-black alphabet strip lining the walls. While my teacher talked, I squirmed in my seat and chewed on the end of my graphite pencils. They tasted sweet and delicious, unlike the ham sandwiches, celery sticks, and oranges that Mom had packed for me each day.

"Garon, it's important to eat a healthy lunch," she said once when I had complained.

"But the other kids eat fun things like cheese and crackers or pizza."

"I'm not concerned with what other parents are feeding their kids. I'm concerned with you. There are plenty of kids in the world who don't have food. I suggest you appreciate your lunches."

In protest, I decided to start throwing my ham sandwiches in the trash each day at lunch until my teacher noticed and immediately notified Mom. I was then forced to sit next to my teacher at lunch and wasn't allowed to play until I finished my sandwich first. My first attempt at rebellion had finished as quickly as it started.

Once we got home from school, Ashoh would come watch

Ebony and me outside in the backyard while Yael rested in his crib. I don't think Mom and Dad ever really trusted us alone out back after the dolphin-pool debacle. Ashoh told us stories of our little cousins in Louisiana: Jessica, Erin, and Ryan. They were our Uncle Mike's kids, Mom's brother. Ashoh said they lived "down the bayou with their mama."

"Why don't they live with Uncle Mike too?" I asked while swinging from bar to bar on the jungle gym.

"Well, it's complicated," Ashoh said. "Ask your mamma and daddy later tonight."

"Do Jessica, Erin, and Ryan go to an international school?"

"No, it's not international like y'alls. Everyone at their school is from Louisiana."

I wondered why there weren't kids from all over the world at our cousins' school.

"What's a bayou?"

"A bayou is like a swamp. And lots of alligators live there. Just like here in South Africa."

I stopped swinging. "We don't have alligators here, Ashoh. Only crocodiles live in Africa." I didn't know a lot, but I knew that much.

Ashoh tilted her head and looked at me skeptically, trying to decide if I was correct.

"Also, why do you say *y'all?* Mom and Dad don't say that."

Ashoh sighed. "It's just . . . that's what people say in Louisiana. Your mama used to say *y'all* when she was growing up."

I looked at her hands positioned on each of her hips. "Ashoh, why are your hands wrinkly?"

"Lord, Garon. You sure are full of questions, aren't ya. I have a good idea. Let's all have some quiet time until we go back inside."

"Sure, Ashoh," I said, flinging myself off the side of the jungle gym and taking pride in landing on both feet. I looked over at Ebony, who had already been having quiet time reading her book on the grass.

HAVING A LITTLE BROTHER wasn't nearly as exciting as Mom and Dad had promised. Yael couldn't play with me, couldn't talk to me, and everyone spent a considerable amount of time fawning over him. I was proud to be a big brother but not sure what to do with him. One afternoon with Mom indoors nursing Yael, Dad called me to the front yard.

"Garon, I took the training wheels off your bike. It's time we learn to ride this thing without them."

I stared at my red BMX bike, then hopped on confidently. As soon as I felt how unstable I was, I gripped the handlebars tighter.

"Ready? One, two, three . . ."

"Don't let go of me!" I shrieked, craning my neck as far back as my cumbersome helmet would allow, only to be overcome by panic-stricken fear as I watched the gulf between me and Dad increase.

"You're doing just fine, buddy. Keep pedaling!" Dad yelled after me.

"No! I'm going to crash!" I saw our front gate getting closer and closer and felt my BMX begin to topple.

"Buddy, use your brakes! Don't put your legs up, put them down to . . ."

I went flying off the side of my bike, my hands grasping at the fluffy grass as I rolled to a flailing stop. "You let me go!" I complained, lying flat on the lawn.

Dad walked over to me. "I have to let you go, Garon, or you'll never learn how to balance by yourself."

"I don't like this. I don't want to ride without my training wheels."

Dad knelt down in front of me. "C'mon, you were doing great. Remember, buddy, you can do anything you put your mind to. You just have to believe in yourself."

That was the first time I can remember Dad saying those words to me. Looking up at his rich brown eyes, I could see that he thoroughly believed it. I trusted him instantly and begrudgingly got back on.

Some evenings just before bedtime, I stood near the French doors of our white den that looked out on the front yard. Mom sat across from me on the cream sofa holding green-and-white flashcards.

"What's two plus two, Garon?"

"Four."

Next card.

"What's three plus four?"

"Six?"

"No, try again."

"Eight?"

"Almost, try again, buddy."

"Why do we even have to do this? This isn't part of my homework," I said.

Mom put the stack of addition and subtraction flashcards down on the sofa next to her. "Garon, every day people come to your father's office and they ask him questions like these that involve math. He has to know the answer. You need to learn it too."

I envisioned Dad sitting at the desk in his office in downtown

Johannesburg at the Carlton Center. I imagined that at precisely the same time each day a man knocked on his door, walked into his office, and Dad stood up quickly.

"What's three plus four, Steve?" the man would say.

"Seven," Dad replied.

"What's six plus five?"

"Eleven."

They would ask him a couple more math problems and then Dad would sit back down at his desk nervously, hoping he got them correct. I couldn't believe someone asked you math problems your entire life, even once you became an adult.

Toward the end of Ashoh's three months with us, we took her to Lion Park, a reserve that offered many activities but of particular interest to me was the opportunity to feed baby lions out of giant-sized bottles. Ashoh, Ebony, and I held the bottles as squirming cubs crawled across our legs to devour milk.

"Heavens to Betsy! They sure are strong," Ashoh said, being pushed around. "Wait until I tell people back in Louisiana that I fed lion cubs. They'll barely believe it."

When Yael was just days old, we had taken Ashoh on a safari in the nearby Pilanesberg Game Reserve and she had marveled beside me at the magnificence of the giraffes as they walked gingerly past our car. But seeing her try to wrangle lion cubs made me belly laugh and I knew that I would miss having Ashoh with me each day. I had become used to her funny-sounding accent and had tried saying *y'all* a couple times while in the bathtub to see what it felt like. It felt weird. After three months with us, even Grace had been able to understand what Ashoh said, and Ashoh, in turn, understood Grace's Zulu accent.

On my grandma's last day with us, I held her tight and gave her a big kiss on the cheek.

"I love you, Garon. Grandpa and I will be waiting for a visit from y'all in Louisiana."

"MY FEET FEEL NERVOUS!" I yelled.

"What do you mean, honey?" Mom asked as she tried to convince me to walk down the steep winding cliffside in the neighboring mountain kingdom of Lesotho. I could feel the small rocks sliding beneath my feet. Mom and Dad, always eager to travel off the beaten path, had decided to retrace their hitchhiking days through southern Africa from their time in the Peace Corps.

"I mean, I feel like I'm going to fall off the side. My feet are slipping!"

"You're fine, Garon," she said in her soft, gentle voice. "Come to me. I'm not going to let you fall off the cliff." That was the thing about Mom: she never seemed nervous about anything in dangerous situations.

Dad drove the Suzuki extremely slowly behind us with Ebony and Yael in the back as Mom walked ahead to make sure the path was wide enough for the car to continue weaving down the mountain range. I made my way ahead to Mom and grabbed her hand. We were on a narrow ridge in the sepia-colored Maloti Mountains. At our high elevation, the cold wind drifted in and out. Sparse green bushes dotted the arid rock-filled terrain around us. As I looked up to my left, a wall of sandstone rock towered above me. On my right, a sheer drop into the valley, where I feared the small rocks sliding beneath my black shoes would cause me to lose balance and fall off the cliff.

"There's enough space to drive farther ahead," Mom announced confidently back to Dad, who gave her a thumbs up.

They were thrill seekers. I slowly turned myself around and tried to hug the side of the sandstone wall as I climbed back into our car. Mom had been right. There was just enough space for the Suzuki to continue winding down the mountain range, and not much else. Once in the valley that night, we linked up with Peace Corps volunteers and slept in our blue sleeping bags on the floor of a church.

Another school holiday, after I turned six, Dad and I took a solo trip west to Namibia.

"Hold on!" Dad yelled as our yellow raft plunged through the rapids, sending us careening to the side. The frothing white water at every turn elated me as Dad and his friends pushed their oars against massive gray rocks to steer us back to the center. The Orange River originated in the untamed mountains of Lesotho and raced west across South Africa. At the southern border of Namibia, it continued west until it spilled into the mighty Atlantic Ocean. The river felt like a wild animal guzzling us at every turn. Whereas the cliffs of Lesotho had frightened me, the rushing water of the Orange River made me feel alive and I screamed out in excitement as we flew down each successive rapid.

Dad put his arms around me. "Garon, I hope when you grow up, you'll always remember this trip we took together."

"I will, Dad," I promised.

After three days of adrenaline by day and campfires at night in Namibia, we returned to Flint Road in South Africa.

Mom gave me a giant hug as she opened the front door. I was so happy to see Ebony and Yael again. Then I watched as Mom's face changed from happiness to concern.

"Steve! He's so sunburned. Look at his face, his shoulders. Look at the back of his neck," Mom said angrily. "Didn't you put sunscreen on him?"

"I didn't think he needed any," Dad said.

My face and shoulders were indeed sunburned and had begun to peel. I had felt the uncomfortable burning sensation the last day of the trip but didn't know what it was and hadn't said anything. Dad, in true oblivious fashion, hadn't noticed.

"Just because he has brown skin doesn't mean he doesn't need sunscreen on a three-day trip where you had him outside for eight hours a day!"

"I'm so sorry, buddy," Dad said, looking over at me. I didn't blame him. I had a great time on our trip. Mom put aloe vera all over my body that evening as I recounted our high-speed ride down South Africa's longest river to Ebony and Yael.

One weekend, the five of us drove in our silver Suzuki north, crossing into Botswana to revisit Mom and Dad's time in the Peace Corps. Botswana was far more rural than South Africa and sandy unpaved roads lay ahead of us for miles. I loved that feeling of being in the middle of nowhere and the uncertainty of never knowing what might be around the next corner. We pulled up outside the school where Mom had taught. She hadn't been back in fifteen years. There were no big walls, painted murals, or attractive gardens like at my international school. Instead, it was a small cement building with no color. I walked beside Mom as she made her way through the dusty courtyard where Botswanan kids my age chased after each other before stopping to stare at us. Then we stepped up from the sand and into the cement school. Mom seemed a bit nervous and giddy. She asked the receptionist if she could say hi to the office staff. Then she walked into the office, with shorter blond hair than in her years before, and said, "Remember me?"

There was a brief moment of silence and then the celebrating began.

"Niki!" "Niki's back!" screamed the Botswanan women who thrust themselves upon her. Mom wrapped her arms around them as though they were her family from a different time. I watched the commotion in wonder and saw how much Mom loved these women as tears fell from her face. They loved her right back, as much as I did. It seemed everyone who met Mom felt the same way. I can remember looking at her surrounded by her friends and for the first time I realized that she had an entire life before adopting us. They had of course told us of their years before in southern Africa, but it had never made sense to me until now.

Her experience teaching young Botswanan children in the 1970s had evolved into quite a different classroom during our life in Johannesburg. Mom was now a sex education teacher for South African young adults amid the developing HIV crisis. Occasionally, Dad would drive us over to Mom's class to pick her up. I would sit in a wooden chair outside her classroom with my legs dangling in the air. Through the glass window of the door I could see her standing before her students, teaching them about safe sex practices. As a result, sex was not a taboo topic in our home, and I can remember hearing the word *sex* well before ever hearing the words *God* or *religion*. I imagine for most people it's the opposite.

"Sex," Mom said, "is a normal, healthy part of life. It's also how babies are made. But it's something for adults, not for kids. It's for when you're older."

I wondered if Ashoh had ever had sex.

THERE WAS SOMETHING extraordinarily special about South Africa that resonated in my young heart. Perhaps because it was the country of so many of my firsts: The first time I realized how much Mom and Dad loved each other was after "Midnight Train to Georgia" faded out. Dad would walk over to that black stereo and put on "The Lady in Red" by the British-Irish singer/songwriter Chris de Burgh. Then he'd walk over to Mom, take her hands, and pull her close to him. Ebony and I would watch near the blue sofa as the two of them would gently sway from side to side together, staring into each other's eyes for even just a moment before they looked over at the two of us. As confident and adventurous as Mom was, when Dad pulled her close to him to dance, I saw her vulnerability. And as they moved softly to the soulful music, Dad too seemed to melt into Mom.

The first time I realized how loved I was and would forever be part of our family was in the late afternoons on weekends. Dad would gently place Yael in the middle of their king-sized bed and Ebony and I would pile in. With Mom on one side, and Dad on the other, I felt protected as they secured the three of us between them. We played with Yael's thin blond hair and asked them lots of questions.

"Why did you name him Yael?" Ebony asked.

"We loved the way it sounded," Mom said.

"Where is it from?" I asked.

"There's a university in the States called Yale. But we wanted to spell it differently for your brother," Dad explained.

"Tell us our adoption stories!" I said, and Mom would launch into a long story of how they found us in the Philippines and Sri Lanka while running her soft hands through my black hair.

"Kids who are adopted are chosen. We chose you. We searched for you and we chose you and we love you. Don't ever let anyone make you feel that somehow it's less meaningful to be adopted than be a biological child, like how Yael came to us."

"That was from sex," I announced, proud of knowing the right answer.

"That's right, honey," Mom said.

DAD HAD CONVINCED Mom to move to South Africa, hoping to be a part of the change of the country. He had bet correctly. I don't remember how I felt the day in February 1990, the year before Yael was born, when Nelson Mandela had been released from prison on Robben Island after twenty-seven years of incarceration, but I knew it was big news. Mom and Dad had talked about it for days thereafter among themselves and each time friends came over, while having drinks on the veranda. And while I couldn't fully wrap my young brain around what it all meant, I knew that I would know about Nelson Mandela for the rest of my life.

"South Africa is starting to understand that black and white people should be given all the same rights," Mom had told me. "Everyone deserves to be treated equally. Anything less is not okay."

We had been given a front-row seat to the slow crumble of apartheid and a movement was underway to unite the country.

"Nelson Mandela will likely be the president here one day. What a great day that will be," Dad said.

After three and a half years on Flint Road and with Dad's contract now complete, we drove to the airport, leaving all I had known and come to love behind. From the back of the car I waved a final goodbye to our house. I don't think I ever thought we would leave. A child's mind can be so inquisitive and yet so naive at the same time. We boarded the aircraft that was to take us northeast to Kenya and then connect onto Europe, where we would catch a third flight to the United States. Ebony jumped eagerly into the window seat just over the wing. I sat in the middle, Mom in the aisle, and Yael and Dad sat across from us. As we prepared to push off the gate, I looked over at Mom, only to find tears streaming down her face.

"Why are you crying?" I asked.

Through a haze of tears Mom held my hand in hers and said, "Because I've loved it here, honey. I've really loved it here."

That memory has stayed with me throughout my life. I remember in that moment looking from her tear-soaked face back out the window. I realized for the very first time that we were actually leaving forever. Somewhere deep in my heart I knew, one day, I would need to find my way back to South Africa.

4

GUMBO

"NIKI AND THE KIDS ARE HERE!" I could hear
Ashoh scream as we approached the yellow
front door of her home on Bernice Drive in the
sleepy south Louisiana town of Luling. Moisture gripped the air
and the smell of slightly decayed leaves lifted from the plush St.
Augustine grass all around us. Luling was a quick twenty-
minute drive across the river from New Orleans, where bald
cypress trees ornately decorated with hanging Spanish moss
created a hauntingly vibrant world below the interstate. Luling
rested serenely along the west bank of the Mississippi.

The house, a two-story red-brick home, sat along a peaceful
street that ended in an idyllic cul-de-sac. As soon as Ashoh
opened the door, we attached ourselves to her. We had last seen
her one year before, when she left South Africa. We then made
our way to hug Grandpa, whom I knew mostly from stories.
Though I couldn't remember him well, I had spent time with
him when I was two years old on a brief trip back to "The
States" while living in Sri Lanka. Ashoh and Mom hugged and
cried while Dad was busy rolling our suitcases up the long red-
brick driveway lined with bushy liriope.

"Come in! Come in! I made y'all some gumbo," Ashoh said.

Dad had made gumbo for us a couple times on Flint Road. I loved the way the white rice soaked into the steaming rich mixture of seafood and okra.

"Now tell me. How was y'alls trip?" Ashoh said. "You must be exhausted."

We spent the rest of the evening sitting around their oval kitchen table sharing stories of the many flights we had taken to get to Louisiana.

Bright and early the next morning, my grandpa, Petie, short with sun-spotted skin and thinning light-brown hair, leaned up against the doorframe of his garage, an unlit cigarette in one hand and a Coors in the other.

"What's goin' on, Rambo?" he asked. I knew he meant me, but I wondered why he called me Rambo. "Ashoh said you kept her busy in Africa." I smirked up at him.

Spanning the length of his tall freezer, Grandpa had posted a five-foot cardboard cutout of three ladies—a blond, a redhead, and a brunette—running down the beach. They seemed extremely excited about something. Across their swimsuits printed in big letters was the same name as the beer he was drinking.

"Those are some good-lookin' gals," he told me. "You gotta find you one that looks like that, Garon." I nodded in agreement to please him.

"Why do you keep the ladies out here in the garage, Grandpa?" I asked innocently.

"Because that grandma of yours won't let me keep them in the house."

Luling was hot and sticky and Grandpa's garage smelled of fragrant smoke. When it met the humidity, swirling upward in the garage, I would cautiously inhale, trying desperately to understand what it was. "This is the only place your grandma will let me smoke anymore," he lamented. I wondered what it felt like to smoke. Mom and Dad had said it was bad and that Grandpa was something called *addicted.* At the edge of his back patio, Grandpa had collected all his old Coors cans in a white bucket. "Wanna smash some?" he asked me.

"Yes," I replied, looking eagerly at the sledgehammer leaning against the doorway.

"Here, let me help ya," he said, lining up two cans. Then he stood behind me and helped me crush the beer cans into small aluminum pancakes. My face lit up with surprise.

"Now don't let your grandma see you trying to do that by yourself or I'll be in the doghouse," he told me.

It became my favorite thing to do with him and I looked forward to it each day. When we were done, I would collect all the crushed cans and pile them together.

"Good job, Rambo. Now I can take them cans down to the store and get some coins for them," Grandpa said.

WHEN I WASN'T trying to inhale Grandpa's smoke in the garage or watching his two schnauzers chase squirrels around his backyard, I was kept busy by the influx of Ashoh's friends who had heard we were "in town" and routinely dropped by.

"Now just look at him! Look. At. Him!" yelled Ms. Pepper in her Cajun accent with a hand on each hip as she stood in the middle of Ashoh's kitchen talking a mile a minute and staring at me. Ms. Pepper was Ashoh and Grandpa's neighbor five houses down who would roll in unexpectedly and command any room she stood in.

"Hi, Ms. Pepper," I said dutifully, looking up at her loose

curly brown hair, Saints T-shirt, and golden cross. In South Africa we had called all our parents' friends "Aunt" or "Uncle," but I had come to understand that here in Louisiana everyone called people "Ms." this or "Mr." that.

"Isn't he just precious?" Ms. Pepper said, shaking her head back and forth. "I tell all my friends, you know Niki and the kids been livin' in Africa! I can barely keep track of y'all. I'm lucky if I get to Mississippi!" Ms. Pepper roared with laughter.

Even at a young age, I loved Ms. Pepper's thick Cajun accent. It wasn't like Ashoh and Grandpa's accent or like anyone's voice I had heard at my international school in South Africa.

On Friday nights, we would all pile into Ashoh and Grandpa's tan minivan with red carpeting and head twenty minutes up the road to a lively seafood restaurant called Spahrs, which was right on the edge of the bayou. I sat with my face pressed against the glass window opening onto the marshy waters, hoping to catch a glimpse of one of the alligators Ashoh had told me about.

In the middle of dipping my catfish in ketchup, I realized I didn't have anything to wipe my mouth with.

"Why don't you go ask the waitress over there, honey," Mom said to me.

I got out of my chair and walked over to the waitress, who was just finishing up her conversation with a nearby table.

"Excuse me," I said, looking up toward her.

"Well hey there, darlin'. What can I get you?" she said.

"Can I please get a couple serviettes?" I asked politely.

"I'm sorry, what is it you need, baby?"

"Serviettes, please."

"Servi— what is it, darlin'?"

Mom rushed over to me and put her hand on my shoulder. "Oh, honey. Here in the States they say *napkins* instead of *serviettes.* Try saying *napkins.*"

"Can I please have some . . . napkins?" I tried again.

"Oh, napkins! Of course. I'll be right over," the waitress said.

"Napkins," I said to myself quietly as I returned to the table. I'd never heard of that. Everyone in South Africa said serviettes.

ON BRIGHT SUNNY DAYS, often when returning from doctors' appointments in New Orleans, Mom and Dad would drive us around Luling.

"Look. That's where I used to keep my cow, Betsy," Mom said, pointing at a small green pasture that ran parallel to the levy. I imagined Mom in the field as a young girl standing on a stool to pet Betsy's head.

"And that was my high school. Hahnville High School," Mom said as we drove by. I stared at the gold and purple lettering and pictured her walking out the doors after school with her friends. I wondered what my life would be like when *I* got old enough to go to high school.

If we were really good, our car would pull into McDonald's and Ebony and I would begin shrieking in happiness while Yael watched our reaction, strapped into his car seat. Nothing in the world tasted as good as a Happy Meal. As soon as the box was in my hands, I would tear it open to see what toy I got. Then, after inhaling my cheeseburger and fries, we would run into the play area, throw ourselves down the slide into the ball pit, and emerge for air only to do it all again. I couldn't believe how lucky American kids were to live just blocks from McDonald's every day of their life where they got toys just for ordering a meal.

As we drove back to Bernice Drive, Mom pointed out an enormously thick, towering oak tree along River Road.

"Look at how beautiful that tree is, guys," Mom told us. "It's been here for hundreds of years."

"So it was here when you were growing up?" I asked excitedly.

"Yes."

"So when you were a little girl, our age, you used to see that tree?"

"Yes, honey. It's always been here," Mom said, chuckling.

I found that incredible. I imagined Mom at my age, sitting in the backseat of Ashoh and Grandpa's car, looking out the window the same way I was, staring at the same oak tree. What was it like for her to grow up here? I imagined her blond hair in pigtails, smiling and laughing. Could she ever have imagined as a little girl that her life would take her away from this small, quiet American town and across the world to Ebony, Yael, and me?

Later that evening at dinner, we all sat at the table, a heap of steaming shrimp at the center. I carefully peeled my boiled shrimp the way Mom and Dad had taught me. I thought it was weird that I could still see their small beady black eyes and I hated the way their antennae whisked against my wrist as I ripped their heads off and cast them aside. Mom and Dad asked about their many friends who still lived in Luling and what, if anything, had changed.

"Well, you can't go over to Paul Maillard Road anymore. The blacks all live that way now. Ain't safe," Grandpa said.

Ashoh nodded in agreement with a shrimp in hand. Mom and Dad glanced at each other and didn't reply.

Why couldn't we go over there? We had just left South Africa, where almost everyone was black.

"WHERE ARE WE GOING?" Ebony asked from the back of the red rental car.

"I'm taking you guys to see your cousins in Des Allemands," Mom said as we sped down the bayou. I wondered what animals, besides alligators, lived in the green murky waters and I imagined what it would be like if I somehow got lost in the thick marsh by myself.

"Why don't they live with your brother?" I asked, trying to remember.

"We talked about that, honey. Remember, it's because Uncle Mike and their mom, Aunt Tammy, got a divorce. Now they only live with their mom."

"Oh yea," I said. While we hadn't seen a lot of our cousins, Mom had made sure while living in South Africa to tell us stories of their life. She'd remember each of their birthdays and sometimes would send them postcards from Malawi, Swaziland, or Zimbabwe.

"Here they are!" Mom said. Jessica, Erin, Ryan and Aunt Tammy were out front of their modest cinderblock home with their other set of grandparents, who lived right next door. We jumped out of the car and gave our cousins hugs. Mom had given us beaded bracelets from South Africa to hand to them.

"Hi, Tammy!" Mom said and they embraced each other. Tammy had long brown hair, sounded like Ms. Pepper, and she and Mom seemed to get along just fine.

"Y'all come inside," Tammy said, leading the way.

Once inside, the two of them talked, and we disappeared into Jessica, Erin, and Ryan's rooms. I wondered if their mom let them go to McDonald's all the time to get Happy Meals. Erin took us to her room and showed us her bed.

"Push on it. Guess what's inside?"

I pushed against her bed and felt the ripple move through and the sloshing of something.

"What is *that*?" Ebony asked.

"I got a waterbed!" Erin said proudly.

"You have water inside your bed?" I asked, full of envy.

"Yea! It's so cool. Do y'all not have waterbeds in Africa?"

I had never heard of sleeping on a bed with water inside it. Between this and Happy Meals, I was convinced that our American cousins had the coolest life. They sounded different than us, looked a lot different than us, and lived in a much different home than us, and yet I felt a strong connection to these three kids whom I barely knew.

SOON THE LOUISIANA SUMMER was coming to a close. I stood in the living room, staring at Ashoh's alluring cherry grandfather clock, waiting for the chimes to sing to me. I was mesmerized as the clock struck six and the golden pendulum swung back and forth. Then I raced to the kitchen for dinner. Grandpa sat at the head of the table, with Ashoh to his left, and the rest of us piled in around the oval table.

"So where y'all moving now?" Ashoh asked as we all sat around a heaping tower of crabs, boiled red potatoes, and buttered-up corn. Ashoh knew as well as we did that the end of summer meant a move to a far-off country.

"Well, Mother, we're moving to Hawaii," Mom said with a grin.

"Hawaii!" Ashoh exclaimed, dropping her crab claw. "Niki, now why on earth would y'all move to Hawaii?"

5

BETWEEN CONTINENTS

"MAINE, NEW HAMPSHIRE, VERMONT, MASSACHUSETTS, Rhode Island, Connecticut, New York," I called out loud. It was our morning game that Dad had created for me to learn the American states from north to south, starting on the east coast. He would say them and I would repeat them as we drove each day from Waikoloa, where we lived, to Waimea, where we went to school.

"You're doing great, Garon! A couple more weeks of this and you'll be able to say all fifty states," Dad said, looking at me in the rearview mirror. Ebony used the thirty-minute ride each morning to snooze with her head resting against the window. Since Dad was between international development projects and we had no new country to go to, he and Mom had decided to try out life on the Big Island.

Most of my new friends at the Hawaii Preparatory Academy, a state-of-the-art private K–12 school, were, not surprisingly, almost all Hawaiian. It was my first time in a school where all the kids were from the same place. The elaborate cafeteria, modern playgrounds, and giant colorful classrooms reminded me of AISJ.

"Garon, where are you from?" my first-grade teacher asked me on my first day of class.

"I . . . I'm . . . I was adopted from Sri Lanka and I moved here from South Africa. My mom and dad say we're American."

No one had ever really asked me to explain where I was from before. I hadn't imagined that the answer would be as complicated as it sounded coming out of my mouth.

"We are very happy to have you here with us. Class, let's all give Garon a warm Hawaiian welcome."

"Aloha!" my classmates said in unison.

"Aloha," I said back shyly with a small wave.

The shores of Hawaii were a far cry from the bush of South Africa. On the weekends, we would snorkel around the beaches in Waikoloa, screeching in excitement each time we saw even the smallest fish. I huffed and puffed while attempting to use my snorkel correctly, never quite getting it right, and most often ended up inhaling ocean water. After I had ingested more Pacific saltwater than I could handle, I ditched my snorkel and rested on the rock walls. My dark-brown eyes chased tanned surfers who seemed to effortlessly wrangle powerful waves. Speeding toward me with the blue swell rapidly rising behind them, it seemed to me that they were from another world entirely.

Yael was quickly moving from a stationary but needy infant to a roaming toddler, and Ebony had mastered the older sister role, bossing us both around and putting on family performances in our living room. I loved following her lead. She made theater programs on folded pieces of paper on which she listed herself as The Director, Producer, Writer, Lead Actor and me—a mere *assistant actor*. I'm sure Mom and Dad had trouble keeping up with the three of us, but they made it look easy. While I had expected to be thrilled by our new home along the Pacific Ocean, it brought a number of unexpected encounters. One evening while Dad was out, Ebony and I sat in our condo reading in the living room while Yael rested in his crib. Suddenly Mom got up and walked to the window.

"Did you guys hear that?" she asked.

I looked around. I hadn't heard anything. "No," I said. Ebony hadn't either, but sensing Mom's concern she looked unsettled.

"No, listen," Mom said, now sticking her head out the front door. I rushed over.

I could hear the distant yelling and arguing in the condo across from us reverberating through the air from the second floor.

"He's hitting her," Mom said quietly to herself.

I heard a slap and a woman crying. Mom rushed back in the door and reached for the phone. "I'm calling the police!" she said forcefully. Within minutes the police were out front in the parking lot between our condo and theirs. Mom told us to stay inside and walked outside to tell the officers what she had heard. I followed. Ten minutes later the officers came back down the gray staircase.

"Is she okay?" Mom asked.

"The lady who lives there says everything is fine. She's not pressing charges," one of the officers said. Then they climbed in their cars and sped away.

Mom walked back in our condo, shaking her head. I could see the anger and disappointment all over her face. I thought that because adults told their kids not to hit, that meant that none of them did it to each other either. While Mom and Dad certainly had their occasional disagreements, I had never seen either of them hurt each other. As I lay in my bed that night, I wondered if the lady across the way was still crying.

Just as I had been excited to get to school each day in South Africa, I now couldn't wait for my school day to start in Waimea.

The Hawaiian kids had welcomed me in quickly and our teacher had taught us songs in Hawaiian while she strummed a ukulele. Twice a week we would board a school bus that would take us to a different part of campus, where we would all take part in swimming lessons. As I sat with my shirt off and my towel on my lap, I noticed one of the other boys in class, Ned, looking my way.

"Hey, Garon. Why are your nipples so small?"

I looked down at my two brown nipples. Then I looked at all the other shirtless boys seated around me. Ned was right, mine were so much smaller than theirs.

"I don't know," I said, embarrassed. I lifted my towel and placed it over my shoulders while Ned and the boy he was sitting next to laughed. When I got home that afternoon, I found Mom and Yael in the kitchen. I sat down on the white-tile floor and pushed Yael's blue and red toy cars toward him. I loved the adorable sounds he made when we played together.

"Mom, are my nipples too small?" I asked, looking up at her.

"What? Are your nipples, what?"

"Too small?"

Mom put the knife down that she had been using to cut cucumbers. "Honey, why are you asking me that?"

"Ned at school said on the way to the pool today that my nipples were small. Then he laughed."

Mom knelt down on the kitchen tile to my eye level. "Garon, there is nothing wrong with your nipples. Everyone's body is different and yours are perfect the way they are."

I smiled, feeling much better. "Thanks, Mom."

Later that weekend I skipped over to a neighbor's condo a couple doors down. His parents were having a barbecue in the backyard.

"Come inside! I want to show you what I found," Taylor said, waving me in. I said hi to his parents and then wandered into the living room.

"This way," he said. I followed him down the short hallway and walked into his parents' bedroom. Taylor pulled the door closed and pointed behind the door.

"Look! These are my parents' guns," he said excitedly. Two rifles lay upright against the wall.

"That's pretty cool," I said, looking at them quizzically. I had only ever seen guns on safaris in Africa, but I never knew that people had them in their houses too.

"Yea, I just wanted to show you."

Satisfied with his show and tell, Taylor led me back outdoors to the barbecue. While the moms sat outside in folding chairs, a number of the dads were crowded around the grill.

"Garon, we're grilling oysters. Have you ever had oysters?" Taylor's dad asked.

I shook my head. "No." I had heard Ashoh and Grandpa talk about oyster po'boys, but I'd never had one.

Taylor's father took his silver spatula, scooped an oyster off the grill, and handed it to me. "Here, you just dig out that middle part and eat it."

I took my fingers and ripped out the center, then dropped it into my mouth. It felt slimy on my tongue and I made a surprised face as the plump flesh popped in my mouth and salty water whirled down my throat. I thought they were delicious.

"Thank you," I said politely.

"Glad you liked it."

One of the other dads was standing around the grill, flush and red, with a beer in hand. "Boy, those will make your penis hard," he said, laughing. The other dads chuckled with him.

I didn't know what they meant. How could an oyster make my penis hard?

Later, I walked back to our condo. "Did you have fun at Taylor's house?" Mom asked while folding our laundry.

"Yea, it was fun. Guess what Taylor showed me?"

"What?"

"He took me to his parents' room and showed me their guns." Mom put the shirt she had been folding down on the sofa, reached for my arm, and pulled me toward her.

"Garon, did either of you pick up the guns or touch them?"

"No," I said, immediately seeing the seriousness in her eyes.

"Honey, thank you for telling me. Listen. Guns are very, very dangerous. Here in America, people can sometimes have them in their homes. If any of your friends ever show you their parents' guns, I need you to go to their parents immediately and have them call me. And never ever touch them. Promise?"

"I promise."

"I need to go talk to Taylor's parents now," Mom said, and she walked toward the front door. I had planned on asking her how an oyster could make my penis hard but sensed that it wasn't the right time.

"Ebony, please watch your brothers. I'm just going next door for a moment." I don't remember ever going to Taylor's home alone again.

"YOU KIDS WANT to see a volcano erupting?" Dad said, standing in the doorway to our room with a knowing smile.

"A volcano!" Ebony and I yelled together, elated at the idea. Yael, who was too young to understand, looked excited at our exuberance.

Later that evening, the five of us stood a safe distance away from the lava flows of Kilauea. It was majestic. I marveled as the fiery orange lava cascaded down the side and spilled into the Pacific Ocean. My young mind felt bad for the fish below, who I imagined were boiling to death. It was and still is one of the most remarkable things I have ever seen. As the sun tucked away beyond the clouds and darkness enveloped us, the glowing orange lava took on a life of its own diving headfirst into the Pacific.

"That was so cool!" I said on the way back to the car. Life on the Big Island—the crushing waves and breathing volcanoes— had revealed a new wonderment of nature, distinctly different and yet equally as alluring as the roar of the African wild.

AS THE YEAR went on, there were more evenings when I found Mom standing with her head outside the front door. The man upstairs would hit his wife and we would hear her cries from above. Mom had called the police once more, but each time they would come down the same staircase and say, "She doesn't want to press charges."

One Sunday afternoon I was sitting in the condo's jacuzzi with Mom while Dad hung out at home with Ebony and Yael. We heard the gate to the communal pool area unlock. It was him. He walked over with his wife and they climbed into the jacuzzi with us. She had long, light-brown hair and smiled at me. He wore a silver chain against his hairy chest and didn't.

"It says *no kids in the jacuzzi*," he said to Mom, pointing to the sign.

I looked at Mom, then stood up to get out.

"No, Garon, sit down," Mom said sternly to me. Then she

turned to him. "I know what it says. I spoke to the property manager and he said as long as parents are here, it's fine."

"But the sign says *no kids in the jacuzzi*," he said combatively. I was intimidated by him but had no doubt that Mom would protect me. His wife, no longer smiling at me, stared into the bubbling water, expressionless.

Mom glared back at him. "If you have a problem with it, go talk to the property manager," she insisted.

We all sat in an awkward silence. Later that afternoon when we got home, Mom told us, "I know he hits her. But I'll be damned if I'm going to let him bully me and my kids."

After just one year of volcanoes, snorkeling, and our neighbor's domestic abuse, Dad got an assignment overseas. "Where are we moving to now?" Ebony asked.

6

DRIFTWOOD

AS OUR PLANE DECELERATED DOWN the runway, I pushed my face up against the window intently. The roar of the reverse thrust exhilarated me. I was seven years old and back in Africa—we had never been to this part of the continent before. There were no other airplanes in sight and the terminal was a small two-room block of concrete. As we taxied forward, my eyes landed on a group of men waving our airplane in. To my surprise, standing alongside them was Dad, dressed in a blue button-down shirt and long brown pants. He waved up toward my window.

"Look! Dad's down there," I yelled through the cabin.

He had flown ahead of us to secure a home and get things ready. As soon as the air stairs touched the ground, Ebony, Yael, Mom, and I rushed down to jump in his arms.

"Welcome to The Gambia, guys!" Dad said, wrangling us. Over the past month I had missed how much vitality he brought to our morning drives to Waimea and seeing his brilliant smile again set me at ease.

After moving through passport control, which consisted of one man sitting at a wooden desk with a stamp, we walked outside and I leapt off the concrete and into the umber earth.

The humidity that had coated my body daily in Hawaii had now been replaced by a dryer warm breeze that became visible as the mahogany dust swirled upward from the ground. We drove out of the airport and the sun started to fade in the West African sky, melting along the horizon into the thick sand roads that lay ahead for miles.

"You guys are going to love it here," Dad promised through the rearview mirror. I could already feel the excitement rising in my body.

Night fell upon Banjul and the only sign of light on our journey were the headlights of passing cars. Soon we pulled up to our new house and stepped out into complete darkness.

"I can't see anything," I said.

"Follow me, guys, I have candles and flashlights in the house," Dad replied.

This would be our new normal. A life with little electricity. I found it mystical, wonderous, and very scary.

We walked through the pitch-black entryway. Dad was careful to show us where stairs lay ahead. Guided by candlelight, we followed him down the long hallway that led to his and Mom's room. And finally three very tired kids, who had crossed the world once more, piled into our parents' bed. In moments we were fast asleep.

I woke up the next morning to Mom's hand stroking my hair and the soothing sound of her voice.

"Hey, guys, wake up. It's your first morning in The Gambia."

I slowly opened my eyes. How long had we slept? The sun was high and filtering through the windows. My eyes quickly settled on two new faces. Crouched down next to Mom was Agnes, our housekeeper, and Juju, our gardener. Their deep, rich brown skin was similar to mine.

"Good morning," they said.

"Good morning," I replied sleepily, knowing very quickly that these two would become my new friends.

Ebony and Yael, always a bit slower than me in the mornings, continued to sleep. I jumped out of bed, eager to get a good look at my new life. A maze of a home, not opulent, but extremely large, revealed itself to me in the light of the late morning. I ran down the long hallway, poking my head in each of the empty bedrooms. Then I raced over to the towering wooden front door, desperate to see the outside.

And what an outside it was. The tropical landscape of Hawaii had been replaced by a dirt wonderland. An enormous cocoa-colored yard wrapped around the entire home, more than enough space for us to run and play. Tall leafy plants leaned against the medium-sized walls that bordered our home. I walked up to the black iron gate and looked out at our neighborhood. I loved that there were no paved roads around us. It was nothing like our wealthy Parkwood neighborhood in South Africa, but instead reminded me of the rough rural roads we used to ride as we made our way through Botswana. In those days I had always felt like a courageous explorer as our Suzuki wheels kicked dirt into the air, and these roads that now surrounded my new home made me feel much the same.

I raced down the cement walkway, finding little enclaves where Ebony, Yael, and I could hide and create our own imaginary worlds. I followed the exterior wall until I came to an opening without a gate and passed through. Adjoining our yard was an entire new plot of coffee-colored land big enough for another home. I soon learned that this was the grounds of our home too, and over the first couple months that space became our utopia. We planted a watermelon garden and spent hours climbing the many mango trees. I would bite into the sour, unripened mangoes, my face wincing with every bite. Short and toned, with a shy smile and kind eyes, Juju allowed me to follow him around the yard as he tended to each plant.

"Juju, where do you live?" I asked.

"I live in a village half hour away."

"Did you grow up there?"

"Yes."

"I want to go to your village sometime. Can I?"

"Yes, if your parents allow."

My curiosity was instantly satisfied by his answer.

"Juju, look, I can stop the water," I said, causing a kink in the hose while he tried to hydrate a nearby lime tree.

"That's very good," he said, holding the waterless hose, waiting patiently for me to release it.

"Juju, now watch me climb this mango tree, okay?"

"Yes. I'm watching you now," he said generously.

Juju was an angel. He smiled graciously and took me along with him, never once showing the annoyance I'm so positive at times he felt.

EACH MORNING AFTER we finished breakfast and brushed our teeth, a blue Jeep Cherokee would pull into the driveway. Standing outside the car was a man we all came to love; his name was Baboucarr. Originally from neighboring Senegal, he was tall, with gorgeous blue-black skin, handsome features, and strong hands. He was Dad's driver and started his weekdays taking us to our school, the Banjul American Embassy School (BAES). Ebony and I would pile into the Jeep and Baboucarr would glance back to make sure we were buckled in. With a contagious smile, he would take his *The Immaculate Collection* cassette out, put it in his player, and we would take off down the sandy roads. Madonna became the soundtrack to our mornings and from the backseat of the Cherokee, Ebony and I begged Papa not to preach and Baboucarr was a virgin touched for the very first time. To this day, when those songs come on, I think of him.

In the afternoon when our school let out, Mom would pick us up in her gray Peugeot, a tiny French car that she loved. We would leap in, recount the highlights of our day, and drive through Banjul to our neighborhood of Fajara. Once coming off the main paved road, Mom would step on the gas and we would shoot through two blocks of sand, trying to make it as far as we could. Inevitably, one block away from the house, the Peugeot would come to a halt and we would feel the wheels begin to spin. Ebony and I would jump out of the car and push it the rest of the way home. This became our normal.

All the sand that filled the city didn't end until it reached the Atlantic Ocean just a short ten minutes from our home. It was here that we spent most of our weekends. Ebony, Yael, and I would trot through the surf, collecting shells, and greet the Gambians who were walking the beach. The beaches of Banjul were untouched, untraveled, and quiet; a stark contrast to the bustle of the touristy Hawaiian beaches we had recently left.

Mom loved walking up and down, collecting pieces of driftwood, and it became our special thing we did together while everyone else played in the sand. Uniquely shaped pieces of wood that had been tumbled through the Atlantic waters had then been tossed along the shore, rendering themselves a piece of art with a smooth exterior. Their unruly shapes captivated my imagination. Where had these pieces of wood started? How long had they traveled beneath the blue currents? I felt that we were similar to them: wanderers of the world, finding our way to the shores of new and unexpected countries.

On occasion Mom and Dad's friends would join us on the beach. One couple, American Peace Corps volunteers who had also found their way to the west coast of Africa, would join us in the late afternoon. They would throw me on the back of their motorcycle and rocket up and down the beach. The speed thrilled me. Ebony and I would boogie board through the blue cresting waves, sand lodging into our legs as we crashed our way into the surf, gulping water, snot running out of our noses, and then diving back into the Atlantic to do it all over again. On the beach under a palm tree sat two white plastic tables and matching chairs sunken into the sand in front of a small makeshift shed just feet away. It was the only place on the beach to buy a Fanta or Coke.

In this tin-roofed shack, a scratched-up black radio sat on the top shelf. As the sun set over the coastline, Lionel Richie's "All Night Long" would come flowing through the dusk air. We watched the sun liquefy into the ocean, the light dimming around us. We had found peace in this tiny country. These weekend nights spent with Lionel Richie, the orange fading of the light and roar of the ocean, was a dream for our little family of five. Africa had once again awoken in me a love that I would chase the rest of my life.

7

BABOONS & CHIPS

THE AROMATIC SOIL OF THE GAMBIAN earth permeated the air. I jumped out of bed at 6 a.m., threw on my black Reeboks, unhinged the big iron gate, and sauntered down the road to the tiny corner store to buy a baguette for our family breakfast. It was my daily chore that Mom and Dad had assigned me. I reveled in my early morning walks because for the first time in my life I felt a certain level of independence. Early morning workers passed me as dawn light crept into the West African sky, nodding at me, and me to them. It was a world of difference from our Louisiana summers, where Ashoh would tell us "Y'all don't talk to strangers" and Ebony and I would watch episodes of *Rescue 911* when our parents weren't looking. We had filled our heads with kidnappings and tales of distress, but none of that fear existed for me as I walked alone through my neighborhood on my quest to get us toasty fresh bread each morning.

Upon returning home, I tossed the baguette down on the kitchen table and checked to see if everyone was up and moving. They were. As soon as we finished our fresh bread with Swiss cheese and honey, Ebony and I piled into the backseat of Baboucarr's jeep and off we went. Rolling through the streets of Fajara singing, the three of us were Material Girls.

PE (physical education) was one of my favorite classes, allowing me the freedom to run, not having to listen to teachers constantly ask me to sit down and focus. The fourteen of us joined our teacher in the grassless soccer field. Just as we were getting ready to form a circle and begin stretching, we noticed the school security guard excitedly heading our way. With a big smirk he held a bag of Lay's potato chips. Trotting behind him was an adult baboon. Naturally, we were all in awe. The guard threw potato chips down behind him as he moved closer to us, and the baboon, who had descended from the canopy of trees that shaded our school, was in close pursuit, happily chomping on each chip as it fell to the ground.

The two of them approached the class and then stopped about ten feet away. Our PE teacher seemed equally amazed at the sighting. All the kids crowded near the baboon in wonderment. He had a grayish-brown tone with beady eyes and a sharp black snout.

"Can I feed him one chip," I asked, looking pleadingly at the guard.

"Sure," he said as he handed me two chips.

At the same moment a classmate who was standing behind me asked me a question. I turned, potato chips in hand, to answer.

When I turned back to feed the baboon, it all happened so fast.

Those glinting eyes locked with mine and the baboon began screeching in a high-pitched tone, baring his fangs. Then with all four legs moving in perfect sync, he sprinted at full speed toward me. I saw the entire movement in slow motion. With one leap, the baboon launched itself into the air, shrieking, and onto my body. His razor-like nails dug into my right shoulder, his left in my other shoulder, his bottom nails scraping at my waistline. My eight-year-old body began to shake and I cried as I dropped the potato chips to the ground. I watched as he bared his teeth and then leveled his face against my stomach, his fangs piercing the skin of my abdomen. I rocked backward and threw my arms out in shock. Then I felt the first blow. The guard, now with his black baton over his head, smashed the baboon in his back. The pressure of the blow compounded the force of the attack. Then again, another slam of his baton, cobbled with the searing pain cry of the baboon as his nails further ripped my skin. And then in a moment it was over. There was complete silence. I stood motionless, tears cascading from my face. My teacher was frozen in horror. With my T-shirt ripped from top to bottom, I looked around me. Hands covering their mouths, my classmates were in complete shock. It was as if all sound drained from the world and suddenly came rushing back to me. The guard was screaming and the baboon raced away from us. I stood there stunned and I felt nothing. Within moments the pain hurtled back to my body and I became very aware of what had just happened. Our teacher rushed to me, yelling, "Garon! Garon!" My mind went blank.

I don't remember much about the moments that followed. The next thing I could recognize was Mom hovering over me, telling me I was going to be okay. I was lying on a bed in the nurse's office with a flurry of adults moving in and out of the room. Mom had raced from our house once getting the call from school. As she tried to get ahold of the emergency line at the American Embassy, I heard multiple adults demanding that the baboon be tracked down and killed.

"No. Don't kill him," I pleaded from my bed. "I don't want you guys to kill him!"

"We have to," someone insisted.

Then I remember Mom driving her little Peugeot as fast as it could move through Banjul. Soon we pulled into the gates of the American Embassy. Moments later I was back on a bed being inspected by the Embassy nurse.

"He'll need rabies booster shots," the nurse said.

"Does he need stitches?" Mom asked.

"No, surprisingly he doesn't. His wounds aren't that deep."

I was pumped full of shots and my wounds cleaned and wrapped. I felt a burning sensation up and down my torso.

Later that evening, I sat at home surrounded by Mom, Dad, Ebony, and Yael.

"Everyone at school knows about it!" Ebony said, wide-eyed.

"They do?" I asked in earnest.

"Yea. Everyone. People kept saying it to me, I heard your brother got attacked by a baboon!"

"Wow," I replied, thinking now for the first time of my classmates who had witnessed the entire attack. I wondered what the next day at school would be like. Would everyone want to know all the details?

Many times throughout my life I have thought about the lack of pain I felt as the baboon cut into my skin. I could see it all happening and yet I felt nothing. When I read stories of assaults, this is where I find peace: the idea that when people are assaulted, whether by an animal or a human, that hopefully endorphins rush through their nervous system, allowing them to leave their body throughout the attack.

Instead of having the baboon killed, a well-known primatologist flew into Banjul, met the baboon, named him after me, and took him away to be reintegrated into the wild. I was thrilled. I was told they made the decision not to kill him at my request. It was a small victory for my young self and one of the first times I realized that my voice really mattered.

MOM AND DAD gave us the greatest sense of self. They both did a wonderful job of making us believe that not only were we worthy but that the things we tried were definitely going to be cool. And so, with Halloween right around the corner and a big party at my school to celebrate, they convinced me that it would be creative and unique if I were a calculator.

"A calculator?" I asked, confused.

"Yes! A calculator. Think of how exciting and fun that will be," Mom said.

"You really think a calculator is a good idea?" I asked.

"Of course, Garon. I can even make it for you," Dad said. "We'll take cardboard boxes and repaint them and then make the buttons black. It'll be amazing."

"I guess I *could* be a calculator," I said, secretly wondering if it was going to be as cool as they promised.

It wasn't. On Saturday afternoon the five of us made our way to the big Halloween party at school. My classmates were running around dressed as dragons, witches, wizards, and clowns. They looked amazing.

"Why are you a calculator?" one kid asked.

"Um, I think . . . well, my mom and dad thought it would be a good idea," I said, still somehow feeling confident.

No one else thought so. It was clear.

I still look back at pictures of me in a black hat and a silver cardboard box with every number on the calculator perfectly stenciled in black and white. Why they thought it was a good idea, I'll never know.

There was, however, one classmate who didn't think I looked ridiculous and her name was Jessica. Jessica was an American girl, freckle-faced, with shoulder-length wavy brown hair. She had begged her mother for a playdate with me and soon it was arranged. Never one to turn down an opportunity to socialize, I eagerly went home with Jessica one day after school. Her mother set up two chairs in the TV room and placed a bowl of popcorn with each of us. As we sat side by side, I was excited to watch a movie. Jessica, however, had other plans. As soon as her mom left the room, she got out of her seat and put my bowl of popcorn on the floor. Then she straddled me and started to kiss me. I flung my back against the chair in shock and didn't know what to do with my hands. What was Jessica doing and why? I didn't like that my upper lip was now wet and it was weird having her eyes so close to mine. After my flail, Jessica looked at me quizzically. Then she climbed off my lap and returned to her chair. We continued eating our popcorn and watching our movie. I was eight years old and it was the first time a girl kissed me.

THE FRONT DOOR flung open one morning.

"I'm sorry I'm late, madam," Agnes, our housekeeper said, completely disheveled. I looked up from the table to see that her face was swollen, with a diagonal cut under her left eye.

"Agnes! What happened to you?" Mom said with great concern, rushing over.

"I was robbed last night, madam."

Her hair was all out of place and the skin around her eye looked painful. My heart sank.

"You were robbed?" Mom said, opening the fridge to get ice for her sores.

"I woke up in the middle of the night and there was a man in my house. He was trying to take my purse, so I fought him."

I looked at her arms. She had bruises and scratches just below her shoulder.

"You fought him?" Mom asked, her eyes growing wider.

"Yes, madam. He was trying to take my purse."

"Agnes, why didn't you just let him take your purse? That's replaceable," Mom said.

I was overcome with sadness knowing that someone had hurt Agnes.

"Because, madam. My purse is all I have."

They were words I have never forgotten. They've stuck with me my entire life. Agnes lived not in a house but in a one-room cement block home. She lived there with her young son, Philip. The two of them on the floor of one room.

I looked around our house at the bounty of food and endless furniture. The two lots of land that allowed us to play freely, and I felt a deep sense of guilt. How did it feel for Agnes to arrive at a home filled with excess each day, leaving Philip to be cared for by others, and to return each night at sundown to her one-room cement home?

Mom took Agnes to the kitchen and continued to ice her eye so the swelling would subside. I tried to imagine how petrifying it must have been to wake up and see a stranger standing above her. I thought about it for weeks.

I had, as expected, fallen in love with Agnes, Juju, and Baboucarr. I had my friends at school and then I would race home to be with the three of them. While they worked, I would follow them around, asking them questions.

"Juju, why are you always eating couscous with Agnes?"

"Baboucarr, what happens if I press this cigarette button on the car?"

"Agnes, what are those scars under each of your eyes?"

WHEN EBONY WASN'T spending time with her closest friends, we took her Barbies on imaginary safaris around the yard and she encouraged me to climb higher into our lofty mango trees. Mom and Dad had well integrated into the international circles, a great mixture of local friends and expats. And Yael, who had started pre-school at the nearby French School, was running around the house saying "Joue avec moi" and enjoying his early life in a country few people had even heard about. But in the coming days, the world would come to know The Gambia.

8

COUP D'ÉTAT

ON FRIDAY, JULY 22, 1994, we had just returned home from school when the news came. Mom called us in from climbing mango trees.

"There's been a coup," she told Ebony, Yael, and me.

"What's a coup?" Ebony asked.

"It's when the military overthrows the government of the country. We need to stay inside the house with the doors locked."

It was hard for me to wrap my mind around what that meant. One thing I always appreciated about Mom and Dad, they told us the truth. A curfew had been announced. There was to be no movement outside of homes after sundown. Agnes raced home to be with her family. Juju agreed to stay with us overnight.

As the sun began to set that evening, Dad still wasn't home. I watched from the window as Juju locked the gates, uncertain of what the night might bring. I could feel an uneasiness building in my body. The streets were eerily quiet. I felt as though something dangerous was all around us and yet I couldn't see it. Upon learning of the news, Dad had been directed along with a number of other Americans to relocate with a convoy to the US Embassy. Once he got there, he was told to remain inside the confines of the Embassy in order to guarantee his safety. The American ambassador, Andrew Winter, had boarded an American naval ship, the USS *La Moure County*, that had coincidentally been scheduled to arrive offshore to facilitate training exercises. In the interest of the president's safety, Ambassador Winter brought the Gambian president, Dawda Jawara, and his wife, Lady Chilel, aboard the USS *La Moure County*. The ambassador had hoped to successfully negotiate an understanding between the Gambian president and the military insurgency.

With Ambassador Winter busy offshore with negotiations, Dad went to the second in command.

"Just like you, I've got my family at home," Dad told the Embassy's executive officer.

He held up his hand. "Stop there, Steve. I know. I understand, but it's better that I don't actually hear the rest. Hang on a minute while I get you a walkie-talkie," he said.

After the sky darkened over Banjul that evening, Dad made his way out of the Embassy gates. He walked quietly along the walls of homes, taking back streets, carefully looking around the corners of intersections, all the way across the city until he made it to our home. That's the kind of person Dad was and still is. The risk-taking I had watched both he and Mom exhibit over the years, which I had often balked at, I now appreciated.

"I'm so happy you're home, Dad!" Ebony said, wrapping her delicate arms around him.

"There's no way I'd leave you guys here by yourself," he said, ruffling his hand through my black hair. Then he walked over and kissed Mom and Yael.

The five of us sat in the living room that evening, happy to be safely together and grateful for Juju.

The next morning, the sun rose on the now embattled country. Across the world people were learning where this tiny African country was. The leader of the coup d'état, a young lieutenant in the Gambian Army, Yahya Jammeh, had recently completed four months of military training at Fort McClellan in Alabama. He had led the Gambian Army's insurrection and now declared himself to be the new leader of The Gambia.

As the days turned into weeks, we now came to accept that we were living under a military dictatorship. Curfew had been lifted and we were able to move about Banjul again, but not without limitations. Each morning as Baboucarr drove us to school, we would be stopped at multiple military checkpoints along the way. A military officer with an automatic rifle would put up his hand and our Cherokee would come to a halt. Then they would check the car. Most times, seeing two kids in the backseat, they allowed us to stay in the jeep. Then they would ask Baboucarr to open the hood and the back. I wondered what they were looking for. As they checked, I looked out the window as adults in other cars were forced out of their vehicles. They stood on the road, surrounded by military officers.

As the months went on, Ebony, Yael, and I got used to our new life under authoritarian rule and Mom and Dad became less strict about our movements. Surprisingly, it became fairly routine. Start the drive to school with Baboucarr, stop the car at the military checkpoints. Wave to them. Open the hood. Open the trunk. Tell them you're going to school. It just became part of our lives. I doubt many people in the world have rocked back and forth to "Express Yourself" with a machine gun less than a foot away from them.

One day after school I rode my bike down near the butcher shop along the main road. Suddenly sirens wailed through the air, forcing me to put on my brakes. A military convoy rolled pridefully along the road, commanding everybody and everything to halt. Young male soldiers sat gleefully on top of military vehicles. I held on tightly to the handlebars of my bike, my palms sweating. One soldier, wearing a red beret, smiled into the crowd, waving his machine gun high in the air. It was Yahya Jammeh. As he turned around, people on the streets cowered in fear. Then he looked down toward the butcher shop and spotted me. Jammeh pointed his automatic rifle at me and the Gambians standing around me. With a sick smile he moved the barrel of the gun slowly from right to left across our faces. It was the first time I had ever had a gun pointed at me. A surge of fear rushed through my body and I wanted desperately to be in the safety of Mom's arms. I froze, staring into the barrel of his weapon as he taunted us, promising myself not to move. Seeing our fear, Jammeh laughed, pointed his gun back up in the air, and continued forward. I'll never forget how powerless I felt. And I'll never forget the enjoyment Jammeh got out of seeing an eight-year-old terrified.

Soon, rumblings began that American contract workers would eventually need to leave with their families. Yahya Jammeh was here to stay and the international community was pulling out.

One evening Mom called us into the dining room.

"Okay, guys, we have some news. We can't live here anymore. Dad has a job offer," she said.

"Where are we going?" I asked.

"We're moving to Jamaica," Mom said, presenting an upbeat demeanor for her children. She was great at always making us believe huge life changes would not only be okay, they would be fun. "It's an island in the Caribbean Sea."

But I was devastated. I had come to love our life in The Gambia. That smell of the warm baguette each morning, the sandy streets that I buzzed around daily on my black Huffy bicycle, and our Lionel Richie sunsets. But most of all I would miss Baboucarr, Juju, and Agnes. I knew I would never see them again.

9
STARTS WITH *N*, ENDS WITH *R*

"I JUST DON'T BELIEVE IN interracial marriage. What can I say?" Podla explained, with her yellow parakeet perched regally on top of her head. Instead of flying directly to Jamaica, Mom and Dad had decided to take us back to Louisiana for a visit. Ebony, Yael, and I loved visiting our great-grandmother in her trailer park less than ten minutes away from Luling, in a tiny town called Boutte. The trailer park was a world away from anything we had ever experienced. I thought it was exciting how close together everyone lived. In Sri Lanka, South Africa, and The Gambia, we had lived behind big walls. In the trailer park, there were no walls and I enjoyed seeing what all the neighbors were up to from any point in the home.

"How can you say that? Look at my kids!" Mom said, annoyed at Podla. "What if they grow up and marry someone of a different race?"

"Niki, it's just the way I was raised. I *don't believe* in interracial marriage," Podla repeated. They continued arguing in the kitchen.

I flung myself back in Podla's La-Z-Boy, extended the footrest, and wished I had one. The entire discussion about interracial marriage had come up because Podla had left *Jerry*

Springer on and his guests were a white wife and a black husband. Podla was Grandpa's mom. To me, she seemed like a character out of a storybook. With the yellow parakeet nesting quietly in Podla's snow-white hair, the two of them moved about the trailer with ease. The bird contrasted nicely with Podla's silky hunter-green muumuu dotted with clusters of pink and blue flowers. When I squinted, blurring Podla's wrinkly face, it almost looked like the parakeet was perching in a natural habitat.

Ebony, Yael, and I would run around the trailer for hours as she and Mom sat at the kitchen table playing cards and talking. I couldn't believe that the air conditioning came from the ground up and spent most of my time standing over the vents, reveling in it as though it were magic. In my mind, Podla was living a glorious life. I wondered what it would be like if we too lived in a trailer.

BACK ON BERNICE DRIVE, Ms. Pepper once again stood in the middle of Ashoh's kitchen. Her eyes always lit up when she saw us and her vivacious personality instantly filled the room with sunlight.

"First Africa, now Jamaica," she said, throwing her hands up in the air. "Maybe y'all can take me with you in a suitcase."

I laughed at the image of Ms. Pepper stuffed in one of our black suitcases as Dad wheeled her down the red-brick driveway. I wished she could come with us to Jamaica.

"You know, Betsy Anne's daughter Brittany got married in Jamaica. 'Course that was her second marriage," Ashoh added in a hushed tone, looking around the room for a reaction.

"What happened to her first husband?" Ms. Pepper asked.

"Well, he probably got tired of her," Grandpa chimed in from the corner with his unlit cigarette.

"Now, Petie, don't say such things! That's not nice," Ashoh said while Grandpa shrugged his shoulders and smirked at me.

Grandpa always knew how to make me laugh. Suddenly there was a knock at the door. Ms. Pepper peered out the window.

"Oh look, it's Eileen. She musta' heard the kids were back from Africa. Everyone wants to see y'all."

Ashoh led Ms. Eileen, who lived a couple houses down the street, into the kitchen. She was slightly more subdued than Ms. Pepper but exuded a similar warmth and charisma.

"I cannot believe how big y'all have gotten," she said, looking at the three of us. We gave her a big hug. "I'll never forget the first time I saw Garon. Just two years old, there he was on the operating table with his little penis. I felt so bad taking away his little foreskin."

Ms. Pepper and Ashoh shook their head empathetically, placing their hands on their hearts. Ms. Eileen was a nurse at a local hospital who years before had been pleasantly surprised to learn that the little brown boy whose foreskin she and others were tasked with removing had been that of her neighbor's grandson. I thought it was weird to have all these women talking about my penis with their hands on their hearts. I looked across the kitchen table at Mom, who was grinning.

That winter Mom's younger brother, Uncle Mike, bought me a pink bike. It was a hand-me-down from a girlfriend's daughter who had outgrown it. I raced out of bed each morning to ride that bike up and down Bernice Drive. Soon I had made friends with a number of similarly aged neighborhood boys and we rode together as a pack. One afternoon we were all hanging out when one of them got angry at me.

"You should just go home, nigger!" he yelled at me. All the other boys fell silent. I felt the pain of his words as soon as he said it. I knew what that word meant. I looked at their five white faces staring back at me. I held my tears that I could feel bubbling below the surface, then jumped on my pink bike and sped back to Ashoh's house. Once I got to the house, Mom opened the door and saw my face.

"Are you okay, honey? What happened?"

"They called me a nigger," I said, bursting into tears.

I watched as Mom's face turned from anger to pain and then she fell apart, pulling me into her chest. I could hear her sobs.

"You listen to me, Garon. No one, ever, has the right to say that to you. They are small-minded. There's nothing wrong with the color of your skin. I'm so sorry. I'm so so sorry," she said, crying. I realized in that moment that somehow their words hurt Mom even more than they hurt me. As much as she wanted to, there was no way for my white mother to protect me from the racism of the town that she had grown up in.

Ashoh stood next to us. "Niki, should we go talk to their parents?"

"No, Mother! Where do you think they learned it from? They learned it *from* their parents. People are so racist down here," she said, shaking her head and holding me tight. Ashoh stayed silent. I continued to cry. The words of that boy and the fact that none of my friends stood up for me hurt more than I'd ever imagined. I had tried to be like them. Weeks before I had even asked Grandpa to buy me a black-and-gold Saints T-shirt so I could look more like them. When the boys said *y'all*, I had practiced saying it under my breath so I might sound more like them. But in the end, my curly black hair and brown skin couldn't hide behind a shirt or a word. They knew I wasn't one of them. With my knees resting on Ashoh's cushioned kitchen chairs, I stared out her front window as the boys rode their bikes up and down Bernice Drive in the days that followed. The gymnastics class in South Africa had been too early. This was the first time I felt the sting of racism by kids my age. While I knew it was wrong, their words had power and they tore at my heart for the rest of our trip.

10

AMBASSADORS

"I DON'T WANT TO REDO the fucking third grade!" I shouted on our tour of the American International School of Kingston (AISK). The vice-principal, our tour guide, stared at me, her mouth agape, then quickly closed it to collect herself.

"Garon, do not swear at school!" Mom chastised me. I knew I would be in deep trouble once I got home. Because I had been among the youngest in my class in The Gambia and had to leave mid-year, Mom and Dad had requested that I redo third grade. At nine years old, I wasn't having it and tried my best to convince them to let me continue onto fourth grade. In the end, they won, I promised to never say *fuck* at school again, and I repeated the third grade.

It turned out to be a good thing because I met one of my best childhood friends there, Amy Moran, a tomboy with a stout build, thick dark-brown wavy hair, pronounced lips, and hazel eyes. Amy and I got along famously. Her father, a Brit, was the European Union ambassador to Jamaica. Her mother, a Palestinian, had a vivacious personality and loved to socialize. Many days after school, I would travel back to the residence with Amy to run around the grounds of her unrivaled, enormous home. Her parents quickly became friends with Mom and Dad and our families began hanging out together regularly. Often, when Mom and Dad would be invited over for a dinner party, us kids would get to come as well. Amy and I would hang over the railing upstairs, watching as people arrived in glamorous eveningwear. She introduced me to the British comedian duo French and Saunders, and we laughed late into the night upstairs while diplomats mingled below us.

Instead of a home like we had in The Gambia, we lived in a giant condominium, like we did in Hawaii. A number of kids from the international school also lived there, which made it an easy place to play with friends after homework was done, Mom's rule. Our white condo was surrounded by an array of lush tropical plants and fluttering hummingbirds that seemed to weightlessly suspend themselves in the air outside our kitchen window. My favorite plant became a large green leafy bush with small clusters of red flowers. I soon discovered if I pulled the flowers off and turned them upside down, I could suck nectar out of the stem. Pink hibiscus flowered all around us and mango trees threw their orangey-yellow fruits on the ground outside our back door.

One afternoon I hung out with my friend Thomas, whose family had relocated to Jamaica from The Netherlands.

"Don't you ever think of running away?" he asked me while pulling a lime off his tree in the backyard.

"Run away?" I asked. "From what?"

"I mean, if I was adopted, I would run away in the middle of the night to go find my real parents," Thomas said sincerely.

"But they *are* my real parents," I said to him. While I hadn't been prepared for being called a nigger, I had been well prepared by Mom and Dad to face questions about adoption. What I couldn't understand is why friends didn't see that I

loved Mom and Dad the same way they loved their parents.
Thomas shrugged. "But they're not your *real real* parents."

"Yea, but they adopted me from Sri Lanka so they *are* my
parents," I fired back.

One day at AISK during recess, Garland, an extremely
upbeat girl whose family had moved to Jamaica from Texas,
asked us, "So are y'all Christians?"

Ebony and I stared at each other, then turned to Garland.

"No, we're American," Ebony offered in response. I nodded
in agreement. We had no idea what Garland was talking about.
When I said previously that I had learned the word *sex* before
God, I meant way before. When we got home, we asked Mom
and Dad what Garland was talking about.

"She asked us if we are Christians," Ebony recounted.

Mom and Dad looked at each other and grinned.

"What are Christians?" I asked, holding Yael's hand. They
chuckled, knowing this day would come.

"You know how in Luling, Ashoh, Ms. Pepper, and Ms. Eileen
all wear those crosses?" Mom asked.

"Yes."

"Well, they are Christians. There are many Christians all
over the world, not just in Louisiana. And it's one of the three
monotheistic religions of the world, meaning they believe in
just one god."

"Right, but there are other religions around the world that
don't believe in a god at all, like Buddhism, heavily practiced in
Sri Lanka," added Dad.

"Yes, or religions that have many spirits, like the Kami of
Shintoism in Japan," said Mom.

Unlike Dad, Mom had grown up with Christianity all around
her. Dad had grown up in a strict but largely non-religious

home in Louisiana. After moving to Botswana in the 1970s, Mom saw how misinterpreted Christianity had been in her life. She felt it had been used to separate people instead of uniting them. She and Dad made the decision not to raise the three of us in any religion.

"Look, guys, we want you to experience many different religions. Then, when you grow up, you can choose to practice one, or none at all," Dad said.

"But do you believe in a god?" I asked.

"No, honey, we don't," Mom said confidently. "But it doesn't matter what we believe. It matters what you believe."

I wondered what I would believe when I grew up. Maybe I would even believe in more than one religion at the same time. Could you do that?

SHORTLY AFTER I turned ten, Mom and Dad took us to one of Jamaica's most desirable locales, The Blue Lagoon.

"No matter how far you try to dive down, you won't reach the bottom," Dad said from the driver's seat.

"No one can reach the bottom or just kids can't?" I asked.

"No one. It's almost two-hundred-feet deep."

Dad was right. The splendid sapphire water of the lagoon was deeper than I imagined possible. After each heaping breath I hurled myself deeper into the water with my arms pointed straight like an arrow. I kicked vigorously as I sunk farther and farther until I became terrified that I was too far from the surface. Then I would throw my arms around in full-blown panic as I clawed my way back to the surface, gasping for air. The lagoon was a mix of warm ocean water flowing in from the Caribbean Sea and icy cold streams from freshwater springs deep below. While Yael floated with Mom and Dad, Ebony and I took turns noting the temperature changes and shrieking every time we felt a frigid current.

BACK AT MY DESK at the international school, I stared impatiently at the clock, waiting for recess to begin. We were all lined up against the wall as the music teacher, Mrs. Belanfanti, stood before us. She was a short woman with close-cut curly black hair and an enthusiasm for creating songs that I thought sounded ridiculous. Amy had agreed with me about that.

"Now, kids, think of how exciting it will be for the seniors to hear you sing farewell to them this year."

I rolled my eyes. We didn't even know the seniors.

"The song I wrote goes like this: 'So sad to say, goodbye today, comeback soon to sunny J-A, your smiles we'll miss, but please remember this, you can always catch a flight three times a day.'" As Mrs. Belanfanti sang, she moved her hands back and forth melodically.

I raised my hand.

"Yes?"

"Three times a day from where?" I asked.

"Sorry?"

"They can catch a flight three times a day from where?"

"From Florida. Air Jamaica flies three times a day from Florida. Any other questions, Garon?"

"No."

Mrs. Belanfanti turned her attention to the entire class, handing each of us a sheet of paper. "Okay, now that you all have the lyrics in front of you, let's sing along together."

I read the lyrics. She had made us sing a song at Christmas

that had sounded equally as dumb as this one.

"One, two, three." Mrs. Belanfanti signaled for us to start. I looked down the line as all the girls began in unison. *I'm not singing this*, I thought.

Suddenly Mrs. Belanfanti's swaying hands came to an abrupt stop. "Garon, is there a problem? Why aren't you singing?"

Mom and Dad had always told me to tell the truth. "Because this song is dumb." The entire line of girls craned their necks forward and stared down the row at me. Instantly I knew I was in trouble.

Mrs. Belanfanti's normally upbeat demeanor and shining smile faded. "Garon, please have a seat immediately." I pushed myself off the wall and walked over in silence to my seat. I knew that I would be in even bigger trouble once I got home.

I was right. That evening at home Mom sat across from me on our blue and white sofa. "Why couldn't you just sing the song?"

"Because her songs are so dumb and she treats us like we are kindergarteners," I said.

"Garon, please. She's a nice lady who is just trying to get the class to sing a song. I expect that when you're at school you respect your teachers and do what they say or you're going to be grounded. Do you understand me, young man?"

"Yes, Mom."

"Good, now when you see Mrs. Belanfanti, I want you to apologize to her and sing her goddamn song."

"Fine," I said with my arms crossed.

That year as the seniors graduated, I stood in line next to the girls of my class with a smile on my face and reminded the graduates that they could indeed fly back to Jamaica three times a day. Mrs. Belanfanti seemed pleased with our performance and as her hands made their last escalation, she turned to face the audience of parents and took a bow.

At the beginning of fifth grade, I was excited to learn that a boy from Brazil would be joining our classroom. His name was Franco, and he was the nephew of the Brazilian ambassador to Jamaica. For reasons not explained to me, he had come to live with his uncle. Franco and I made friends quickly and very soon I found myself downstairs at the Brazilian residence playing Sega with Franco in a TV room outside the luxuriant pool area. Hanging out at ambassadors' residences had now become completely normalized. I didn't look twice when event crews and staff showed up to set up for a diplomatic event. I did, however, notice that on the weekends the Brazilians had pool parties that looked slightly different than anything I had seen at the European Union ambassador's residence. The men and women wore revealing swimsuits, sipped attractive cocktails by the poolside, and danced soulfully to alluring music. As my eyes shifted from Sonic the Hedgehog out toward the pool area, I noticed for the first time that I was attracted to the sexiness of it all. The Brazilian residence had, without intention, awakened something within me at ten years old that felt new and exciting.

Months later, I was invited to hang out at the house of a Swedish friend who lived in our same condominium. He was a bit older than me, more Ebony's friend, but we got along really well. We lay on two different sofas as he flipped through channels.

"Do you want to watch porn?" he asked.

I hesitated. "Sure," I said casually, not wanting to admit that I had never seen porn before.

He changed the channel. Rollerblading down a sidewalk alongside the ocean was a blonde, completely naked, with big breasts and a clit piercing. She looked like one of the women that Grandpa had posted across the freezer in his garage. I lay on the sofa, slightly aroused but perplexed. While aware of a clitoris from the many biology books Mom had left around the house over the years for us to peruse, I had never seen a pierced clit before.

"Do your parents let you watch this?" I asked naively, knowing that it seemed secretive.

"Don't worry, they're taking a nap upstairs. I watch it all the time," he said.

I oscillated between being turned on and wondering why she'd forgotten to wear her helmet. It was a confusing evening.

JUST AS IT had in all the other countries, our time in Jamaica was coming to a close.

With Dad at the end of his contract, but searching for another international assignment, they made the decision that we would move to Louisiana for a year.

"We'll live near Ashoh and Grandpa?" Yael asked eagerly.

"Yes," Dad said, picking him up and giving him a big kiss on the cheek.

We were delighted. A chance to really see our grandparents every day. What could be better than that?

11

BERNICE DRIVE

I ROLLED BACK ON THE FLOOR of Ashoh and Grandpa's den, roaring in laughter. Lucille Ball was one of the funniest people I had ever seen. I loved her perfectly timed facial expressions. I especially loved the relationship between her and Ethel, played by Vivian Vance. By day I watched *Doug, Rugrats,* and *Saved by the Bell.* Then at night I would dive onto the floor of the den glued to *Nick at Nite.* Overseas, Mom and Dad's rule was that we could only watch VHS tapes of cartoons, and only if they were in French. By comparison, American TV was a dream.

Mom and Dad bought the home seven houses down from Ashoh and Grandpa's on Bernice Drive, fulfilling our dream of being able to see our grandparents every day. They had even bought us an apricot miniature poodle puppy. Ebony, Yael, and I fell head over heels in love with her. I had wanted to call her Jazz, after the sensational music genre that had been birthed in New Orleans. Yael, now six years old to my eleven, wanted to call her Sheebee for reasons he couldn't communicate. Mom made us compromise and call her Jazzbee. Each day after I returned from school, I would chase Jazzbee around the house, dutifully finish my homework, and then bike down the street to Ashoh and Grandpa's house.

"America is just the best country in the world," Ashoh told me one day as she perused the obituaries of the New Orleans newspaper, *The Times-Picayune.*

"But how do you know that?" I challenged her.

"I just do. It's just what I believe."

"But you haven't been to *that* many countries, so how would you know that America is the best country?"

Ashoh looked at me annoyedly as she took a deep breath and folded the obituary section. She firmly believed that children should not question adults.

Another afternoon I was playing with the set of black umbrellas that sat next to Ashoh's front door.

"Garon, do *not* open those in the house!"

"Why?"

"Because it's bad luck," she said, with her hand on her hip.

"How do you know it's bad luck if you've never done it?" I pressed. I'd never heard of these rules in Africa.

"It just is! It's bad luck to open an umbrella in your house, everyone knows that."

With my eyes firmly locked on Ashoh, I took the black umbrella and opened it to completion in the foyer. I was sent home immediately.

But in the moments when I wasn't finding ways to challenge Ashoh's authority, the two of us would sit on the edge of her bed and sort through old pictures. I loved seeing black-and-white photographs of Mom when she was a little girl and my Uncle Robby. Uncle Robby was mom's younger brother who tragically died when he was seven years old. Ashoh and Grandpa had chosen a weekend to move houses in Louisiana. Podla had offered to watch Mom and Robby for the weekend so they wouldn't have to juggle moving and the kids. At the time, Podla lived on a large piece of land near a lake. Mom, who was ten at the time, decided to play hide and seek with her brother. She counted while he hid. After an unusually long time Mom gave up trying to find Robby and, sensing something was wrong, called Podla. Podla and her husband ran into the lake, believing perhaps Robby had drowned. They couldn't find him. Later, they went to open a big refrigerator that was stashed in the garage. Robby lay inside motionless. He had suffocated to death while trying to hide in the old fridges that had a locking handle on them.

I have known that story since before I can remember. I sat next to Ashoh, staring at a picture of her young baby boy with bright eyes. I wondered what our family would be like if Uncle Robby were still alive today. Years after Robby's death, my Uncle Mike was born. He and Mom loved each other very much, but there was always something missing. That something was Uncle Robby.

"I can still see his little hand waving me goodbye as he left that weekend," Ashoh told me. Hearing her say that shredded my heart into pieces. I reached over and held Ashoh's hand. We sat together at the edge of her bed in silence as tears rolled down her cheeks.

Now old enough to smash Grandpa's beer cans by myself, I spent many afternoons by his side in his smoky garage while Ebony talked with Ashoh in the kitchen and Yael chased the schnauzers around the backyard.

"Your grandma said I had to slow down my drinking. Now I got these here Coors *Lights*," Grandpa said, holding one up to show me. "How many years until you can have a beer?" he asked.

"I don't know. I think if we move back to Africa, I can drink alcohol when I'm eighteen. But Mom and Dad give me a sip of wine sometimes at dinner."

"How old are you now?"

"Eleven."

"Here," he said, handing me his Coors Light. "Just take a taste of this one. Can't hurt you."

"Thanks," I said, pressing his can to my lips. Beer tasted strange to me and while I didn't like it, I made sure to pretend it was good to please him.

"Now don't tell your grandma. She'll get her panties all in a twist."

When we weren't outside in the garage with the dogs, I followed Grandpa into the den. He would sit back in his green La-Z-Boy positioned next to a small table and a penny gumball machine. I loved his gumball machine.

"Here's a penny," he said, placing the copper coin in my hand. "Grab yourself a gumball, Rambo." That was how Grandpa showed me he loved me. Not by saying it, but by giving me small things or sharing his alcohol.

Then the two of us sat together as he flipped through the channels. "There's a good movie on Lifetime. Let's watch that." My time with Grandpa always felt special. While at times he was a man of few words, there was an understanding between the two of us. I just got him, and I liked his humor. Grandpa reached down to the wooden handle on his recliner and extended the footrest. We sat there together for hours watching Lifetime: Television for Women.

DOWN THE STREET at 100 Bernice Drive, we had settled comfortably into our own two-story red-brick home. Uncle Mike came over many afternoons after he got off work and I watched as he and Mom laughed together on our back patio, recounting old stories. I sensed that over the years they had needed each other more than time and space had allowed. The love Uncle Mike had for his older sister was evident. On weekends, just as we had done in South Africa, the five of us would all pile into Mom and Dad's same king-sized bed, snuggling up with each other.

"Did you guys ever think we would live in Luling?" Mom asked, running her hand through my lengthy black hair. I loved when she stroked my hair while I lay close to her chest. I could hear her heart beating. It felt like the safest place in the world.

"No!" I volunteered. There was something absolutely charming about living in the same southern Louisiana town where Mom had grown up.

Some days after school we would ride in the backseat of our red Honda Accord to the homes of her childhood best friends. I would sit on their sofas staring quizzically at the taxidermy deer heads that hung proudly from the walls. Mom and her friends drank sweet iced tea and gossiped about their high-school years.

"Where's Troy now?" Mom asked.

"He married Jennifer from the cheerleading squad. Remember her? They live a couple streets over," her friend said.

"And what happened to Tommy?"

"Oh, you'll never believe it. He married Diane from the 4-H Club. They have two kids at Hahnville High School now."

It seemed everyone that had grown up in Luling still lived here, except for Mom. Her friends leaned forward on the sofa with enamored faces as Mom told them about our five-day trek through the Kathmandu Valley in mountainous Nepal with Ebony and I riding on the backs of Sherpas. Or visiting friends who lived on a wooden houseboat on Dal Lake in Kashmir, floating on colorful shikaras by day with the Himalayas in the distance.

"Niki, you gotta come to the reunion this year. No one will be able to believe all the places y'all been in the world. Some of us never been out of the country."

BACK ON BERNICE DRIVE, Dad had bought me a red lawnmower and leaf blower from a store called Home Depot. I was ecstatic. I couldn't believe that in America there was one giant orange store where you could buy anything and everything you could want for your house or garden.

"All right, Garon, I'm going to teach you how to cut the grass," he said, pushing the mower and talking in a loud voice above the roar of the motor. "It's kind of like sweeping, you go back and forth systematically so you don't miss any spots."

I spent hours outside in the thick Louisiana heat pushing that mower back and forth in my safety glasses. I loved how the St. Augustine smelled as it fractured into pieces and dispersed through the swampy air. I waved excitedly to neighbors as they drove by smiling. We had always lived behind towering walls in Africa or contained condos in Hawaii and Jamaica. I loved how open and social American neighborhoods felt. When I finished cutting the lawn, I took the leaf blower, pointed it at my mouth, and allowed the jet of air to rapidly inflate and deflate my cheeks, interrupted by fits of laughter.

One day there was a knock at the door. Mom and I opened it. It was Dane, one of the five boys I used to ride my pink bike with two and a half years prior, before moving to Jamaica. His mother was standing alongside him.

"Hi! Welcome to the neighborhood. Dane wants to know if Garon wants to come play with him."

Mom looked at me. "What do you think, Garon?" I could see the worry building in her eyes.

Dane was not the boy who had called me a nigger that summer. And while he hadn't stood up for me when it happened, he had always been nice to me. "I want to go play."

Moments later Dane and I were riding our bikes up and down Bernice Drive just like old times. He had a sleek Mongoose that was cooler than any bike I had seen.

"Guess what? I'm in BMX dirt-jumping competitions now," he told me. Some days Dane would take me out to an open tract of land alongside the railroad tracks just behind our neighborhood. I would watch in envy as he would do tricks, swinging his bike around in the air as he hurdled over mounds of dirt. Here I had thought my leaf blower was amazing. I might as well have been wearing my calculator costume standing next to him. *Dane is so much cooler than me*, I thought.

Eventually Dane introduced me to some new kids in the neighborhood, and weekend nights we would split up into two groups and play cops and robbers, running from yard to yard trying to catch each other. Crickets chirped in the background as the moist night air drifted slowly down Bernice Drive. The streetlights lit our path as we darted across the road, hiding behind neighbors' cars or trying to conceal ourselves behind leafy bushes. I didn't look like any of these kids and I sure didn't sound like them, but I felt like we had been friends for years. It had only been six months but just as it had in South Africa, The Gambia, Hawaii, and Jamaica, Louisiana began to feel like home.

NEXT DOOR TO US lived a very conservative southern pastor with his wife and two daughters. Heather, about my age, twelve, had short brown hair, pale skin, and was rail thin. We would see them often, and while our parents were cordial, we didn't socialize together. My window faced Heather's window on the second floor, and one day she threw a paper airplane out her window and at the glass of mine. I went downstairs to see what it said. It was a love note. Later, when I saw her in the space between our two houses, I thanked her for her note but told her I didn't feel the same way about her. Looking back, I wonder what her southern pastor father would have thought of her writing love notes to the brown Sri Lankan kid next door. Also, I admire how straightforward and mature she was at a young age to write me in the first place. I was nowhere near as mature.

ASHOH, WHO FOR YEARS lamented to Mom and Dad that I had never been baptized, felt it would be productive to continually remind me.

"I'm just so sorry that you never got baptized, Garon," she told me one afternoon while eating her daily saltines and drinking a Coke.

"Why? We're not even religious," I shot back.

"Well, I *still* think your mama and daddy should have gotten you baptized."

"Why do you care so much?"

"*Because* I believe, if you're not baptized, you're going to Hell."

"So you think I'm going to Hell?"

"Well, Garon, I don't *want* you to, but yes. The Lord says anyone who isn't baptized is going to Hell. It's very clear," she said, motioning toward her Bible.

I wondered quietly to myself if the Lord had said anything about jerking off on the floor of your grandma's bathroom. The previous Saturday all five of us had spent the evening at Ashoh and Grandpa's house for a dinner of boiled seafood. While Mom, Dad, Ashoh, and Grandpa were preparing dinner in the kitchen, I was watching *Nick at Nite* with Ebony and Yael. Suddenly I felt myself getting hard and afraid I wouldn't be able to conceal my boner at the seafood boil, I made my way to Ashoh's bathroom, closed the door, and carefully locked it. The smell of pumpkin and cinnamon filled the air from the crystal bowl of fall potpourri that Ashoh always kept in there. I lay down on her tan carpeted floor, pulled down my shorts, and started stroking up and down. Not one minute into my happy place, I heard Ashoh's voice just outside the door.

"Garon? You in there?" she said with a brief knock.

"Yea," I said, trying to mask my heavy breathing and sound as normal as possible.

"Dinner's ready."

"Okay!"

Once I heard her footsteps trail away, I spit on my hand and continued stroking. Masturbating really was the most amazing feeling and I wished I had discovered it years before. While Mom's sex education books had said it was perfectly normal, I was sure it wasn't the most normal thing to do on the floor of your grandma's bathroom. A couple minutes went by of rolling my eyes back in pleasure as I slid my hand up and down. I felt a rush building, the muscles in my shoulders and arms beginning to tense as I moved my hand faster, and then just as I was about to come, I heard her voice again.

"Garon? What on earth is taking so long in there?" Ashoh said, leaning against the door.

But it was too late. "I'm coming!" I said, trying to appease her question, and then shot all over myself.

"Okay. Everyone else is already at the table. You sound out of breath."

I could barely respond. I had been lifted off Ashoh's tan carpet, launched through the pumpkin potpourri, out her bathroom window, across Luling, and back inside.

"I'll be right there," I struggled to say, my chest rising and falling rapidly. Then I closed my eyes and lay motionless on Ashoh's bathroom floor, reveling in my newfound ecstasy.

ONE DAY AS I was cutting the edge of our property line, Heather's pastor father was watering his garden. He turned around without turning the water off and accidentally sprayed my shirt.

Once all my chores were done, I rode my bike over to Ashoh's house with a devilish grin.

"Guess what, Ashoh?" I asked upon arrival.

"What, honey?" she said, holding the *TV Guide* in one hand.

"I got baptized today." Ashoh put the *TV Guide* down on the kitchen table and walked over to me in her pink floral muumuu and white house slippers with a confused look.

"You did?" she asked cautiously.

"Yea. I was mowing the lawn and Heather's pastor father squirted me with the hose," I said, smiling.

"Garon! It's not funny to make jokes about a pastor and God and baptism," Ashoh scolded. Once again, I was sent home.

ON A TYPICAL hot, sticky Louisiana summer night, after a year of living on Bernice Drive, Dad sat us down at the kitchen table.

"Guess what, guys? It's looking like our next move will be to Kampala, Uganda."

"Back to Africa!" I yelled excitedly. But as soon as I said those words out loud, I realized how much I had come to enjoy living in Louisiana. Louisiana and Africa were worlds away from each other, yet somehow I felt like I now fit in both. As I lay in my bed at night I journeyed back to The Gambia and remembered how wonderful our life with Juju, Baboucarr, and Agnes had been. *I could love living in Africa again as easily as I could continue living here*, I convinced myself.

Weeks passed and I finally told Dane and the rest of my neighborhood friends that we were probably moving to Uganda. They didn't know where that was. I had lived in southern Africa, western Africa, and now I wondered what our life in eastern Africa would be like. I knew that Uganda was home to mountain gorillas, and I imagined what it might be like for the five of us to trek through the dense forests in search of a silverback. Mom would surely lead the way.

One evening as Ebony, Yael, and I were chasing Jazzbee around the house, Mom and Dad called us into the kitchen. "We have some news." This was it. We were moving to Uganda. I had come to accept our nomadic lifestyle and I felt a rush of excitement wind through my body.

"We didn't get the job in Uganda," Dad said. My nascent excitement came to an abrupt halt. *That's okay*, I reassured myself. *We get to continue living in Luling.*

"Instead, we're moving to the Middle East. We're moving to a country called Jordan."

12

THE RED LIGHT DISTRICT

ON OUR WAY TO ONE of the most conservative regions of the world, we stopped to spend time in perhaps the most liberal. "Ladies and gentlemen, we'd like to be the first to welcome you to Amsterdam's Schiphol Airport," the KLM flight attendant announced. The Netherlands. Mom and Dad had taken us through Amsterdam over previous summers in transit across the world. This time, however, we would be spending a full day and night here.

Amsterdam was everything that Luling wasn't. Mysteriously tall Dutch people rode their bicycles in an organized fashion around us. Goth men and women walked by unnoticed, gay couples kissed openly, mixed-race families held hands without being stared at, and the smell of marijuana drifted into the air from nearby cafés. No one in the family was more enthusiastic than me to be in this supremely liberal environment. Yael and I spun around and watched as hundreds of people of all types rushed past us outside of Amsterdam Central Station.

Mom and Dad guided us through the Red Light District, where provocatively dressed women filled floor-to-ceiling window frames above.

"Remember, kids, here prostitution is legal. It's a really good thing because the government can make sure the women are working in a safe environment. They also have access to contraception and can be tested regularly to protect their health." The sex ed. teacher from South Africa in Mom was still thriving. I laughed to myself, imagining what Ashoh's face would have been like had she been with us. She could barely handle my joke about the pastor and his hose. These ladies in windows would have surely sent her over the edge. Grandpa, on the other hand, would have loved it.

At every canal bridge the five of us would stop and watch the boats pass beneath or alongside us. When Mom and Dad wandered into one of the many gift shops, I walked up to a turnstile postcard holder that stood invitingly outside. The first postcard was a picture of Holland's windmills against a bright blue sky. I spun it gently. The second was a postcard that read "The Netherlands" above an endless field of radiant yellow, red, and orange tulips. I pushed it around a third time. A picture of two men having sex slid in front of me. The postcard read "Welcome to Holland" above their bed. While I knew of homosexuality from all the sex education books that had occupied our homes for years, I had never seen an image of two men in bed.

"Whatever you guys are is fine with us. If you're gay, straight, bisexual, whatever, we will always love you," I remembered Mom and Dad saying to us in The Gambia.

I looked closer at the postcard. The men were both well built and extraordinarily handsome. I liked how one's muscular arms looked against his lovers equally toned back.

"This is the freest place in the world," I said out loud. There wasn't a chance in hell you would stumble upon a postcard of two guys having sex in Luling.

"Yes, it is," Mom replied, surveying the city.

"I love it here," I announced. The people of Amsterdam didn't seem to care about their differences. They moved about the city uniquely themselves, side by side, without judgment.

13

THE HASHEMITE KINGDOM

EBONY, YAEL, AND I WERE lying together in our king-sized bed when the noise rose through the air and soared over the city of Amman.

"Allahu Akbar!"

Mom came through the door and jumped in bed with us. She smiled as the *adhan*, or call to prayer, rang for the very first time in our ears.

"Listen to how beautiful that is. It happens five times a day," Mom said. It was the most captivating and mystical sound I had ever heard in my twelve years of life.

"Your father and I first heard it after the Peace Corps when we took a ship to India and then trekked through Pakistan and Iran during Ramadan."

The words to the call to prayer echoed through my body until I, completely jet-lagged, drifted off to sleep. It was our first day in the Middle East. The next morning, just as I had done in so many countries before, I jumped out of bed and made my way downstairs with Jazzbee to see what our new city looked like. It was still early in Amman and a gentle fog filled the air. I looked across the street at the light-sandstone-colored buildings that filled our neighborhood, Shmeisani. We would live here in an apartment until Mom and Dad found a house for us. A yellow taxi with Arabic writing had pulled up down the hill below me. I stared at the unfamiliar Arabic lettering and wondered what it said. My eyes followed the winding road that snaked throughout the city's rocky desert hills. I then glanced down at the ground where Jazzbee was sitting. It wasn't like the red soil of South Africa or the sandy roads of The Gambia. Here, both the soil and the buildings existed in attractive multitudes of brown. Louisiana had been so moist and verdant, but here there was no grass for as far as the eye could see.

That evening we took a stroll through a road in Shmeisani that was lined with small bustling shops. Lively Arabic music flowed from stores where balloons and toys hung from the ceiling entrance above colorful fabrics and brass and copper coffee pots. It seemed there was something for everyone. I had never heard Arabic music before and while I couldn't understand a word, I was instantly seduced. Heat climbed off the sidewalk as we passed the largest column of meat I had ever seen rotating on a vertical spit near orange flames. A man used an extremely long knife that looked almost sword-like to carve the slow-cooked meat off and tuck it away in a warm piece of flat bread for hungry customers. All around us Arabic words were being spoken in rapid succession. I knew that I too would soon learn this seemingly magical language that sounded distinctly different from the Sinhala and Tamil of Sri Lanka, the Zulu and Xhosa of South Africa, or the patois of Jamaica. There was an undeniable enchanting quality to Jordan that breathed life all around us.

WITHIN WEEKS, the three of us had settled into the American Community School of Amman (ACS Amman), where I was once again surrounded by kids from around the globe. My new schoolmates were from France, Oman, Canada, South Korea, Germany, Japan, Ireland, and Lebanon. I woke up excited to get to school each day, the ultimate place to socialize. My favorite seventh-grade class by far was language arts, expertly taught by a tall American woman named Joyce Kasim. Most of the kids thought Ms. Kasim was strict, but I thought she was both strict and enthralling. She taught me words like *ubiquitous* and *relinquish*. She guided me thoughtfully as I wrote my research paper on the topic of my choosing: honor killings. Ms. Kasim made me feel like I could accomplish anything, and she inspired me to delve deeper into literature and to speak clearly and with purpose. I hoped to be as intelligent as she one day.

One afternoon while riding the bus home from school, Laura, a German girl who was in high school, turned around to look at me.

"Have you been out in the sun for a long time?" she asked me. I looked over at Ebony for confirmation. Was this girl talking to me?

"Me? No, I haven't," I said, intimidated by her and her friend sitting next to her.

"Well, you're so much darker than a few weeks ago. It looks like you were burned in an oven," she said, giggling, then turned around to continue laughing with her friend.

I looked at Ebony. She, I'm sure equally intimidated, ignored it. Laura was so much older than me. I felt powerless.

When we stepped off the bus, Mom was outside waiting for us. She took one look at my face.

"Garon, what's wrong?" Even when I was trying to be strong, Mom could always read me.

"A girl on the bus said I looked like I was burned in an oven."

This time I didn't cry. Mom sent Ebony upstairs.

I watched Mom's face morph into pain. "And how did that make you feel, Garon?" she asked me, her voice breaking.

"It made me feel terrible," I said, suddenly bursting into tears. I pushed my face into her blouse.

As soon as she saw me cry, tears began falling from Mom's face, just as they had that day in Louisiana. She sat me down next to her on a curb outside our wheat-colored apartment building.

"Garon, I hate that people say these things to you. It hurts. It feels terrible. But you have to know how beautiful you and your skin color are. My worry is that this racism is going to follow you your entire life. There may come a time when you're older, if you fall in love and marry someone of a different race, that even their parents may have a problem with you. I hate that." While Mom had likely expected racism to rear its head in her hometown, she wasn't prepared for it to happen so quickly at an International School in the Middle East.

Mom held my hand as she stood up, then walked with her arm around me to the elevator.

Once upstairs in our apartment, I sat in the kitchen while Mom stood by the phone in the living room. I knew it was about to go down.

"I will not tolerate it! Do you understand me? I will not tolerate this!" Mom yelled into the phone at the principal of ACS. "Her name is Laura, according to my son she is German, and this is what she said to him on the bus ride home today. My daughter, who is a sophomore in high school, heard it too," she continued. While sweet and somewhat reserved, Mom was an attack dog when it came to protecting her children.

The next day the principal called me into his office. All I

wanted to do at school was socialize with my friends and have a good time. I knew the situation was escalating.

"Garon, I'd like to apologize to you for what happened on the school bus yesterday. We don't accept that kind of behavior and bullying from other students. We have contacted Laura's family and are dealing with it."

"Thank you," I told him, relieved to be sent back to class.

At lunchtime, I was sitting outside with a number of other middle-schoolers when I heard rapid footsteps approaching us.

"Hey! You're the little shit from yesterday." It was Laura. "The school called my parents and now everyone thinks I'm a fucking racist!" she yelled at me. My friends all sat there in shock at this tall high-schooler screaming at us.

"Don't talk to me," I said defiantly. I wished I'd had the courage to yell at her on the bus the day before. Her friend was standing beside her once again.

"You better tell the principal that I didn't say that. I am not racist!" Laura yelled.

"I'm not saying anything!" I yelled back. She stood there fuming, then turned and left.

Later that year Laura left the school and returned to Germany. I never found out if it was because of the situation or if she just had to leave. It wasn't uncommon for kids to leave mid-year when their parents got assignments in other parts of the world.

MOM AND DAD had been scouting homes and had finally settled on one. While I had voiced my opinion of wanting to live in the middle of the urban hustle and bustle, they chose a gigantic two-story home about fifteen minutes outside of the city on a rocky hill with breathtaking views. Standing in our upstairs living room my eyes drifted across the rolling barren landscape.

While the neighbors directly next to us lived in homes like ours, a winding dirt road wove through the hillside and our most visible neighbors there were a Bedouin family who lived in a sizable canvas tent alongside their sheep and goats. The Bedouins were Jordan's nomadic people, who lived off the land and the animals they took care of. I waved to them each day as I rode past them on the bus to school. Jazzbee, who we rarely sheared, looked a lot like some of their lambs.

We quickly learned that besides the Jordanians and Palestinians who surrounded us, the two other nationalities that were prominently featured in Jordan were Sri Lankans and Filipinos. Why? Because they were the housekeepers. Most wealthy Arab and foreigners' homes were looked after by women from the countries of my and my sister's birth.

After establishing his team at work, one of Dad's first orders of business was to host an elaborate dinner party at our house. Mom disliked this part of international life the most. While she enjoyed talking to people, she didn't like the pomp and circumstance that surrounded so many of these events and she limited Dad on how many she would be willing to host. Rarely did she want to spend time in the evenings going to events. Instead, she preferred to be home with her children. For Dad, it was part of his job and he knew he had to make the appearances.

"Someone's at the door," I told Dad. He'd been socializing in our living room with a number of Arab guests who had already arrived. I followed him to the door to open it. Standing in the entryway was a tan-skinned man, dressed elegantly, who exuded excitement at seeing Dad, his boss. As he extended his hand to shake Dad's, he simultaneously handed me his black coat with the other.

I began to take his coat. "Oh, this is my son. This is my son, Garon," Dad said, clearly understanding what was going on.

The man, deeply embarrassed, hastily pulled the coat back and I could see the dread in his eyes.

"I'm sorry. Of course," he said in a thick Arab accent. He now turned his eyes to mine and made an effort to enthusiastically shake my hand. "Nice to meet you."

I learned in that moment, at thirteen years old, that whether it was the apartheid government of South Africa, five young white American boys in Louisiana, the German female high-schooler on the bus from the international school, or my dad's adult Arab colleague, racism didn't present itself in one way and wasn't restricted to one country. I had grown up thinking Grace, Baboucarr, Juju, and Agnes were beautiful, strong, and loving. To me, they had even more protection from the sun, just as I had, and it seemed cool, like having on extra armor. But now I realized that much of the world didn't see it that way.

WE TRAVELED TO some of the most incredible sights in Jordan. Mom and Dad's good friends Pat, an American from Vermont, and her Palestinian husband, Hamed Bakir, had two boys, Abdo and Hytham. Our two families traveled five hours to one of the most scenic deserts in the world, Wadi Rum. The fiery red sand and colossal rock formations create what the world has come to know as The Valley of the Moon. *Lawrence of Arabia* was filmed here, *Red Planet*, *The Martian,* and *Star Wars.* As kids we took off running into the iron-oxide-laden sand, convinced we'd arrived on another planet. Together with Abdo and Hytham we would crawl up the sandstone and granite rock trying to find the coolest nooks and towering views of the desert dream world below.

One morning I woke up in my tent to the sound of bells, movement, and Jazzbee barking. I unzipped the tent to reveal a caravan of majestic camels and their Bedouin owners moving at a steady pace past the rippled sand dunes that we'd spent the evening running down. They nodded and waved in their ethereal white robes and keffiyehs. Suddenly, Jazzbee jumped out of my tent and took off, sprinting after the camels. I threw on my shoes and ran screaming into the desert after her. I couldn't keep up. After ten minutes of unsuccessfully trying to catch up to the caravan, I looked around me, defeated. In every direction Wadi Rum continued for miles and I was quickly losing site of our camp. I saw our silver Honda CR-V moving glacially through the sand toward me. It was Dad.

"I can't find her," I said sorrowfully.

"Hop in, buddy. If you keep going any farther, I'm not going to be able to find you. Let's go back, get some things together, and then go search for her," Dad suggested.

As we glided across the cayenne-pepper-colored sand, I looked out the window, searching desperately for my pup from Louisiana whom I so loved. Her apricot-reddish hair camouflaged perfectly into the desert landscape, making it impossible for me to spot her. I got out of the car and dejectedly walked back to my tent. There lying on my sleeping bag in a deep slumber was Jazzbee. She had run after the caravan of camels, then made her way back to camp to rest, and I had lost her in the mirage of the desert. I picked her up and buried my face in her curly fur. I thought we had lost her forever.

"GUESS WHO'S MOVING to Jordan?" Mom asked us one day, her face beaming with happiness.

We all looked at one another. "Who?"

"The Morans are leaving Jamaica and coming here!" Amy's father, Jim, would now become the European Union's ambassador to Jordan. Mom was ecstatic to have Amy's mother, Randa, back with her on the other side of the world. I, too, couldn't wait to see Amy. And on the turn of the millennium, our two families celebrated the last days of 1999 once again in picturesque Wadi Rum. Randa and Mom jumped in the front of the Moran's Montero, and we kids took turns matching up in pairs. I stood on the backseat next to Amy, the top half of our bodies hanging out through the sunroof. Then Randa gunned it, and we sped through the Jordanian desert. With our hands above us, and our heads leaning as far to the side as we could, we screamed in excitement as the Montero raced uninhibited back and forth across the cinnamon sand under the night sky. It was a moment to remember.

The Hashemite Kingdom of Jordan had turned into our newest home, filled with friends, family, and an immense amount of love. From our anchor in the Middle East I traveled to Syria with the family, Greece and Lebanon for speech and acting competitions, and Egypt each year to run the 200m and 400m against other teenagers from Europe, the Middle East, and Africa.

NOW FIFTEEN, I dated, and I use the word *dated* lightly as it was all mostly innocent, an American girl whose parents were diplomats and had come to work in Jordan. Her pale skin, light eyes, and straight hair contrasted with mine. Her name was

Rachel and I had found myself attracted to her from the first time she walked into ACS. My ninth grade English teacher, Vicky Jalamdeh, whom both I and the entire school loved, had told my parents: "Garon seems to be a little distracted in class lately. There's a girl here from New York who just arrived."

Upon returning from the parent-teacher conference, Mom sat down next to me.

"Honey, Ms. Jalamdeh says you've done really well in her class, but you seem to be a bit distracted lately. Is there a reason for that?"

"No," I answered, wondering how Ms. Jalamdeh had known.

"Are you sure? She said that maybe it's because there's a new girl. Rachel?"

I smiled awkwardly as Mom grinned back, fishing for information.

"Okay, I'll try to focus more," I said, sighing.

"So who's Rachel?" Mom asked now, giggling.

"No one, Mom. She's just a girl in the class. It's nothing," I said, blushing.

On weekends, Rachel would give me hand jobs at friends' houses under the blanket while we all watched movies together. Moments after the movie would start, Rachel's hands would quickly and quietly find their way beneath the blanket. She would unbutton my jeans, slide the zipper down, pull my cock out, and start jerking me off. I cautiously scanned the room to see if my friends sitting on other sofas could see the movement of the blanket going up and down, but they were focused on the movie. Rachel seemed equally excited to have my cock in her hand and to be doing it in a public space. After a number of times of secret living-room hand jobs, I tried to return the favor, but she would always gently move my hands away from the button of her jeans.

Later, a stunning girl, Nora, moved from Washington, DC, and started at ACS. She had big soulful eyes, skin the color of mine, and sensual lips. At lunch we would find each other and flirt in the hallway. When our lips touched, it felt intoxicating. So many years later, I still remember her as one of the most wonderful kissers.

And then there was Vassia, who was originally from Cyprus. I met Vassia the first year we arrived in Jordan, when we had both sat in Ms. Kasim's class together. We kissed once in middle school while playing truth or dare but there was nothing sexual between us. Now freshmen in high school, we had a lasting friendship, and one that I would come to depend on in the coming years. Vassia had long, voluminous chestnut-brown hair and a sassy demeanor. I liked her confidence right away. Her mother, whom I called Ms. Endrie, worked at the Embassy of Greece and had moved Vassia and her sister, Ellie, to Jordan.

One morning when I wasn't feeling well and worried about missing out on the social aspect of school, Mom convinced me to stay home with her and rest up. By the early afternoon I had improved, and the two of us went to lunch in an area of Amman called Sweifieh, full of shops and cafés. I used to do this thing to make Mom laugh. As she was driving, I would mimic the motion of her hands on the steering wheel and move my feet in step with hers from the accelerator to the brake. She found this hilarious and would laugh uncontrollably each time I did it.

"Stop, Garon! Stop!" she would say, wailing with delight. Of course, I continued. After one of these moments one day, after the laughter had subsided, Mom said, "You know, honey, when Ms. Connie and I were in college, on the weekends we would often go hang out at the gay bars."

"Oh yea?" I said, interested in the story to come.

"Yes. We went there because all the most handsome men hung out there. And they were the most fun," she said.

That was it. No story. No follow-up. Nothing. I wondered why she'd chosen that moment to tell me that story.

14
THE RETURN

I PEERED OUT THE PLANE WINDOW. How did these titans transport me across the world with such ease? Airplanes were a mystery to me, and each time I flew I was completely seduced by the experience—the speed, the majesty. We had cruised above Saudi Arabia, Oman, spent hours crossing the Indian Ocean, and finally we were landing in Sri Lanka. I had been adopted from this island at ten months old, left for South Africa at age three, and was now returning twelve years later. Mom and Dad looked over at me lovingly. I imagined it was overwhelming for them, bringing their fifteen-year-old son back to the country of his birth, the city where they'd first met me.

The rush of humidity swirled around us as we walked to the restaurant patio of the Galle Face Hotel, one of my parents' favorite places. A lovely green lawn stretched out until it met the water's edge. The Indian Ocean, with its full vigor, danced in shades of sapphire ahead of us. A giant marble black-and-white chessboard sat in the center of the garden.

"Want to go check out the chessboard with me?" Yael asked.

"Yea. Let's go." I had waited many years for Yael to grow older. Five years younger than me, I had often just seen him as

Mom and Dad's baby while I spent most of my time with Ebony. But now, with Yael at nine years old, I felt that he and I were entering a new chapter together.

Once we finished ordering, Yael and I playfully leapt from square to square, a terrace of black and white surrounded by moving color. Fanning their brilliant blues and greens, male peacocks strutted through the palm trees. I understood why Sri Lanka was often called The Pearl of the Indian Ocean.

Our second morning the five of us stood in front of 7 De Soysa Avenue in Mt. Lavinia. Dad made an attempt to see if the owner was home and would let us in the gate, but no one was. Instead I stood at the edge of the driveway, staring through the same white metal gate with purple bougainvillea flowers cascading off the sides of the wall, marveling at the home where I had been given the gift of a family.

"Garon, the day we adopted you we came back to the house, we rolled a big burgundy-and-beige bamboo mat out on that front lawn, and the four of us played here for hours," Dad told me.

"That's right. We stared at you taking your whole new world in. We couldn't believe that after nine months of paperwork, you were finally ours," Mom said, putting her arm around me.

"And then the trouble started," Dad said, laughing. "After the first couple days you didn't want anything to do with anyone besides me."

I laughed.

"I would try to hold you and you would start screaming," Mom said. "Then Dad would hold you and that was all you wanted. He carried you around this house for days, until you got comfortable."

I looked over at Ebony and Yael, who were taking it all in. I ran my hands through Yael's smooth hair. I hoped he never felt left out of our adoption stories. In my mind, his arrival was so special in its own way: completely unexpected to Mom and Dad, who didn't think they could have a baby naturally, and he had been born in such an exceptional country.

"Remember the bandicoots that used to crawl above the ceiling?" Ebony asked.

"I can't believe you remember that, sweetie!" Dad said. "They made so much noise at night."

"Yea, I used to be really scared of them."

Mom took my hand in hers. "We fell in love with Sri Lanka so easily, Garon. I remember you eating Mr. Twan's food with him in the kitchen. You would shove rice and curry in your mouth, swallow it, and then suck in air as hard as you could because it was so spicy. Then you would reach for more and do it all again. We all laughed so much looking at your little face," Mom said, smiling.

Throughout the years, as Mom and Dad came across photographs of our time in Sri Lanka they always showed them to me. Mr. Twan was in a couple of the pictures and I could still see him standing in the kitchen in his blue-and-white-striped sarong. Where had life taken him? I wished we could see him now. My closeness with Mr. Twan had set in motion more than a decade of meaningful relationships with all the others: Grace, Juju, Agnes, and Baboucarr.

Mom and Dad had always made it clear that if Ebony and I were interested in searching for our biological parents, they would help us in any way they could. But in my case, there was virtually no information to go on. By the time Mom and Dad had met me at the Jayamani Malnutrition Center in Colombo, the government had issued me a name, Gamini Mirihella, but no birthday. My parents had been given the opportunity to create a birthday for me and so they did. They decided that my birthday would be November 29. But because I'd been abandoned on the steps of the hospital in Kegalle, with no one to claim me, there were no biological parents' names on my birth certificate. My identity, in essence, had been created. When people find out that my birthday is not actually the day I was born, they are often surprised. Over the years, I've just gotten used to it. I do occasionally wonder which day of the year I was *actually* born on, but I've also accepted that I'll probably never know.

I agreed that it would be interesting to travel back to the orphanage in Kandy, Tikiri Sevana, where I had stayed for the first few days after being abandoned. We pulled up to the orphanage gate, and beyond it I saw dozens of little kids waiting to see who their newest visitor was. They ran up and down the unpaved driveway, laughing and smiling. As I walked through the gates, the kids rushed me, jumping up and down. I stared at the little boys. I couldn't believe how much I looked exactly like them. Some played in the dirt outside while others slid across the hard floor of the orphanage on their bellies. I tried to imagine myself here as an infant. Who had taken care of me? Who had decided I was too malnourished to stay?

Mom and Dad were inside talking to the head caretaker. They flipped through old decrepit books, searching for the names of children and dates of arrival. They couldn't find me. It was no surprise; my stay here in Kandy had been stunted. As I continued to play with the young orphans with whom I'd established an initial rapport, I heard footsteps behind me. I turned around and two women with long black hair, dressed in yellow and blue sarees, stood in front of me. They started speaking Sinhala rapid-fire. I couldn't understand what they were saying as they began to touch my face and stroke my hair. I was uncomfortable and shifted my eyes beyond them to Mom and Dad for a second, who looked on from the office. I bowed my head to allow them to access my hair more easily as they ran their fingers through it. Then they started crying. I could see the tears building in their eyes and sliding down their cheeks. They caressed my forehead, my chin, my ears, saying words in Sinhala. Mom and Dad walked over.

"No one's ever come back, honey," Mom said, looking at me.

"They said they've been working here for longer than you've been alive. So they would've taken care of you even for a couple days when you were small," Dad added.

I didn't know how to feel. I looked at the tears that rolled down their faces and understood that I needed to allow them to have this moment. I didn't remember them, I couldn't, I was too young. But I found my peace in the eyes of the little girls and boys who sat around us, watching. To the women of the orphanage, one of their kids had finally come home.

As I looked beyond the orphanage gate at the lush green hills that surrounded us, I wondered if my birth mother had ever walked these winding broken roads. Maybe she had walked them holding the hands of her other children. Did she have other children? If she did, did I look like them? I envisioned her with rough hands and a worn face from a lifetime of some form of manual labor. Almost certainly she was impoverished. And selfishly I wondered, Did she still think of me? Or had so much time passed that her memories of me had faded into darkness? I imagined that a mother would never forget her baby, but perhaps the pain of losing a child hides in one's soul. Had there been more information, we could have searched for her. But with no real name and no birthdate, it was close to impossible. Back in Colombo, we searched for the Jayamani Center but couldn't find it. I wondered if years of civil war and no funding had led to its shutdown. What would have happened to kids like me who arrived there in search of a last chance? I would have liked to see where I spent my first year of life; what it looked like, what it smelled like.

On one of our last evenings in Colombo, we got together with family friends who had been neighbors at our apartment in Shmeisani during our first months in Jordan. They were a Sri Lankan-Irish family who had recently moved back to Sri Lanka and opened an Irish pub in Colombo. Their daughter, Ruwena, had a mischievous smile and flirtatious eyes. In years before I had certainly had a crush on her, but nothing ever happened in the brief time we lived near each other.

"I'm going to take you and Ebony out for an hour for a ride around Colombo," Ruwena told us.

I looked over at Mom and Dad, who were talking with her parents. "Don't worry, I already asked and your parents said yes."

Thirty minutes later Ebony, Ruwena, and I rode together in the back of a bright-red tuk-tuk as its three wheels wove in and out of the bustling city traffic. The tropical evening breeze off the Indian Ocean swirled around us and neon lights lit up bars and restaurants on every corner. Young men and women who looked just like me made their way in and out of stores and restaurants. I looked closely at the older men, closer to Grandpa's age. Their thick jet-black hair had been replaced by equally thick white hair. I hoped that many decades in the future, as I aged into my seventies, my mass of black hair would turn as strikingly white as theirs. And I wondered what my life would have been like had I never been adopted. Given that I was born in Kegalle, two hours away, maybe I would still live there in the highlands. Without a family and perhaps limited education, surely I would have struggled to make money going into adulthood. It was hard to imagine myself living in Sri Lanka, dressed completely differently, speaking Sinhala or Tamil, and never knowing Mom, Dad, Ebony, Yael, or the far corners of the world I had grown up in.

Our short holiday was over, and as our plane climbed back into the skies above Sri Lanka, I gazed below at the country that had brought me into the world. And still that nagging question lingered in my mind. Did *she* leave me on the steps of that hospital or was I taken from her arms by a disapproving family member or a stranger? And the dreaded question: Was she even still alive? As the island disappeared beneath the clouds, the faces of the young toddlers at the orphanage in Kandy looped in my head. In some strange way, I felt that they were a part of me, and I was a part of them.

15
SURAJ

IN JANUARY 2001, UPON OUR return from Sri Lanka, one of the people I love most in this world walked through the front door of our home and into my life. His name was Krishnan Putalath Suraj, or as he liked to be called, Suraj. Suraj was a twenty-one-year-old who, at the encouragement of his mother, had left his native India to come work in our home in Jordan. His mother, Molly, a robust and hardworking woman, had cooked at our home, helping Mom the occasional time that she'd agreed to host a dinner party. Suraj had kind eyes, light-brown skin, and stood much taller than me. He spoke English, Malayalam, and Tamil. Now a freshman in high school, I was happy to have someone older to hang out with at home. Ebony, months away from graduating from ACS, was either with her best friend Sara Yoder or purposely locked in her room away from her brothers, listening to Third Eye Blind or Dido. Yael had a rich social life of his own and was either hanging with his international crew from school or collecting turtles that burrowed in the rocky hills surrounding our home and relocating them to our backyard.

During Suraj's first three months in our home, I found myself looking forward to time spent with him. I asked him questions about growing up in India, just as I had done years earlier with Grace, Juju, Agnes, and Baboucarr. Only this time, much older, my questions were more thoughtful—and most importantly, I listened closely to his answers.

"What city were you born in, Suraj?" I asked him one afternoon while hanging out in the kitchen together.

"I was born in Kerala in 1978."

"And how many years did you and your mom live together before she moved to Jordan?"

"Soon after I was born, my mom came to work here in Jordan for money."

All my other housekeepers had lived in the countries where they were from. I tried to imagine just how difficult it would have been for Molly to leave her four young children and move to the Middle East to be able to provide for them.

"How did it feel to have your mom so far away from India?" I asked him.

"You know, we were so happy when my mom would come visit us in Kerala for her vacation. Because I don't have a father, we lived with guardians. At the same time, we were scared because our guardians would tell my mom all the things that we did wrong that year," Suraj said, laughing.

"And what about your brothers and sisters. Where are they?"

"I have an older sister and an older brother in India. In 1991, we moved from Kerala to a village in Tamil Nadu called Mettupalayam. Our little brother's name was Kannappan. He was the baby. Me and my older brother, Solly, played together and we didn't let Kannappan join with us.

"Why didn't you let him play with you?"

"We kept saying, 'You are smaller, go away, go away.' It was

October 1, 1993, and I was with my group of friends and Kannappan wanted to come also. Usually I ignored him and told him to leave, but that day I didn't ignore him."

I thought of where I had been in October 1993: we were still living in The Gambia.

"We found a farm where there was a sort of dam, where the owners collected rainwater for their crops. There were fourteen of us and many of the kids started to undress and jump into the dam. No one knew how to swim so the kids were holding on to larger pieces of dried wood that were floating. I was also planning to jump into the water. But at the time, I had ripped a lemon off a tree, wanted to finish it, so I sat on a wall and watched everyone. Kannappan took off his clothes and jumped in the water. My brother was always faking things. Sometimes he would pretend to cry and then would start laughing when we checked on him. He was funny and he was really smart. But he would always pretend. So he jumped in the water and after a few seconds he came up with big eyes and waving both hands. Then he went down again. We all thought he was just making it up. I am lying down on the top of a wall eating a lemon watching him come up and down, up and down. Then he went down for the last time and he never came up."

I stared at Suraj in disbelief. And while his voice held strong, I could see the pain in his eyes.

"Then what happened?" I asked, completely consumed.

"All our friends started feeling scared. We asked who could swim and get him. Most couldn't. A couple boys jumped in, but they said there were plants at the bottom and they couldn't find Kannappan. I started to run the three kilometers to my guardian's house. I saw a guy on the road on a bicycle and told him what happened. He put me on his bicycle and took me to my guardian's work. I told him the story and they called the fire service. One hour later the fire service got there. I was also there. After some time they found Kannappan. I still remember his hands as they brought him out. It was a terrible time for me and Solly, all of us. You know it is still very hard to think about his death. It is very hard for me. Kannappan was ten. My mother was here in Jordan. We still miss him."

I stood motionless in the kitchen. I hated that Kannappan had died while Suraj watched, not understanding the pain he was enduring as he took his last breath. I tried to imagine what Kannappan was thinking in those last moments, drowning, while no one helped him. And how Suraj must have felt, knowing that had he just jumped in, maybe he could have saved him. And of course, Molly. I didn't want to imagine the pain she went through here in Jordan, alone, while she learned that her youngest son had died in India. I told Suraj about Uncle Robby and how Mom had lost him when they were young. Suraj's willingness to be so open with me set the tone for how quickly we became close to each other. I felt an immediate bond with this man, just seven years older than me, who looked like he could be my big brother.

16

NIKI

THREE MONTHS INTO THE NEW YEAR, having experienced some abdominal discomfort, Mom went to see her doctor. After various tests, her doctor suggested that she get her gall bladder removed. She desperately wanted to feel better before June, Ebony's graduation from ACS Amman. Dad and Mom sat all of us down and explained that she was going to have surgery and that it would take some time for her to recover afterward. *That's fine*, I thought. *I'll help her around the house and get her recovered as fast as we can.* The night before her surgery I was sitting at the kitchen table while Mom sat over by the phone.

"Garon, I'm scared to go in for this surgery," she said to me. This surprised me, as I couldn't remember another time when Mom told me she was scared of something. Throughout our lives, she'd been the one encouraging all of us to be adventurous.

"Don't be scared, Mom. It's going to be fine," I promised her.

"No, Garon. It's going to hurt for a long time afterward," she replied.

I listened to her words. She genuinely seemed afraid. As a kid I can remember the thing that made me saddest was thinking of Mom in pain. When living on Flint Road in South Africa, I had a nightmare so vivid that I've always been able to remember it. Mom and I had just finished shopping at CNA, a stationery store where we often bought our school supplies. We walked out of the store onto the busy street. Suddenly, Mom fell through an exposed grate in the sidewalk and she crashed fifteen feet down below into a cavernous den of scorpions. I jumped in after her, screaming and begging to be close to her. Scorpions and snakelike centipedes encircled us. It was pitch-black but slowly my eyes began adjusting and eventually an orange light illuminated the cavern. I saw Mom lying down on the ground, badly injured. Black soot lined her face and she was grasping her arm, which had snapped in half in the fall. I was bawling, sitting a foot away from her, calling out her name. An older man with sparse gray hair stood just beyond her.

"Why are you crying?" he asked sinisterly.

"Because I don't want her to die," I said, amid a rush of tears.

It's amazing how a dream I had when I was five has stayed with me throughout my life.

The morning of Mom's surgery, Ebony, Yael, and I left for school as usual. We knew that Dad would be taking Mom and we would get an update once we arrived home. I didn't worry at all throughout the day. I knew she'd be fine, and I would help her when we returned. When we arrived home, Mom still wasn't back and Dad came by himself. He called us together.

"Your mom's done with the surgery, but she's not feeling well, so she's going to stay in the hospital overnight," he told us. "Randa and I will be with her."

That seemed normal enough. Perhaps if she were feeling better in the morning, we could go see her.

I went back to school the next day and that evening Dad told us we could come see her. He warned us that she was still in a lot of pain.

I can still remember walking into the Amman Surgical Center in Jordan. It had the same smell that most hospitals have, a very sterile odor. The three of us made our way to her recovery room. There she was, lying in bed, Dad by her side, and her doctor encouraging her to get out of bed.

"You have to get up and try to walk, Niki," Dad said.

I looked at her face. I expected her to be in a certain level of discomfort, but I wasn't expecting to see her in excruciating pain. Her eyes squinted as she tried to stand up, and she bared her teeth in an effort to take a step while crying out.

"I can't, Steve. This hurts too much. Something's not right," she countered, her eyes red.

"Just try to take one step, Niki," the doctor urged.

Ebony, Yael, and I stood there in the corner, my heart beating faster. I had seen Mom cry before of course, but not out of pain. It's a very different sound and it cuts right through your bones.

As she tried to move forward, she saw us off in the corner for the first time. "Hi, kids," she squeezed out, with tears rolling down her flush cheeks.

"Hi, Mom. How are you doing?" I said, aghast and trying to think of something to say.

But she couldn't answer me. Instead she held her abdomen and began to cry harder. A lump grew in my throat. I knew something was very wrong. Her pain became too severe to watch and it quickly became clear that we needed to leave.

"Hey, guys, why don't you go outside and I'll meet you in a moment," Dad said. I looked at Ebony and Yael, who looked as shocked as I was.

"Okay. Bye, Mom. I love you," I said, trying not to cry. "We're taking good care of Jazzbee," I blurted out. As we left the room, my eyes filled with tears. Ebony, Yael, and I had a hard time talking as we left the hospital.

That afternoon, instead of returning to our house, we went to the Morans' home. Each time I started to think about Mom, I blocked out the pain that would surface, assured that Dad and her medical team would take care of her. Later that evening Dad came to pick us up. As we drove our normal path that led us outside the city, our Honda CR-V was completely silent.

"Look, guys, Mom and I have always believed in telling you the truth. The truth is, something is wrong with her. She shouldn't feel like this after the surgery. They took her back into surgery today to see what went wrong, discovered they'd punctured a hole in her small intestine, and now she's in ICU."

I stopped breathing. ICU. ICU? I sat stone-faced, staring at the back of Dad's seat. Then, out of nowhere, Yael's young voice asked the question I never thought possible.

"Is Mom going to die?"

I wanted to look at Yael, but I couldn't move. Dad was silent for a moment.

"I . . . I don't know, guys. I don't know what's going to happen," he said slowly.

It had never once occurred to me that it was that serious. I could feel the heat rise in my body. *No, this isn't possible. Mom can't die. This isn't an option.*

None of us spoke once we got home. Dad got us ready for bed and then told us he was going to stay with Mom in the hospital. Yael and I chose to sleep in Mom and Dad's bed that night. Ebony slept in her own room.

"I'll be back to take you guys to school in the morning," Dad promised, walking away. Then he stopped and turned back to us. "I love you, guys."

I lay in the bed next to Yael in the exact spot where Mom had read bedtime stories to him each night. I wanted to say something to him, but I didn't know what to say. The images I had seen of Mom in excruciating pain circled through my mind. I tried to calm myself, but it wasn't possible. I don't remember when I finally was able to drift off to sleep.

At 5:30 a.m. I woke up startled and leapt upright in bed, gasping. The bedroom was still dark and Yael still beside me. I put my hand on my chest. I had never in my life sat upright in bed like this so suddenly. It felt like a gust of wind had rushed through me. The room was silent. Quickly I remembered that Mom was still in the hospital and Dad was with her. I fell back into Mom's pillow, knowing that it was my job to take care of Yael in the morning.

The sun drifted in from the bedroom balcony and I hustled to get my brother up and ready. We did our best to get everything together, hoping for an update from Dad. Yael and I were the first down to breakfast. I ate with him at our kitchen table.

"Maybe after school we can go see Mom," I said, looking at him.

"Yea," his ten-year-old voice returned.

As we were finishing breakfast, I heard the downstairs door open and close, followed by footsteps up the stairs. Dad walked into the kitchen.

"How's Mom?" I asked, trying to be upbeat.

"Can you boys meet me in the living room," he said quickly. He was calm and I looked forward to his news. "And tell your sister to come down."

I raced upstairs and knocked on Ebony's door.

"What?" she said in her usual morning teenage-girl annoyance.

"Dad says to come downstairs quickly. He's going to tell us how Mom's doing."

Yael and I were first into the living room, and we jumped onto the biggest couch next to Dad. A minute later, Ebony arrived and sat on the couch across from us.

"So. How is she?" I asked again.

"Oh guys," Dad said, his voice shattering. Then a guttural sound rose without control from deep inside him and, bursting into tears, he choked out, "Guys, your mom died."

A rumbling cry lurched out of him. It was the worst sound I've ever heard and to this day brings me to tears if I think of it.

The room went hazy. Pain rose through my body and tears cascaded down my face. I could no longer see in front of me and I heard the cries of Yael, who fell into Dad's arms. Ebony's eyes welled up as she tried to keep from breaking down.

"I'm so sorry, guys!" Dad cried, feeling as if he should have prevented all of it. I felt like I was suffocating.

What I wouldn't know for fifteen more years is the pain that Dad went through that morning before he saw us. For *fifteen years* my pain sat too close to the surface to ask him what he had seen. Many years later across the dining-room table, he told me this: After getting us set up for bed, he went back to the hospital that evening. There was a sofa directly outside of the ICU window. Hooked up to monitors, Mom was sleeping after the last-minute surgery effort to fix her small intestine and stabilize her body. Dad half slept, half watched over her throughout the night. Then around 5:30 a.m., when something had pushed me upright in bed, Mom's pulse started crashing. The alarm sounded and Dad watched as nurses and doctors rushed into ICU to her bedside. He ran up against the glass window and watched as the defibrillator came out and the

YOU'LL ALWAYS BE WHITE TO ME

medical team tried desperately to shock her back to life. He stood there watching in horror, unable to do anything as Mom took her last breath.

When the door opened, the doctor walked out with his head down and toward Dad.

"You killed my wife," Dad yelled through his tears. Many years later when he recounted this story, I struggled so hard not to cry in front of him. Not because I didn't want him to cry, but because I wasn't sure I could handle seeing him cry again.

We all sat in the living room in silence.

"Mr. Moran is downstairs with his driver, Mohammed. You guys have a choice to make. You can come to the hospital to see your mom if you want. Or you can stay here," he offered, wiping his face.

"I'll come," I said.

"I'll come," Yael said.

"I don't want to come," Ebony said, shocking me.

I didn't understand it then, and it would take me many more years to understand how people process death so differently.

Yael, Dad, and I walked downstairs. I couldn't feel myself moving, it was almost as if my actions were automatic. As we stepped outside the door, Amy's father was standing there. It was clear he'd been crying. He pulled me close to him.

"I'm so sorry," he said.

"Hi, Mr. Moran," I managed to get out.

Dad sat in the middle, his arms around Yael and me in the back of the ambassador's car. Mohammed drove us, Jim sat next to him, and the five of us moved through Amman in complete silence. I stared out the window. My childhood nightmare had come true.

Upon reaching the hospital, I took off, running up the stairs, desperate to find Mom. As I approached the glass doors of ICU, I could see Amy's mother, Randa, inside. She was pacing back and forth, yelling in Arabic over the phone, tears overtaking her face. I flung open the door and ran into her arms and began to sob. She pulled me and Yael into her.

"Do you guys want to go into the room individually, or all together?" Dad asked.

The pain was almost more than I could stand. I looked to Yael and read the answer in his eyes.

"All together," I said.

I took a deep breath and knew my life would never be the same. There she was. Now out of her hospital clothes, in which I had seen her crying just a day before, she lay motionless in her bed. The elegant long-sleeve black-and-yellow-patterned blouse that she'd left our house wearing now covered her upper body. Her eyes were closed. I rushed over to her.

"Mom!" I cried. "Mom! Mom! Mom!" I gently positioned my face over hers and kissed her forehead and her lips.

"I love you so much" I said, begging her to hear me. I remember seeing a delicate stream of blood trickling from her nose.

Yael climbed up onto her bed and he nestled next to her, his tears falling onto her blouse. I stared at her face, trying to memorize every angle, every wrinkle, the softness of her lips, the woman who had in every way given me a second chance at life the day she'd met me in Sri Lanka. My heart fractured as I watched my little brother cry above her.

As Yael and I prepared to leave her for the last time, I grabbed hold of her hand and ran my fingers across hers. I reached over one more time, kissed her lips, and whispered, "I love you, Mom." Then I walked toward the door but turned to see her one more time. There are no words to express the feeling of knowing you will never see your parent's face again. I took one last look, then walked away.

When we got back to our house, it was as if all the light had been sucked out of our home. Suraj and Molly were standing quietly at the top of the stairs. As I looked into Suraj's eyes, I knew instantly that he knew the pain I was going through. I hugged them both and without words walked to the living room. Randa and Dad had come back with us, and she was on her phone contacting the world.

"In the next hours, lots of people are going to come over," Dad said. "Then, you can choose. You guys can fly back to Louisiana tonight to be with Ashoh and Grandpa, or you can wait with me for a couple days while we prepare Mom's body to fly home to the United States."

Ashoh and Grandpa? I crumbled inside. In my own grief I hadn't even thought of Ashoh and Grandpa, who I knew would be destroyed. I rushed upstairs to Ebony's room and pounded on the door.

"Dad says we can either stay a couple days or go back to the States tonight," I shouted as she opened the door.

But Ebony was already one step ahead of me. I looked around her room. Clothes were piled on her bed and she was pulling things out of her chest of drawers.

"I'm going back tonight. You and Yael can do what you want, but I want to go back tonight," she replied. It surprised me that she'd already known the options. These hadn't even occurred to me.

"People are coming over, Ebony," I said. She looked annoyed. In the Middle East when a death takes place, friends and family come immediately to bring food and sit with you for hours. The extrovert in me found comfort in this. The introvert in Ebony hated that.

I ran back downstairs to find Yael, who was sitting on the sofa crying. I went over to him. Then there was a pounding on the door. It was Mom's friend Pat.

"What the fuck happened!" she yelled, tears spilling down her face.

"The surgeon made a mistake and punctured a hole in her small intestine . . . and . . . and she died." That was the first time I had said it out loud. Ms. Pat rushed to hug Yael and me.

Over the course of the next fifteen hours, teachers from school, friends from our class, neighbors we were close to, neighbors we barely knew, people from various NGOs, people from various embassies, people from the Jordanian government, people from Dad's work, all piled into our house, coming and going, the biggest banquet of food you've ever seen. It was surreal.

At 12:30 a.m., Mohammed once again arrived with the ambassador's car. With Dad in the front next to Mohammed and Ebony, Yael and me in the back, we journeyed through the moonlight early morning hours to Queen Alia International Airport. Dad and Mohammed escorted us through security, into the gate area, and to the door of our Lufthansa flight, which would carry us first to Germany and then to the United States.

"I love you guys so much," Dad said. Fifteen years later, during that same conversation, he would tell me, "You can't imagine. You just cannot imagine what it was like coming home from the hospital that morning knowing I had to tell the three of you that Mom died. That was the hardest thing I've ever had to do in my entire life."

"You guys be strong, your grandparents will be waiting for

you on the other side," Dad told us. "I'll be in Louisiana with Mom in a couple days."

We had trained for this our whole childhood. Mom and Dad had coached us repeatedly, making us guide them through Chicago O'Hare, Amsterdam Schiphol, London Heathrow, Frankfurt, and Brussels, asking us, "Which way do we go now to get to our gate? Left or right?" or "How do we get to Gate 17F? Take us there." We had been well prepped and knew how to cross the world by ourselves. As we sat in the three seats on the Airbus that would take us to Europe, there were three violet flowers in the seatback pocket in front of us. I looked around. They weren't in any other seats.

As we ascended out of Amman and into the skies above the Middle East at 3 a.m., Yael and I cried endlessly. It didn't seem possible.

Ebony looked over at us. "Stop" she said, not knowing how to manage her own emotions, much less her two brothers. Many years later she would tell me, "I was worried if I couldn't get you guys through this first flight, how were we going to make it through the next two?" By the time we landed in Germany, I felt I didn't have the energy to cry anymore.

From Germany we traveled to Washington, DC. Finally we boarded our last flight, taking us down through the southern United States and into New Orleans. As the sliding doors opened at the arrivals hall, there stood Ashoh, Grandpa, and Uncle Mike. They rushed over to us and the six of us fell into each other's arms. Somehow, the pain that circulated between us was comforting. We had flown nearly seven thousand miles to get to them. Thirty years before, Mom had left this airport in search of an international life bigger than herself. We were the result of her dreams.

At Mom's funeral in a crowded church in Luling, Dad read a letter he had written out loud. He began:

My Dearest Niki,
I begin this letter, the saddest I will ever write, in a haze of tears as I gaze from the cabin of the plane that will carry you to America for the very last time. I'm thankful that no one is sitting next to me; it makes it easier to believe that you are still here with me, as you have been through so many other journeys. I will be your guide on this one as you have been mine so often over the three decades of our life together.

I watched on, my heart in pieces and feeling as though I couldn't breathe. As Dad spoke, he was able to give those who had known Mom as a young girl and teenager growing up in Louisiana a glimpse into her life across the globe.

Fifteen minutes later, and without a dry eye in the church, he read:

We are now over the snowy hills of Eastern Canada, homing in on JFK. You and I have avoided JFK for years. But perhaps it is fitting to have you return to American soil via JFK, for it was from that airport 28 years ago to the week, that we first embarked abroad on the journey of a lifetime.

Your hair was longer then, your eyes never brighter, flaming with excitement. Remember how hours later, on the other side of the Atlantic, we all rushed to the windows to get our first glimpse of Africa and imagine our lives ahead. It was a heck of a ride, my love. Thank you for taking me along.

When we get home, we will have a ceremony in your honor, a celebration of life. I may read this letter if I can get through it. People will come and they will hear about a little girl from Luling, Louisiana, who for some reason went out and touched the world. A woman barely 5 feet tall, but fearless, who became a giant in the lives of many. She did not have to do this; she probably did not intend to. She never sought an ounce of credit for what she did. She just did it, nonetheless.

It was all too much for me to handle. I tried hard to subdue my incessant cries and I watched as Ashoh and Grandpa clutched their chests in agonizing pain.

When the service was over, I looked into Grandpa's swollen eyes. "They said the second time it would be easier. It isn't any easier. I loved your mama."

17

THE SILENCE

OPENING THE DOOR TO MY BEDROOM in Amman, everything was as I had left it. The silence of my room and the pain in my heart was overbearing. I looked out across the hills to the few city lights that flickered in the distance. I was fifteen years old and I would need to begin learning how to live without her.

In the weeks that followed, I tried to hold my head up at school the best way I knew how. My friends rallied around me and I found comfort in those closest to me, like Amy and Vassia. I could sit with them, not say a word, and they knew the storm churning inside me.

One afternoon during lunch break, Amy and I journeyed up to the third floor where the year before we had completed our middle-school classes. We opened a tall blue door and walked into the classroom of our former math teacher, who was also our high-school track and field coach.

"Garon, come here." Stacey Johnsen was extremely tall with long, wavy blond hair. She led us to a circular gray table and the three of us sat down.

"I'm just so sorry that your mom passed away," she said, leaning into me. "How are you doing?"

"I'm okay," I said, looking across at Amy, who knew I wasn't.
"I'm just . . . I . . ." Then I felt a surge in my chest and a
complete loss of control as tears came leaping from my eyes
and my voice crashed. "I just miss her so much," I cried out
loud. It was the first time since Mom's funeral that I had cried
in public. I had been trying so hard to keep it all together.

"Oh no," Ms. Johnsen said, immediately scooting her chair
next to mine and throwing her arms around me. She motioned
for Amy to come closer. I glanced up at Amy, who had tears in
her eyes watching me breakdown. Amy and I had experienced
so much happiness together starting all the way back in
elementary school in Jamaica. She had loved Mom in the same
way that I had loved Randa. And she had never seen me like
this.

"I'm so sorry," I said, trying to regain control.

"Don't be sorry. We are here for you, Garon. We will
continue to be here for you," Ms. Johnsen said. With both of
their arms around me, I knew I had two choices: to succumb to
this acute soul-wrenching pain or find a way forward.

At home, the silence of our house was deafening. I walked
past Mom and Dad's room and day after day expected her to
walk out and hug me. Dad, grieving himself, did a wonderful
job of trying to be two parents. For so long he had relied on
Mom for the more emotional side of parenting. Little boys
raised in America in the 1960s weren't taught to be emotionally
in-touch parents the way women were. Now, through his own
struggle, Dad too was learning a new role and I admired him
for it. Outwardly, he projected a sense of strength. I never saw
him cry in front of us again and he still greeted us every single
day after work with that kilowatt smile that I so loved and
depended on. Consumed by my own grief, I don't remember

thinking much about him and what his journey was like. Even as I write this, I now think back on him during that time from an adult perspective: lying in his bed, night after night, alone, without her. Did he cry himself to sleep too? I'm sure he did. I wish I could have helped him somehow, but I was too broken myself and I was still a child.

I've long said, after someone dies, the days and even weeks that follow are filled with love and people around you: constant companionship. But it's when they all leave, when the house grows silent, that's when you are really forced to deal with what has happened.

I found peace in quiet moments walking with Yael and Jazzbee through the dusty roads that weaved farther up into our barren hills. There had been many afternoons over the past three years when Mom had called me from downstairs.

"Garon! C'mon."

"Where are we going?" I'd yell from the upstairs living room.

"It's time for an evening walk through the hills."

"I don't want to go," I'd say.

"It's a family walk. All of us are ready. I'm not asking you, honey. I'm telling you to come down here and get your shoes on."

I had begrudgingly complied and rolled my eyes as I put my shoes on. Now I would have given anything to walk alongside Mom just one more time.

Near the top of the hill Yael and I stepped off the path and into the brown soil anchored by white desert rocks. Jazzbee dug furiously beneath them and occasionally uncovered desert tortoises as large as an adult hand. Yael and I took the terrified tortoises from Jazzbee's mouth, protecting them from our little apricot poodle who sat with a wagging tail, proud of her hunting abilities.

"I miss Mom so much, Yael. I know you do too," I said, putting my arm around him.

"I can't believe she died," he said, his young voice cracking.

"I can't believe it either. It still doesn't feel real. I keep thinking she's going to come back." As I looked at Yael's tear-streaked face, I realized just how much he looked like Mom. With her gone, for the first time, I saw her face so distinctly in his: they had the exact same light-brown eyes, dirty blond hair and smooth jawline. She emanated from his eyes.

ONE DAY AFTER SCHOOL, Dad invited an American woman named Virginia Foley over to our home. She and her husband, Larry, were diplomats in Jordan and he worked for USAID, the United States Agency for International Development. Virginia was soft-spoken, gracious, and had a trusting quality about her. She was a grief counselor and sat with all of us as we discussed the great emptiness we felt without Mom. Yael, who had just turned ten the month before Mom died, sat in the stairwell near the living room. I can still see his blond hair poking out behind the wall as he tried to listen in. Dad had told us if we didn't want to take part, we didn't have to. My little brother, the baby they once thought they couldn't have, was heartbroken and wanted to keep his distance. Virginia brought calm to our home and her trusting eyes allowed me to express the immense pain and sorrow I felt.

Suraj was the first face we would see when we got home from school. He would make us food, make us laugh; he brought levity to our often somber house. I started to see him as more than my housekeeper and friend, but as an older brother.

I don't think that when Suraj arrived in Jordan at the very start of the year, he could ever have imagined himself jointly parenting three American children after their mother died. Dad now hired his mother, Molly, to cook for us multiple times a week. Having the two of them consistently in our home brought a warmth that we desperately needed. Together, we all became a family.

18

SEPTEMBER 11

THE AFTERNOON OF TUESDAY, September 11, started like any other. Dad had flown to the United States to take Ebony to college. She would be attending The University of Chicago. With the two of them gone, Yael and I were spending a lot of afternoons at the Morans' house, and this day was no different. We piled onto the bus and made our way to the residence in Abdoun. Amy and I walked inside and put our schoolbags down. Stephanie, her younger sister, ran out and shouted, "Quickly, come to the living room!" We darted into the living room, where Yael was already sitting with Amy's younger brother, Thomas. I looked around the room, trying to understand what was happening. The ambassador, Randa, and the kids were all staring at CNN as the second airplane crashed into the South Tower. Headlined across the bottom of the screen was AMERICA UNDER ATTACK. I read it over and over.

I immediately thought of Ebony and Dad. They were going to spend some time in Manhattan before continuing on. Were they there? Smoke billowed from both towers now, and the CNN commentators were virtually speechless.

"Wow, that's so cool," a young Thomas said, reacting to the

dramatic images on TV that seemed more like an action film than real life.

"Don't say that, Thomas! People are dying!" Mr. Moran thundered from across the room. Thomas cowered down. Mr. Moran's eyes were filled with anger at his son's statement— fear that the world had just entered into unchartered territory. I knew that this would have serious and lasting effects. And I was sure that Mr. Moran was running all sorts of scenarios through his head. I looked over at Yael, who was staring at the TV intently. *Should we go home and try to call Dad later?* I wondered. *What if they are still in Manhattan?*

Then, seen around the world, a video that has haunted a generation, the Twin Towers gave way and crumbled to the ground, creating an ash cloud that engulfed lower Manhattan. It was unbelievable. Like so many people, it is an image I will never forget: people running frantically, covering their faces with their shirts, red and blue emergency lights disappearing into massive amounts of smoke and fire.

Within an hour, from outside the protective walls of the ambassador's residence, drumming and singing began in the streets. I could hear it rising above the walls. It was the sound of some, not all, people marching through the streets, celebrating the attack on the United States. Why? It came down to Middle Eastern politics. Jordan, a country with a significant population of Palestinians who were refugees, felt that the only way Israel was able to carry out their occupation was because of the deep line of financial and military backing that the United States offered to Israel. And here, finally, the United States had been struck. Israel's ally was faltering, and so there was celebration.

Politics or not, I was disheartened. How could anyone be

celebrating when we just watched thousands of people die before our eyes on television? These people had nothing to do with the foreign policy decisions of the United States. Standing behind the secure walls, I felt a sudden and intense urge that I had never felt before. I wanted desperately to be in the States, back in Louisiana with Ashoh and Grandpa on Bernice Drive. As a child, I was never particularly patriotic, but in this moment I wanted to be with other people, Americans, who felt similarly violated. They had just woken up to an unthinkable reality, and here we were, seven hours ahead, at the end of the afternoon, with cheering outside our walls.

"I hope Dad and Ebony are all right," Yael said, looking up at me.

"I'm not sure if they're in New York or New Orleans. I'm going to find out though, okay?" I said, trying to comfort him.

Yael and I returned to our home that evening to Suraj, who made us a warm dinner and took care of us.

"Suraj, did you hear what happened?" Yael asked him as the three of us sat in the kitchen together.

"Yes. I saw there was an attack on America today. It was in New York, yes?"

"And in DC at the Pentagon. This is really bad, Suraj," I said. "I wonder what's going to happen now?"

Dad called to tell us they had left Manhattan two days before and were now in Luling with Ashoh and Grandpa. I was relieved. I wished I could talk to Mom about what the world had witnessed today. She had left from our lives just five months ago and I had never felt so alone. But I knew my job for now and years to come was to watch over my little brother. And so I did.

19

MOHAMMED

SOPHOMORE YEAR OF HIGH SCHOOL, I had become good friends with a guy my age at a local school nearby. His name was Mohammed. He was handsome, athletic, with well-faded black hair, and about my height. We had mutual friends and so most weekends we would end up at the same house parties to pre-game, then restaurants and bars for a long night out.

One Saturday afternoon, I went over to Mohammed's house to hang out. He had suggested that we watch a movie. We got some food from his kitchen, said hi to his parents, and then headed upstairs to his bedroom. Mohammed turned on the movie and we both lay in his bed side by side. While we had spent many nights out in group settings, this was the first time we had decided to hang out alone. About thirty minutes into our film, our blue-jeaned legs began to touch. But instead of moving away, something told me to keep it there. Staring straight ahead, I began wondering why he hadn't moved his leg either. Maybe he didn't actually realize they were touching? After a couple minutes, I casually moved my leg away from his. We both continued staring straight ahead at his TV. Minutes passed and I was now completely in my head, wondering what had just happened. And why had being close to him felt so good? I daringly moved my leg back to touch his and this time I made sure it would be unmistakable. Mohammed didn't move. My heart started to race. My mind started to flash through all the past year and a half, meeting each other out at argileh cafés on the weekends, laughing with all our friends, and talking on the phone in the evenings.

Our legs were now unquestionably connected, and I was both exhilarated and terrified. It was as if I could feel electricity moving between the two of us. I could feel my hard-on pressing against my jeans. All this time we had been friends, had there been something more? We'd had our socks on and my legs reached just above his ankles. I'm not sure where the courage came from, but all of the sudden I found myself sliding my foot from just above his ankle down along his foot. I fully expected him to pull away and say, "What are you doing?" But he didn't. He kept his leg there and soon, as if all my unrealized adolescent dreams were answered, Mohammed slowly started sliding his foot against mine.

The movie was as good as over. For the remainder of the film we both pushed against each other deliberately. Never once did we look at each other. Those first moments of awakening are as if you have entered a different world entirely. I wanted so badly to turn and kiss Mohammed, to rip his shirt off and feel his chest against mine, but I didn't have the courage. I was afraid that if I did more, it would end. This small action of our feet moving against each other's was infinitely more sexual for me than anything I had ever experienced with a girl. We stayed together like this until the credits rolled. Then, we got up as if nothing had happened, and went downstairs to put our plates back in the kitchen. Later that afternoon I returned to my home on the hillside. I was sixteen, and subconsciously I had been waiting for a moment like this since the evening I jerked off on the floor of Ashoh's bathroom.

The next day after school, I went to find Mohammed at Chili House, a casual restaurant a lot of kids went to once our schools let out. It was the same as it had always been between us. We joked, we laughed, but my mind raced around and around, wondering how he felt? I couldn't get him off my mind.

That evening I called Vassia and detailed the events of the weekend to her.

"It's perfectly normal," Vassia told me. I pictured her hands waving wildly in the air. "It could be just a phase, or it could be forever and anyway it's healthy to experiment," she continued.

I loved that about Vassia. I could tell her absolutely anything and it would be met with a very matter-of-fact answer and without judgment.

"So what should I do?" I asked.

"Just keep doing what you're doing with Mohammed and let's see what happens," Vassia said, confidently owning every inch of the sex therapist role I needed her to play.

The next week I invited myself over to Vassia's house after school. As was typical, we would make our way into her condo, plop ourselves in the kitchen, and she would start pulling out delicious food for us from her fridge. Ms. Endrie came home earlier than usual from her day of work at the Greek Embassy. I was always happy to see her bright face. Besides my cousins Jessica, Erin, and Ryan, Vassia was the only person I had ever known whose parents were divorced. It seemed to me that between Vassia, her mom, and her sister, Ellie, there was more than enough love to go around.

After eating on the kitchen counter, we slid down and headed to her room. We tossed ourselves on Vassia's bed. As had become a custom earlier in the year, we watched *Crazy/Beautiful*, a film starring Kirsten Dunst and Jay Hernandez. Halfway through, and fresh off the experience with Mohammed, I turned to Vassia.

"Vass?" I said, trying to get her attention.

"Yea?"

"I think I'm bisexual, or . . . yea, bisexual. It's not a phase. Also, I think Jay Hernandez is really hot."

"Me too! He's so hot!" she squealed, delighted that I was talking about men with her for the first time.

"Let's not tell anyone about this, though." I made her promise.

"Okay, I promise, I won't."

"Jay Hernandez's eyes are just beautiful," I continued. "And his . . ."

"And his smile, and those lips," Vassia announced, reveling in the shared experience.

It was a moment in time where I knew, in some small way, my life had changed.

ONE FRIDAY EVENING back in Amman along with a big group, we made our way to Blue Fig. We sat at a long table, eating our favorite dish, New Orleans Blues. It was a beef patty with melted cheddar cheese, a sort of chipotle sauce, and french fries. I had no idea why they called it New Orleans Blues. It didn't taste like anything I'd ever eaten in Louisiana. I spent much of the evening moving between engaging conversations with Amy and Vassia and glancing over at Mohammed, who was sitting a bit farther down the table with some friends from his school. How had I not noticed him before? Was I really bisexual? Was I gay? Or was it just something about Mohammed in particular?

At the end of the evening, a number of us decided to go back to Amy's home. We could stay up late and drink more vodka on her balcony.

Around 2 a.m., we all decided to call it quits. While Amy climbed in her bed nearest the balcony doors, we decided that Mohammed would sleep in the other bed across her spacious room. I volunteered to sleep with a comforter on a giant rug between the two. Once I was convinced Amy was asleep, I crawled into bed with Mohammed. Then again, it all happened as it had the first time at his house. Snuggled up closely to each other, we pressed our legs against each other and I felt the courage to kiss him slowly building. Only this time, after about ten minutes, Mohammed moved away from me. I was disappointed but moved back to the comforter on the floor. I had hoped that tonight we'd be able to face each other and actually acknowledge what was taking place. That didn't happen.

The next morning, I was back home on the hillside.

"How was last night, buddy?" Dad asked.

"It was fun," I replied.

"And how were Amy and Vassia?"

"They're great. It was a good time."

But it wasn't the girls I was thinking about. I went to our computer and logged on to MSN Messenger. Mohammed was on.

(Me) *Hey man. I was thinking we could talk about what happened the other night at your house.*

(Mohammed) *What are you talking about?*

My heart sank. It was one thing for him to not want to continue anything, but to pretend nothing happened, that didn't feel great.

(Me) *Can we just talk on the phone?*

(Mohammed) *Sure. Call me in a second.*

I moved to the kitchen where our phone was, making sure both doors were closed and that neither Dad nor Suraj were around. I dialed Mohammed's number and after the first ring he answered.

"Hey, listen, man. I know this is different, but I wanted to talk about what happened the other night," I said.

"I'm not gay," he replied defiantly.

"Okay, Mohammed. I'm not saying you're gay, but at least, let's talk about it. I don't know what I am. I mean, I might be bisexual. I don't know. I've never done anything like this before," I said, completely honestly and confused.

"I'm not gay. Can we just forget about this?" Mohammed repeated.

"Sure. I just don't want this to change our friendship, okay?"

"Sure. Okay, Garon. I have to go." He hung up the phone quickly.

And with the silence on the other end of the line, I knew I had lost Mohammed as a friend forever.

In the weeks that followed, Mohammed and I didn't talk to each other much. We were both invited to the same parties on the weekends. I would show up and he'd be there on one side of the room with people from his school. I would be there with my crew. Neither of us would go up and say hi, it was just too awkward.

As sophomore year was wrapping up, there was one more surprise. Amy called me one evening.

"Guess what?" she asked.

"What's going on?"

"We have to leave Jordan. My family has to move to Belgium."

"Fuck."

I knew that losing Amy and the entire Moran family would be really hard. But this was the way of the international school life. At any moment one of your closest friends could be whisked away to another country, forcing you to redefine your world without them. In Amy's final note to me, she wrote:

Can you believe it's been 8 years? What the hell am I going to do without you next year? I remember when you walked into the 3rd Grade in Jamaica in the middle of the year. You were this skinny boy with a bad hairdo and the squeakiest voice I have ever heard. You have seriously had a big effect on my life. The tragedy with your Mom and the way you handled it showed me how to be strong. I love you

What Amy didn't realize was that she, along with Vassia, had very much held me together since Mom died. If I projected strength, it was surely feigned. I still cried myself to sleep most nights, sometimes stuffing the edge of the comforter in my mouth to muffle the sound of my cries.

20

THE MURDER

ON OCTOBER 28, 2002, Dad pulled Yael and me into the living room.

"I need to tell you guys something. Virginia Foley's husband, Larry, was murdered this morning in their driveway. They are saying it looks like it was a terrorist attack. She was there for us. Now we need to be there for her."

I was speechless. It was hard to believe. Virginia, who just a year and a half before had sat in our living room, graciously allowing us the space and safety to talk about Mom's death, was now the one living an unspeakable loss, the murder of her husband. Larry had been getting ready for work that morning. As he emerged from his house to get in his car, he was shot multiple times in the face and body. Virginia, hearing the shots, had run out to the carport and found her husband.

That night, just as so many people had arrived at our house the day of Mom's death, we pulled up to Virginia's home. There was security, press, and a line of people making their way into her residence. As we walked up to the house, I could see the blood-stained carport where Larry had been murdered. I held Yael's hand tight. Virginia was standing at the front door, dressed in white, hugging both Arabs and foreigners who had come to support her. I didn't want to look at her eyes; the pain of her loss and the way he was executed was too heavy. But I knew I needed to. When I got up to her, I wrapped my arms around her.

"I'm so sorry, Virginia. I'm just so sorry," I said.

"I know. I know," she said, hugging Yael and me tightly. I felt a wave of understanding move through our bodies.

The woman who had brought calm and empathy into our home was now about to embark on a nightmare of her own. And her journey would unfortunately become international news.

Weeks later, on December 14, 2002, BBC reported:

> *Police in Jordan have arrested two men in connection with the killing of American diplomat Laurence Foley in October. . . . Announcing the arrests in a statement on Jordanian television, [Jordanian Information Minister] Mr Adwan said that Libyan Salem Saad bin Suweid had shot Mr Foley. . . . He said that his accomplice, Jordanian Yasser Fathi Ibrahim, had waited for him in the car. Salem Saad bin Suweid had entered Jordan using a fake Tunisian passport after being trained in al-Qaeda's camps in Afghanistan. The minister said that investigators had found guns and ammunition used in the attack in the men's possession. They included a revolver and silencer, machine guns, grenades and $18,000 – the first instalment of $50,000 which was allegedly being provided by al-Qaeda to fund their operations.*

The same day, CNN reported:

Al-Adwan said the two men would be tried in a state security court and would face the death penalty. According to [a Jordanian government] statement, "bin Suweid and Ibraheem confessed that they are members of Osama bin Laden's al Qaeda organization, and are affiliated with bin Laden's lieutenant, Ahmad Fadeel Nazal Al-Khalayleh, known as Abu Musa'ab Al-Zarqawi." . . . The Jordanian government said Zarqawi "had devised an operational program for the two perpetrators to carry out terrorist operations against embassies, diplomats, foreigners, security officers and other strategic targets in Jordan." . . . Sources also told CNN that in the course of the investigation, authorities uncovered evidence of other al Qaeda sleeper cells elsewhere in the Middle East and that evidence is being pursued by Jordanian and U.S. authorities."

I knew Virginia was devastated and had returned to the States. I couldn't imagine dealing with both the personal loss and having the international press take your heartbreak to the world. I hoped, just as she had comforted me once, that those closest to her now offered her solace. I had always known a terrorist attack was possible in Jordan, but it didn't quite hit home until Larry was murdered. Each afternoon as Dad returned from work, I would stare at him quietly when he was moving about the house. I would try to imagine what our life would look like if he too were killed; I wasn't sure I could survive that.

WHEN THE UNYIELDING PAIN of losing Mom got too hard junior year, I found refuge in two of my best friends. I now ran around Amman with two guys I had become close to: JJ and Saleem. JJ's family were South Korean diplomats who had recently relocated from Romania. From the moment he arrived in our small class, I knew that he and I would be friends. JJ was highly intelligent, laughed easily, and liked parties as much as I did. Saleem was Palestinian and had spent a considerable amount of his childhood in Libya. He was kind-hearted, soft-spoken, and loved a good time. The three of us started off most weekend nights together. I would call Saleem, whose parents had recently given him a new luxury car. JJ and I had taxis.

"Saleem, what's up?" I would start each call.

"I'm on my way to pick you up, man," he would say without me even asking. Saleem and I lived on completely opposite sides of the city. That boy would drive out of the city, wind up our hillside in his Mercedes, and pull into my driveway. I'd jump in, thank him, play "Breaking the Habit" by Linkin Park, and then we'd roll back into Amman to JJ's house.

"Do not say *fuck* when we go into JJ's house," I reminded Saleem one evening as we pulled up.

"His parents are so sweet, and you said *fuck* when we were talking to them last time." Saleem laughed hysterically, remembering. Once upstairs at JJ's we talked to his parents and his sister briefly. Then the three of us began our night out on the town.

Eventually we would link up with Vassia and a number of other friends from ACS. We all had fake IDs, which we'd secured at the end of sophomore year, allowing us to access bars and clubs across Amman. Many evenings we would start at Champions, the sports bar at the Marriot Hotel, or Blue Fig or Shamrock, a bar that poured strong drinks and had a great dance floor. Most Thursdays and Fridays ended with drinking late into the night at one of our friends' homes, lounging around pools, on elegant terraces, or in palatial living rooms while parents went on international business trips. To put it simply, the local kids whose parents could afford the exorbitant tuition of the International School were rich, and the foreign kids' parents had been put up in lavish homes by their employers. Either way, it made for a memorable high-school experience wrapped in unintended opulence. All we cared about was being together. These evenings moving from party to party in Amman are some of my favorite memories of life. A Cypriot, a Palestinian, a Sri Lankan-American, and a South Korean, growing up together in a region of the world we never expected to come to.

21

THE INVASION OF IRAQ

ORDERING JORDAN TO THE NORTHEAST was a country I had always wanted to visit: Iraq. In March 2003, news came that the United States had invaded the nation. There were grave disagreements among the international community as to whether it was a good idea. I myself wasn't sure, but I also knew how hated Saddam Hussein was in the region. Immediately rumors began of mandatory evacuations of Americans in Jordan. Those rumors came true, and late one evening I sat on a KLM flight once again watching Amman disappear below me as we raced into the sky toward our connecting city: Amsterdam. It was my first time back to Amsterdam since our trip five years before as we made our way to the Middle East for the very first time. As Yael and I walked around outside Amsterdam Central Station, this time without Mom, I was painfully aware of how much our life had changed.

We caught our connecting flight across the Atlantic. With the war next door, our life in Jordan now seemed uncertain and what lay ahead was unknown. I found a sense of peace aboard this flight; airplanes always made me feel at home. I sat next to a garrulous, middle-aged, heavyset blond from Texas who, it was obvious, was a tourist coming back from her first trip to

Europe.

"Where are you coming from?" she asked loudly.

"I'm coming from Jordan," I said more quietly. She stared at me blankly. "It's in the Middle East," I confirmed to her wondering face.

"My word. Has anyone ever told you that you look just like one of the terrorists from September eleventh?" she asked.

I stared at her in silence. I couldn't believe what she'd just said. I couldn't even fake a smile. She leaned over to her travel companion.

"Brenda," she called, prodding her arm. "Doesn't he look like one of the terrorists from September eleventh?" She giggled.

Brenda, who was the quieter of the two, leaned forward and looked at me, then smirked and sat back. I felt disgusted and on display for their amusement. I turned away from the two Texans abruptly and stared forward into the seatback ahead of me. I wanted to say something in response, but I didn't know how to handle the situation. We were aboard a flight headed for the United States and she had compared me to the terrorists who had crashed American jetliners into the World Trade Center and the Pentagon, killing thousands. I had initially not been able to go into that gymnasium in South Africa because of the color of my skin. That boy in Luling had called me a nigger while the other boys watched. But I had never imagined someone would compare me to a terrorist: a word that connotes the slaughter of others for political gain, leaving in their wake the devastation of families and the incitement of fear. As we crossed the Atlantic, I wondered why these two women from Texas felt they had the license to call a brown teenage boy something so abominable.

We landed at Washington Dulles and so began the loneliest

two months of my life. The big public high school in Virginia, just across the river from DC, that I attended was nothing like the American School in Jordan. While the students there seemed nice, they didn't want to make new friends so late in the year. I couldn't blame them for not caring; we lived in two separate worlds. One morning when the Pledge of Allegiance sounded over the PA, I stood quietly not saying a word. It felt disingenuous, given the war and our displacement.

"Some of you may not agree with what the United States is doing, but you should still be saying the Pledge of Allegiance," my science teacher said after, looking only at me. Still, I refused.

At lunch, for the very first time in my life, I sat in the library with no one to talk to. I missed JJ, Vassia, and Saleem, and I longed to be back in the Middle East. One day a week I was able to get out of school an hour before the bell because I had completed more than my share of electives at ACS. Without a school bus to take me home, I walked the thirty minutes through suburbia to our apartment. One day I stumbled upon a well-maintained graveyard and walked in. I stared at the names of the deceased on each headstone and wondered what their stories had been.

Strangely, this graveyard soon became my sanctuary. Each week I made my way to a different part of the cemetery, then lay down on the narrow concrete path that bordered the graves and stared into the sky. I imagined how much the buried had meant to their loved ones; their names proudly displayed in granite: *Loving Father & Husband, Connor. Forever Loved. Never Forgotten, Thelma. In Loving Memory, Henry.* How had they died? Old age? Cancer? Or accidentally like Mom? The heat rising off the concrete warmed my back and I felt a sense of peace and tranquility lying among people who had experienced the full spectrum of life before me. I wasn't alone when I was with them.

Luckily, two months later, even though the war raged on in Iraq, it was determined that Jordan was relatively secure. We were finally allowed to return.

"Make sure when you're riding around in taxis, if the drivers ask, tell them you're Canadian," Dad warned Yael and me as we crossed the Atlantic yet again.

The first day back I returned to my favorite spot inside our home. I looked out the second-story living-room window as I had done so many times before. The call to prayer rang over the dry hills of Amman, echoing in my soul. I was back home.

22

NEW LOVE

SURAJ CAME INTO THE KITCHEN SMILING in a way I'd never seen before. I looked at him, knowing that something was up.

"Garon, I met someone," he said. "I really love her and I want to marry her."

I was thrilled for him.

"Tell me all about her, Suraj," I said eagerly.

Her name was Banu and she was from Kandy, Sri Lanka. She had arrived in Jordan the same year as we had, to work as a housekeeper. Suraj had arrived three years later to work in our home and met her at a concert. They had fallen in love.

Within weeks Suraj brought Banu over to meet me and I saw the love between them. Her dark radiant skin was similar to mine and her blue saree with gold décor highlighted her natural beauty. She was strong and she was kind. I was thrilled that Suraj had met someone to share his life with.

AS A SINGLE PARENT, Dad had done an outstanding job of filling our injured home with love. But sometimes the absence of Mom was too much for me to bear and I'd escape across town to Jay and Tina's. Jay was my English teacher at ACS and his wife, Tina, was the kindergarten teacher. They had previously taught together in Brazil. I became Tina's teacher's assistant, taking seventeen screaming five-year-olds out to play for an hour each morning. When they had gotten enough exercise, I would bring them back into class and help them with colorful activities. The opportunity to be Tina's teacher's assistant was an elective offered to high-schoolers. Not only did I love hanging out with her, but I thoroughly enjoyed being around the silliness and laughter of the kindergarteners. It reinforced in me the hope that one day I would have a child of my own. Very quickly Tina, Jay, and their two young sons, whom I would occasionally babysit on weekends, became my second family. The loss of Mom had drained so much from my life, but Suraj's devotion for Banu, and Tina and Jay's tenderness toward me, had sparked new light into my world. Sometimes you find sustaining love in unconventional situations.

ONE EVENING JJ, Saleem, Vassia, and I met a bunch of other friends from ACS at Shamrock. We grabbed drinks and sat down at a high-top table near the dance floor. No sooner had I taken my first sip than I looked across the bar and there he was. Mohammed looked devastatingly handsome with his black hair pushed back and a fitted navy-blue T-shirt that held tight to his muscular arms. I had missed him greatly. While evacuated to the States, I had forced myself to stop thinking about him, about us, because I knew it would never go anywhere. I missed being his friend and how effortlessly we had laughed together and gotten along. Seeing him now, I was as attracted to him as I had been that afternoon on his bed. Mohammed walked over to a table. Soon a girl approached him and locked her arms around his waist. Then they began to kiss. I felt a lump in my throat and a heaviness in my chest. I had wanted so badly to kiss Mohammed. From where I was, although my view of her was partially blocked, I felt like I recognized her. I walked closer to see who it was. It was Rachel. I stopped moving. Rachel and Mohammed were now a thing? I stared at the two of them kissing passionately, his hand moving slowly through her hair, hers down his back, jealousy coursing through my body; The first girl I had been with in high school and the boy I had fallen for later. Who did I want to sleep with more: Rachel or Mohammed? In times before, I would have said I didn't know. But on this night at Shamrock it all became very clear to me. I knew that I would have chosen to be with Mohammed over and over again. Vassia looked over at me knowingly. I had never told JJ and Saleem about Mohammed mostly because I was afraid of how they might react. Many years later, I know I could've told them, and I should have.

FOR OUR SENIOR TRIP, our class boarded a flight that took us to the only landmass in Egypt that is part of Asia. Through my track and field competitions over the years, I had come to love Egypt. On this trip, however, instead of Cairo, we flew farther south, to the tip of the Sinai Peninsula on the Red Sea: Sharm El-Sheikh. JJ, Saleem, and I roomed together. By day we indulged in opulent brunches and swam in the sea. In the late afternoons, we rode four-wheelers through the desert, stopping at dusk for tea with the Bedouins we met along the way. And at night we smoked pot as quietly as we could from our balcony overlooking our Egyptian resort. I knew it was my last big trip with my boys and Vassia. I was in heaven. We flew back to Jordan with full hearts, a lasting headache, and an awareness that everything was about to change.

My six years in Amman were coming to an end. My roof in Jordan was flat, with a generous amount of space to move around, and many evenings I would sit by myself gazing across to the city. With my secret stash of Marlboro Lights, I turned west in the direction of the United States. What would my life look like in a few short months on the other side of the ocean? JJ was going to Michigan, Saleem to Connecticut, and Vassia to the United Kingdom. We would stay in touch, but it wouldn't be the same. The friendship we had nurtured here in the Hashemite Kingdom was so organic, and in some form we had raised each other. Now it was time for our paths to diverge. Never could I have guessed the life that lay ahead for me.

As the breeze rushed through the dusk air, pushing my cigarette smoke away, I thought about how much my life had changed in the six years since arriving in the Middle East. I looked out across the hills and landed on our neighbors' tents, the beautiful Bedouin family. We had lived in such close proximity for six years and yet we lived so differently. I wasn't from Jordan, and I wasn't from Sri Lanka, and I didn't feel American. Where was I from? I'd been accepted to The University of Texas at Austin. Maybe, just maybe, I would know what it meant to be an American soon.

The morning of graduation I looked around my bedroom. I had spent a legion of hours in this room writing research papers, working out, learning lines for acting classes, and stretching for the 400m in Egypt. I had cried myself to sleep countless nights, begging the world to give me back Mom, knowing it was never possible. Jazzbee had nestled close to me, allowing my tears to soak into her apricot fur. I felt that Dad had done an exceptional job of guiding me. Years before in South Africa, when I had tumbled off my red BMX, he had knelt down in front of me and said, *Remember, buddy, you can do anything you put your mind to. You just have to believe in yourself.* Over the years he had told me that time and time again, and I believed him. Now, eighteen years old, he sat beside me and said, "Garon, remember, I want you to go out into the world and always believe in yourself. You can do anything. And don't forget that the point of college isn't to get a degree. The point of college is to learn to critically think on a higher level. Question everything. I'm so proud of you. Mom would be so proud of you."

The American Community School of Amman graduates each senior class in a spectacular manner. Our senior class met at school, piled onto a bus, and we all headed to Jerash, a former Roman city in Jordan. We were graduating in the ancient Roman amphitheater, a dramatic desert landscape surrounding us. In pairs of two, we walked out between the majestic columns of the amphitheater, the sun slowly setting around us, our parents cheering from the stone seating. At my side walked a remarkably kind girl with an exquisite sense of fashion from Taiwan: Sheau Shan Wu. I had always liked Sheau Shan, and we had talked occasionally together at school, but we largely ran in different social circles. Looking back, I wish I had invested in a deeper friendship with her and the others who weren't necessarily part of my crew. There were only twenty-nine of us in The Class of 2004. It would have been easy to include everyone all the time.

I looked down to the band playing below and there, on the drums, was Yael, crying ever so quietly. He watched his older brother walking toward him, but in reality I was walking away. The little boy who in South Africa I had hoped was a new toothbrush or a parachute, and who I had come to love so much, was playing the music to my exit. He and I both knew that I would no longer be able to take care of him in the same way.

23

MS. JOLIE

INSTEAD OF FLYING TO LOUISIANA after graduating from ACS, I decided to spend my last summer before college in Amman. While interning at Dad's office, my new boss, Diane Scott, a tall, warm, freckle-faced woman with silver streaking through her light-brown hair, walked over to my desk around lunchtime. Diane had moved to Jordan from Seattle looking for adventure, unexpectedly landing a job as the communications director. From what I could tell, everyone loved her.

"Hey, Garon. There's an event we've been invited to at the Royal Performing Arts Center tomorrow. Angelina Jolie is going to be there. Do you wanna come?" Diane asked casually. I looked up from my computer screen and stared at her, trying to comprehend the words that had just so nonchalantly come out of her mouth.

"I'm sorry, what did you just say, Diane?"

"The Royal Performing Arts Center event is tomorrow, and Angelina Jolie is going to be there; want to come?" she repeated with a smile, enjoying the effect her offer had on me.

I smirked back at her. "Angelina Jolie is really going to be there?"

"Yes. She's going to be there with Queen Noor," she said

with a chuckle. Queen Noor. I had sat next to her daughter, the princess, in my global history class during the one semester she attended ACS Amman.

"I would love to come with you, Diane, thanks," I said, trying not to bubble over with excitement. I didn't get any work done the rest of the day.

Why was I so thrilled at the prospect of seeing Angelina Jolie in person? Besides thinking her portrayal of Lisa in *Girl, Interrupted* was one of the best performances I'd ever seen by any actor, Angelina Jolie was truthfully the first high-profile person who I had seen adopt a child. I hadn't often seen the composition of our family reflected in the experiences of others. When I first saw photos of Angelina Jolie with her Cambodian-born son, I saw a reflection and I was moved.

I also knew that she was a United Nations Goodwill Ambassador and had traveled the world visiting conflict zones and refugee camps. While many people felt that she was sort of *weird* or *strange*, I honestly identified with her brutal honesty in interviews. Her wild-child element with the black clothes, bold statements and tattoos was bridged with a humanitarian soul; she cared deeply about the world.

The next afternoon, I jumped out of the shower, threw on my black shirt, and took a quick taxi ride to the Royal Performing Arts Center. Diane was waiting for me outside with her usual smile and upbeat attitude. As we walked into the auditorium, I noticed that she had tickets for seats in the very center, third row, a perfect vantage point to watch the night unfold. An announcement came over the surround sound in Arabic and the hundreds of conversations came to an abrupt stop. I was staring at the stage, expecting someone to walk out, when all of a sudden the people behind us stood up and started clapping.

I turned around and there she was. Tall and absolutely as gorgeous as any picture or film I had ever seen of her, Angelina Jolie, dressed in a long black skirt and blouse covering most of her arms, was walking alongside Queen Noor in a sort of regal procession. The auditorium darkened and a performance ensued. It was all in Arabic, and mostly local teenagers as actors. Once the performance was over, Queen Noor spoke, and then the moment I had been waiting for arrived. Angelina Jolie made her way to the stage and stood facing the audience, who applauded wildly. As she spoke, she came across as genuine, heartfelt, conveying her excitement at being in the Middle East. Then, once she finished, the audience erupted in applause and about two full minutes of chanting "An-ge-li-na" in an Arabic accent began. I smiled, sharing in the excitement of the Jordanians and Palestinians who surrounded us.

"Garon, get out of your seat and go say hi!" Diane said.

"No way, Diane!" I said, laughing it off. "How am I going to do that?" I asked, finding humor in the impossibility of the idea.

"Just get out of our row and walk up to the stage. We are so close and she's right there," Diane encouraged.

I was no longer laughing. Diane was serious. I shook my head in disbelief and with a grin and the nervousness of an adolescent boy, I got up, excused my way through our row, walked up to the stage, and planted myself three feet in front of Angelina Jolie. She stood slightly above me, still smiling, laughing, and waving at the auditorium.

"An-ge-li-na!" they continued chanting.

It occurred to me that if I said "Angelina" there would be no way she would hear me in the roar of the room. So instead I took one step closer, looked up, and quietly said, "Hey, Ms. Jolie." She heard me instantly. Her head tilted down and her eyes connected with mine. She smiled kindly and with the warmest demeanor said hi to me. We stood there for what was an incredible couple seconds in my teenage world. She was radiant and supported important policies that focused on helping people struggling to make it in the world. I was completely enchanted. Still today, I don't follow many high-profile people, but I have keenly followed her life and work with the United Nations High Commissioner for Refugees (UNHCR) for years. It is my hope that one day I can have a conversation with her. I am glad that someone who I believe to be an asset to this world has earned such visibility, allowing her to elevate the voices of others around the globe.

MY LAST EVENING in Amman, JJ and Saleem came over to be with me. Dad had taken Yael back to visit Ashoh and Grandpa in Luling. Vassia had already left Jordan for the summer and we had promised to see each other again soon. The three of us laughed about all the trouble we had gotten into together in high school; we were excited about what lay ahead. Without even knowing it, these two—my dearest friends—had taken care of me in the wake of my devastating loss and filled my lowest moments with happiness and laughter. I knew, regardless of where life took me, I would always remember them.

With my bags lined up next to the door, I heard a beep downstairs: my ride to the airport was here. I gave JJ and Saleem one last long hug in my living room. It was nearly 12:30 a.m. and they were going to stay the night at my house, leaving the next morning. Waiting for me at the door was Suraj.

"Bye, Garon," he said, holding me close. I didn't want to let him go. The man who had arrived as our housekeeper had turned into my family.

"I'll write you as soon as I get to the States, okay, Suraj?" I said. I had created an email account for him so we could stay in touch. "I love you. Thank you," I said, memorizing his eyes.

I'll never know what it was like for a man in his early twenties, who I perceived at my young age to be far older, to be so poised, to be so responsible with us kids, and to treat us so well while working in someone else's home an ocean away from the only life he had ever known.

As I rode in silence to the airport, Jordan was dark and tranquil. Stars high above the desert landscape lit our path along the muted roads. I thought back to when we had first arrived six years before with Mom and Dad. I saw her in my mind, nestled in bed with the three of us, encouraging us to listen to our first call to prayer.

PART TWO

24

A FOREIGNER

M Y INTRODUCTION TO TEXAS was an opportunity for the gods to highlight that I was nowhere near as American as I'd hoped to be. It was one of my first Saturday mornings at the University of Texas at Austin. My roommate Joey was a fun-loving violin major from Alaska with a lip ring. He had already left by the time I'd woken up. I went to raise the blinds in our tiny dorm room that we shared seamlessly: we had both agreed it would just be easier if we left our stuff all over instead of cleaning it up. The sun drifted into the room and I watched intently as hundreds of students walked past my window, all apparently headed in the same direction. I looked around quickly. Was there a fire alarm that I slept through? I ducked my head out into the hallway. There was no one around. Back at the window I noticed that none of the students looked alarmed; instead they looked happy, and they were all strangely wearing the same burnt-orange T-shirt with the university logo on it. *Maybe there's a campus event I wasn't invited to,* I thought as I climbed back into bed.

Later that day when Joey returned, I asked him where everyone had been this morning.

"Um, it's game day, man," he said with a perplexed look on his face.

"It's what?"

"It's game day."

"Okay. What is that?"

Joey laughed. "Garon, it's when everyone goes to the football game. Actually, to tailgate first, then to the game."

"Oh!" I said, trying hard to convey that I knew at least, in part, what he was talking about.

But what was tailgating? And how was I to know that literally the entire campus went to a football game every Saturday. That right there was my introduction to American college life. I felt like a foreigner. And in almost every way besides my US passport, I was.

As the second week began, I wrote an email requesting to meet with a guidance counselor to chart out my classes for the year and look into changing my major to political science. One afternoon I arrived at the offices of the guidance counselors, signed in, and then stood in the hallway outside. For a couple minutes I stood there alone and then three people walked in. Two men and a younger woman. I smiled and said, "Hi," added a quick "How's it going?" and they were kind and polite back. We stood within three feet of one another, all waiting for the counselors to finally come out. Suddenly, a woman rushed out, excitedly greeted the three of them, and said, "Someone will be right with you." Then she approached me, less smiley, and said, "Garon Wade?"

"Yes. Hi," I said.

"Please follow me," she muttered, far less enthused.

We left the hallway, disappearing through the big set of double doors. Once on the other side, her face lit up. She stopped walking and turned to me.

"Oh my god! Can you believe who that was!" she yelled passionately.

"Know who . . . who was?" I asked, confused.

"The guy who was standing there with you?" she added, appearing more befuddled than I was. I looked back at the now shut doors.

"No. Uh. No, who was that?" I asked.

"What? That was MC Hammer!" she exclaimed. Clearly she'd been holding this in, desperate to shout it from the rooftops. "His daughter is thinking about coming here!"

"MC Hammer?" I questioned, staring blankly at her. "Who is MC Hammer?"

The guidance counselor stared at me with a bewildered look. She then glanced down and started shuffling through her papers, which had my name on them.

"Garon. Where did you say you're from again?"

"I just moved here from the Middle East."

And with that, she turned, nodded, and continued walking toward her office. I understood very quickly that everyone, except for me, knew who this guy MC Hammer was. I was definitely not from America.

As the weeks went by, and turned into months, I felt homesick. In Jordan I had enjoyed such an easy time making friends. And the days of hanging out at stylish bars and chic restaurants wasn't really a thing in American college life, it seemed. I soon realized that Vassia, JJ, Saleem, and I had socialized in high school the way late twenty- and thirty-year-olds do in the States. On Friday nights, Joey would always invite me to come with him to a friend's dorm room to drink beer. He was kind to ask and I went with him a number of times. But the other kids talked only about football, cars, and American TV shows and I found it a struggle to relate. Their school trips had been to Galveston or the panhandle of Florida. Mine had been to Athens, Beirut, or Damascus. They weren't sure where that was. When they asked me what kind of cars I drove in high school, I explained that we took taxis everywhere, Saleem's Mercedes, or had our friends' drivers. That was met with silence. And when asked who my favorite player was, I explained that I didn't like football. That was met with confused looks.

It was all unchartered territory for me, and as the months went by I had the good fortune of making a few friends whom I related to. But as soon as I was finding my rhythm, freshman year was over, I was moving out of the dorms, and into a building off campus.

THE TEXAS HEAT came in waves during the summer and I felt much better living in a building called The Castilian, off campus. I decided that I wanted to find a summer job and I went from store to restaurant filling out job applications. One day the phone rang.

"Hello, Galon?"

"Yes, this is Garon."

"Hi, Galon," the women said. "Can you come in for interview at Thai Noodle House?"

"Absolutely, I'll be there," I said excitedly.

The Thai Noodle House was a charming, casual restaurant a short walk from The Castilian. It was owned by two Thai sisters, and one of their sons was the cook. While I wasn't a connoisseur of Thai food, I had eaten plenty of it overseas, in a variety of countries, and felt I could learn it well. I went to my interview and a week later *Galon* was written on the server schedule above the cash register.

25

THE GUY ON THE DUCATI

AT THE THAI NOODLE HOUSE, I met a group of people in their late twenties whom I got along with right away. Harmony, an Asian-American woman with a bubbly personality and a cool sense of style, had been assigned to teach me the ins and outs of service at the restaurant. Among other things, she showed me how to make Thai iced tea, which we were allowed to drink whenever we wanted and without paying. The intense sugary concoction rushed to my head each time I drank it. One afternoon as we were making the rounds, Harmony pulled up next to me behind a bookcase where we downed our Thai iced tea in between tables.

"There's this really hot guy with a blue Mohawk that comes in here for lunch every day. A lot of us have a crush on him," she said.

"Oh yea?" I asked, wondering why this guy had come up out of nowhere.

"Yea. I totally want to fuck him, but guess what?"

"What?"

"He's gay."

"Oh."

I thought now was as good a time as ever.

"Actually, Harmony, you know what? I'm into guys too," I said.

Harmony's smile widened just as Vassia's had that day in her room in Amman. I was learning quickly that there was something about girls liking boys who liked boys.

"Oh, that's great!" she said, putting her Thai iced tea back down.

Days later as I had just finished delivering food to a table and rushed back to the water station, I heard the roar of a motorcycle. I looked out the window and saw a tall, extraordinarily handsome, well-built white guy with a blue Mohawk and Ray-Ban glasses. He slid his Ducati into the parking lot with ease. Harmony raced over to me.

"That's the guy I was talking about. That's Chad. He's so fucking hot!"

With the water pitcher in my hand, I stared as he got off his black Monster 620 Ducati and strolled effortlessly into the restaurant. Once the door swung open, I made sure not to stare in his direction at all.

"Look! He sat in your section, Garon. Now you get to take his order," Harmony chided with a sly smile.

"What? No," I countered, intimidated by his clear sex appeal and unsure what to do with Harmony's excitement.

I took a deep breath and approached the table as nonchalantly as I could.

"Hey, how's it going? What can I get you to drink?" I asked while trying to decide if he was as attractive up close as Harmony had made him out to be. He was.

He glanced up at me. He had light-brown eyes and an extremely chiseled face, covered with scruff. "I'll have a regular iced tea, please, and the Pad Thai with tofu," he said, then turned toward his phone.

"Sure." I nodded and left to grab his drink. I could barely look at Harmony, who was in the midst of serving tables, still maintaining her sly grin, no doubt wondering what had been said. While I absolutely thought he was attractive, it didn't seem in our six-second exchange that he felt the same. Harmony would be gravely disappointed. Later I returned to his table with his steaming dish, and as I placed it down in front of him, he lifted his gaze from his phone.

"Are you new here? I haven't seen you before," he said with an intensity in his eyes. I immediately felt myself becoming flush and nervous.

"I'm, yes. I just started here," I stammered.

"Cool. I'm Chad. What's your name?"

"I'm Garon."

"And where are you from?"

I have this very strange feature where I don't sweat almost at all from anywhere on my body, except for from my nose. I could feel my nose becoming moist and I felt Harmony's eyes locked on to me from across the restaurant.

"I'm, uh, well, I was adopted from Sri Lanka, my parents are American, but I grew up in South Africa, Hawaii, The Gambia, Jamaica, Louisiana, and Jordan. I just moved here from Jordan," I said, wondering why I had just laid out my entire life.

"That's really cool," Chad said.

While he ate his tofu, I made sure my other tables were well taken care of, finding myself stealing glances of him whenever I could. He was confident, direct, and he carried himself with a sexiness that I hadn't really seen before. He also had a masculinity that I hadn't seen in the majority of the out gay guys on campus. And he was older. I didn't know how old, but I knew he wasn't in college. That was instantly attractive.

As I approached Chad's table to give him his check, I once again tried hard not to appear nervous.

"Hey, good to meet you, Chad. Here's your check," I said, handing it to him.

"Nice to meet you too. Hey, do you want to hang out with me sometime this weekend?" he asked.

Fuck. I wasn't prepared for this at all. I just stared at his gorgeous face and scrolled through about twenty different things one could say in this moment. Did I want to hang out with him? Absolutely.

"Oh, sorry, man. No, I can't. I've got a lot going on," I blurted out. As soon as I heard the words come out of my mouth, I could not believe it.

"Okay, cool," he replied. And with that, Chad paid his check, walked out, jumped on his Ducati, and roared off.

Harmony was peering out from behind the Thai iced tea corner at me as I approached her with a defeated face.

"Sooooo, what happened?"

"Harmony. I think he just asked me out?"

"Ahhhh!" Harmony shrieked. "What did he say?"

I recounted the events of table ten to Harmony, who was clearly living vicariously through every word.

"So, you said no?" she asked in disbelief.

"Well, I didn't say no, I just said I was busy," I said, rolling my eyes, realizing what I had done.

"So you don't want to hang out with him?" Harmony pressed.

"No. Of course I want to hang out with him, I just, I wasn't prepared," I said, regretting the whole interaction.

"Okay, who cares! Next time he comes in, you're going to

have to ask *him* out," Harmony squealed, loving the entire situation.

I stared at her in silence, realizing that if I ever wanted anything to happen, Harmony was one hundred percent right. Fuck. As the weekend went by, I wondered about Chad. What was he doing? How did I go from having virtually no friends and not liking Austin to loving my new place of work and being asked out by basically the hottest guy I had seen since moving to Texas? The next week at lunch, I heard the black Ducati roar up, and I knew I had to do it. I had never really asked a guy out before, though. I mean, he had asked me first, so it couldn't be that hard. Surely he would say yes. Only this time Chad didn't sit in my section. If I were going to go talk to him, I would have to intentionally go over to his table. Halfway through lunch service I forced my way over to where he was sitting.

"Oh hey, Chad!" I said, pretending I'd just seen him for the first time. Yes, guys play these bullshit games too.

"Hey, Garon, how's it going?"

He had remembered my name. That was a good sign.

"I'm great, man," I said.

Then an awkward silence took over, where I realized he wasn't going to push the conversation forward and once again I hadn't planned. I felt my nose start to heat up and my neck and shoulders tense.

"I, um. Hey, I uh, well, actually, I wanted to say . . ."

Chad just looked up at me with a blank stare.

"I wanted to say, well, you know how you asked me if I wanted to hang out last time, and I said I was busy? Well, actually, I'm not that busy anymore. If you want to hang out sometime, I'm around," I stammered. What a disaster. I sounded like a fucking idiot.

"Sorry, I can't. I'm seeing someone," Chad said and returned to his phone.

"Oh, okay. Well, cool then," I somehow managed to get out as I turned away from the table as quickly as I could. Harmony was staring at me with big eyes as she delivered Tom Kha soup to another table.

What the hell had just happened? I continued waiting on my other tables, now completely distracted and unfocused. It was my fault for being ridiculous in the first place. As I passed by his table, Chad called out to me. I walked over reluctantly, but with my best "How can I assist you?" face. Maybe he needed his iced tea refilled.

"Hey, Garon. I am actually seeing someone. But we're not exclusive. Let me give you my number," he said with all the confidence in the world.

The nineteen-year-old in me found it supremely attractive. Before I could see the situation for what it was, there I stood, giving Chad my phone number in the middle of Thai Noodle House with Harmony beaming with pride, or horniness, from behind the Thai iced tea station.

I called Chad two days later and we met at a restaurant in downtown Austin later that weekend. He was everything I hoped he might be. I learned that he had gone to Princeton, lived in New York City for years, working his way up to partner, had recently lived in Barcelona, and had moved back to the United States to be closer to his parents. On paper, he was wonderful. I had spent the year feeling unable to connect to American students and disliking the dorm room kegs and frat parties that seemed so coveted by my classmates. Here, sitting before me, was a thirty-nine-year-old—yes, twenty years older—Ryan Gosling lookalike who was worldly, educated, and extremely charismatic. The weeks that followed opened a door to a world I'd never experienced. Chad and I became a couple, and for the first time in my life I had a boyfriend.

THE FIRST SIX MONTHS were wonderful. Chad and I covered the town together, eating at all the most unique restaurants in Austin and walking around the Colorado River on the weekends. In meeting him I had returned to the social life I had known for so long in Amman. We flew up to New York City on occasion to spend time with his family, and spent many evenings talking over how fortunate we were that our lives had intersected. I did notice that Chad had very few friends. Occasionally, a friend would fly in from Montreal, or another friend would meet up with us in NYC, but generally speaking he had very few people he felt close to. I thought initially that this was strange, but I just chalked it up to the fact that he had recently relocated from Barcelona and hadn't had the opportunity to build lasting friendships.

As the months moved on, I also noticed that if I had plans with friends from college, he had to be a part of them. There was very little room for me to do any socializing by myself. On nights when we did eventually agree that he would hang at home, he would become irritated late into the evening if I didn't text him when I got home. This behavior concerned me because while I was, and still am, an extrovert and enjoy being around people fairly regularly, I am also extremely independent. The next morning, we would talk it over. He would hug me and tell me he loved me and that he was sorry for being so possessive. I rationalized his possessiveness as attractive.

A year later Chad told me that his parents were moving down from New York to live in Austin. With Dad and Yael still in Jordan, and Ebony finishing at the University of Chicago, I welcomed the idea of greater time spent with his family. Chad's father, Benjamin, was a lovely, gentle, athletic man who was kind to me and who I looked forward to seeing at our regular weekend brunches at their home. Chad's mother, Helen, on the other hand—a star violinist who'd wanted so badly to make it big but instead settled down to do the important job of raising Chad and his three sisters—was a different story. Helen had a very inauthentic disposition. To the casual observer, she had a sunny exterior, but I learned very quickly that she was a seasoned alcoholic who strongly resented her husband and felt he hadn't provided an opulent enough life for her. Chad would tell me stories of how as a child he would overhear Helen yelling at Benjamin, "You call yourself a man? You're not a man!" while the children huddled in the living room. Chad's youngest sister sat with her hands covering her ears. As a result, she had put all her faith in Chad's New York success, and to her, he had achieved it. He had made partner at a high-profile asset management firm in his early-thirties and retired just a couple years later.

Each Sunday as we arrived for brunch, Chad would immediately gravitate toward his mother in the kitchen and I would head into the office toward his father. The four of us would, for the most part, stay separated until it was time to eat. At the table, Chad would endlessly compliment the food while Helen explained to everyone the never-ending line of ingredients that the recipe *called for* and how she had decided to make small changes here and there. Benjamin and I would mostly eat in silence, and I would ask the occasional polite question about their week or try to redirect it to whatever housing project Benjamin was working on.

ON FRIDAY EVENINGS, Chad and I would often go out to El Chile, a delicious, lively Mexican restaurant on the east side of Austin. El Chile had wonderful fish tacos and a creative lineup of margaritas. As we drank and talked about life, we laughed and shared stories of our families. But as the night grew longer and Chad downed his Herradura, I began to notice that he became a completely different person. He became a monster.

If he made a comment about someone or a social issue, and I disagreed, he would fly into a rage. The first couple of times it happened I decided to change the subject, which would generally allow him to ease out of his fit of anger in the middle of the restaurant. But as time went on, I stopped caring as much. Coming from a family where Mom and Dad had not only offered but encouraged us to have our own opinions and make convincing arguments to support them, I didn't feel that I should have to walk on eggshells around my own boyfriend.

One evening at El Chile, he made a statement, I offered an opposing opinion, and this time I didn't change the subject. Chad's face filled with rage and in the middle of the restaurant he began yelling at me. Everyone around us stopped eating and turned to our table. He barked at the waiter to get the check. Completely embarrassed, I followed him out of the restaurant, knowing that something wasn't right.

In the morning when I thought Chad might be apologetic, he wasn't. He seemed to never really be able to take responsibility for his outbursts. Occasionally, in place of brunch, we would be invited to his parents' house for Sunday dinner. Helen would be drinking to excess, her feigned sunny demeanor disappearing as she sank into a state of annoyance and depression. It was disconcerting to watch. Her voice would get deeper, her happiness gone, and before I was able to see what came next, Chad would make sure we got up and left. The first time I watched her transformation, it sent a chill up my spine. He was just like her.

Chad and I would go through days of intense connection, but then the outbursts became more regular at home. Anytime he drank alcohol, I would see the monster within him begin to rise. One evening when he was complaining about his mother and her alcoholism, and angry at me over something trivial, I decided to take the conversation to a place where it should have gone months before.

"Chad, what I really don't understand is this: you complain about your mom. But the irony in all of it is, you *are* your mom. You both get drunk and start judging people and yelling at people. You're the same," I told him.

"You have no idea what you're talking about, Garon. You're not even a smart person. Look at you, you go to The University of Texas. You didn't go to an Ivy League school like me!" he shouted.

"Actually, Chad, I didn't apply to any Ivy League schools because the deal with my dad was, if we went to a state school, and got in-state tuition after a year, he would pay for all four years. If I went to a private school, I'd have to take out loans," I said calmly.

"You know what you are, Garon? You're like a hot car. Fun to ride but not much going on inside," he said, hurling his anger at me.

I thought this incredibly strange. The last thing I had ever seen myself as was a hot ride. And I knew in that moment that our relationship had entered an abusive stage.

"Chad, say whatever you want to say, but you and your mother are exactly the same. You are both alcoholics and the fact that you can't see that you're exactly the same, putting people down to make yourself feel better, that right there is the problem. If you're this unhappy, maybe you should think about no longer drinking because clearly you can't handle it."

"Shut up, Garon! Shut the fuck up!" he yelled. We were standing across from each other in the kitchen, my back to the kitchen door, which led outside.

"Don't talk to me like that, Chad. I'm sick of this shit. You thinking you're better than everyone. I hate the way you talk to people, and this is the reason you have no friends. It's the reason I can't bring you around *my* friends. You are, for some reason, a deeply unhappy person, and I think you need to get some help," I said to him, defiantly.

Chad took a step toward me.

"Shut the fuck up, Garon, I swear, shut the fuck up or I'll . . ."

"Or you'll what, Chad? You'll what?"

"Shut the fuck up or I'll kill you," Chad said.

The room went silent. I had never imagined anyone would say that to me. What was frightening was that he said it with certainty. Inside, I was terrified. He didn't take his gaze off me. I thought about walking out the back door, but in that moment I knew that if I backed down, I would have lost forever. Chad wanted to control me. He had been trying to control me since the day we met. That was clear. I wouldn't let him. I took a deep breath and stared directly at him.

"Okay. You're going to *kill* me, Chad? Really?

He stared at me, his breathing becoming deeper.

"How fucking ridiculous. To say, you're going to kill me. Who says that to another person?"

"Garon, I swear to God," he warned.

"Chad, you drink. You get angry. You lose control. And then . . ."

And that's when it happened. Chad pounced on me. He took his left hand and locked it around my throat, violently slamming me up against his kitchen door. He then took his right hand, brought it together around my neck, and started choking me. Our eyes were less than an inch apart and while mine grew wide in terror, his eyes grew narrow and focused. "I told you to shut the fuck up," he whispered, squeezing my throat tighter and tighter.

In many ways it felt similar to the baboon attack in The Gambia. I could vividly see Chad's face. I could feel his hands clamping down around my throat. A surge of adrenaline swept through my body. I shifted my eyes to his wrists. I grabbed them with my hands, trying desperately to pry them away. But I couldn't do it. He was taller than me, stronger than me, and I could feel the breath inside me leaving.

"Stop, Chad. I can't breathe," I gasped.

I looked into his eyes. There was no remorse. He gripped tighter. And tighter. I made one last attempt to rip apart his grasp, but he had me.

Suddenly I felt his hands release from my throat and his eyes widened. I gasped for air and felt my lungs spring back to life. The house was silent. Tears I hadn't even felt were rolling down my face.

Chad took two steps back now and was staring at me in shock. He pulsed his hands, extending his fingers in and out, looking at them in disbelief. I noticed his breathing was heavy. My eyes darted around the kitchen, landing on my phone, wallet, and keys near me. I grabbed them, never taking my eyes off Chad. Then I flung open the kitchen door that led to the outside.

"I'm . . . I'm sorry. I'm sorry, Garon . . . I . . ." Chad repeated through deep breaths. He looked around his kitchen. It was almost as if he wanted to believe someone else had done it.

"I can't believe you just did that. I *cannot* believe you just did that!" I yelled, grabbing my bike.

"I'm sorry. I don't know what—"

"Just leave me the fuck alone, Chad," I said. I studied his body language. He wasn't a threat anymore. The monster had left him. I slammed the gate, jumped on my bike, and got the hell out of there as fast as I could. I took stock of my body. My breathing was heavy and my throat hurt. But I was alive.

As I zipped out of his neighborhood, Hyde Park, and biked down near campus, I realized it was a lively Friday night. Students walked together on the sidewalk laughing. All the warning signs were there for months on end. I had just chosen not to believe them. I knew better than to be with someone like him. I had been taught better. I was disappointed in myself. I wiped tears away from my chin.

Once I made it to the home I had rented near campus, I parked my bike, went inside, and locked my door. I called my friend Melissa who lived nearby. I explained the situation to her and she said she'd be right over. But by the time I saw Melissa's red car pull into the driveway, there was a knock at the door.

"He's standing at your front door," Melissa said over the phone. "I'm not going anywhere. I'm going to stay right here in the driveway."

I stared at the locked front door as Chad knocked repeatedly.

Having Melissa outside the house gave me a level of comfort. I knew if Chad tried anything, she would call the police.

I opened the door. "What?" I said curtly.

"I'm so sorry." He had been crying. "I've only ever done that once before to someone else. I'm not here to bother you, I just wanted to make sure you're okay."

Once before? I thought? Which other boyfriend had Chad threatened to kill and then tried to?

"I'm really sorry," he said. "I really do love you."

I looked into Chad's remorseful eyes. Then, and it's hard for me to even write this, I opened the door and let him walk into my house.

"Melissa, I really appreciate you coming. It's okay now. I'll catch up with you tomorrow," I said.

I hung up the phone and watched her slowly, and reluctantly, pull out of the driveway. Melissa was considerably older than me and I often wonder what she thought at my poor decision making in that moment. Many years later, I would have the unpleasant opportunity of being Melissa, the friend who showed up after an assault. I was Melissa for two different people, and both times I told them my story and encouraged them to leave. They both left their abusers.

The question is Why? Why did I open that door and let Chad back in? Looking back, I wish I'd had the strength to tell Chad it was over. To tell him to leave. But as I stared into his tearful eyes, I remember feeling pity for him. He was nowhere near the confident man Harmony and I watched climb off his Ducati and strut into the Thai restaurant a year and a half before. I felt he struggled because Helen always expected him be the person who she wished Benjamin had been for her. He treated people poorly in an effort to make himself feel bigger and better. Maybe I would be the one to help him see a different way forward. Of course, I was wrong.

When Chad attacked me, he didn't just try to hurt me. He was trying to kill me. He didn't hit me—he tried to stop me from breathing. To this day, I have nightmares about him. I see him staring at me from across a restaurant and I am desperately trying to get away from him. I also wonder if he has ever tried to kill someone else because I know he's capable of it. That monster lives within him.

I think back to those nights in Hawaii when as young boy I would stand outside the door with Mom as she listened to our neighbor across the way hit his wife, her cries ringing through the air. I stared up at Mom and watched her devastated face as she dialed 911. Growing up, I could never understand why the neighbor's wife chose to stay with him. And here I was, making the exact same choice.

Chad and I continued to date. I'm embarrassed and disappointed to write that.

26

THE WORLD OF NEWS

NOW A JUNIOR AT UT AUSTIN, I committed myself to earning a degree in political science. I chose to focus my area of study on political violence and international relations. As such, some of my favorite classes were Political Violence of South Asia, Suicide Terrorism, and Introduction to the European Union. After a life living across the globe, while my personal life was falling apart, I found happiness in revisiting global issues.

Suicide Terrorism. That professor taught me to critically think in a way that I had never before been exposed to. He explained about the grooming of young people into suicide terrorism. He compared the reverence of famous people and celebrity culture in the United States to the propaganda in certain countries. "In the US, kids grow up idolizing famous people, actors, singers, etc. We see them on TV, in posters, in films, at awards shows. In a select number of other countries, heads of organizations recruit young people with posters. Posters with the faces of suicide terrorists who are heralded as heroes. You, too, can be just like them, you see. Your legacy will live on and everyone will know your name," he explained. I remember how powerful that comparison was. A chapter of human psychology carefully slipped into political violence. It made me understand how important it was to consider *how* people arrive at doing what they do, not just what they do. I studied Prime Minister Benazir Bhutto of Pakistan and Indira Gandhi of India. And in delving into the political chaos of various countries and paying close attention to the contemporary journalists who continued to cover Iraq and Afghanistan, I decided to start down the road to become a television reporter.

Luckily, UT Austin allowed for credit for internships outside of the university and so after much calling and semi-begging, I landed a spot as an intern in the New Media Department of the Austin NBC affiliate, KXAN. I learned an enormous amount at KXAN thanks to the director of the department, Charlie Ray, a short southern gentleman whose demeanor very much resembled Leslie Jordan from *Will and Grace*. Charlie quickly took me onboard and I found myself as his temporary assistant, going over his schedule, coordinating his needs with different departments, and keeping track of the number of impressions for each story. All of it I found greatly interesting. It also coincided with then Senator Barack Obama and Senator Hillary Clinton's debate during the primary at the UT, which was thrilling.

And at KXAN I learned a young life lesson: often times, people only want to help you if you can do something for them or, to be more blunt, if you'll sleep with them. New Media sat on the second floor, and one floor down was the newsroom. There, the TV reporters hustled in and out of the station with their cameramen, chasing stories and drumming up ideas. One reporter in particular, a tall auburn-haired woman named Ava, started doing the rounds on the second floor on the two weekdays that I would be at KXAN. Each time I was at my desk, Ava would make her way around for a casual conversation.

"So why did you choose this internship?" she asked.

"Well, I originally wanted to be an intern in the News Department. I want to be a TV reporter, but they only had openings in New Media. So here I am," I replied.

"Oh, well, if you want to come with me on stories, I mean, if Charlie will let you, I'll show you around," Ava offered with a smile.

I was elated. The entire reason for doing these internships, beyond learning the ins and outs of the news business, was to develop a reel that I could then pitch to TV stations once I graduated, landing myself a job as a reporter.

"Thanks so much, Ava. I really appreciate that." She offered exactly what I needed.

Over the next couple of weeks, Ava and I would talk in the office. She was extremely thoughtful, and I wondered why she would spend such a considerable amount of time talking to an intern who wasn't even in the newsroom.

"Garon. Want to come with me while I cover Bill Clinton speaking this Thursday?" Ava said one day as she slid past my cubicle.

"Are you kidding? Of course I want to. Thank you, Ava."

"Great, meet me at 5 p.m. on Thursday, near the quads. I'll get you in with the rest of the press."

With the press to see Bill Clinton? Yes, please. "I really can't thank you enough."

"Sure. You can come with me on stories anytime," Ava said, smiling as she walked out of the office.

I DECIDED TO break away and go have lunch at Whole Foods, a twenty-minute walk away from KXAN. The Whole Foods in Austin, though I didn't know it at the time, was the flagship location where it had all started. I made my way through the sliding-glass doors and into the hot food line, filling my plate with rice, chicken, some vegetables, and looking for a place to sit after paying. Most of the individual tables were taken, but I noticed to my left a long communal table with space available. My eyes landed on a woman eating, wearing a giant tan sunhat, and I carefully seated myself onto the bench directly next to her and began eating.

I thought about UT, and how I'd arrived a short three years ago, unsure of what I might focus on. I now felt slightly accomplished, having talked my way into this internship, and was tremendously excited to see President Bill Clinton speak later in the week, thanks to Ava's selflessness.

As I ate, the woman next to me, whom I hadn't spoken to, was finishing the last bites of her meal. She lifted her head to wipe her mouth and out of the corner of my eye, it was as if my brain realized it before I could understand what I saw. *Is this . . . is this . . . Sissy Spacek? Not possible. Why would Sissy Spacek be sitting shoulder to shoulder with me at Whole Foods?* Trying hard not to turn my head, I ran through the ridiculous list of reasons I had assumed it was Sissy Spacek. Then she raised her head again, her sun hat tilting.

I saw her small iconic triangular nose, her high cheekbones that accentuated her already naturally beautiful features, and her piercing light-blue eyes. As she got up to leave, she carefully arranged things on her tray. I struggled whether to say hi or not, not wanting to invade her privacy in such a public space. My mind raced back to her films we had watched in Banjul,

Kingston, and Amman. Films like *The Long Walk Home*, the touching story set in Montgomery, Alabama, in the 1960s: a white mother who stood alongside her black nanny during the bus boycotts. Mom and I used to watch it over and over. As she got up, I felt myself rise from the bench at the same time, and I turned to face her as she stepped out from the table. Then in a whisper I said, "Excuse me, I'm so sorry to bother you, but are you Sissy Spacek?"

Those crystal-clear blue eyes turned to mine and clearly worried that I was going to completely lose it, she didn't utter a word. Instead she smiled genially, maintained eye contact, and nodded her head in acknowledgment, the brim of her sunhat moving up and down.

"Wow, it's really so nice to meet you," I said, still whispering. "I wanted to tell you, when I was growing up, my mom and I watched all your movies together." She smiled widely now and took both my hands in hers, a move that, frankly, surprised me. I think she was just so grateful that I was keeping the conversation to a whisper.

"Thank you so much," she said.

"I really appreciate the work you've done," I continued.

"Thanks, it's really so nice to meet you," she said, still holding my hands. There was a calmness to her, and an affinity, and an almost maternal vibe as we exchanged words.

"You too. Have a nice day," I offered.

And just like that, as quickly as it happened, we were each on our way. I sat back down at the communal table to finish my meal and glanced after her. She was recycling her plastics and putting her tray away where it belonged. *What an endearing spirit she has,* I thought.

27

ASHOH'S GAY EDUCATION

I STOOD ON THE FRONT LAWN of Chad's house and called Ashoh in Luling. As the years had passed, I had stopped challenging my grandmother as much, choosing instead to listen to her stories more often. We had grown close as adults, and I was thankful for the year we had both lived on Bernice Drive allowing that bond to form, despite not always seeing eye to eye.

"How are you, Ashoh?" I could hear an afternoon talk show in the background.

"Well, I just got back from my day out with the Busy Bees."

"With who?" I asked, confused.

"The Busy Bees! My group of ladies. We go out antiquing and then have a nice lunch together."

"That's sounds fun, Ashoh," I said. I had indeed forgotten that Ashoh was a proud member of the Busy Bees. "Did you have a good time with them today?"

"Oh, heavens yes. Now what about you? Do you have a girlfriend yet?" she asked. That question surfaced each phone call since starting college and I simply said no. But I knew it was time to tell her. She deserved to know, and I didn't like lying to her.

"Actually, Ashoh, I want to tell you something. I'm not really into girls."

There was a lengthy silence.

"You don't like girls? Then who do you like?"

I thought it was implied.

"I like guys, Ashoh. I'm gay."

Another long pause.

"Well, are Ebony and Yael gay too?"

I burst into laughter. It wasn't the follow-up question I expected. "Why would Ebony and Yael be gay too?" I said, not able to compose myself.

"I just don't know who's what anymore in today's age," Ashoh said with a long sigh. I imagined her sitting on the edge of her bed, clutching her rosary. "What can I say? You like what you like."

I could tell she wasn't thrilled, but she wasn't sad either. And that was a win.

"Thanks, Ashoh. I've wanted to tell you that for a while," I said.

"Well, I'm glad you told me. Your mama used to have a good friend that lived over in Mimosa Park who was . . . like you. I can't remember his name."

She had just said *gay* a moment ago. I wondered if it was the first time she had ever said it. "Oh yea?" I asked. "Where is he now?"

"He died of AIDS."

"I'm so sorry to hear that. I wish I had known more about his and Mom's friendship."

"Well, your mama loved him."

"Ashoh, can you tell Grandpa for me or do you want me to?" I asked.

"I'll . . . I'll tell Grandpa," she stammered.

"All right, thanks. I love you, Ashoh," I said.

"I love you too, Garon."

28

AVA'S BOYFRIEND

THURSDAY CAME AROUND and in the late afternoon I raced through campus and met Ava on the quads where she had asked me to. Shortly thereafter, she arrived with her cameraman.

"Ava, thanks so much for doing this. I really appreciate it," I said.

"No problem. Just one thing. We're going to go over there to meet some reporters I know," she said, pointing toward the press platform. "Pretend to be my boyfriend, okay?"

Boyfriend? I was completely taken aback. Why would she want me to pretend to be her boyfriend? I remember feeling like I didn't have an option. Here was this journalist who was willing to get me a press pass and take me on the press line to watch President Clinton speak. She was the whole reason I was here, and I had asked for this favor. Now she was using me as some sort of social currency. As I've gotten older, I've realized that this was just a fraction of the shit that women deal with in the company of powerful men who promise them opportunities and an open door to success. This, at least, is how it starts. In 2008, there was no #MeToo movement. Although the American activist Tarana Burke had coined the phrase two years prior, it wouldn't find its way to popular culture for over a decade.

"Your boyfriend? Uh, okay," I said.

"Great! Yea, my boyfriend," Ava confirmed.

The two of us walked over to a group of other female TV reporters, who Ava hugged as they all complimented each other's clothes. Then she brought me in.

"This is my boyfriend, Garon."

The women smiled enthusiastically, we shook hands, and I smiled back at them. After a while Ava turned back to the women.

"No, I'm just kidding, he's not my boyfriend," she said, giggling as she placed her hand on my shoulder.

I looked at Ava, completely confused. The women who had initially believed it now started nervously laughing. I had made the quick uncomfortable commitment to pretend to be her boyfriend at her request. Now, without notice, she had changed her game. I felt like an object for her amusement. I laughed along with the reporters, not knowing what Ava wanted out of me now. It was all very strange and I didn't quite understand it, but I knew it was a means to an end. Ava seemed pleased with herself.

Bill Clinton, who had his own #MeToo legacy to battle, was a spectacular orator. I had, of course, seen him speak on television growing up, but in person he was even more compelling. The charisma that people speak of politicians needing, he has in spades. He stumped for Hillary Clinton effectively, and more importantly the crowd adored him. It almost seemed effortless as he related stories and made people laugh. I stood on a press platform alongside the local ABC, Fox, and CBS affiliates and the national press who had traveled in, watching their every move and hoping one day that I might be in their place.

The next week at KXAN, Ava strolled into the New Media Department. Dressed attractively in a black skirt and stylish blouse, she rested up against the wall across from my desk. I thanked her again for the opportunity.

"So what did you do this weekend?"

"I just hung out with my boyfriend," I replied. We had never spoken about my personal life before.

Ava's face shifted. There was a long, awkward silence.

"Cool. Your boyfriend," she said. I could see her mind swirling around the word *boyfriend*.

From the look in Ava's eye, I knew that was the last time I'd see her. And it was. From that day forward she never returned to the second floor. No Ava leaning up against the wall on her breaks, no offers to take me on stories, zero interaction. It was unfortunate because I very much liked hanging out with her. I always knew it was a risk to come out to people at work because they might discriminate against me for being gay. But I had never considered the idea that I would be not helped at work, or not have opportunities extended to me because I wasn't available to women. That was a first.

AT HOME, my junior year was quickly coming to an end and Chad and I had our ups and downs, though mostly downs. He hadn't attacked me again, but he continued to get drunk most nights and tried to control me with his words. One afternoon I ran into his ex, Santiago, a handsome Mexican. Chad had introduced me to Santiago the year before, we both liked each other, and the conversation was always easy. He and Chad seemed to get along well and the three of us had dinner a number of times together.

"Chad and I are headed out to dinner on South Congress on Friday. Want to come with us?" I offered. Santiago had always been a pleasure to be around and to be honest, I enjoyed dinner even more when he was there. He was kind. He was sincere. He was everything Chad wasn't.

"Actually, Garon." He paused. "I appreciate you inviting me, but I'm trying to get Chad out of my life."

I nodded my head. I wanted to ask him more, but I didn't. His words were enough, and I felt there was an understanding between the two of us as we looked at each other. I knew that Santiago had seen the monster in Chad too.

One day after eating lunch at Whole Foods, Chad and I were pulling back into his driveway when Chad saw a woman letting her dog poop on his grass. He rolled down his window.

"Don't do that!" he yelled.

The woman turned around abruptly, completely caught off guard.

"I'm sorry, what?" she asked.

"Don't let your dog shit in my yard. That's disgusting!"

"Oh, I . . . I'm so sorry," she stammered, pulling her dog away while trying to clean the mess off the grass.

Chad rolled up his window.

I knew in that moment that I had chosen, *chosen*, to stay with a terrible person. How someone talks and interacts with strangers says so much about their personality and integrity. That night at El Chile, when Chad had screamed at me in the middle of the restaurant, should have been the end of it. I should never have allowed myself to continue to date him. Look what it had all spiraled into.

"You're just going to talk to her like that?" I said angrily.

"What is your problem?" he asked.

"It's so embarrassing and it's rude, Chad. You're a rude person. How can you talk to people like that?" I said, shaking my head.

The relationship, steeped in acrimony, was over. I knew it and he knew it. This led into a lengthy, exhausting fight. We decided to end our relationship. Santiago had said the words that I needed to hear.

29

A WAY OUT

WITH MY INTERNSHIP AT NBC over, I shifted to an internship at Austin's Fox affiliate, FOX7. I thought it would be a worthwhile learning experience. And it was. It was FOX7 that gave me the opportunity to begin compiling my newsreel, which I needed to send out to prospective TV stations after I graduated from UT.

Being single felt like freedom. I went on a dates with Aiden, the handsome Austin hipster who tried to read me some of his poetry after we had sex. And Chris, from Philly, who never worked out but somehow his abs rippled under his smooth mocha skin. I worked out daily and couldn't get mine to make a notable appearance. And my favorite, Keith. Keith was the most *Texas* guy I dated. He had intense bluish-green eyes and always wore flannel and blue jeans. On weekends he would take me out to the farmland where he had grown up. We took his four-wheelers out under the Texas sky and looked up at the stars. Surveying the landscape, I thought about how different our childhoods had been.

One weekend, Ebony and I agreed to meet in New York City for a weekend of fun with our sweet cousin Sandra. Sandra lived on the Upper East Side, was thirteen years older than me, and had known and loved Mom. By day, Ebony and I walked the streets of Manhattan thrilled to both be single and together in one of the world's most wondrous cities. As we walked along 5th Avenue and approached Tiffany, we simultaneously spotted an undeniably attractive doorman and analyzed him.

"He's straight," Ebony said.

"No, he's gay, Ebony," I told her. "When we walk by him, we'll both say hi and then we'll know."

As we passed by him, we both gave him a flirtatious hello. His eyes floated across Ebony's and locked on mine.

"How you doing?" he said with a devilish grin.

"Fine, you're right, he's gay just like every other attractive man in this city," Ebony said, lamenting. I laughed.

In the evening we drank wine, ordered Chinese food, and smoked with Sandra, leaning out of her fire escape. We waved as the cable car moved right past her window, taking people back and forth from Roosevelt Island. Sandra was generous, free-spirited, and had a wonderful sense of humor. Late into the night the three of us shared stories of Ashoh and Grandpa, and of Mom. It had been seven years since we lost her. While I had never wanted to know the name of the surgeon in Jordan who ended Mom's life, I had truly forgiven him. I knew there was no way I could continue living a happy life with any hate toward him in my heart.

During my three days in New York I realized that I needed to get back to living in a big city. Spending time with Ebony and Sandra had given me much needed perspective.

Finally, it was my last semester at the University of Texas. All the political science majors were considering their next step. I sat in my Politics of Contemporary Africa class and remembered rolling through the sandy streets of The Gambia with Baboucarr, following Juju around our dirt wonderland, and eating couscous with Agnes. I still missed them and I wondered where life had taken them. I wished they could know that fourteen years later I was sitting in one of my last college classes, thinking of the three of them.

"Are you planning to go to law school after this?" the guy sitting next to me asked.

Law school? There was no way. I was ready to get out into the world and start working.

"No law school for me, man," I said. "Are you going to law school?"

"We're all going to law school, Garon," he said, looking around the room at the rest of the class. "If you're not going to law school, then what are you going to do?"

"I'm going to be a TV reporter," I said.

IN MY LAST MONTHS of college, much to my disappointment (and that of probably everyone reading this memoir), I got back together with Chad. The only reason I can imagine I did it was out of feeling like I wanted a natural ending to our story instead of a breakup. Chad told me he wanted to give us one more chance and apologized for losing control. He acknowledged that he had a drinking problem and wanted to try to be better. If Chad and I ended because I was moving, it wouldn't be a failure, is the way I rationalized it. I would never have to deal with the feelings of him giving up on me, or me giving up on him. It doesn't make sense to me now. And it was as poor a choice as it seems.

In my last two weeks, with my internships at NBC and Fox complete, I sat on the wooden floor of Chad's house and carefully packaged my newsreels. As I sealed each FedEx box, I looked at the destinations. They were all across the United States.

"So you're not even going to apply to any stations in Texas?" Chad asked, sitting on his green sofa and scanning my list of cities.

I looked over to him, knowing this moment would mark the end. "No, I'm not."

"You're not even going to give it a shot and give us a chance to continue together?" he asked.

"Chad, I need to move back to DC and be with my family for a while until I get hired somewhere. I can't come back here."

Dad and Yael had left Jordan and moved to DC. Ebony had graduated from The University of Chicago and moved to DC as well. I did miss them and desperately wanted to be near them again. The other truth was that I needed to leave Chad forever. If I stayed in Austin, I feared that somehow our stories would become entangled yet again. After four years in Texas, I packed up my apartment and Chad offered for me to stay with him for my last two days. This was surprising, as we were hanging on by a thread. As expected, we didn't get along at all.

On the morning of my departure, I woke up early, got all my things together, and soon it was time. Chad was sitting outside on the front porch as the taxi pulled up. We had fought the night before. I picked up my bags, then turned to look at him.

"I'm sorry things ended the way they did, Chad. I hope that in the future, maybe after some time, we can find a way to stay in touch," I said.

Chad sat there, expressionless. "I hope you have a good flight," he said. It was a cold response and it hurt, but it summed up the disaster of a relationship that we had.

I turned to walk down the gray stairs of the porch I had once bounded up so many times in excitement to see him. "Bye," I said, turning away from him and stepping into the taxi.

"Bye," Chad said quietly. We knew it was the last time we'd ever see each other.

As I rode away in the taxi, I don't remember whether I gave a final wave or not. I do remember feeling a huge wave of relief. It was over. For so long I had wanted to find a way out, but I was never strong enough. A lot of that was absolutely my fault. When I had found myself alone, and in a great space, Chad had found a way back into my life and persuaded me to come back to him. But this time was different. There was no going back.

30

COLUMBIA HEIGHTS

THE HOT JULY SUN POURED into Washington, DC, and I journeyed for miles on foot from Columbia Heights down to U Street, through Dupont, and into Georgetown. It was the chapter of my life I had longed for, for years; no more schooling whatsoever and an exciting unknown path of life that awaited me. Some afternoons I would sit in Dupont Circle and people-watch for hours. Workers, sweating profusely in their black suits, made their way into inviting coffee shops, crowded restaurants, and modern office buildings. Families visiting DC wandered into the circle, looking in all directions, deciding where to go next. Homeless people slept on park benches. Nearby, a game of chess that seemed to span much of the day took place at another table, with people swapping in and out. And in the grass under the trees of the circle, girlfriends and boyfriends, boyfriends and boyfriends, girlfriends and girlfriends, leaned into one another, basking in the sun that had finally arrived in full force to enrich this vibrant city. I was thrilled to be back in a big city, and one that, in my mind, held so much promise.

Ebony had kindly but reluctantly agreed to let me come live at the house she and her two friends, Nick and Karl, were renting on the corner of 11th and Harvard. The deal was that I would live with her, job hunt, and hopefully sooner rather than later move out on my own. I assured her that I had sent out all my newsreels to various TV stations and was hoping to hear back soon.

Karl and Nick—except for being tall—stood in stark contrast to each other. Karl was markedly more serious, quiet, and seemingly more responsible. Nick, on the other hand, was extremely outgoing, never quiet, and, whether drinking copious amounts of whiskey or not, filled my ears with stories of the classics, which he was studying. I appreciated their generosity in letting me stay at the house. Many mornings, after they had all left, I made an effort to do the dishes or organize the home, and hopefully be seen as less of an intrusion than I felt I might be.

Here I was, my own agent in a new city with the possibility of a new experience at every corner. The hopeful boy who had left the Middle East four years before, and in some form had lost his way in Texas, was coming back. I could feel myself returning in the quiet moments as I stood pensively outside the White House, Library of Congress, and on the marble stairs of the Supreme Court. My evenings were spent on dates with handsome strangers and in quality time with Ebony, Dad, and Yael. The four of us reminisced about our life on the other side of the world, and we spoke of Mom together. Each of us had figured out our own way to continue living with the pain of her loss. That pain resided just below the surface in all of us. The four of us had been apart for so long. I hadn't realized how much I needed them.

31

IS HE OR ISN'T HE?

I LEFT EBONY'S HOUSE AND WALKED the four short blocks to the Washington Sports Club, WSC, on the corner of 14th and Irving. I always enjoyed the late-afternoon walks to the gym, watching as black and Latino teenagers in their khaki uniforms, leaving late from afterschool activities, moved slowly in groups across the neighborhood. People of all ages, many with earbuds in, rocked to their music, dodging honking cars on their way home. And those who had arrived home from one of the many colleges hours before now sat on their steps with a drink in hand, while others walked their dogs to nearby parks. I had been in Washington for two months and had very quickly fallen for Columbia Heights.

The WSC was, as usual, abuzz with the youth of DC running in unison on treadmills in an effort to make their bodies as powerful as their minds. It was a city of high achievers, that was for sure. Columbia Heights itself is one of the highest point in the city, and the gym's giant sprawling windows ran the length of the block. People on striders and weight machines could work out with a floor-to-ceiling view and do free weight routines while watching the District teem below. As the sun began to set over the capital city, the fire sky lit the glass-lined perimeter of one of the city's busiest streets, 14th.

Never one to have a workout plan, I made my way around the gym in a disorganized fashion, moving from shoulder press to triceps extensions and then to bicep curls. Just as in all my years of schooling, I had a hard time focusing on and dedicating myself to a routine. Soon, I made my way over to a glute machine, lay down, and began my effort to sculpt a better ass. Listening to my playlist, my eyes moved about the room and landed on a strikingly tall, brown-haired boy in a white T-shirt who was rowing four machines over from me. He was classically handsome, very well built without being over-muscled, and rowed with a great amount of force. I stopped staring at him for a moment and continued working out, but when I went back to look at him he was staring back in my direction.

Fuck. He saw me looking.

I pretended for a moment that I hadn't been, and then of course, as boys do, I looked again, and he continually looked back as he rowed. But there was no smiling. He seemed serious, confident, and before I could figure out my next move, he averted his eyes, finished rowing, and moved on to another part of the gym.

Well, I missed that opportunity. *Maybe he's straight. Is he straight? No, he's gay. Actually, he's probably straight.* This, as many of you may find surprising, is the thing that all gay men have to go through when looking for interested partners. Is the guy gay, or straight, or just European? Is he bisexual? Honestly, sometimes it's impossible to tell.

I didn't see Mr. Tall for the rest of my workout, though I did do a lap around the gym looking for him. *Perhaps he's already left,* I thought to myself. Finished with my workout, I made my way to the locker room. As I walked up to my locker I looked to the right and to my surprise, there was Mr. Tall. We made eye contact with each other a number of times as we changed, but yet again no one said a word. I'm usually quite confident in these situations, but the fact that there were a number of other guys changing around us made it slightly awkward and I didn't want to force it. Mr. Tall put his gym bag over his shoulder, looked at me with that same stone-cold, serious face, then turned and left the gym.

Well, that was strike two. He's gone and I didn't say hi, and I probably won't see him again for months. Shaking my head, I threw my clothes in my locker, wrapped a towel around my waist, and headed for the showers.

After a steamy shower, I put on clean clothes, gathered my stuff, and headed out of the WSC. The gym sits on the third floor of the building. I walked down the first set of open stairs that looked upon the large lobby, where people were continually coming and going. As I made my turn down the second set of open stairs, I looked down to my right and there, leaving the second-floor Target and heading down the escalator, was Mr. Tall. I looked down at him. He was still remarkably handsome and stood (I later learned) at six-feet-five, towering above the people around him. Suddenly, and very unexpectedly, he looked up from the escalator toward the staircase and once again caught me staring.

I stared back at him this time, wanting to see if that intense stoic expression might change. It didn't. Time to change gears. I smiled and waved down to him on the escalator below. Mr. Tall's eyes became less serious, and to my surprise, he smiled and waved back.

He's definitely gay, I told myself. I made my way past Target and onto the escalator. He was now standing near the double doors that led to 14th Street, waiting. I reached the large glass doors and pressed them open.

"Hey, I'm Garon," I said, extending my hand. "What's your name?"

"I'm James," Mr. Tall said, seeming far more approachable and with a kindness that was completely juxtaposed against his towering figure and serious eyes. I looked up at him. His face looked like it had been sculpted. He had high-angled cheekbones, slightly fuller lips than your average white guy, and light-brown eyes. He was drop-dead gorgeous.

"Where are you from?" James asked.

"I was adopted from Sri Lanka, grew up in Africa and the Middle East, but I just moved here from Austin," I said. I've still never figured out a succinct way to answer that question.

"Wow," he said.

"What about you?"

"I'm just from Upstate New York." We laughed.

"So, can I get your number and we can hang out sometime?" I asked.

"Sure." We exchanged numbers.

"Where do you live?" he asked me.

"I'm staying at my sister's place on 11th," I said, pointing across the street. "You?"

"Oh, I live a couple blocks this way, on Monroe," James said, pointing in the opposite direction.

"Nice. It's really great to meet you," I said. God, he was handsome. With that, I turned away and we walked in opposite directions. Before I got to the first intersection, I turned back to look at him again, and he was doing the same. We laughed, turned, and kept walking our separate ways.

32
MATCHBOX

THE FOLLOWING WEEK I SAT across from James at a high-top table at Matchbox, an American bistro known for its sizzling woodfired pizza in the heart of Chinatown. It was nice to finally be at eye level with this giant and he smiled more easily now.

"So tell me again all the places you're from," James said teasingly.

"Well, I was adopted from Sri Lanka, then we moved to South Africa, Hawaii, The Gambia, Jamaica, Louisiana, and then I graduated from high school in Jordan. My dad worked in economic development."

He nodded and said, "Wow, that's quite a list of countries."

"How long have you lived here in DC?" I asked.

"I've lived here for ten years."

"And where did you live before?"

"The Philippines."

It wasn't the answer I was expecting. James had just gotten even more intriguing.

"My sister was adopted from The Philippines. She was born in Cebu. Where did you live?"

James looked as surprised as I had been a moment before.

"Really? I lived in Makati for a year. I was working there," he said.

I looked across at James as he spoke. He was an alluring combination of his towering physical presence and then a voice quality that was slightly nerdy, which I unexpectedly found myself attracted to. I couldn't take my eyes away from his cheekbones, so angular and defining. And he was erudite; that, I gleaned very quickly.

I learned that besides The Philippines, James had lived for a brief time in London. He had previously worked for Harmon Kardon and traveled extensively for work, spending quite a bit of time in Japan, Ukraine, Germany, South Korea, Hong Kong, Taiwan, Mexico, and China. As a young boy he was raised largely by a single mother who worked two jobs in the small town of Rotterdam, New York, to take care of him and his sister. James had found his own way out and into an international life.

I remember thinking he was different than all the rest, and I liked him right way.

We chatted nonstop throughout the meal, and when the bill came, James asked, "Do you still have some more time to hang out?"

"Sure," I said in a controlled way, though internally I was elated that he, too, didn't want the date to be over. "What did you have in mind?" I asked.

"Have you seen the Constitution before?"

"No," I answered, but it was absolutely something I had wanted to see since arriving in DC.

"Would you like to go see it? We're just a couple blocks from the National Archives," James suggested.

Who is this guy? Sexy and into the Constitution. Yes, please.
I was glad that he had gathered over lunch how much I, too,

cared about politics. It was the perfect suggestion.

"I would love that," I said.

As we walked side by side, I could feel the chemistry. It filled the air between us as we walked to the National Archives, an exquisite structure of Corinthian columns and home to two enormous bronze doors that even dwarfed James. When it was our turn to step up to the four airtight glass cases that held the Constitution of the United States, I felt an overwhelming sense of gratitude. The United States was not perfect, and many of the founders who had asserted in the Declaration of Independence that "All Men Are Created Equal" had written those words while owning black women, men, and their children as slaves. I've often felt that this is one of the first things kids should be taught when learning about American history. That people aren't exclusively good or bad, and that the truth often lies somewhere in between. The Framers should be remembered as much for their gross abuse of black people as they are for the inception of the country. Those two things are not mutually exclusive.

The United States had enshrined in its founding documents a free press and freedom of speech. I had lived for years in countries that didn't honor these fundamental values. Even if imperfect, the document I was standing next to made me proud as it appealed for each generation to come closer to creating "a more perfect union," especially when it came to race. And while there was much work to be done, Senator Barack Obama had clinched the Democratic nomination for president of the United States and the excitement in the air around Washington was palpable. I certainly was eagerly anticipating Election Day.

I looked up at James, who was carefully, thoughtfully, reading through the Bill of Rights alongside me. When we were done, we exited the cold, dark rotunda and arrived back into the hustle and bustle of the streets of Penn Quarter.

"That was incredible. Really, it was. Thanks," I said, reflecting on what had been a truly wonderful moment.

"You're welcome," James said. "I guess we should head back to the neighborhood."

We were approaching the metro entrance to Navy/Archives. "This was pretty smooth. Do you take all your dates to lunch and then to the National Archives?" I said jokingly.

James turned to me and said gently, "Oh. This isn't . . . this isn't a date."

My heart sank. Did he just say *This isn't a date*? I was speechless. My brain expected him to follow it with a laugh and tell me he was joking, but he said nothing.

"Well, what was it then?" I asked playfully.

This had the potential to be extremely awkward. *Did he think we were just friends? Had I completely misread all the chemistry at Matchbox?*

"It's not a date because I'm with someone," James said thoughtfully, trying to make the situation a bit better.

"You're with someone?" I wasn't computing. "Oh! Like you have a boyfriend?" I asked, realizing what he meant.

"Yes, we live together," James said.

I understood the complexities of relationships and certainly within the gay community the non-exclusivity that often is part of the rules of gay couples. I respected that.

"Okay," I said, understanding that he liked me, I liked him, but it couldn't be anything serious. "So, do you guys have an open relationship then?" I asked, shifting gears.

"Yes, we do," James said. I could tell he was glad that I had been able to put it all together and not gotten upset.

"Well, then why don't you come over to my place," I

suggested. If I wasn't going to date this gorgeous guy, I at least wanted to sleep with him.

James and I rode the green and yellow Metro line, racing under the city back into Columbia Heights. The awkwardness of the moment had passed, and we were back to talking about our families and time spent in other countries.

When we reached Ebony's house, as expected, no one was home. I locked the front door, and we went up the stairs. The chemistry I had sensed earlier at Matchbox and the Constitution played out wonderfully.

33
SLIDING DOORS

IT HAD BEEN FOUR MONTHS since I had sent off all my reels to various news directors. No one was interested. Just like in the acting world, TV journalists sometimes have agents. Determined not to give up, I researched agents and submitted myself to Nancy Shafran, the vice-president and senior agent of the NWT Group.

I was pleasantly surprised when days later the phone rang.

"Hi, Garon, this is Nancy Shafran. I've looked at your résumé and newsreel and I'd like to talk to you about representation," she said. Nancy had a kind demeanor over the phone, and I could also ascertain that she was well experienced and, to put it bluntly, she knew her shit. I needed her expertise and she was easy to talk to. Later that week I signed with her. While I was open to almost anywhere in the country, I impressed upon her the fact that I'd prefer to stay within two to three hours of driving distance from DC.

IN THE WEEKS that passed, I saw James a number of times. We would take long walks around the city together. I didn't ask about his relationship and understood that they had some level of agreement.

"Garon, I wanted to tell you something. It's not just that my boyfriend and I are in an open relationship. We are actually in the process of breaking up. I'm trying to get out. It's just tough because we own the house together and are both living there until we can sell," he said. I understood.

This was welcomed news to me. I had very quickly taken a liking to James and had stopped going on even casual dates with anyone else. I loved spending time with him in Meridian Hill Park discussing international politics. In my mind, he was very much the whole package.

One afternoon we were sitting in a DC favorite, The Diner, in Adams Morgan. The Diner is a place people flock to at all hours of the day or night for comfort food in a warm, familiar atmosphere. James and I were sitting along the bar, eating and talking about his recent trip to Fort Lauderdale.

"Have you ever been to Lauderdale?" he asked.

"No, I haven't. The only place I've been in Florida is Orlando for Disney when we were kids."

"South Florida is incredible. My friend Richie lives in Lauderdale, and I was down with him right before I met you. I love the beach life down there. My grandparents used to have a house west of Lauderdale. When I was a kid, we would drive down from New York to visit," he said. "Maybe we could go to Lauderdale together someday."

"I'd love to do that together. That would be great. By the way, question. James is a bit formal, does anyone call you Jamie? Because I'd like to call you Jamie," I told him.

"Actually, my entire family calls me Jamie," he said, laughing. And from that moment, he was Jamie to me.

FALL IN WASHINGTON was undoubtedly the most picturesque time of the year. Yellow and orange leaves float through the city, turning the once gray roads into vibrant avenues. The cooling wind flows off the Potomac River and glides easily through the neighborhoods. I, like everyone else, took unnaturally long walks from Columbia Heights into Mt. Pleasant, up the impeccable Belmont Drive and into Kalorama Heights.

One afternoon while at home, my phone rang.

"Hey, Garon, it's Nancy. I have an interview for you at an affiliate in Salisbury, Maryland."

My first interview. I thanked Nancy, hung up the phone in excitement, and then googled *Salisbury* to find out exactly where the hell it was. I rented a car and made the two-and-a-half-hour drive out of DC, across Chesapeake Bay, past Easton, and into Salisbury, a college town just forty minutes from the coast. I settled into my hotel room for the night, anticipating my interview the next day.

The next morning I woke up early and eagerly showed up to the TV station. While I had imagined the interview would be mostly verbal, I was taken to a room, given a pen and an assortment of questions, and asked to write for an hour and a half. I didn't answer the questions as well as I wanted to in the allotted time. The verbal portion of the interview went terribly, I stumbled incoherently through most of my answers, and when I returned to my hotel room I collapsed on my bed.

Later that evening, Jamie called.

"How'd it go?" he asked.

"I'm not getting this one. I was a disaster," I told him.

He assured me there would be more opportunities. I hoped he was right.

"Remember that I'm leaving for London the day after

tomorrow. I'll miss you, but I'll be back in ten days," he said. "I probably won't be able to see you before I leave. I have a lot to get done."

I understood. A lot had changed since we'd met two and half months before. We had become extremely close.

"I'll miss you too," I said, then paused. I pulled up another window on my laptop and searched flights from Washington to London.

"What are you doing?" he asked.

"Question. Let's say I could get myself to London while you were there. Would you want to hang out, or what that be too much? It's totally fine if you don't," I asked daringly.

"You would come to *London*? I would love that!" Jamie said. "Are you serious, Garon?"

"I don't know. I need to see what flight prices look like," I said. I could tell he liked the spontaneity. And I was glad he was open to the idea.

"The only thing is, I can't have you stay with me because I'm going for work. The whole team is staying together at this giant manor an hour outside of London," he reminded me.

"No, that's okay. I have friends from high school who live in London. I'm sure I could stay with my friend Vassia," I said.

"It's the day after tomorrow. If you can pull this off, that would be amazing," Jamie said excitedly.

"Let me see what I can do," I said. We hung up and I turned to my laptop.

34
ELEPHANT AND CASTLE

MY FLIGHT TOUCHED DOWN AT London's Heathrow Airport on a chilly day in October. The Heathrow Express rocketed me through the countryside and into Paddington Station. I had made the mistake of forgetting that the Tube doesn't have escalators like the DC Metro. I had brought along a large black suitcase without wheels and needed to change trains multiple times. I huffed and puffed up and down the stairs with my overweight suitcase, browsing signboards and arrows until I found my train to Elephant and Castle.

Emerging from the Underground, excitement vanquished jet lag. I couldn't wait to see Vassia; it had been four years. I arrived at a two-story brick row house with a red front stoop and knocked politely on the large wooden black door.

"Gaarrron!" Vassia yelled, flinging the door open and throwing herself into my arms. She still smelled the same and her face hadn't changed one bit. I kissed her on both cheeks and instantly it felt like old times.

"How was your flight? Come to the kitchen, you have to eat something!" she said, pushing my luggage to the side and leading me down the hallway.

"This is Danai, Kyriakos, Maria, and Nita!" she said,

introducing me to her tribe. I was officially in a Greek home. All except for Nita. Nita was from Indonesia, lived in North London, and was hanging out at the house for a couple days. They were all warm and welcoming. I took a deep breath and realized how much I had longed for this kind of diversity over my four long years in Texas. I had missed being surrounded by people from across the world.

"Garon, do you want some coffee?" Danai asked.

"Sure."

"Where are you from?" Kyriakos asked in earnest.

They were kind and lovely, exactly as I would imagine any friends of Vassia's to be. As for Vassia, we picked up right where we had left off years before. We reminisced about JJ, Saleem, and so many of our other classmates, and relived our crazy nights in Jordan. I was so grateful to be sitting in front of her again. But mostly, as I stared back into her brown eyes, I saw a person who *truly* knew who I was. She had known me and known Mom. She knew the pain I had gone through, and was still going through, without her in this world. She knew the fears I had, the strength I held, and that I had lost my way in Texas. Through it all, she loved me the same way in this group house in London as she had all those years before in her small bedroom in the Middle East.

Two days later, after a lively dinner with the Greek-Indonesian crew, I made my way to Waterloo Station, with high arched ceilings and glossy geometrically designed floors. I browsed through destinations until I found mine: Fleet.

I texted Jamie.

(Me) *Leaving London now. Should be in Fleet in an hour.*

(Jamie) *Great. Heading to a late dinner with the team. The Hotel is called The Elvetham. Told the front desk to expect you and to give you a key to my room. Just text me when you get here.*

I wove through the dark countryside. It was the late-night train, and only ten other passengers sat around me. As we pulled into smaller towns along the way, sparse lights were visible in the distance. One by one, passengers disembarked. Soon, there were only two of us left. I reveled in the sense of adventure of going through these small English towns, unsure of what my destination might look like. I pressed my head against the cold glass of the window and thought back to how unhappy I had been five months earlier in Austin with Chad. I knew at the time I needed to get away from him, to move up to DC. But nowhere in those plans had I ever imagined myself across the Atlantic again, riding a train late in the evening out of London and into the English countryside.

"The next stop is Fleet. Please mind the gap as you exit."

I stepped out onto the empty platform and inhaled the country air. It smelled fresh and I could tell horses were nearby. It was as if the earth out here could breathe. Above, free from smog and light pollution, the black sky enveloped me. A lone taxi light glimmered in the parking lot.

We rode in silence through country roads. I couldn't see much of anything out the window save for some fence-lined pastures. Minutes later we turned a corner and there, looming in the distance, surrounded by absolutely nothing, was an extraordinary manor: The Elvetham. I thanked my driver and climbed out of his car. I walked up to the front desk, where a man and woman were pleasantly waiting.

"Good evening, how are you?" I asked them both.

They smiled and added a gracious "Hello, sir."

"My name is Garon Wade. I'm here to see one of your guests,

James Suriano. He's at dinner and said he would leave a key at the front desk for me."

"Yes, good evening, Mr. Wade. He did, indeed. Will you be staying the night here?" the man asked.

"Yes," I answered.

"Brilliant. Now, Mr. Wade, are you aware that there is only one bed in the room?" he asked.

Well, I didn't expect that question.

"Yes, I'm aware."

"And are you okay with that? Or would you prefer a room with two beds?" he pressed on.

What is going on?

"No, I'm fine with one bed."

The two of them glanced at each other, then opened a drawer, produced a key, and handed it to me. I could tell from their eyes they had questions as they stared at me in my white V-neck under my long black trench coat and black boots.

"Please feel free to relax over there at the bar. Our bartender Thomas will be happy to serve you a drink, and we will have someone show you to your room shortly," he said.

I thanked them both. As I walked into the adjoining room, I could feel the two sets of eyes following me.

"Hello, sir, I'm Thomas. What can I offer you to drink?"

"Hi, Thomas. I'm fine actually, thank you. I'll just wait here for a moment," I said politely.

"Are you sure? A gin and tonic? Perhaps a cup of tea?"

"No, thank you."

"Where are you joining us from?"

"I just came from London."

"Oh, wonderful, sir," Thomas said. I liked him. He seemed much nicer and more comfortable with me than the two at the front desk.

A moment later a bellhop arrived. I thanked Thomas and followed the bellhop through the manor up two flights of stairs and to Jamie's room. I closed the door behind me and a huge smile lit my face. The room smelled of a mixture of Jamie and his cologne. I looked around the small bedroom. On the far side of the bed a radiator warmed the space just below a large window. A wooden writing desk sat quietly in the corner. On top of it, I found a note.

Garon, can't believe you are here. I'll be back from dinner soon. Can't wait to see you.

I took off my trench coat, hung it up in the wooden armoire, and waited patiently for Jamie to arrive. Ten minutes later, I heard the key in the lock slowly turn; the door pushed open and there he was. Jamie was all smiles as he quickly pulled me close to his chest. We hugged, then looked at each other with the same knowing grin we had across the table at Matchbox two months before.

"You're actually here," he said, holding my hand. I could see the excitement in his eyes.

"I can't believe it either. I'm so happy to see you," I told him.

We collapsed on the bed and immediately started recounting all that had happened since I left the unfortunate job interview in Maryland. He wanted to know how I had managed to get such a last-minute flight to London, and how my first two days with Vassia had been. I had plenty to tell him.

"There was one thing. The front desk people asked me some strange questions," I told him.

"What did they say?"

I repeated the entire conversation and Jamie began laughing. "Oh my god!"

"What?" I asked playfully.

"They think you're a prostitute from London!"

"What!" I said, scoffing at the ridiculousness of the idea.

"Well, think about it. First of all, there are no brown people here. Brown guy arrives at ten at night from London with no bag."

It was true. I would be returning early in the morning to Vassia's house and had not brought a bag.

"You're wearing a black trench coat and told the front desk a guest left a key to his room for you," Jamie said, seeing the trench coat hanging in the closet behind.

I started laughing. He was right. It was very Julia Roberts in *Pretty Woman*. And of course, it couldn't have been further from the truth. We had a good laugh and then Jamie asked, "Do you want to go on a walk around the manor? It's beautiful outside."

"Yea, let's do it," I said, putting my prostitute trench coat back on.

The two of us stepped outside into the quiet darkness and found our way to a walking path that wound throughout the manor. I looked up. The towering red-brick building rose high like a castle and we marveled at the architecture and quiet beauty of our surroundings. The stars glistened in the sky and, with the help of the moon, lit our pathway.

"This is incredible," he said.

"I can't believe we met at the gym in Columbia Heights and are standing here together right now," I told him. We looked around at the desolate English countryside. It felt right.

The next morning, I woke up at 6 a.m. to leave The Elvetham before Jamie's team would rise and make their way to breakfast. Jamie called the front desk and asked them to summon a taxi. I kissed him goodbye and agreed that I'd come back later that evening. It had rained overnight and the grass around the manor was damp. A thick fog held tight to the air. As the taxi slowly pulled up, I looked toward the lobby and two faces were staring out at me. I was still wearing my white V-neck under my black trench coat. Jamie was right, they definitely thought I was a prostitute. *At least I'm a high-class hooker*, I thought, stepping into the car. *Sleeping with clients at castles: that's the way to do it.*

BACK IN ELEPHANT AND CASTLE, Vassia and the Greek crew took me to delicious restaurants, bustling pubs, and showed me a wonderful time around the city. I returned to The Elvetham for just one more night and fully accepted my status as the London call boy who was good enough to come two nights in a row. By the weekend, Jamie, finished with work, joined me in London. Together, we checked into the Marriot Marble Arch. It was the first time we truly had a place to be together. Not Ebony's house, not his house in the midst of his breakup, but instead a place for the weekend to call our own. The first afternoon after having lunch, Jamie had an idea.

"Want to walk by Madonna's house?" he asked.

"Sure," I said. "Are you a big Madonna fan?"

"Huge. Huge Madonna fan. Every time she goes on tour, I go to see her twice."

Instantly, I thought of Baboucarr.

"The first time I ever heard Madonna, I was in the backseat of a Jeep Cherokee in west Africa. My dad's driver, Baboucarr, loved her. Ebony and I rode all the way to school singing 'Like a Virgin' and 'Papa Don't Preach.'"

"Is that why you're gay?"

"Probably," I said. We laughed.

We passed by Madonna's home in Marylebone and Jamie was ecstatic.

"One day I'll take you to one of her concerts," he said. I loved that idea.

Later that afternoon, I introduced Jamie and Vassia to each other at an intimate pastry shop on Old Compton Street. It was important to me that they liked each other, and they instantly did. He now had a face to put to the name that I said each time I recounted a story of my years in Jordan. I hoped one day I could introduce him to JJ and Saleem also.

Jamie's favorite restaurant in London was an unassuming Japanese restaurant a couple blocks away called Matsutake. We sat shoulder to shoulder with other diners, sipped on miso soup, and tried an excellent array of sushi. I told him how Mom and Dad had lived in Tokyo for a short time before they adopted Ebony, and how I had dreamed of going to Japan one day. He, in turn, told me of his month and a half working in Nagoya and Tokyo and how fascinating Japanese culture was to him.

Soon enough, it was time to return to Washington. We flew on the same day, on two different flights, crossing the Atlantic simultaneously in parallel flight paths. It was a wonderful metaphor for our situation: unable to be together immediately but moving side by side and trying to get to the same place.

BACK IN COLUMBIA HEIGHTS, I was sitting on the counter in Ebony's kitchen, talking to her as she cooked.

"How was London?" she asked.

"Remember that guy, Jamie, who I went to hang out with there?"

"Yes," she replied. By now, she had met Jamie a couple times.

I smiled. "One day I'm going to marry him, Ebony. And when I do, remind me that I told you this," I said confidently.

Ebony stopped stirring and looked up at me quietly. I could tell she didn't believe me. My somewhat impulsive nature stood in sharp contrast to her calculated, methodical decision making. Our birth, or rather adoption, order was showing.

35

BARACK OBAMA

TUESDAY, NOVEMBER 4, 2008, was exhilarating. I, along with much of the nation, had become extremely excited for Barack Obama to become the next president of the United States. And no city on earth was as excited for election night as the District of Columbia. It felt like the Super Bowl had come to Washington, with parties starting early that morning after people rolled out of bed and continuing on throughout the day. I was ecstatic and hoped history would be made that evening.

Ebony went to an election-watch party on U Street while Nick and Karl had gone to parties of their own. I chose to stay at the house by myself and watch the returns. I had yet to make many new friends in DC, and while I would have loved to spend election night with Jamie, he was in the air, en route to Fort Wayne, Indiana, for work. I felt badly that he couldn't be in the District on the night of the election, knowing how much he would have enjoyed it.

At 8 p.m. I watched with excitement as Obama won Pennsylvania and then Ohio. By 10 p.m. he had won Iowa. "No Democrat has won Virginia since 1964," said George Stephanopoulos. "No Democrat has won North Carolina since

1976. That he's competitive this late in the evening says so much," he added. And then finally I turned to CNN as Wolf Blitzer spoke, "Barack Obama, forty-seven years old, will become the president-elect of the United States." I started screaming by myself in Ebony's house. The scenes from Grant Park in Chicago, New York City, and Washington, DC, filled the screen.

Jamie had just texted me that he had landed in Fort Wayne. I called him.

"Obama won! Obama won!" I yelled.

"I know! We were in the air and the captain announced it just before we landed. You know what's funny? There's little old ladies here at the airport in Fort Wayne who hand out chocolate chip cookies to passengers as they arrive. When I got off the plane, they were handing out cookies to us and saying to each other, 'It's a sad day for America.'"

We laughed. "I wish you were here. I'm so fucking happy he won!"

"Me too. Now go and have a great time," Jamie said.

Another call came through. It was Ebony.

"He won!" she screamed.

"Yea! We have a black president!" I yelled, jumping throughout the house.

"Quick, come down to U Street. I'm outside of Busboys and Poets, everyone is freaking out, and the party is moving into the street," Ebony said.

"I'll be there!" I said, hanging up, throwing on my shoes, and taking off out the door.

I sprinted through Columbia Heights, down 11th Street and onto Florida Avenue. Adrenaline coursed through my body and all around me people were screaming in happiness and cheering on every corner. At 14th Street, I turned left and ran down to Busboys and Poets. Amid the crowd, I found Ebony, and we ran into each other's arms, jumping up and down.

"We have a black president!" I shouted.

"I know! I know! Can you believe this?" Ebony yelled joyfully.

Washington was in ecstasy. Shoulder-to-shoulder couples and friends were crying and hugging. People came pouring out of bars and restaurants on the corner of 14th and V, merging into the crowd of people equally reveling in the Obama win along U Street. I'll never forget it. Standing next to Ebony I thought of Mom and how she would have loved this night of change in the country of her birth. I quickly texted Dad, who had heavily canvassed for Obama in Virginia. He had chosen to stay at his home across the river to watch the returns, and he was equally thrilled. I thanked the world for putting me in Washington on this evening. Perhaps the only other place with this much enthusiasm would have been Grant Park in Chicago, where the Obamas were making their very first appearance as the next First Family. Above me, a young black guy had climbed on top of a bus stop and was celebrating with one arm outstretched in victory as people cheered him on from below. It was time. It was far past due time. For the first time in the history of the United States, black and brown people felt seen on a level that was unprecedented. I shared in that feeling.

36

ASHOH'S REPUBLICAN LOYALTY

THERE WERE, HOWEVER, TWO PEOPLE in our family who weren't celebrating the historic election. I knew Ashoh and Grandpa wouldn't be happy with the Obama win. On more than one occasion Ashoh had reminded me that she was a proud card-carrying member of the Republican Party.

"I've always been a Republican woman, and I'll be a Republican woman until the day I die," she once told me. I figured I'd call to check up on them. I promised myself I wouldn't be the one to bring it up, though.

"Well, I guess y'all are excited about the big news," Ashoh said, wasting no time in instigating the conversation.

"What news?" I lied.

"The news of Bara... whatever his name is, winning the election."

"His name is Barack Obama, Ashoh," I said.

"I heard they are going to replace the rose garden with a watermelon garden," Ashoh commented snidely.

My mouth dropped.

"Ashoh, that's really, really, really racist," I told her.

"I didn't come up with it. It's just what I heard at the beauty parlor," she deflected.

"Well, you heard wrong. Why don't like the Obamas?"

"I just don't! And neither does your grandfather! He's so upset he had to rest in his La-Z-Boy."

"Ashoh, he's always in his La-Z-Boy. What exactly is it that you don't like about Barack Obama?"

"Now, Garon, you know I don't talk politics!" Ashoh said.

"But *you* brought it up," I said.

We hung up the phone, both equally annoyed at each other.

37

DO YOU PLAY BASKETBALL?

EBONY HAD GRACIOUSLY OFFERED to host Thanksgiving. I asked her if I could bring Jamie and of course she said yes. This would be the first time my family would meet Jamie, and he them. I was especially excited for Jamie to meet Yael, who was now in his senior year of high school in Virginia. Dad would be there, along with my dad's older brother, my Uncle Mike (yes, I have two Uncle Mikes), and my Aunt Rose Anna, who were driving up from North Carolina. It was the first Thanksgiving we had all spent together in years.

Jamie and I walked up the beige metal stairs to Ebony's house, me carrying bottles of Malbec and Jamie cradling a basket of artisanal bread that he had baked.

"Ready to meet the family?" I asked.

"I'm ready."

We knocked on the door and it soon swung open. It was Dad. I watched as his eyes landed on mine, then traveled high above to meet Jamie's. I could tell he wasn't expecting him to be so tall. I knew, in typical Dad fashion, a comment, probably relating to basketball, was coming.

"Hey, Garon!" he said with that infectious smile.

"Hey, Dad, Happy Thanksgiving!" I said, hugging him. "This is …"

"And you must be Jamie! Wow, you're tall. You play basketball, man?" Dad asked happily.

"No, no basketball," Jamie said kindly, shaking his hand. "Nice to meet you, Steve."

We walked in together and I introduced Jamie to Yael and the rest of the family. Jamie seemed to effortlessly move from conversation to conversation throughout the evening. As wine, food, and conversation flowed, Dad recounted how often times, when he showed up at the door of a middle-aged white couple who looked very much the same as him, the couple expressed surprise that Dad was canvassing for the progressive black senator from Chicago.

With Jamie now deep in conversation with Dad, I took the opportunity to slide a couple chairs over to sit with Yael.

"What do you think about Jamie?" I asked, resting my arm on Yael's broad shoulders.

"He seems really cool. So easy to talk to."

"That's one of the things I like about him the most. Not pretentious. Very down to earth. I've been excited for the two of you to meet. How's senior year going?"

"I've had a great time playing football. Besides that, I've just been smoking weed and applying to colleges."

I laughed. "Where are you thinking of going?"

"Actually, I want to go to UT Austin."

I moved my arm from his shoulder and nudged him. "That's so great, Yael. I had no idea you were interested in UT. I learned a lot there in my political science classes. And you'll love the football culture. I never got into it, but everyone else loved it.

"I can't wait."

I looked at the little blond boy whom Mom and Dad used to carefully position in the middle of their bed in Parkwood before

Ebony and I would come running in and pile around him. "My god, I can't believe it's time for you to go to college. I can still remember when you came home from the hospital in South Africa."

Yael smiled. "What about you? You're going to be a TV reporter?"

I sighed. "If anyone will ever hire me, then yes." We laughed together, clinked our wine glasses, and continued sipping on Malbec. Down the table Dad and his brother were having a lively conversation.

"All of these people denying the fact that he was born in Hawaii, it's born out of racism," Dad said loudly.

"You're absolutely right, Steve."

My Uncle Mike, a history professor and department chair at Appalachian State University, had spent a good portion of his career researching race relations in the South. In Jamaica, I could remember staring up at the green jacket of a book nestled at the center of our cedar bookcase, *Sugar Dynasty*, in which he wrote at length about slavery, the Civil War, and the post-war labor regime in the cane fields. As the Wades do, we rambled on about politics and culture late into the evening. At some point we shifted from the racism surrounding Obama's candidacy to Dad's stories of hitchhiking with Mom from Botswana to Kenya, and later from India to Germany.

"Niki and I spent two weeks on buses, trains, and in the backseats of other people's cars from India, through Pakistan, Iran, Turkey, Bulgaria, Yugoslavia, and Austria. When we got to the border of Austria and Germany, we stood on the side of an eight-lane highway; two thin, hungry American backpackers looking for one more ride. We held up a cardboard sign that said, NEW YORK. You guys wouldn't believe the faces of the motorists who zoomed by us. Finally a woman, a professor from the University of Berlin actually, who said she couldn't stop laughing at our sign, pulled over and told us to jump in," Dad recounted. "She told us, we made her day. And of course, she had made ours."

I had heard the story a thousand times growing up, but I never tired of seeing the excitement in his eyes as he remembered.

I leaned back in my chair and took a moment to take it all in. I was truly happy. Outside, the last leaves had fallen from the trees, and winter was sweeping into the District.

38

THE FIVE-YEAR PLAN

"I HAVE A QUESTION FOR YOU," Jamie said.

I smiled. "Okay, go ahead."

We were at Oyamel, a charmingly decorated Mexican restaurant in Gallery Place that boasted some of the best guacamole in town. It was, as usual, full of people. Unable to find a table, Jamie and I sat down at the blue talavera-tiled bar looking out at the Christmas shoppers running in and out of stores. It was a great escape from the freezing wind sweeping down 7th Street.

"Where are you with kids?" Jamie asked.

My smile moved into a slight nervous laughter.

"I . . . Kids. Look, I've known I've wanted to have a child since I was little boy. It's definitely something I want. But right now, I'm not in a place financially or career-wise to take care of a kid."

It was as honest as I could be. As the guacamole melted in my mouth, I remembered the occasional afternoon when I had walked with Juju along the sandy streets of The Gambia to pick Yael up from his French pre-school. I loved taking care of him on our walk back home. I knew then that one day I would want to be someone's father.

"Do you want kids?" I asked Jamie, now realizing that perhaps he *didn't* want children and this would be a deal-breaker.

"I've never wanted kids... until now. Throughout my twenties when people would ask me if I wanted kids, I said no. But now in my thirties, I've had a complete change of heart," he said.

"And why the change?" I asked.

"Well. For years I've taken care of this little boy here in Washington who I call Mr. Nick. Mr. Nick is originally from Thailand and his mother is sisters with my friend Tuk, who I once worked with here at the Red Cross. On Sundays I would take Mr. Nick to The Diner with my friends. In the past year or so, I started to have dreams of having a kid. When I wake up, sometimes I think it's about Mr. Nick, but I'm realizing now that it's not. And it's made me think about what I want. And I do. I do want to have kids."

It was music to my ears. I hadn't been prepared to bring it up so early and I was glad Jamie had.

"Would you want to adopt or do surrogacy?" I asked.

"Definitely adopt. I only want to adopt."

"Good. Me too. Only adoption," I said.

While I was glad surrogacy was an available option to people, I knew how much being adopted from the Jayamani Center in Sri Lanka had transformed my life. I wanted to give another child without a home the opportunity that had been given to me. And I was thrilled that Jamie felt similarly.

"What if we come up with a five-year plan? Five years to get everything together. I want to be in a place where I can be well established in my career and have enough money not to worry about being able to raise a kid," I suggested.

"I like that idea, and maybe it'll happen in less than five,"

Jamie said. I smiled lovingly at him.

I held his hand in my one hand, ate Oyamel's delicious guacamole with the other, and felt strongly that I had found a partner to move through this life with. Still, job-wise, things were uncertain.

THREE WEEKS BEFORE Christmas, Nancy called me once again.

"Garon, I have an interview for you at an ABC affiliate in Harrisonburg, Virginia. The news director, Ed Reams, wants to have a phone interview with you first, and then if that goes well, he'll have you drive down to Harrisonburg," she said.

"Thanks, Nancy, that's wonderful." Then, once again, I hung up the phone and googled *Harrisonburg, Virginia.*

A week later, after a successful phone interview, I took the train down to Charlottesville, Virginia, just across the mountain ridge from Harrisonburg. I discovered that my former teachers from ACS Amman, Jay and Tina, were living there with their sons. I couldn't wait to see them again. As my Amtrak pulled into the station, Jay stood outside waiting for me. I was overjoyed to see him. Jay had taught me so much in high school, speaking passionately about Ralph Waldo Emerson and introducing me to the work of Joyce Carol Oates. After they'd finished teaching at ACS Amman, Tina and Jay had moved with their boys to Syria. After only a couple months, American soldiers in Iraq had illegally crossed into Syria. The Syrian government shut down the International School and gave the teachers a week to get back to their home countries. So here they were, temporarily living back at their home in Charlottesville.

Reunited after all these years, I was thrilled to be sitting in the yellow living room of their cozy two-story home with the four of them. They told me of their brief months in one of the oldest cities in the world: Damascus. I remembered on a family trip years before how Mom gently placed her arm around mine as we bartered for colorful rugs in the open-air markets of Damascus.

"It's a game, Garon. Make your last offer, they'll decline, and we'll walk away. They'll eventually follow us." She was right. "Isn't Syria marvelous, honey? You're standing in one of the oldest civilizations in the world."

From Damascus, we had travelled to Aleppo. From there, Mom and Dad wanted to cross the country again, south to Palmyra. Ever seeking adventure, they ditched paved roads and instead took our SUV straight across the Syrian desert to reach the ancient Roman city. Along the way, we met extraordinarily friendly nomads, who showered us with smiles.

Now, surrounded by the two teachers who had shown me such love in the wake of Mom's death, little did I know that in just two years, this country would be devastated by war and become the epicenter of one of the world's largest humanitarian disasters. To this day, I still think of those welcoming faces I met in the Syrian desert, wondering what happened to them: Did they join the resistance or become refugees displaced internally? Were they forced into camps in Jordan or Lebanon or, worse, killed by the Assad regime, ISIS, or al-Qaeda? I can still see the warmth in their eyes and I'll always remember them.

Jay and Tina's boys, Jonny and Leo, were growing up fast. Leo was no longer the baby whom I once cradled in my arms as he sucked on his bottle of milk and drifted off to sleep. Seeing Jonny brought back fond memories of taking Tina's kindergarten class out to play each morning at ACS Amman. Jonny had been in his mom's class and I often played beside him while he plunged his shovel repeatedly into the sandbox. My nights of babysitting these two boys in Jordan seemed long ago.

The next morning, Tina drove me across the mountain ridge into Harrisonburg, known mostly for James Madison University. The ABC affiliate, WHSV, sat in the town square across from a courthouse, an Ethiopian restaurant, a few bars, and what was once an old dance studio. With the exception of my year in Luling, I had never lived in a small American town. I liked how the Blue Ridge Mountains framed the whole place. It was only a two-hour drive to Washington. I felt I could be happy here for a couple years and I could drive back to DC on weekends to spend time with Jamie.

The WHSV studio was very attractive. The well-designed newsroom was surprisingly up to par with that of NBC and Fox in Austin. I sat down with Ed Reams for an interview, and it was a complete reversal of my experience at the TV station in Salisbury, Maryland. The interview was exclusively verbal, his questions thoughtful, and my answers flowed easily just as they had during my initial phone conversation with him. As I walked out of his office, I knew I had landed the job. Tina, who was waiting outside for me, was eager to hear all about it. We talked about how different living in this slice of Americana would be compared to our life in the Middle East. It's always been that way between us. I once told Tina, "If anyone in this world has come close to being a maternal figure for me since Mom died, it's you." I still call her every Mother's Day.

WASHINGTON IS DEVASTATINGLY beautiful at Christmastime. To this day, I do my best to travel to DC around the holidays. Back in the city, Jamie and I walked through Georgetown, then Dupont, and later along New Hampshire Avenue, checking out a number of embassies. Windows were adorned with twinkling Christmas lights, red ribbons shined brightly on the doors of cafés, and Christmas cheer spread through the city like wildfire.

My phone rang, it was Nancy. I knew why she was calling.

"Garon, congratulations, WHSV has made you an offer. They want you to start in the New Year."

My time spent at NBC and Fox in Austin had paid off. For me personally, the New Year brought a lot of promise.

"I'm so proud of you," Jamie said, with his long arms wrapped around me. "Congratulations. I'm taking you to dinner. What kind of food do you want?"

"How about Indian?"

"I know an amazing place," he said.

And it was. Rasika was one of Washington's best Indian restaurants. Not only was the food mouthwatering, but the décor was alluring, with white linen tablecloths against a light golden-beige interior. White and red strands of glass hung vertically from the ceiling, adding to the hot spot's already seductive atmosphere.

"You did it," Jamie said, raising his gin and tonic to meet my martini.

"I wanted this so badly. Hard to imagine it's actually happening."

"Where do you want to be in ten years in this career?"

"I want to work for CNN."

"Then do it," he said with a smile.

I reached across the table and held his hand. "I'll drive up on my weekends to see you?"

"Of course, and I can drive down too sometimes."

I laughed. "Once or twice will probably be enough. It's a small town. I'll be wanting to come back to DC every weekend."

Even in those early days, Jamie supported my dreams in a way that no one had ever authentically done before, besides Dad. I genuinely felt he believed in me.

"Okay, now about Christmas. I'll be here with Dad, Ebony, and Yael. Are you excited to go back to Rotterdam?"

"Not really," Jamie said. We laughed.

"C'mon. Everyone's going to be really happy to see you. I'm sure your mom can't wait for you to come home."

As for DC, perhaps as exciting as the advent of Christmas was the inauguration of Barack Obama. This year, that holiday cheer would carry straight into late January.

39

LIVE SHOT

O N TUESDAY, JANUARY 20, 2009, I maneuvered through an elaborate auditorium full of high-schoolers. My cameraman and I filmed the reaction of students' faces in real time as Barack Obama took the oath of office on a giant screen that dropped down from the top of the auditorium. I tried hard to appear calm and unemotional as I did my job, but I could feel tears welling up inside of me as he spoke those sacred words: "Preserve, protect, and defend the Constitution of the United States." To see a person of color speak those words was overwhelming, and to see the excitement and jubilation of the largely white high-schoolers was a testament to our changing times.

The best part of my job at WHSV was, without a doubt, hanging out with my cameraman, David Johnson. Tall with light-brown hair, Dave was an easygoing guy from Indiana who had a charming laugh; we got along like we had been friends for years. One afternoon after shooting a story together, we were riding back to the station.

"So this weekend, Tia is having one of her girlfriends over for dinner. I thought that maybe you could come meet her. She's gorgeous and I think you two would actually be a really good match. I talked to Tia about it, she thinks so too," he said, confirming the confidence both he and his wife had in the idea.

Dave and I had talked about many things over my first few weeks in Harrisonburg, but my dating life hadn't come up yet.

"Thanks, Dave. I appreciate you guys thinking about me, but I'm gay," I said, smiling.

Dave whipped his head toward me, his mouth agape, "Dude, whaaaaat!?" he said. "I had no idea! Why didn't you tell me?"

"I don't know, man, it just didn't come up," I replied. We laughed about it the rest of the way to the station.

"I can't wait to tell Tia about this," Dave said.

My start at WHSV had been exhilarating. I loved the element of live TV and feeling the pressure of needing to get it right while on air. Every day led to a new set of stories and I covered everything from manslaughter cases to new local government regulations, home fires, to interviewing US Senator Mark Warner.

But I soon realized that there was a side to TV journalism that was deeply unappealing to me. Each day started off with a morning or afternoon meeting where the news director, executive producer, producers, and reporters all sat together and pitched ideas for news of the day. If there was a fire, or a shooting, the excitement would grow in the meeting if grave injuries or casualties were announced, making it an even bigger story. I found this repulsive and hard to stomach. One day I was assigned to go to the home of a mother whose son had just been shot. I felt it invasive and wrong and I could feel my disgust in the pit of my stomach as I put the microphone in front of her face and asked, "How do you feel?" *How the fuck do you think she felt? Her son had just been shot.* I left the front steps of her home disheartened and feeling a disconnect from the enthusiasm of the journalists around me from other networks who were riding high off the big news viability of the story.

A week or so later, as the auto industry was crashing, a local auto dealer was going out of business. It had been decided in the morning meeting that I would roll the story on the dealership going under. I went back to my desk and made the necessary calls to establish contacts and lock in an interview. As I was about to leave to shoot the story, the advertising team walked into the newsroom alongside the news director.

"Garon, we can't have you do the auto dealer story anymore," I was told.

"Why not? I just got the interview lined up and I'm about to leave," I said.

"You can't do this story because they are one of our biggest advertisers," the head of advertising told me. My news director nodded his head in agreement.

I stared at their faces, knowing how unethical the decision was. But I had no say, no choice.

"All right. I'll find another story," I said reluctantly.

It was a major turning point for me. Perhaps naively, I had never considered this business side of TV journalism. Of course it existed, how had I not seen it? And I didn't enjoy asking families who had lost their homes to fires "How did it make you *feel* to see your house burning to the ground in front of you?" The thing with TV reporting is that when you build a story, or what is known as a *package*, you are given roughly one minute and fifteen seconds to tell that story through what is called *SOT*, or sound on tape. These are essentially emotionally vulnerable moments during which the subject of the interview might break down and say, "Everything is lost. My whole life is gone," while crying. Or "I don't know how I can live without my son. He was my baby," while sobbing. It's the kind of moment in TV journalism that you are taught to ask questions to elicit. When you achieve it, it is considered TV gold. I wasn't interested in any of it, and I kicked myself for not realizing it during my internships at NBC and Fox in Austin. I had been blinded by ambition, but reality had set in. There were parts of the industry I valued. Reporters at the scene of a natural disaster or an unfolding event speaking directly to the camera without trying to solicit emotional interviews—that was worthy. Political reporters holding elected leaders accountable—that was worthy. War correspondents and photojournalists in the field moving with militaries and exposing conflict to the world—that was worthy. But not this. And I didn't want to ask people how they felt about their kids being shot to get to a section of a career I'd feel better about. I knew in the recesses of my body, it wasn't right for me.

While I was unhappy about my cold realization about this career I had worked so hard to get into, Dave kept me laughing the entire time. We would ride to live shots bitching about the executive producer or how ridiculous the choice to run with a certain story had been. One day as we were riding around, Dave started asking questions about my life in the Middle East.

"Did you like living in Jordan?" he asked.

"Yea, man. I had so many great times there in high school," I told him, then proceeded to detail the carefree evenings spent running around Amman with JJ, Vassia, and Saleem.

"There was an American girl who I was friends with at Goshen College. She grew up in Jordan," Dave said.

"What was her name?" I asked.

"Sara Yoder."

"Sara Yoder!" I yelled, turning to Dave.

"Yea, why, do you know her?"

"Do I know her? Yea, man! Sara was my sister's *best friend* in high school."

Dave and I broke into our usual laughter and continued sharing stories. It seemed too crazy a coincidence to comprehend. A reporter and a cameraman driving through central Virginia, thousands of miles away from the deserts of the Middle East, and we had a friend in common who was Ebony's best friend.

On Friday afternoons, I would walk out of the TV station and excitedly drive back to DC to see the family and to hang out with Jamie. Huddled in our puffy jackets together, earmuffs on, we walked with a hot beverage steaming in our hands. Jamie was still traveling a lot for work and would watch my live shots from his laptop in various hotel rooms across the country. He also understood my growing dissatisfaction and the moral complexities I had about the career. I couldn't leave, though; I had worked too hard to get into it.

40
ASHOH'S THRONE

ON ONE OF MY MANY two-hour drives back to Harrisonburg, I called Ashoh in Luling. Beyond a fleeting "Merry Christmas" conversation in December, we hadn't talked at length since she accused the Obamas of planting a watermelon garden. I hoped time had healed our little spat.

"Well, how's your reporting job going?" Ashoh asked thoughtfully.

"It's going well. I don't love the job as much as I thought I would, though."

"I'm sorry to hear that, honey. I thought you always wanted to be a reporter?"

"I did. Anyway, how are you, Ashoh?" I said, trying to change the subject.

"Well. I'm not great now that the Obamas are actually *in* the White House."

Oh fuck. Here we go.

"What did he do to you now?" I asked, rolling my eyes. She was eating saltines, I could hear the crunches.

"Well, ever since he became president, when I go to the grocery store, the black people who bag my groceries just think they are better than me."

I almost drove my Honda CR-V off into a ravine.

"Ashoh, why would you think that people who are bagging your groceries feel that they are better than you? They are *equal* to you," I said, trying to bring a sense of logic to the conversation.

"I don't know, Garon! Ask them. I can just tell by the way they look at me."

"And how do they look at you?" I asked, now fully regretting that I had called.

"They look at me like they are better than me because Obama is now president," Ashoh repeated slowly.

I inhaled and held it in for three seconds, then released slowly.

"Ashoh. You're telling me that hardworking black men and women who are bagging your groceries feel they are better than you because Obama is now the president?"

"Yes."

"I think you're making it all up in your head. I think you're upset because a black man is finally the president of the United States," I said to her directly.

"I don't have any problem with the blacks! Your grandpa is the one who doesn't like them. It's *the Mexicans* I don't care for!"

Oh. My. God.

"You know what, Garon? I think we had better talk another time," Ashoh said. She hung up the phone.

I was wrong. Time had not healed anything.

41

THE CRASH OF CONTINENTAL 3407

O N FEBRUARY 12, 2009, CONTINENTAL 3407 was making its approach into Buffalo, New York, when the turboprop stalled and crashed into a home, killing all forty-nine passengers onboard. It was a huge national story and I was asked to cover it in the local market. I was sent to a nearby airport to interview a pilot who flew a similar plane, and to get his thoughts on what had occurred. Little did I know that this would be an enormous turning point in my life.

After shooting the interview, I told the pilot how fascinated I had always been with airplanes, as I flew back and forth across the world as a kid. He graciously asked me if I wanted to walk with him into a hangar where a number of private planes were kept and tour the jets. I was elated. He took me inside a Citation and a Falcon. I felt like a kid in a candy store. Something immediately clicked inside for me. As I drove back to the station, I vowed to find my way into the aviation world. But how?

In March I had a weekend off. Jamie was going to be working in Fort Lauderdale and asked me to come meet him. I looked at my work schedule to make sure I hadn't missed anything. Just as I was about to book my tickets, at the bottom of the page I saw it. *On Call: Garon Wade.* It meant that while I had a weekend off, I was expected to stick around in case anything went on that required additional reporters. I looked at pictures of the alluring coastline and the vast maze of magnificent waterways that comprised Fort Lauderdale, then back to the schedule.

Fuck it, I thought. I booked my flight to Fort Lauderdale, called Jamie, and we celebrated.

"You should hang out with my friends for the first day in Lauderdale since I have to work late. Then go with them to the party in Miami on Saturday. I'll meet you in Miami."

MY PLANE TOUCHED DOWN at Fort Lauderdale/Hollywood International Airport on a bright, sunny Florida day. The rush of humidity against my skin felt sublime compared to the frigid air of Harrisonburg. I met Jamie's friends, whom I had met before in DC, and we kicked off a lively weekend in paradise. Lauderdale was sensational and even more captivating than the pictures. Vibrant orange, yellow and pink plants filled neighborhoods beneath towering palm trees. The turquoise water rushed to meet the pristine sand as visitors relaxed on restaurant terraces staring out at the Atlantic. Three-story yachts cruised confidently through the intracoastal waters. And the sun truly never seemed to stop casting its powerful rays upon us. The next day we went to a big party in Miami and later Jamie arrived. We ran into each other's arms and walked up and down the beach, endlessly marveling at the beauty of the waves crashing along the south Florida coast.

That evening, I looked at my phone. A snowstorm had hit DC, and Central Virginia and my flight the next morning had been cancelled. I had a number of missed calls from the TV station. I knew instantly I was in trouble. And there was a text from Dave.

Hey man. There was a crazy snowstorm and you're on call. Ed's been asking people where you are.

Fuck me.

I called the news director and prepared to be berated. He was livid.

"I apologize, Ed. All the flights to Washington are cancelled and I'll make sure that I get on the first one possible. I apologize," I repeated.

It wasn't good. On the return flight I rehearsed four different ways to say sorry. When I landed in DC, I rushed out to my car and drove the two hours into Virginia as fast as one can in a snowstorm to get to your boss who is sitting in his office, irate and waiting for you.

When I arrived in snowy Harrisonburg, I threw my stuff into my apartment and raced over to WHSV. I walked up to Ed's door, took a breath, and prepared to be yelled at.

"Sit down, Garon," Ed said curtly. "You were on call. We had a giant snowstorm. But instead of being here, you were in Miami," he said with restraint. He was fuming, I could tell.

"You're right, Ed. I honestly have no excuse and I'm very sorry," I said deferentially.

"Do you realize that there are colleagues of yours who were enjoying their weekend who I had to then call in because you were in Miami? Dave was one of them."

Shit. I hadn't thought about that. He was smart to drive home the point mentioning Dave. Ed knew how close my cameraman and I had become.

"There are hundreds of young journalists around this country who would die for your job. But I picked you. I chose *you*. If you don't want to take this seriously, I'm sure there are other young journalists who would want your job more than you."

I sat quietly. My eyes dropped down reflectively. It occurred to me that perhaps Ed had said what I needed to acknowledge. I looked back up at him.

"I'm sorry. You're right, Ed, you're right. There are hundreds of people who want this job more than me. I think you should give them that chance," I said.

Ed stared at me, speechless. It wasn't the answer he was expecting.

"No, Garon, I'm not firing you," Ed assured me with a confused look.

"But you're right. I'm not sure I want to do this anymore. I don't think this industry is really for me," I said. "Look, I've been here three months, I've tried it, but it's not working out."

"Wait. Let's back up. I'm upset that you left when you were on call, but I'm not asking you to leave."

"I know, but I think I *need* to leave. Can I have an hour or two to think about this?"

Ed sat back in his chair, seemingly shocked by the turn the conversation had taken.

Sighing, he said, "Okay. Go think it over."

I rushed back to my apartment, sat on my couch, and called one of the other reporters I had quickly grown close to while in Harrisonburg.

"Garon, you have to do what you feel is right. If this isn't for you, it's not for you."

"I really want out," I told him. I knew I had a two-year contract with the ABC affiliate and I had no idea how to get out of that, but one thing was clear since my experience in that hangar of private jets. I wanted to stop being a TV journalist.

I made my way back to WHSV.

"Come in," Ed said, this time more subdued.

"I really appreciate that you took a chance on me, Ed. But you're right. There are people out there who want this job, and I don't even want it. I want to resign," I said.

Ed stared at me in what I can only describe as disbelief. I had a feeling he had never been in a situation where a reporter had quit in front of him. It was true that people would die to have this job. Competition was extremely high and it was a notoriously hard industry to get into.

Ed let out another large sigh. "Are you sure?"

"I'm sure." I had always been able to make extremely big decisions very quickly.

"Okay," Ed said, throwing his hands in the air. "Go call your agent."

Shit. I hadn't even thought about Nancy. She would be so disappointed. Once home, I reluctantly called her, pacing around my kitchen.

"Nancy? Hi. I don't know how to tell you this, but I just quit at WHSV."

There was a short silence on the other end of the phone.

"What? Why? What happened, Garon?" Nancy asked thoughtfully, but I could tell she was completely taken aback.

I explained the situation. She said, "Let me call your news director."

Moments later Nancy called me back. "Okay, well, Ed asked me if you're going through a midlife crisis or something."

"I'm twenty-three. I sure hope not," I said. "Nancy, I am so grateful that you chose to represent me and that you got me this job. But this entire industry isn't for me and I want to leave."

After more conversation, Nancy eventually understood what I needed. "Let me see what I can do in terms of the contract," she said.

The next day, Ed called me into his office. "I've spoken to your agent and the general manager. Will you at least stay two more months until we hire and bring in your replacement? Then we will void the contract."

"I can definitely do that, Ed. Thank you for understanding," I said. And with that I walked out of his office and immediately felt an enormous weight off my shoulders.

Over the next two months, I reported on stories as best as I could. My saving grace was Dave. The hardest part about leaving was knowing that I wouldn't see him anymore. On my last day I finished my final live shot and said goodbye to everyone. I walked to my car and got in. It wouldn't start. I needed to get to DC and on to the airport for a flight in the evening. Jamie and I had agreed to meet in California the next day. Dave came over and gave me a jump. We ended off in the way we had begun, with Dave by my side, always willing to help out with his charming laugh and easy smile. I hugged him goodbye one final time. As I drove out of Harrisonburg, my years of wanting to become a reporter had come to an end almost as quickly as my first news gig had begun. It felt as though I had gone through a marriage that had started with such elation and expectation and very quickly and unexpectedly ended in divorce. But I knew there was something better out there for me; something that was more true to who I was.

Two hours later, I saw the Washington Monument to my left. I knew that whatever lay ahead in my future, it would be here in DC. I parked my car at Washington National Airport (DCA) and boarded my flight to California.

42

THE PACIFIC

JUST AS WE HAD DONE the year before at The Elvetham, I waited for Jamie at his hotel. Only this time, in place of an English manor shrouded in darkness, I sat by a refreshing Marriott pool basking in the southern California sun and overlooking planes as they climbed off the departure end of the airport's runway. San Diego reminded me of Fort Lauderdale minus the humidity.

"Buddy, how you doing?" I heard his voice.

"Jamie!" I got up from the chaise and ran over to him. We stood face to face and hugged for the first time in almost a month. He looked handsome as usual.

Although we'd been able to see each other on weekends while I was in Harrisonburg, it hadn't been enough. I had missed him deeply.

"You ready to go to Laguna?"

That was the plan: to jump in the car and take a ride up the Pacific Coast Highway to one of his favorite places, Laguna Beach, somewhere I'd never been. I grabbed my bag and we left the pool for the parking garage, got into the rental car, and buckled up.

Once we were underway, Jamie asked, "So what are you going to do now?"

"I don't know. I want to do something with airplanes," I said as a United Airlines jet departed just above us.

"That's one of the reasons I love staying at this hotel—you can watch the planes take off and land all day," Jamie said. "Do you want to be a pilot?"

"No, not a pilot. I want a family and I don't want to be gone that much."

"What about an air traffic controller?"

"An air traffic controller? What is that?"

"You know, they work up in the tower at airports and control all the airplanes."

I wondered how I'd flown between Asia, Africa, Europe, and into North America so many times throughout my childhood without ever hearing about this profession. Jamie told me as much as he knew about it.

"Well, if you're interested, when we get back to DC, you should try to go up into Washington Tower," he suggested.

"That's a good idea," I said, grasping his hand and looking out the window.

THE CALIFORNIA COAST is sensational in a way that the east coast is not. The hills and jutting rock formations that form the coastline are breathtaking. I wondered what it would be like to wake up each morning in one of these exquisite homes tucked into the side of a cliff overlooking the Pacific Ocean. The floor-to-ceiling glass residences seemed an impressive feat of architecture and design. The views must have been spectacular. An hour and a half later we arrived at our hotel in Laguna Beach: La Casa del Camino. The multistory beige stucco facade was nicely offset with red terra-cotta tiles. From the spacious wooden rooftop terrace overlooking the sea, I gazed across as far as my eyes could take me. I thought of the seventeen years before, when Mom and Dad had taken us across the world to live in Hawaii, my first time along the Pacific. We were such a young family then in Waikoloa, full of excitement for the future and adventure. I do this thing often: I try to imagine myself at a younger age with the world whispering in my ear what is to come. Of course it's impossible, but it helps me see how we never really know where our paths will take us. I imagined our condo in Waikoloa: Ebony, Yael, and I racing around our living room. How would my life have changed had I known I only had eight more years with Mom? It would have sent me into a spiral, but I also would have appreciated her more. I would have held her hand more often at night, kissed her cheek longer before running off with my friends, and told her I loved her as if it were my last time. This is both the delightful and devastating fact of life: we never truly know what's next.

Laguna Beach had a sleepy surfer vibe to it against the backdrop of wealthy homeowners. The ocean, however, was a spitfire, drumming up some of the most powerful waves I had ever seen anywhere in the world. Jamie and I threw a neon-green frisbee up and down the beach and then allowed ourselves to get pummeled by the colossal waves. The waters off the coast of California were freezing compared to the Atlantic waters off the western coast of Africa. As each wave aggressively tumbled me, I reveled in the rapturous control it took of my body and then fought hard to return to the surface.

Jamie and I spent three days in Laguna, reading each morning over a continental breakfast on the patio of a cozy bakery waiting for the foggy marine layer to lift. We watched attractive surfers ride the waves in the morning, strolled through the restful town's surf shops in the afternoon, and devoured exquisite Italian food in the evening. It was the perfect Reset button.

43
AIR TRAFFIC CONTROLLERS

BACK IN COLUMBIA HEIGHTS and once again nestled comfortably in Ebony's house, I applied for work at a number of restaurants and cafés along 14th Street. I thought I would go back to waiting tables until I could figure out what I might want to pursue within the aviation world. I imagined how it might go at each interview when I would undoubtedly be asked where I had worked before. I would say, "I was a TV reporter for an ABC affiliate, but I didn't like it and quit." Each time I rehearsed it in my mind, I realized that no one would believe me. I was sure they would think I got fired and wonder why.

One afternoon, I revisited the conversation Jamie and I had about air traffic controllers as we were driving by San Diego Airport. I googled what I could and found various numbers for Washington Tower. Over a series of days, I made a number of unsuccessful calls, leaving voice messages, which no one returned. Finally, realizing that it probably wasn't going to happen but willing to give it one last shot, I dialed the remaining number.

To my surprise, a soft voice answered.

"Can you be here at 3 p.m. on Wednesday?" she asked.

"Yes, I can. Thank you so much," I replied.

Just before 3 p.m. that Wednesday, the Metro pulled into the airport. I had flown out of DCA on and off for years. It's the airport closest to DC and immensely busy with a wide range of domestic flights. Always in a rush to get through security and get to my gate, I had never noticed the giant alabaster-colored tower that can be seen right as the Metro pulls into the above-ground station. I wondered how I'd never seen it before. I made my way to the main terminal, courtesy of the moving walkway, to the entrance of Washington Tower, where I checked in with tower security. Five minutes later a woman named Cindy Dymond met me.

"Hi, are you Garon?"

"Yes, great to meet you," I said, shaking her hand.

Cindy was nice without being overly friendly. She explained to me that she was a controller at DCA and had been for much of her career.

"The chief asked that I bring you by his office before you go up," Cindy told me matter-of-factly.

"Sure," I said, not knowing why the chief of Washington Tower would have any interest in talking to me.

Cindy walked me through the entrance of the tower's administrative offices over to a large corner office.

"He's here," she said, poking her head in the doorway.

A tall, exceptionally well-dressed black man in his fifties got up from his desk and walked toward me. His name was Donnie Simons.

"Nice to meet you," I said as we shook hands.

"Have a seat, Mr. Wade." He pointed toward two chairs in front of his desk and we sat down. Cindy stayed in the doorway, leaning against the frame. "What brings you to Washington

Tower?" His soft but confident voice was powerful.

I had not planned for any of this.

"I just recently heard about air traffic controllers and I wanted to see what the inside of a tower looks like," I explained.

"But you're a reporter, correct?"

I was completely caught off guard.

"I *was* a reporter. Yes." How did he know that? Who was this guy?

"Well, we can't have you going upstairs and then reporting on what you see," Donnie said very directly.

"As of right now, I am *not* a reporter. I'm not even employed. I quit my TV job recently because I didn't like it," I said, trying to clarify the situation.

Donnie's eyes searched my face. He was deciding if I was telling the truth.

"Okay," he said, standing up and extending his hand. "Enjoy your tour." His grip was firm and strong.

I thanked him and began to walk out toward Cindy, who looked bored and annoyed that she had been asked to give me a tour. I couldn't blame her. Then I heard Donnie's footsteps behind me.

"Just one more thing, Mr. Wade. Come back to my office when your tour is over. Cindy, bring him back please," he instructed, and Cindy and I both nodded in acknowledgment.

Cindy had me follow her down the well-appointed front offices, leading me to an elevator. When we reached the top, we walked up two more staircases and finally approached the door to the tower cab.

"Please make sure your phone is off," Cindy said.

"Okay," I acknowledged, scrambling for my phone.

As I stepped into the tower cab, it was as if everything

around me became silent and my eyes searched to understand the world I had just entered. The tower, 229 feet in the air, had enormous glass panes allowing for a 360-degree view. A breathtaking view of Washington sat beyond those windows. And in front of me, an assortment of men and women stood with microphones secured along their ear and extending to their lips. Beyond them, on three runways, aircraft from US Airways, Delta, American, and United, looking as small as toy airplanes, landed and departed in a high-speed, perfectly synchronized dance. As one plane lifted off a runway, another, hugging the river below, landed in perfect time. Still another waited on the intersecting runway, ready to roll as soon as the intersection was clear and they were given the instruction. Helicopters whirled around the airplanes, and with calm and confident voices the controllers issued second-to-second instructions, making it all happen.

"American 986, Washington Tower, traffic landing Runway one-five, traffic four-mile final, Runway one-niner, line up and wait, be ready to roll," one controller said. "Delta 65, good afternoon, Washington Tower, favor the east bank of the river, square your last turn to final, traffic holding in position, Runway one-niner, cleared to land," he continued. "United 1660, fly heading 170, contact Potomac Departure, good day."

It was—and to this day still is—*the* sexiest thing I have ever seen. I looked at the faces of these professionals, who, after twenty-three years on this earth, I had never even known existed. These are the pros Jamie was talking about: air traffic controllers. The tower crew was a great combination of ages, races, and gender.

"Want to watch for a couple more minutes?" Cindy asked, then walked over to an area where I assumed she'd been working.

"Yes, please."

DCA sat on the winding Potomac River. The Washington Monument and US Capitol Building, with its eminent political stature, stared at me from across the water. Maryland sat in the distance to the east. To the north, I could clearly see the White House; and to the west, the Pentagon in Virginia. I imagined how many times I had flown in and out of this airport. Sitting in my seat reading a magazine or watching a movie, imagining the pilots somehow had a map to get us from Washington to New Orleans, Boston, or Los Angeles. But no, air traffic controllers moved these airplanes at every moment, even on the ground as they taxied to and from the runway.

"Brickyard 1650, give way to Delta from the right, Runway one-niner, taxi via kilo, november, sierra, hold short of Runway one-five," another controller directed. "Cactus 48, you now have a release time of zero three void at zero five into Atlanta, cross Runway one-five and monitor tower, good day."

I was entranced by what seemed like a foreign language I had never heard of.

"American 460, Washington Ground, turn right on juliet, foxtrot, kilo, hold short of your alley, the Gulfstream is holding for you," instructed another controller.

After each instruction, the planes, as if they were remote-control cars I had played with as a child in South Africa, complied immediately.

I felt that I had entered an alternative world: one of speed, precision, and unfathomable power and responsibility. The multitasking ability of these people was even more mesmerizing than the breathtaking view.

"Ready to go?" Cindy asked. I took one last glance around the tower at what I believed was the most otherworldly thing I'd ever witnessed. Then I turned and followed her down the stairs, into the elevator, and back to Donnie Simon's office.

"So, what did you think?" Donnie asked, inviting me to sit down again.

"I . . . that . . . that was surreal," I stammered, still processing what I'd just seen. Donnie chuckled.

"So, you're not employed, right? Do you think you'd like to be a controller?"

What was this guy talking about?

"I . . . I mean, I think it's amazing. But I don't have any training or knowledge of aviation or any background to do something as incredible as that," I said, falling all over my words.

"But you were a reporter, so you're used to having an earpiece in your ear and listening to multiple things at once. Would you be interested in trying?" Donnie pressed on.

I couldn't believe this. Was he serious?

"Yes, I would be interested," I said, trying to conceal how daunted I was by his offer.

"Garon, tell me a bit about yourself," Donnie said.

I told him my life story. Adopted. All the countries. Political science at UT Austin and how I had become a reporter and then quit.

"Okay. Let's do this," Donnie said. "I'm going to set up a time for you to go to Departure Control next week and sit with controllers there. Sit with them, watch it closely, and then call me and tell me how you feel. If you like it, there's a test you can apply to take that will assess your aptitude to be a controller. Sound good?"

I was still confused by the entire interaction. "Yes," I said, feigning confidence. "Thank you so much, I appreciate you taking the time to talk to me." Donnie gave me his card, and I

YOU'LL ALWAYS BE WHITE TO ME

left. I cleared the tower security once more and walked toward the Metro entrance, wondering what the hell had just happened. As I boarded the Metro, I looked up at the giant tower above the terminal. I watched as passengers hustled by on the platform, paying it no attention as I had done so many times. If they only knew the world that existed in that tower high above them in the sky.

That evening Jamie came over to Ebony's house, eager to hear all about it.

"Jamie. That was the most unbelievable thing I have ever seen," I told him, shaking my head.

"I've always wanted to go into a tower. What does it look like up there?"

"The planes all look like toys and are moving so fast. The air traffic controllers are telling every single airplane what to do. I had no idea it worked this way. And the view! Oh my god, Jamie, you wouldn't believe the view of Washington from up there."

"That sounds amazing. You look so happy."

I put my hand on his knee. "I just can't believe I've never known about this world. Thanks so much for telling me about it in California."

THE FOLLOWING WEEK I did my normal run through the city, which took me down to Logan Circle. As I was jogging on P Street between 14th and 15th, I spotted a man who looked familiar to me sitting quietly by himself outside a Starbucks. I couldn't quite place him. As I got closer, I realized it was CNN's Don Lemon. Out of breath, I stopped by his table.

"Hi, you're Don, right?" I asked.

He put down the paper he was reading. "Hi. Yea, I am." His

eyes searched my face, trying to remember if he knew me from somewhere.

"We've never met. I'm Garon. I used to be a reporter and watched your stories in our newsroom. You've done a lot of great work."

"Thanks so much," he said kindly.

"Okay, I gotta go. Great to meet you," I said, taking off.

"Nice to meet you too," he said, waving as I left.

I was happy to have met him. Later that afternoon at Ebony's house, I pulled Don Lemon up on Facebook and decided to write him. I told him that I'd enjoyed meeting him and was sorry to take off as soon as I said hi but I was trying to finish up my run. He wrote me back later that night, asking if I wanted to join him for breakfast the following morning before he left town. It was a compelling offer, as I would have liked to sit and talk with him. I knew that he had grown up in Louisiana and I would have liked to hear stories of his childhood in the state I so loved. Unfortunately, though, the next morning was the day Donnie Simons had arranged for me to go watch controllers work at Departure Control. I wrote Don and explained as much. I also wondered how I'd never met a Don before and suddenly had met two Dons in one week: both tall, powerful black men.

THE NEXT MORNING, Jamie and I drove out to Departure Control, officially known as Terminal Radar Approach Control, or TRACON. It's a slight misnomer, as TRACON deals with both approach *and* departure control. From the passenger perspective, once the plane is rolling down the runway, becomes airborne, and starts climbing out, the tower transfers control of the aircraft to TRACON, who climbs your flight through all the other traffic in the sky until your plane nears cruising altitude. Conversely, once your plane leaves cruising altitude and begins its descent for arrival, TRACON controls your flight as it descends through all the other traffic in the sky until they transfer control over to airport towers like Washington Tower. I learned all this while sitting there mesmerized in the enormous dark building where, unlike the tower, controllers sat with their face inches away from radar screens issuing instruction after instruction to all the pilots in the sky. "American 56, turn left heading 16c." "Climb." "Descend" "Increase speed." "Reduce speed." I held my headset close to my ear, watching as the pilots of every major carrier listened to the controller's instruction, read it back to the controller to ensure correct communication, and complied, changing the climb, descent, speed, or direction of the aircraft immediately. It was mesmerizing. How many people had known this world existed?

Just as Donnie had requested, I called him later that day.

"This is Donnie speaking."

"Hi, Mr. Simons. This is Garon Wade. I was in your office last week and—"

"Garon! Yes. What did you think?"

"I thought it was spectacular. Really fascinating. Thank you for arranging it."

"So, do you think you'd like to take the air traffic control test?"

I stared at the phone. *What am I doing? And why is this guy so sure I could be an air traffic controller?*

"Yes," I said, and then stared at myself in disbelief in the mirror across from me.

"Wonderful. The next ATSAT, the Air Traffic Selection and Training Test, is much later in the year. I'm going to find out more information and be in touch. In the meantime, there are books you can buy to study for it."

I thanked Donnie, ended the call, and fell back on Ebony's bed.

I also got a call that week from one of the cafés along 14th Street for a waitering job. I went to the café the next day for my interview.

"So, Garon, tell me a bit about your work experience," the manager asked.

"Since January I've been working as a TV reporter, but didn't like it, so I quit. I moved back to DC and came in here the other day. I think it's a cool place, and I think I'd like working here," I said confidently.

And there it was. The blank stare that one could only understand to be: *You were a TV reporter and you quit to become a waiter at a café? Surely you got fired.* I left the café convinced that there was no chance of landing the gig.

That evening, however, the manager called to offer me the job. I knew I would need to move out, again, of Ebony's house and find my own place. Jamie was still tied up in the real estate he and his ex had bought and neither had moved out yet. Jamie had been traveling sometimes for weeks on end and had barely been home to deal with the property fallout. I thought about what would make me happy. I looked out the window at a city I loved, but I also knew that it would be hard to live here on $12/hour. Suddenly, I had an idea. I picked up my phone and dialed Jamie.

"Hey, what's up?" he said.

"I'm good. Question."

Whenever I said *Question,* Jamie knew I had some crazy idea that would probably end up happening, just as I had suggested our time in London together. It made him both slightly nervous and intrigued, as he loved the impulsiveness of it. It was something, he would tell you himself, that he's not as inclined to be, but he appreciated how much I was.

"If I moved to Fort Lauderdale, since you're traveling every week anyway, would you still date me?" I asked boldly.

"Yes, definitely," he said.

"So, instead of coming back to DC most weekends, could you fly to Lauderdale and we could hang out by the beach?"

"Are you kidding? I would love that!"

I was thrilled that he was onboard with the idea. I loved Washington, but money didn't go far here, and I knew whatever job I could get at a surf shop or restaurant in Lauderdale, I could live on down there and—the best part—be by the ocean.

"I'm going to do it, Jamie. As long as we can be together, I'll do it. And I'm going to study for this air traffic control test and take it later this year."

"I think that's so cool," he said. "You should call up my best friend, Richie, and see if you can stay with him until you get a place," Jamie suggested.

"I just got back to DC and now I'm leaving again," I said with a sigh.

"Garon, if I could go live at the beach, I would. Go do it now while you have the time, study hard, and have fun. I'll fly there as often as I can."

44

LAS OLAS

ON A HOT JUNE AFTERNOON, I watched as we descended out of the clouds and flew parallel to the breathtaking shoreline of south Florida. White boats sped along the brilliant turquoise water below and the yellow sand seemed to effortlessly melt into the Atlantic Ocean. We flew west out over the swampy Everglades, which instantly reminded me of Louisiana, swung around, and landed in Fort Lauderdale.

Richie, just a bit taller than me, with curly brown hair and an exceedingly friendly demeanor, met me with a big embrace. He had been raised in a small town in southern Virginia and carried that southern hospitality into Lauderdale. Twenty minutes later we were at his condo, Pine Crest Village, in Victoria Park. Pine Crest could not have been more beachy if it tried. The yellow four-story Key West–style condo sat surrounded by swaying palm trees and opened into a charming courtyard. From Richie's balcony, I sat high above the courtyard that housed a soothing aqua-blue pool and a well-used gym. Tanned neighbors lay out basking in the warm sun. I thought back to the first time Jamie had told me about staying with Richie in Lauderdale, when we'd sat together at The Diner in DC. I now understood completely why he had succumbed to its undeniable allure.

It took me five minutes to drive from the condo to the beach. Once there, I dropped my towel on the sand, ripped off my shirt, and threw myself headfirst into the enticing warm ocean. I held myself underwater as long as I could. When I came up for air, I knew that yet another chapter of my life had begun. It was the middle of the week and the beach was quiet and peaceful. The fluffy light-colored sand lay in sharp contrast to the busy road just beyond it, where cars cruised by slowly—the drivers no doubt checking out the spectacular view of the ocean, or maybe the attractive women and men jogging by, or both. Along the sidewalk, people sat casually on the restaurant patios of The Ritz and The Hilton, watching as the calm waves lapped at the shore. I spun around in the aquamarine water, my feet sinking into the sand below. Just three months before, I had been stuck in shitty Harrisonburg at a job I didn't love and had flown down here on a whim. Now I was living here. It's always surprising where life can take you.

Lauderdale was not hard to fall in love with and I did so very quickly. Richie had agreed to not only let me stay with him but to become his roommate, as he was traveling constantly and could use the extra cash. The casual pace of life, tropical drinks, and opulent yachts cruising through the intracoastal waterway was a strange mix with the crashing housing market that seemed to overtake the city. On a drive around Victoria Park or any of the other neighborhoods up or down the beach, foreclosure signs were everywhere. I found work at a small clothing store along Las Olas, a bustling street of restaurants, bars, and stores that stretched from downtown to the coastline.

One afternoon at the beach, I met a guy also in his twenties who was interning in the hotel business for the summer. Alejandro was from Spain, and when I referenced him to other people, I affectionally called him Spanish Alex. We became fast friends. While he had been living in Spain, he was originally from the Canary Islands. Alex was staying in a multimillion-dollar three-story home three blocks from Richie's condo. He was friends with a property manager who was looking after a wealthy client's home for the summer and had offered Alex the place all to himself. And this is where one of the most fun summers of my life began. Alex and I were in very different situations. He was single and an excellent cook, whereas I was in a relationship with Jamie and couldn't cook to save my life. He was extremely shy and didn't approach guys on the beach easily, while I had no problem talking to strangers. We made a deal: I would strike up conversations with guys at the beach and hook him up, and he would cook amazing dinners for me at his palatial home. It was a sound arrangement.

Most days, I would work at the clothing store until three, then Alex would pick me up on his yellow Vespa and we would ride down to the ocean. The two of us would stay at the beach, playing frisbee, talking to strangers, and floating in the waves until the fiery sun started to fade over Lauderdale. On the weekends, Jamie would fly in and Alex would throw big pool parties at the house. Richie, Jamie, Alex, and I made many new friends from around Lauderdale and had an unforgettable time.

Oftentimes we found ourselves at the home of Bill Yule and Barry Ball. Bill and Barry were much older than all of us, in their seventies and eighties. They had led remarkable lives as singers working on cruise ships traveling around the world. They had started in the late 1960s, performing together as The Gentry Brothers for the next thirty years. Bill and Barry had to pretend to be brothers because the world would not accept them as a couple. They had been together for almost fifty years and were an inspiration to all of us.

Barry ran one of the most successful agencies for cruise ship talent: Barry Ball Artists. As a result, their home was always filled with wonderful singers, acrobats, and dancers. Jamie and I, less inclined to theatrical performance, would stand in the back of their living room with drinks in hand and take it all in. Being in their home transported me to a world that morphed into an artistic hybrid of *The Bird Cage* and *Moulin Rouge*.

And when we weren't running around Lauderdale, I would sit by the pool and study air traffic control for hours. I convinced myself that I could learn anything and did simulation after simulation on my laptop dispersed between speed/time/distance equations. My favorite were fractions that moved across the screen at rapid speed. There would be a category to hit: say, even numbers between 16 and 360. As fractions of all kinds moved across the screen, if the numerator fell into that category, you would need to enter them as quickly as possible. The computer tested how many you could identify in an allotted amount of time. Word came that the next available ATSAT would be in October in Baltimore, and I waited to hear if I would be granted a seat in the exam room.

One afternoon I was driving along Sunrise Boulevard in Richie's car (which he'd been kind enough to let me borrow for the summer while he was mostly away) when I realized I needed gas. I pulled into a Shell station, filled up, then took off. Moments later my phone rang. I didn't recognize the number.

"Hello, this is Garon," I said, wondering who it might be.

"Hey, Garon. This is Donnie Simons from DCA. Are you driving along Sunrise Boulevard in Fort Lauderdale, Florida?"

What the hell? This man, who had known I was a reporter before I ever told him, now knew that I was driving along Sunrise Boulevard in Lauderdale? I knew he was powerful, but not this powerful.

"Donnie, yes. Yes, I am," I stuttered, completely bewildered and looking around me to see if somehow he was in a car beside me.

"Okay, well, a woman just called me and said you just left the Shell station near 15th. You left your wallet on the top of the car and it flew away as you drove off. She picked it up for you and there were two business cards in there. One of them was mine. She called me. Anyway, she has your wallet and wants to return it to you. She'll be waiting for you outside the front entrance of Publix on 15th and Sunrise in a blue SUV. Here's her license plate number."

I was completely speechless. This man, who believed I could be an air traffic controller, had his busy day in Washington interrupted by a woman in Florida who had watched me leave my wallet on the top of my car and drive away. How could I convince him that I could keep track of seven to ten jetliners at the same time, each with 160 humans on board, when apparently I couldn't even keep track of my own fucking wallet?

"Thank you so much, Donnie. I ... I really appreciate you calling me," I said, deeply embarrassed.

"So why are you in Lauderdale?" he asked.

Oh shit, more questions.

"I moved down here to study for the test by the beach."

By the beach? Who says that to a person who is trying to get you into one of the most competitive and stressful jobs in the world? One affliction I have always had is that I tell the truth, even if it sounds ridiculous or conversationally inappropriate.

"Lauderdale sounds nice. Have you heard about the test?" Donnie asked. "They've scheduled it for October in Baltimore. I'll do my best to see if I can get you in there."

I thanked him profusely, hung up the phone, tried to understand the serendipity of what had just happened, and drove to Publix to retrieve my wallet. When I got my wallet back, I opened it up. There were only two business cards in there. One was Jamie's. The other was Donnie Simon's. I'd wished that the Good Samaritan had called Jamie so I didn't seem like such a fucking idiot. But I knew that by calling Donnie, this caring stranger had ironically placed me back in Donnie's mind.

Sure enough, weeks later, I got an email offering me a seat in the air traffic controller exam room.

45

THE EXAM

LIKE ALL GOOD THINGS, MY summer of fun was slowly coming to an end. Spanish Alex had returned to Europe. I thought about him each time I passed the opulent home where we had partied all summer. I had wanted to stay in Lauderdale as long as it took to get the opportunity to take the test. I had played hard and studied harder. I felt as prepared for the ATSAT as I could be. One afternoon in early October, I boarded my flight for Baltimore.

I arrived at the FAA's Air Traffic Selection and Training Test, which would vet potential air traffic controllers for the nation. I wasn't nervous until I arrived, and then of course it all set in. There were far fewer candidates than I had imagined. Only fifteen people sat in the hotel conference room alongside me. I thought of Donnie Simons and how much he believed in me. Years of middle school, high school, and university had taught me how to read textbooks, listen to lectures, think critically, and regurgitate information. This exam was completely different. The ATSAT is an analysis of your multitasking ability. Each of us candidates was positioned in front of our own computers and told that the test would take multiple hours and we would be timed. There were no calculators allowed, which I knew in advance, and we were only given a pencil and multiple sheets of paper.

The test began. I worked through what seemed like endless speed/distance/time equations in my head, occasionally jotting them down on paper and trying to work at a reasonable pace. Then the fractions, just as I had trained for in my simulations. They flew across the screen. On the keypad next to me I entered as many numerators as I could, as fast as I could, knowing I was being timed for speed and accuracy. As time passed, I began to relax a bit more in my chair, realizing that I was actually enjoying the test. I had always hated the rote reading and memorization of textbooks, demonstrating on tests that you'd only memorized the information by recalling the templated answer.

This, though, was dynamic and high speed.

Perhaps my favorite section was the multiple conveyor belts dropping down the letters *A, B, C,* and *D* simultaneously and in different colors. At the bottom of the belts were boxes. I had to group the same colors and in the order of *ABCD* as fast as I could on four different moving conveyor belts. In another section, planes emerged in close quarters to one another and I needed to guide them in all different directions, ensuring they never hit. It was the first test I've taken in my entire life where I felt invigorated and excited. After many hours, the FAA exam came to completion. I went back up to my hotel room, packed my things, and flew back to Lauderdale. As we soared down the east coast of the United States, I stared out the window and wondered who was controlling our Airbus and if I would ever become an air traffic controller. My performance on the test was either going to open a door into this highly competitive profession or keep it firmly shut. And if I did *not* exhibit the aptitude to be an air traffic controller, what was I going to do instead?

I KNEW THAT winter would soon be arriving in Washington. Though I had fallen in love with the easygoing beach culture in Lauderdale, there was a frenetic energy in DC that occasionally I missed. And I longed to be in the same city as Jamie. After all, this was only supposed to be a temporary stop. Still, I told myself I wouldn't return to DC until a job offer came through. I had been applying over the past months to various aviation-related positions, where I could work around airplanes while I waited for my test results. If I did well on the exam, a seat at the US Aeronautical Academy would be available to me.

Right after Thanksgiving, Frontier Airlines offered me a job as a ramp agent, loading baggage onto jets at DCA. I took it. As I flew away from sunny Lauderdale, I looked down below at the dazzling coastline. I was proud that I had taken the opportunity to live the Florida beach life for five months, and I was sure that Lauderdale would be a place in the world I would return to in my years ahead.

46

WINTER IN WASHINGTON

L OADING CANINES AND EXTRAORDINARILY HEAVY packages of oysters was the most surprising part of the ramp agent job at DCA. The daily oyster pallets made me markedly stronger. I had never before considered food being flown from state to state on commercial aircraft. As for the canines, as each pet crate was carried out to the loading belt, I would go over and talk calmly to the dog, who was either sedated or panting, heavily traumatized by the experience. Then I would carefully position the crate in the cargo hold and wish the dog well. I remembered as kids how concerned Ebony, Yael, and I were as Jazzbee sat below us in the cargo hold the year we left Louisiana for our new life in the Middle East.

I would look out from the cargo door of the Frontier Airbuses and survey Washington Tower. Prior to taking the ATSAT, Donnie had advised me that there were two successful categories: *Qualified* and *Well-Qualified*. Anything below that would not lend itself to becoming an air traffic controller. Even then, he added, the FAA was basically only taking candidates who scored in the *Well-Qualified* category.

The winter air mixing with the smell of jet fuel was addictive. I thoroughly enjoyed being up close and personal with these enormous flying giants. I had come back to Washington so many times, each return feeling like a homecoming. This time, however, Dad and Yael were no longer around. Dad had taken an assignment in Lahore, Pakistan. Yael had graduated and was attending UT Austin. I missed them both but was happy that Ebony had continued to make Washington her home, studying at American University's law school.

One afternoon I received an email from the FAA. I did a double take upon receiving it. I had scored *Well-Qualified.* I reflected on all the hours of studying I had logged, in between riding waves, in Lauderdale. Jamie and I celebrated at home with a bottle of Sangiovese. But most of all, I was happy that Donnie Simons had taken a chance on me and that I had lived up to his expectations.

AFTER CHASING EACH OTHER from Washington to London, Virginia, Florida, and back to Washington, Jamie and I finally moved in together in Colombia Heights, where it all started right on 11th Street. I couldn't believe that after all the travel I had managed to find my way back to the street I loved, just four blocks up from where I had first lived with Ebony.

We lived on the corner of 11th and Park, in a tall, tan three-story row house. Our front balcony faced a lively dog park, and six steps separated us from the busy foot traffic of the sidewalk. Each evening as the sun set over the District, I parked myself on our front steps and watched the city wind down. It was especially gratifying to finally have a place to call ours. We didn't have much furniture: just a kitchen table and chairs on the first floor, a king-sized bed upstairs, and one big sofa downstairs in the finished basement. The three bedrooms upstairs were cozy and close. Sometimes Jamie and I would just sit together quietly and remark on this winding journey we had taken to finally be able to live together.

With *Well-Qualified* in my pocket, I eagerly awaited the Aeronautical Academy's invitation to have a seat in their highly competitive three-month intensive training. If step one was achieving *Well-Qualified* on the ATSAT, step two was proving yourself at the academy. Not all who attended made it. The big question was, When might I go? And from everything I read, it sometimes took a year or longer to get a seat.

I enjoyed loading luggage, dogs, oysters, and even the occasional coffin on planes, but as time went on and still no academy date, my muscles had become strong yet my wallet was weak. I went searching for more money. I left Frontier Airlines and took a job as the assistant manager of Bike and Roll, a bike tourism company that rented bikes for the many visitors who piled into Washington wanting to explore the National Mall. They had multiple locations and I ran the operation in a cool-looking building: a green glass helmet-shaped building that sits in front of Union Station. There, I learned basic sign language to accommodate the students of nearby Gallaudet University.

In the summer, Jamie asked me if I wanted to go home with him to Rotterdam to finally meet his family.

"Of course I do," I said.

Jamie had told his mom, Denice, about me in the weeks before, prepping her for my arrival. I was the first non-white boy he'd ever brought home and to some degree that concerned me.

"Where's he from?" Denice had asked Jamie, surely expecting an American city.

"Well, it's complicated. He was adopted from Sri Lanka."

"Sri Lanka? Where's that?"

Jamie had showed her where Sri Lanka was on the map. It was the first time she'd heard of the island in the Indian Ocean. A week later his phone rang.

"Hi, bud. I just wanted to say that I was drinking my tea this morning, looked at my tea bag, and realized the tea is from Sri Lanka!" Denice exclaimed.

Jamie shook his head. He later relayed the story to me, smiling. I thought it was endearing. It reminded me a lot of those months in Luling when Ms. Pepper or Ms. Eileen had stood in Ashoh's kitchen waiting to hear tales of the lives we were living in the far corners of the world. My summers, combined with the one year we lived in Luling, had unknowingly prepped me for my first trip to Jamie's hometown.

47

DENICE

ON A STICKY SUMMER AFTERNOON, Jamie and I landed in Albany, New York, the closest big city to his family's small town of Rotterdam.

"Are you ready?" he asked.

"I'm ready. I'm excited."

We walked out of the concourse and then toward the exit. For those who haven't been, the arrivals area where one might meet a loved one at the Albany airport is shockingly busy. People hung from the stairs with *Welcome Home* signs and others huddled together for their first glimpse of a family member.

"Wow, this is like Heathrow," I jokingly told Jamie as we approached the arrivals area.

"It's because nothing happens here, Garon, and everyone's excited when someone comes home," he said. Jamie wasn't fond of Rotterdam. I, on the other hand, felt a great sense of adventure, knowing I was going to spend the weekend in a small American town in the northeast.

"There she is," Jamie said, waving to her. I hung back so he could walk toward her first. She gave him a giant hug, then turned to me.

"Hi, Garon!" she said warmly and hugged me.

I hugged her right back. "Hi, Denice! So nice to finally meet you."

Jamie and I had talked about this on the flight before.

"Hug or handshake?" I had asked him.

"You can do whatever you want, but I think she'll probably shake your hand the first time," he had said. I was happy she'd gone for the hug.

Denice was a gorgeous strawberry-blonde with thick shoulder-length hair, brilliant blue eyes, and smooth, lustrous skin. Jamie had surely gotten this from her. Everywhere we went, people always looked at Jamie's face and asked, "How is your skin so smooth?"

That evening, we sat around Denice's kitchen table in her three-bedroom home where she lived alone. She had prepared a decadent Italian meal. I looked around the modest house and realized how differently Jamie and I had grown up. Jamie had lived in this house since he was twelve years old. He'd told me how they always had enough but never anything extra.

"When Mom got done with the bills every month, she had five dollars left over for herself," Jamie had said.

To me, it seemed like their home was filled with a lot of love, and I imagined Jamie moving around the house as a teenager. Denice had so many questions for me. She seemed fascinated with my life spent living around the world.

"Have you ever been back to Sri Lanka? What was it like in the Middle East and throughout Africa?" she asked. "When you were in Egypt, did you see the pyramids?"

I told Denice of my years running the 400m in Cairo near the banks of the Nile River, and I explained how much my years living in Amman had molded me into the person I was. I had just as many questions, or more, about her life here in Rotterdam. In that way, we seemed quite similar.

"What does it feel like to live in the same town for both your childhood and as an adult?" I asked.

"Well, this is all I've really ever known. I was born here, grew up here, and raised Jamie and his sister here in Rotterdam," she said in her soft, sweet voice.

"I think there's something really cool about that. You have such continuity of friendships and relationships in one place. I've always wondered what that would have been like."

"I think how you grew up sounds much more interesting," Denice said with a laugh. She was adorable.

"Jamie says you work nearby?" I asked.

"Yes. I work a quarter of a mile away. I could walk if I wanted to. I even come back to the house for lunch most days."

"How long have you worked there for?"

"I started there as a secretary in 1984 and worked my way up to be a risk manager."

I did the math. Denice had been working at her same job five minutes away since before I was born in Sri Lanka. I thought of all the years growing up, circling the globe. She had gone back and forth each day between her home and that same office in this small town. It reminded me of Ashoh and Grandpa's life in Luling; no matter how far across the world I traveled, Luling always seemed to be frozen in time once I returned.

THE NEXT MORNING, Denice's boyfriend, Sherman, arrived. Sherman was a Jewish guy who had been raised in New York City and later worked there as a burn surgeon. He had an earring in one ear, lived across the border on a lake in

Massachusetts, and was extremely progressive. I instantly felt comfortable with him.

"We're going to my grandma's house after breakfast," Jamie said. Once we had all finished eating together and learned more about one another, Sherman kissed Denice, said goodbye, and headed home.

Two hours later, I sat inside Jamie's grandma's house, beside her on her sofa. The only thing I had been told about Barbara was that she'd just returned from a stint in the hospital but was doing much better. Jamie and Denice were now in deep conversation across the living room with one of his three aunts who had stopped by. It was awkwardly quiet on the sofa between me and his grandma, so I decided to break the ice.

"So, Barbara. I heard you just got out of the hospital. How are you doing?" I said, smiling.

Barbara, a tiny woman with cropped white hair, turned to me. "We don't talk about that kind of thing in this house," she said and then promptly turned away.

Fuck.

We sat in silence again. I tried to think of something else to say, but I was so taken aback by her reaction that after enough time had passed, and it was clear there was no recovery, I just continued sitting there motionless in painful silence.

Moments later, perhaps feeling the same awkwardness as I did, Barbara offered me a drink.

"There's some wine in the kitchen," she said directly.

Maybe she's forgiven me, I thought. I actually kind of liked her confidence, but I was decidedly intimidated by her. I went to the kitchen and looked around for bottles of red or white wine. There were none in sight.

Jamie walked in. "How's it going?"

I quietly told Jamie what had happened. He laughed.

"You're not allowed to talk about anything serious, nothing medical, nothing about sex, and definitely not about anyone in the family who has died," he said.

"Well, that sure would have been nice to know ahead of time," I said, still glancing around for the hidden wine.

"Listen, when my grandfather died, the family had a lunch at the house in honor of his life. I couldn't go because of work. My cousin Theresa said it was the strangest thing because not once did anyone mention him. You're just not supposed to talk about it," Jamie said, finding the whole thing humorous.

This stood in sharp contrast to my family, where we talked about everything.

"Okay, well, good to know," I said. "By the way, your grandma said there's wine here, but I couldn't find any."

Jamie smiled knowingly. "You're standing right next to it."

I spun around and there behind me was a large box of Franzia wine on the counter.

"It's Franzia, Garon. You're not in the city anymore. This is what people think is good wine here," Jamie said with a smirk.

"I'll drink anything now that your grandma just chastised me," I said.

The following day we drove over to Jamie's sister's home. Melissa was hosting a lunch for everyone, and their father, Jamie Sr., would be there. Jamie had told me that both Melissa and his father were fundamentalist Christians and ardently disagreed with homosexuality. While I knew that many people of his father's generation held these antiquated views, I had a harder time understanding his sister's opposition. It was especially ironic given that Melissa had spent much of her youth lusting after Ricky Martin, with posters of him splashed across her bedroom walls. Jamie's father had made it clear to him from an early age that gay people were not to be respected.

"When I was ten, I was riding with my dad in his truck. We pulled up to a toll booth and in the car next to us were a gay couple holding hands. My dad had this crazy reaction. He started laughing and pointing at them and saying to me, 'Look at them! Can you believe that? Can you believe that!' It was as if a giraffe had walked across the highway in Upstate New York," Jamie once told me. "He also used to drive me in the back of his cop car into Schenectady to Jay Street, where the gay bars were. As we'd pass by, he'd say in a disgusted tone, 'Jamie, this is where all the gay people are.'"

This is going to make the Barbara debacle seem like a walk in the park, I thought.

Melissa's home was busy and full of relatives. I was very quickly introduced to Jamie's father. While Jamie is six-foot-five, his father, whose parents immigrated to the United States from Italy, is about my height, five-foot-seven, and in the summer is quite tanned.

"So nice to meet you," I said, shaking his hand.

"Nice to meet you too," his father said.

Alongside being a fundamentalist Christian, a former cop, and telling Jamie as a young child that people from India were dirty, black people were bad, and gay people were to be mocked, the only other thing I knew about his father was that each year his church took a mission trip to build homes in various countries. According to Jamie, in previous years his father had been to China and Honduras. It seemed a reasonable thing to ask him about and truly, I was interested in his international experience.

"Jamie tells me that each year your church goes on a mission trip. I'm curious, how do you decide which country has the most need in any given year? Is there a list of countries and specific needs that you can meet?

"Oh, it's not hard. We just pray about it and we go wherever the Lord sends us," he said, very matter-of-factly.

I paused, trying to make sure my face didn't move or register as anything other than interested. Stupidly, I wasn't prepared for such a religious response. *Of course that's his answer. He. Is. A. Fundamentalist. Christian.* I should have just ended it there, but regretfully I continued.

"Right. But, like, when it comes down to booking the tickets, how do you decide one destination over another?"

"The Lord tells us where to go," he told me again.

I had nothing. We stood together in silence.

I thought it ironic that this man, who had such a strong dislike for so many minority groups here in America, traveled each year to assist people in other countries.

Jamie once told me, "I can remember being twelve years old. There was an area called Hamilton Hill that was really impoverished. He would drive me and Melissa through that neighborhood in the back of his car, pointing out all the black families. 'Look at how filthy they are,' he would say to me. Another time, I was in his truck driving through an area closer to our house. He saw a black teenager walking through the neighborhood in the afternoon. We followed that little boy. 'They don't belong in this neighborhood,' my father had said. Imagine, Garon. Two of us in a big truck with a gun rack across the back, driving right behind that little boy who was doing nothing but walking home by himself from school. Imagine how scared he must have been."

I remembered Mom's words again, that day in Jordan when

the German girl on our bus told me I looked like I was burnt in an oven: *Garon, my worry is that this racism is going to follow you your entire life. There may come a time when you're older, if you fall in love and marry someone of a different race, that even their parents may have a problem with you.* I knew Jamie's father wasn't happy that he had brought a boy home, and I'm sure it was even worse that the boy was brown.

Melissa came barging into the living room to announce, "Dinner's ready!" I was thankful for the interruption. We were all seated at a large dining table. There was a long prayer. *That,* I expected. Then, just as I had filled my plate and was about to eat, I heard Jamie's father's voice from down the table.

"So, Garon. Jamie tells us you used to be a reporter?"

"Yes. I used to be. Not anymore, though."

"Who did you work for?" his father asked. The entire table leaned forward and looked in my direction.

"I worked for an ABC affiliate."

The table was silent.

"He worked for the enemy!" his father said, erupting in laughter. The rest of the table laughed in agreement.

I tried my best to fake a laugh and then focused in on my mashed potatoes. Jamie looked at me apologetically. Was it too late to mention that I had interned at Fox before that?

The next morning, I woke up beside Jamie at Denice's home, in his tiny bedroom that he had grown up in. Denice had a wonderful assortment of fresh fruit and waffles waiting for us at the table. I had often wondered what it would have been like to be able to go back to a home you had grown up in. I imagined there would be memories at every corner. Denice had gotten up early to put together this breakfast, so thrilled that Jamie was back in Rotterdam. Her thoughtfulness and love for her son reminded me of Mom. Had she lived, I know she, too, would have been so happy to have Jamie and I wake up and stumble out to breakfast together. I remembered that day shortly before her death, when she and I had spent the day in Sweifieh before driving to our house on the hilltop.

You know, honey, when Ms. Connie and I were in college, on the weekends we would often go hang out at the gay bars. We went there because all the most handsome men hung out there. And they were the most fun, she had told me.

I realized now that back in Jordan, Mom had known me better than I knew myself. She wanted her oldest son to tell her he was gay, and I wish I had known then and could have. She died knowing who her son was but without him being able to tell her that. It is one of the things I regret most. But in her loving and gentle way, she was telling me it was okay.

I sat down at the kitchen table next to Jamie's mom. "Denice, how old was Jamie when you knew he was gay?"

"Oh, I always knew," she said, pouring me coffee. "Probably going back to the time he was five. He was different than all the other boys up here and he was far smarter than them too. He didn't want to do the things they did, he wanted to play with his sister's toys. I kept trying to give him more boy toys, but he didn't want them. It was just something I sensed."

"And how did you feel when he came out to you?"

Denice and Jamie looked at each other. "I don't really think he did, I just always knew," she said.

"Yea. I had a boyfriend, Dean, and he and I were always together, and I think one day you asked if Dean was gay. I said yes. Then you asked if I was gay, and I said yes," Jamie said, looking at his mom.

"And then?" I prodded.

"And then nothing," Jamie said. "I don't think we really talked about it," he said and then began laughing, knowing what I was thinking. I shook my head. Denice smiled warmly as he laughed. It seemed that there were a lot of things people just didn't talk about in this family.

I looked past Denice's shoulder out the kitchen window at her sizable backyard.

"Garon, we used to have an above-ground pool out there and Jamie would spend all summer swimming with Melissa and their beagle, King. I loved watching them splash around and have a great time. All I really ever wanted was to have kids," Denice told me.

"You knew that as a little girl?" I asked.

"Yes, I couldn't wait to be a mom and I had Melissa when I was nineteen and Jamie when I was twenty-two."

I wondered quietly if Jamie had told his mom that he, too, now wanted to have kids. Given their family policy of not talking about significant things, I guessed he probably had not.

I liked how well the two of them got along. They shared the very admirable quality of wanting to take care of those closest to them and they were both extremely hard workers. I could see him in her, and her in him.

On Sunday afternoon Denice drove us to the airport. It was time to head back to Washington. I liked her a lot. It was clear to me that Jamie had been raised by a strong, smart, loving woman.

"Bye, bud," she said, with tears filling her eyes.

"Bye, Mom."

I wished he knew how much I would have given in my life to be able to speak those words again. It had been nine years without her.

48
ASHOH'S SIX WORDS

WHILE I HAD ENJOYED MY ADVENTURE into small-town America, I was grateful coming through the terminal at DCA to be among the diversity of Washington. I thanked Jamie for taking me to meet his family. I marveled at how far he had come from his Rotterdam beginnings.

"I used to sit and think about how I was going to get out of that town, Garon," Jamie said. "I knew my education was the only way out."

His education had taken him first to New York University, then SUNY Albany, and finally Johns Hopkins. I was proud of him.

When we got back to 11th Street, I decided to give Ashoh a call. I also felt it was time for me to finally tell her about Jamie. The phone rang a number of times. I imagined her trying to reach for the remote in the darkness of her room to pause QVC, the home-shopping channel, before answering.

"Hello?" she said.

"Hey, Ashoh, it's me."

"Well, hey there. How are you?"

"I'm great. How are you?"

"I was just getting ready to say my rosary. What are you doing?"

"I just got back from a trip to New York. By the way, Ashoh, I have something to tell you."

"Oh?" I could hear the skepticism in her voice.

"I'm dating someone. I've been dating someone for a while and his name is Jamie."

There was the usual long silence and then a frustrated sigh on the other end of the phone.

"Jamie, huh? Is he at least white?"

I'm not sure why I was stunned, but I was stunned.

"Ashoh, did you just say, 'Is he at least white?'"

"I surely did."

I shook my head.

"I mean, he is white, but that's not why I chose him or why I'm dating him. And it's sort of hurtful to hear you say that because—I'm not white," I said.

"Oh honey, you'll always be white to me."

And there it was. Words that I never expected to hear. Words that Mom would have hated, that went against everything she spent her life working toward. And yet, they were words that, for Ashoh, were meant to convey *I love you and I always will.*

I lay in bed later that night and thought about what sat behind those six words. *You'll. Always. Be. White. To. Me.* She had raised a white daughter who had married a white man, and they had traveled the world, adopting brown babies and living in black countries. All those summers when we had traveled thousands of miles back to Louisiana, Ashoh had waited eagerly by the door for our arrival. When she saw us, her two brown grandchildren and her white grandchild, she hugged us all tight the same way, tears streaming from her face in happiness. And yet, to somehow love us, to feel like we were really hers, for more than twenty years her mind needed to view us as white kids. If we were white, we were hers; and if we were hers, we were lovable.

I've never really been able to get past those words. They cut to the bone, yet they were said with the deepest love. It's the kind of love we expect a grandmother to shine on her grandchildren. I've long wondered why I couldn't have just been brown to her and loved the same. I had loved Ashoh since the first time I could ever remember her, visiting us on Flint Road in South Africa. I had never needed her to be darker like me to love her as much as I did.

PART THREE

49

TIFFANY BLUE

ONE NIGHT WE WERE INVITED out by friends to a big dinner in Logan Circle. The long wooden table and leather chairs at Logan Tavern on P Street were filled with people who had moved to Washington from around the country. Some we knew, some we didn't. Across the table from us sat a handsome Dominican-American guy named Giovanni. Giovanni was a fourth-grade teacher at the Oyster-Adams Bilingual School in the city. He seemed kind, was outgoing, and fun to talk to. Jamie and I were seated next to a couple from North Carolina: Matt and Anne Gialanella. I sat next to Matt, while Jamie sat near Anne. They had gone to Wake Forest University together, and after a brief stint in New York they made the move to Washington for work. The five of us hit it off right away and talked most of the evening together.

"How long have you and Jamie been together?" Matt asked me.

"It's been three years," I told him. "Actually, we're flying to Fort Lauderdale this weekend and I'm proposing to him. He doesn't know."

"Wow!" Matt said, trying to make sure Jamie and Anne didn't hear. "Congratulations!"

I had been planning to propose to Jamie for some time and had secretly been shopping for an engagement ring. Except for two friends who had agreed to house the ring at their condo, I had told no one else that I was going to ask him to marry me, not even Ebony, Yael, Dad, or Denice.

ON THE FLIGHT down the east coast, I stared out the window and thought about our story. It had been three years since Jamie and I had met at the Washington Sports Club in Columbia Heights, and our individual paths had taken us away from each other so many times. Yet we always found our way back to one another. Our relationship wasn't perfect. He thought I was messy to some degree because I often left my jeans on the floor in the corner and after I used our sink he would often complain that there was "so much water everywhere." I didn't like that he was such a taskmaster: it seemed that on days off he had to cross off every single errand on his list before making time for things the two of us wanted to do together. By the time his list got to "us," the day was almost done and it felt like an afterthought. But when problems arose, I felt we both did a wonderful job of communicating.

Jamie and I rarely argued because of something that I dreamt up months after meeting him called "the boyfriend check." Once a month during a happy time—a time when we would be laughing together in bed or having a wonderful conversation over dinner—I would say, "Time for a boyfriend check, Jamie. How are we doing? Is there anything I've been doing that has annoyed you? Or is there anything you want me to change or work on?" Instead of letting frustrations build and waiting until an argument for it to all come to the surface, the boyfriend check allowed us to talk about issues in our relationship when we were in a good place. I had learned the hard way with Chad that keeping everything bottled up and allowing it to erupt during a monumental argument was a poor way to handle a relationship. I wanted to do better with Jamie. He would express any frustrations he had during the boyfriend check, then I would reciprocate. Our conversation was anchored by two open minds, caught up in an enjoyable moment, and talking honestly about how to be better as a couple moving forward. It worked for us. I knew that no matter what challenges we would face down the road, the two of us would have a great shot at tackling them together because of our ability to pre-emptively communicate. And there was one more thing: somewhere deep in my heart I had this resounding feeling that if Mom had not died, and if she had met Jamie, she would have looked at me and said, *Garon, this is the guy for you.* These two things led me to want to ask Jamie to marry me. But how?

With my head against the airplane window, I thought of what I wanted to say to Jamie. I wanted him to know that while we had grown up so differently thousands of miles away from each other, I truly felt like he was made for me. Maybe I would start talking about growing up in Africa and how I never could have imagined the turns my life took that allowed us to meet each other. Each time I rehearsed something, it felt memorized and strange. I decided I would start in Africa and work my way toward our life together in America and speak honestly and truthfully in the moment so it didn't sound contrived.

Jamie had been able to get out of work a day earlier and had flown ahead to hang out with Richie. I had texted him just before my departure, asking if we could walk along the beach at

night after I landed. He had agreed. I thought all the way back
to my senior year in Amman, when I would sit on the roof of
my home on the hillside, overlooking the arid landscape, the
skyline just beyond. How I would turn west toward the United
States and wonder what life had in store for me. A lot had
happened in seven years.

My airplane yet again touched down in Fort Lauderdale,
which now felt like a second home to Washington. Jamie rolled
up in Richie's BMW and I jumped in.

"Welcome back to Lauderdale, buddy," Jamie said. We both
loved it here so much. "How was your flight?"

"I love flying down the east coast at night. The lights are
stunning."

"Are you sure you want to go to the beach? It's almost 10 p.m.
We usually just go in the morning."

My nose started to sweat. "Yea. Let's go the beach. We never
do that at night and I'd really like to."

"Are you sure?"

"Yea, I'm sure," I said as I pulled my backpack closer, which
held the ring.

Parking at the beach, Jamie got out of the driver's seat, and I
quickly opened the backpack, took out the Tiffany Blue box, and
stuffed it in my pocket.

On the beach where Spanish Alex and I had spent our
summer, I looked at the night sky meeting the horizon of the
Atlantic. You almost couldn't tell where one ended and the other
began. Massive cargo ships drifted offshore, their bright lights
piercing the darkness. As we walked, the reflection of the moon
glistened on the ocean and the salty breeze enlivened me. A
brief rain shower had moved up the coastline, leaving the sand
a bit damp. I looked around. There was no one else on Sebastian

Beach, just the way I wanted it.

"Hey, do you want to sit down?" I asked Jamie at one point.

"No, I don't want to get my shorts wet," he said. *Typical,* I thought. I could feel my nervousness building.

Finally, after walking farther, I asked, "Do you want to sit down now?"

"No, I'll stand."

Jesus Christ. Why won't he just sit the fuck down?

Finally, with my nose sweating profusely and unsure of how to get the giant to sit with me, I turned to him. "Jamie, who cares if your shorts get wet, just sit down with me."

"Okay," he said, and we positioned ourselves side by side, staring out at the moonlit water.

"You know, on the flight down here, I was thinking about growing up in The Gambia. Those days walking along the coast collecting driftwood with Mom are some of the best memories of my life. I never knew then where my life might take me."

Jamie leaned into me.

I then began a long, incoherent speech about growing up in Jordan, meeting him in Washington, our time in London, and everything that came after that. I looked over at Jamie, who had a strange look on his face. The only way I can explain it is, he looked concerned. Clearly, this is why people rehearse what they're going to say when they propose instead of just letting it flow in the moment. Realizing that I was rambling and hadn't struck the tone of someone who was proposing, I reached into my pocket, pulled out the box, and handed it to him. He opened it and I could see the answer in his face instantly. His eyes lit up with excitement as he gasped and stared back at me. Oddly, we had talked about having a child together, but we had never really spoken about getting married. I was so caught up in his astonished face that I forgot to continue speaking.

"You have to ask, Garon," he said.

"Oh!" We began laughing. "Will you marry me?" I asked him.

"Yes," he said, giving me a giant hug and kissing me. We sat on the beach, staring out across the Atlantic, and talked about the many things we wanted to do together in our life. I thought back to the day after I had arrived from London and was sitting on the counter in Ebony's kitchen on 11th Street. I remembered how confident I was when I told her, *One day I'm going to marry him and when I do, remind me that I told you this.*

I couldn't wait to tell Ebony and the rest of my family. As we drove back to Richie's condo, I asked, "Did you know that I was proposing to you when I started talking?"

"No, Garon. You were acting so strangely that I thought you were breaking up with me." We laughed all the way into Victoria Park.

50

AMERICA'S HEARTLAND

CLOSE TO TWO YEARS AFTER I had walked away from my job as a TV reporter, the FAA offered me the opportunity to become an air traffic controller by granting me a seat at the Aeronautical Academy. I was overjoyed. It had been a long road and one full of uncertainty. I had trusted my instincts that day in Harrisonburg, covering the crash of Continental 3407, and it had paid off.

In early March, I said goodbye to Washington yet again as I flew to the heartland of the country: Oklahoma. Oklahoma City, a flat Midwestern capital with a sparse skyline, was home to the United States Aeronautical Academy. I had been hired to work at Manassas Tower, an airport about an hour outside of DC, which landed and departed mostly private aircraft. But I would have to take tests and run simulations nonstop at the academy for close to three months before reporting to Manassas Tower the last week of May. That was, *if* I made it.

The very first day, I woke up in my hotel room at the Wyndham Garden Inn at 5:30 a.m., arrived early to campus, and found my class. I looked around the room: there were twenty-one of us, all men, and just three of us were minorities. Two more men walked in and introduced themselves as our instructors. Then a woman walked in with a far more commanding presence. She was tall, moved with confidence, and spoke fast.

"Good morning, and congratulations, you've arrived at the Aeronautical Academy. Out of the thousands of people we tested across the country, the twenty-one of you have been selected by the FAA this round to become air traffic controllers. There's a couple more classes of new recruits down the hallway, but overall, as you can now see, getting selected to hold a seat here is an achievement in itself. I'm going to take a guess here and say that all of you have spent your life being told to sit still, stop moving, and focus." Her eyes searched the room.

I couldn't believe it. Yes, that is exactly what Mom and Dad had been told by my teachers since my first school days in South Africa: *Garon needs to stop moving as much. Garon needs to sit down, sit still. Garon needs to learn to focus more often.*

"If that's true of you, well, bravo, you're in the right place. It's the reason you were selected. You see, we don't want you to sit still, stop moving, and focus. In fact, we need the opposite. We need you to be able to watch seven different situations happening at the exact same time. At the end of your almost three months here, some of you will make it, some of you will not. Welcome to the academy." Then she turned and walked out.

She was a department head and she took my breath away. I was twenty-five. It was the first time in my life anyone had verbalized that they understood the way my brain worked, calling it an asset instead of a fault.

Over the next three months, the twenty-one of us operated as a unit, learning from one another's mistakes and successes and taking countless exams together. We watched video after video of real-life airplane near-misses and crashes and listened to tapes of pilots in distress. We studied how to resolve emergencies, cracked windshields, loss of engines, bird strikes, and wind shear. We were taught what to do during hijackings, terrorist attacks, and how to move the president of the United States. We rehearsed fighter jet maneuvers. And finally, we learned how to issue instructions to pilots fast and effectively, and to identify the performance differences of, say, a Boeing 777 to an Airbus 321, to a Gulfstream to a King Air to a Cirrus. On the ground and in the air, we were taught how to listen closely for pilot errors, and how to keep airplanes separated from each other while moving at lightning speed. I thought back to that day I had met Donnie at Washington Tower. It was hard to imagine I was finally here.

At lunch, the twenty-one of us broke up into groups and roamed the campus. The Aeronautical Academy was the preeminent training ground for not only the United States but much of the world. One day I saw the controllers from Afghanistan walking together. Another day at lunch a group of Italian controllers were eating nearby us. And later, controllers from India. I loved seeing us all together. It reminded me of my international schools in Johannesburg, Banjul, and Amman. In the evenings, occasionally a number of the guys would go to strip clubs.

"Garon, we want you to come with us but we're not sure you'd enjoy it," one of the guys said.

"Why wouldn't I enjoy it?" I asked with a straight face while knowing what they meant.

They hesitated, with shy smiles. "Because . . . you're gay."

I laughed. "That doesn't mean I can't go out with you guys."

So one Friday night we sat in a row next to a stage where a redhead with big breasts and a black G-string danced in front of us.

"Garon, have you ever had a lap dance?" one of my friends asked.

"From a girl? No."

"I'm buying Garon a lap dance!" he announced. The rest of the guys cheered.

"No, no. I'm fine, man," I said with a smile. "Really, I'm good."

"I'm doing it!" he said. Seconds later the redhead strode over to me with seductive eyes and began moving sensually.

"Hey baby, how you doing?" she whispered. All the guys had their heads craned down the row.

"Hi, I'm good," I said, looking up at her and then down the line to my friends' exhilarated faces. This seemed to make their night even better.

"You like my titties or are you an ass-man?" she asked.

I've been asked a lot of questions in my life, but this was a first. "Um, actually, I'm gay."

"Well, your friends over there paid for this, so I'm going to give you a dance, baby," she said provocatively. Before I could say anything else, she squatted down in her heels, grabbed my face, and buried it between her breasts. When I didn't move, she grabbed me by the back of my hair and rocked my head back and forth.

"You can motorboat me," she whispered.

I pulled my head away from in between her breasts to look up at her. "I can *what?*"

By this point all the guys were dying in hysterical laughter. Then she grabbed her breasts and buried my face in them once again.

"All right, that was . . . you are . . . great. Thank you," I said, coming back up for air.

She tilted her head and studied my face. "They were telling the truth. You really are gay," she said, running her hands through my hair. "Too bad for us."

"Thanks, nice to meet you." *Did I just say 'nice to meet you'?* Ugh.

"You're welcome, sugar." As soon as she stood up and returned to the pole, all the guys piled over my shoulder, hugging me and patting me on the back.

"Did you get anything out of that?" one of them said.

"Not a thing."

"*Nothing?*" he asked, chuckling.

"Sorry to disappoint, man. Still gay."

AS WE WAITED for our instructors to arrive in the classroom the next morning, apparently my night out with the boys was the big topic of the day. "Yo! Garon motorboated a stripper for the first time last night," they told the other guys who hadn't been able to come.

They threw their fists in the air. "Yea!"

"I'm glad you're all so excited. Now you guys have to come to a gay club with me," I said.

"Whaaaat!" they responded, laughing. Most of the twenty-one guys had come from small towns across the country, and I was the first gay guy they had knowingly befriended. They had certainly never been to a gay club. The following weekend, ten of them followed me into their very first club in a small gay area of town in Oklahoma City. Fifty or more people danced at the center of the two-tiered large oval club as bartenders steadily poured drinks, swapping bottles back and forth as rapidly as air traffic controllers needed to make decisions.

"I'm a bit nervous," one of my friends said as we stood waiting in line.

"About what?" I asked.

"Just, what if a guy hits on me?"

"Have you ever hit on a girl who doesn't want you?"

"Yea."

"And what did she say?"

"She said she wasn't interested."

"Same thing, man. Just be polite and tell them you're straight. By the way, there will be a lot of girls in there. There's always bachelorette parties at gay clubs." He seemed surprised by that.

Sure enough, an hour later as I drank my vodka soda, I looked around at a number of the guys who had found girls to dance with. The others hung out with me by the well-lit bar that wrapped around the dance floor, talking about airplanes over drinks. I watched their eyes move across the dance floor as shirtless guys grinded up against each other, flashes of strobe lighting snapshotting the evening.

"What do you think?" I asked one of my buddies, a guy from a small town in New York, not far from Jamie's Rotterdam."

"You know, Garon, this is actually pretty cool. I've never really had a gay friend."

"I hope I'm your first of many," I said. "Cheers, man."

Over another weekend, Jamie and I decided to meet in Fort Lauderdale. While he had offered to fly to Oklahoma, I knew I needed a break from the academy and to get back into a bigger city if even for just one weekend. And a whirlwind weekend it was. We took walks around Victoria Park in the mornings, swam in the turquoise waves in the afternoons, had dinner with Richie and Bill and Barry in the early evenings, and had as much sex as we could at night to make up for lost time.

With the weekend behind us, I jumped on a flight to Houston, where I would connect on to Oklahoma City. This was my first time back in Texas since three years prior, when I had left Chad and UT Austin. With a fairly tight connection, I hustled to find my gate. Once in my gate area, I slumped against a pillar, took out an air traffic control textbook, and started studying while I waited for boarding to be called. Within minutes I noticed a number of security agents arriving at the gate area. I occasionally glanced up, wondering why there was more than the usual security presence. I looked around and all the other passengers had noticed it too. Just as I decided to ignore it and continue memorizing how to launch successive departures six thousand feet down the runway with fifteen degrees of divergence, I heard a voice.

"Excuse me, sir."

I looked up. Two security agents were standing before me.

"Yes? Can I help you?" I asked.

"Sir, this is one of the worst parts of our job, but we need to take you away for questioning," one of the men said.

I was completely caught off guard. "For questioning? Questioning for what?"

The other security agent stepped forward. "Two women in this waiting area called security because they said they are scared of you."

"Scared of me?"

"And they also said you are reading some kind of book on how to detonate a bomb aboard an aircraft."

I felt everything start to move in slow motion. I glanced

down at my textbook, at the faces of the two security agents, and then around the gate area, where all the waiting passengers for both this flight and the many other flights in the concourse were staring at me.

"But I'm . . . I'm," I stammered. "I'm reading a textbook on air traffic control. I'm an air traffic controller in training at the US Aeronautical Academy."

"I'm sorry, sir, we just need to follow procedure."

My mind went a thousand miles an hour. Surely this wasn't happening again. Someone else had looked at me and decided I was a terrorist. I felt the heat rise in my body and my muscles started to tense. I wanted to confront whoever had decided to judge me this way so publicly and cause me such embarrassment. But I also knew that if I got angry, I would be seen as an even bigger threat and thus legitimize their concern. In these moments it becomes absolutely imperative that you behave in the most agreeable manner possible to assuage the fears of everyone, or you'll end up confirming their stereotype. You might feel enraged, but if you show anger, they will immediately think you're guilty. An angry black woman. A young brown guy who is surely dangerous. A black man who feels belittled by the world and wants to take it out on everyone else. We don't have the luxury of being publicly upset like others do.

"Look, I have this badge," I said, reaching into my bag. "This is my Federal Aviation Administration badge. That's why I'm flying back to Oklahoma City, to return to the US Aeronautical Academy."

The two agents stared at me.

"We still have to take him in," one said to the other.

I looked at them both and felt the weight of hundreds of eyes staring at me in the concourse. The second agent took my ID and read it. Then he looked at me again.

"No. Let's just leave him alone. There's nothing wrong here," he said to his colleague. "We apologize, sir. We were just doing our job."

"Thank you," I said. As they walked away, I couldn't bring myself to look around the gate area again. I felt ridiculed and embarrassed.

Fifteen minutes later, along with the other passengers and my two anonymous accusers, I boarded my flight. It had been eight years since those other two women from Texas aboard the flight from Amsterdam to the United States had called me a terrorist. It was worse this time because I was so publicly humiliated. And the ridiculousness of imagining that someone reading a book about how to detonate a bomb on an aircraft would actually read it while standing in plain sight of the entire waiting area—I still have no words for that. I wondered what would have happened had I called security on two white American women whom I feared. Would security agents have taken my charge as seriously? Would they have tried to detain them? I doubt it.

51
MOMENT OF TRUTH

UPON RETURNING TO THE ACADEMY, my classmates and I worked day and night to prepare ourselves for our two final PVs, or performance verifications, which we knew was a make-or-break moment. Supervisors and air traffic managers from around the United States would be flying in over the next days to watch us work. We needed to pass both simulations. If we failed one, we were given one final PV (aka "the last chance") to prove ourselves. Stories of people who had failed their last-chance PV spread through the academy.

"One of my friends who was here before us told me that someone in their class failed their last-chance PV. Security was literally standing outside, took their badge, and escorted them to the front gates of the academy," a classmate relayed to all of us.

I didn't want to be that person. Immersing myself in the world of air traffic control without any aviation background was hands down one of the most difficult things I'd ever done. But I had worked extremely hard, prepared for this moment, and felt confident that I would perform well. On the eve of the final simulations, I reviewed how to integrate helicopters into the flow of my commercial jet traffic and rehearsed correct wake turbulence spacing between aircraft of different weight classes to ensure that the tornado-like air movement off the wings of the lead aircraft wouldn't flip the jet behind it.

The morning of my PVs, I joined the rest of my classmates in a large waiting room. For the first time in three months, we were all quiet. Some guys drank coffee peacefully in the corner while others flipped through last-minute notes. I bounced my leg up and down while seated in my chair, glad that my name had been selected to be one of the first in the testing room. I couldn't imagine sitting for hours in this state of nervousness. My stomach was in knots and I knew that regardless of the countless exams we had taken, it all came down to these simulations.

"We've taught you everything we can," said Roy Hillen, our tall, slim instructor with an affable smile, graying hair, and glasses. "Now it's time for you guys to go into those simulations and show them that you are the next generation of air traffic controllers." Over the months at the academy we had a number of instructors, but Roy was by far my favorite. He was masterful in the way he taught us how to control airplanes and had a long and successful career as a controller at Chicago O'Hare to draw stories from.

"Garon Wade." With the call of my name I took a deep breath, got out of my seat, and walked into the simulator. I briefly greeted the FAA examiners in the room and took my position. The first of two was my Ground Control simulation, moving the departures to the runway, arrivals away from the runway to their respective gates, and issuing instructions to the many airport vehicles that requested movement around the airplanes. As soon as the timed simulation began, I felt my body relax. I called out instructions rapidly and confidently and listened carefully for pilot readbacks. After thirty minutes of talking I knew I had done well, and for the first time in days a relaxed smile stretched across my face.

"Time!" the FAA examiners said, noting the end of the simulation. "Congratulations, you've successfully passed the Ground Control simulation." I thanked them, felt a huge weight off my shoulders, but also knew not to relax too much as I had one more to go.

An hour later I was called into my final simulation. This time it would be on Local Control: the controlling of arrivals entering the airspace, lining them up on two parallel finals, as well as clearing departures for takeoff on both runways in between arrival slots. It was what we had trained so hard for. I thought of my time reporting at WHSV, Jamie, Donnie Simons. They were all part of the journey I had taken to get to this moment.

"Are you ready, Mr. Wade?" a new FAA examiner asked.

"Yes, sir."

The simulation began and within seconds I was in the thick of it. Props calling me, requesting entry points into the traffic pattern around the airport. Commercial jets reporting a seven-mile final, requesting landing clearances. Helicopters calling from the middle of the airport, requesting to cross active runways and to work in the airspace amid the other traffic. Departures lined up short of the runway, waiting for me to build four-mile gaps in between my arrivals using speed control. Listening carefully to make sure pilots read back correct hold-short instructions as they approached a runway where I was seconds away from landing an aircraft. The minutes flew by and at times I felt like I was ahead of it all and then there were times when I felt it was catching up to me. Air traffic control is about excellent timing and making countless decisions at the same time. Often, even though you hear a request from a pilot, you store it in your memory and prioritize six other departures and arrivals, and then come back to the first request. You must choose the way you want your sky to work and commit to it. In the very last minutes of the simulation, I was landing Southwest and issued a specific exit point to the pilot. Very quickly afterward as I saw his speed reducing, I instructed an airport vehicle to cross the runway downfield, seeing that there would be no conflict.

"Time!" the FAA examiners said. I took an enormous breath and ran my hand over my face. I was completely exhausted and felt as though I had run a marathon. It was over, though. I had come here to do what I needed to.

"How do you feel you did?" the examiner asked me.

"I think I did well," I said, reflecting on the previous half hour of judgment calls.

"I'm so sorry, Mr. Wade. I'm not going to be able to pass you."

My heart stopped. I opened my mouth to speak but nothing came out. Heat rose through my body and I felt sick to my stomach.

"You largely did well, but in the end you issued the exit to Southwest and he never responded. I know you saw his speed reduce on the runway, but without the pilot acknowledging compliance to your instruction, it doesn't matter. Then you instructed the airport vehicle to cross the runway. You had a runway incursion."

I stared at the FAA examiner in disbelief. It felt as though it was happening in slow motion. I could see his mouth moving, heard his words, but it didn't feel as though I was even in the room.

GARON WADE

"I'm sorry. I'm going to have to fail you here and you will have the option for a last-chance performance verification," he said. Then he extended his hand toward me. I stood up, still feeling as if I were outside my body, shook his hand, and without a word walked out of the simulator. Once in the hallway, I looked down to the room where so many of my classmates were waiting. The FAA examiner was correct about everything. That's the thing about air traffic control. You can get ninety-nine things right, but if you make one mistake, it's not good enough. In the real world, it means hundreds of people die in an instant. I stared down the hallway and forced myself to walk forward. When I reached the room, a number of guys who were still waiting jumped up from their seats.

"How'd it go, Garon?" they asked. I stood there for a split second and stared at them, knowing that I would not only acknowledge my own failure for the first time, but I would add anxiousness to their simulation.

"I failed it."

Roy got up from his chair and asked me what happened. I told him. Classmates had been going through the simulations all morning and I was the first who had failed one. Roy's face tightened and he genuinely looked sad.

"Garon, it's not the end. You have a last-chance simulation. One more shot. I'll go find out when it is," Roy said, leaving the room.

I sat back in my seat and put both of my hands on my head. I had prepared so well for these simulations, but I hadn't prepared to deal with how I felt after failing one. I was now headed for a last chance. The rest of the day I watched as classmates came back from their second PVs.

"How'd it go?" I asked them, trying to put on a brave face.

320

"I passed." I stood up and hugged them. We had all been here, away from our respective families, for three months. We had become a unit. And I wanted to celebrate their happiness in this moment even though inside I was torn apart.

"Congratulations, man, you did it," I told each of them. By noon, two of my other classmates had failed and it was established that all three of us would be given last-chance simulations.

At lunch while the majority of the class was celebrating, I went outside the doors of the building to a spacious patio. I looked up at the blue sky and took a deep breath. Suddenly the door opened behind me. It was Roy.

"Garon, I just talked to the schedulers and they can't do it tomorrow. They've listed your last-chance simulation for the day after tomorrow."

"Thank you so much, Roy. I appreciate it." A part of me felt as though I had let Roy down. We stood together in silence.

"Listen, Garon. I hate this part of the academy. You take all these tests over three months, but it *all* comes down to these two simulations. I've been watching you all along. You are one of the best students in my class. You've done an excellent job here. You can absolutely do this, I know you can."

I nodded. "I really appreciate everything you've taught us, Roy. I'm not giving up, I promise."

Once Roy left, I pulled my phone out and dialed Jamie. I had told him I'd call him by noon to let him know.

"Hey, buddy!" he answered in an excited voice. "How'd it go?"

For once I paused the way Ashoh always had.

"I failed the second one, Jamie."

Neither of us spoke for quite a while.

"What happened?" I could hear the sadness in his voice. I explained the last minutes of the simulation.

"You get a last chance though, right?"

"Yes. I was hoping it would be tomorrow, but they needed to schedule it for the day after tomorrow. So I'm not going to be able to fly back to DC tomorrow night as planned. I was really looking forward to seeing you and celebrating."

Saying those words made me feel the weight of the situation.

"Okay, listen, buddy, go home and relax. Then go back in there and give it all you got."

"I will."

THE NEXT MORNING, many of my classmates came over to say goodbye.

"I'm going to miss you, Garon. You can do this, man. Let me know once it's over," one of my friends said as he hugged me.

In the afternoon, I went over to a condo where another classmate was staying. He was getting ready to drive back to Indiana.

"I've had a great time here with you," I said.

"Me too. Stay in touch, Garon. You've done so well all along. Go knock it out of the fucking park tomorrow."

The rest of the evening I sat quietly in my room trying to rebuild my confidence. Before I drifted off to sleep, I decided to focus on being grateful that I had one last chance instead of the failure.

The next morning, once again I re-entered the simulator. This time there were far more evaluators there. An FAA examiner with a pixie cut and a model-like face sat to my left. Another FAA examiner, a tall, older southern gentlemen with a black suit, sat to my right. A number of other people moved about the room.

"Mr. Wade, this is your last and final simulation on Local Control. Do you have any questions before we begin?" she asked.

"No. Thank you." I took a deep breath, held my push-to-talk transmitter in my right hand, and adjusted the boom of my microphone that draped down over my left ear and positioned the mic in front of my lips.

"Let's begin."

Just as before, I immediately got calls from smaller aircraft miles away from the airport requesting entry points into my airspace. I set a sequence. I pulled commercial traffic down both finals toward the parallel runways and used speed control to adjust the spacing between them. I shot helicopters across the runways at precisely timed moments, and put departures in position on the runway, holding them to cross other airplanes downfield before I cleared them for takeoff. I changed jet traffic to different runways, allowing me to depart multiple airplanes in rapid succession, spacing them six thousand feet apart and turning them fifteen degrees away from each other as required. I gave it all I had and pushed hard until the very last second.

"Time," the female examiner called out. I looked around the room at their faces. No one spoke.

"Mr. Wade, please follow this gentleman. He will escort you upstairs." A man was waiting by the door for me. I followed him, trying to replay each command in my head to see if I had made another error somehow. He led me into a small room on the second floor.

"We will be right with you. The examiners will be replaying

the simulation to ensure accuracy," he said as he left the room, closing the door behind him.

I slumped back in my chair, exhaled, and stared at the wall ahead. I had no idea what was about to happen. I thought I did well, but I'd thought that the last time too and then failed. My mind began to race.

I've wanted this so badly, but if I failed, I'm going to thank them politely, go back to DC, and figure out something else, I thought. I ran my hands up and down my arms as five, ten, and then fifteen minutes rolled by. And I thought of Jamie. I knew that he would be waiting for my call.

Suddenly there was a rapid knock at the door as it swung open. The FAA examiner with the pixie cut walked confidently into the office and extended her hand.

"Congratulations, Mr. Wade, you are now an air traffic controller."

A giant smile leapt from my face and I breathed freely. "Thank you! Thank you so much! I didn't know if . . ."

"Did you think you'd made a mistake?" she asked with a smile.

"No. But I definitely second-guessed myself as I sat in this room."

"Listen. At one brief point you began to get a little behind the curve, but you very quickly pulled it all together. That's exactly what we need controllers to do. Every controller at one point or another loses the picture. What we are looking for is to see how quickly you can pull it all back together. You did an outstanding job."

Her words filled me with joy as I thanked her and walked downstairs to find Roy in his office.

"Garon! How'd it go?" he said, standing up quickly and walking toward me.

"I did it, Roy. Thank you so much for believing in me."

Roy's face lit up. "I knew you could do it. And I've always believed in you." Roy shook my hand. "You're going to make a fantastic controller. I can tell. Stay in touch."

I made my way down the hallway to find my other two classmates who had just completed their last-chance PVs.

"We made it!" they said with their arms high in the air. The three of us hugged, sharing in our elation, and then said our goodbyes.

I walked back outside to the very same spot on the patio and dialed Jamie.

"I did it!" I said quietly into the phone, feeling the exhilaration rise through my body.

"Yes!" Jamie yelled. "I knew you could do this, buddy. Congratulations, you're an air traffic controller."

It had been a long road since quitting my job that day at WHSV. The road ahead had taken many unexpected turns, but I had known then that there was something far better out there for me.

The next day, I said goodbye to Oklahoma City, connected at Chicago O'Hare, and arrived back home in Washington to our house on 11th. When I got to the front steps, Jamie opened the door with that same smile he wore after not seeing me for a while. We hugged each other tight. We both knew that it was the last time we would ever need to move away from each other. We had done it for three years. From this point forward, we would always live under the same roof.

"I have something for you," Jamie said, leading me downstairs to our family room. Beside the beige sofa was a table made of carefully chosen pieces of light-colored driftwood anchored by a thick circular sheet of glass.

"That is so beautiful," I said, my eyes following every rough edge and sharp turn of the wood. While narrower at the bottom, near the top it branched out as if a hand were holding the glass top. "It's for me?"

"It's to remind you of your days in The Gambia collecting driftwood along the beach with your mom. I know how much you love those memories of her."

I looked between the coastal table up to Jamie's light-brown eyes. I had never expected a gift as meaningful as this. It was one of the nicest things anyone had ever done for me.

52

ASHOH'S FOOT

WITH THE PRESSURE OF THE Aeronautical Academy behind me, I decided it was time to call Ashoh and tell her about our engagement.

"You're getting married, huh?" I sensed a hint of judgment in Ashoh's tone. "Well, that'll be nice."

"I hope you'll be able to come. I'd really like to be with you and Grandpa on our wedding day. We're not sure yet where the wedding will take place, but it will be here in the United States and I can arrange all your flights and hotel," I offered.

"The thing is, Garon, my foot hurts," Ashoh said.

Was that all she could come up with?

"Well, you have some time. It won't be until next year. I hope as we get closer to the date, your foot will feel better and you and Grandpa can come." I knew she was in a full-blown panic over being invited to her first gay wedding. An *interracial* gay wedding. Imagine that.

"I'd like to come, I'd really like to," Ashoh said, lying through her phone. "I'll just have to see how my foot is."

There was silence.

"Now who proposed to who?" she asked.

"I proposed to Jamie."

"Mmm-hmm. Well, that's nice."

"By the way, Ashoh, I'd really like for him to meet you guys before the wedding. What do you think about us coming for Christmas?"

An even longer silence passed through the phone.

"Garon, I'm not so sure that's a good idea."

"But why?"

"I just don't think Grandpa would like that too much."

"You don't think Grandpa would like what?" I pressed.

"I'm fine with it, you know, the gay thing, but I don't think your grandpa would be very comfortable if you brought Jamie here."

"But, Ashoh, if I can't bring him, then I have to choose between Christmas with him and Christmas with you guys and I don't want to do that."

"I'm sorry, Garon. I just don't think it's a good idea."

53
WEDDING PLANS

T HE REST OF THE SUMMER back in Washington was spent making wedding plans. Jamie and I made lists of people we wanted to invite from all over the world. We decided that we would have a destination wedding and bring all our guests to sunny Fort Lauderdale the following year.

By the end of summer, I was in the thick of controlling live traffic on two parallel runways at Manassas Tower. As is the procedure each time you begin in a new airport, an instructor stood by my side, ready to over-key my microphone in case I gave an instruction that could result in airplanes crashing. It's the way controllers learn. Everything that Roy Hillen had taught me at the Academy in Oklahoma City had allowed me to excel. In a strange way, I felt that controlling live traffic was easier than controlling in the simulators at the academy because I knew that I had to get it right or people could die. Whereas my job as a TV reporter sometimes left me feeling as though I were preying on the misfortune of others, being an air traffic controller allowed me to *protect* human life and it was indescribably rewarding. The stakes were so high and that pressure forced me to learn and adapt rapidly. There's no rehearsal in air traffic control. Planes are converging at hundreds of miles an hour and not only must you figure out a plan immediately, you better have a backup plan ready in case the first one doesn't work. The thrill-seeking nature of Mom and Dad that I had experienced as a kid as they led us through the Maloti Mountains in Lesotho, or white-water rafting in Namibia, I realized that I, too, now shared. I reveled in the adrenaline rush that came from having six to eight aircraft enter my airspace at roughly the same time and in seconds increasing speeds, reducing speeds, having aircraft maintain various altitudes as they climbed above another or descended below traffic; creating order out of chaos in the sky.

While Manassas Tower wasn't much to look at, it was an incredible place to start learning. A much smaller airport than Washington National or Washington Dulles, it brought in a wide range of smaller aircraft. I witnessed my first two incidents while working there. One afternoon, a Saab 340 ran off the runway during landing. No one was hurt, but the aircraft was damaged as its gear sunk into the ground. Another time, a young woman who was flying her first solo crashed the wing of her airplane into a taxiway sign on landing. It rolled off the runway and buckled into the grass. Holding my breath, hoping she was okay, I watched through my binoculars as she climbed out of the cockpit, sat on the grass, and put her head in her hands.

As summer was winding down, Jamie's dad and his wife, Christine, on their drive back from Williamsburg, Virginia, asked Jamie if they could stop by our home one afternoon while I was at the tower. They were all sitting around our kitchen table when Jamie's father told him that he was making a big mistake in getting married. Not specifically to me, but to a guy. He tried to convince him yet again that it was wrong, and against God's plan, urging reconsideration.

Jamie had told me stories of his father's aptitude for binary thinking. He'd burned Melissa's books and Jamie's music when he didn't agree with it, tossing them in the campfire. He'd yell at Jamie for reading anything with a globalist bent and even encouraged him to avoid college and instead take a manual labor job. One summer on a visit to his father's parents in Davie, Florida, they drove into Fort Lauderdale to celebrate a special occasion. When Jamie had expressed admiration for the sprawling estates on the yacht-lined canals near the restaurant, his father cautioned him that living in wealthy neighborhoods was not something that Jamie would ever be able to achieve. It was as if his father wanted to perpetuate the anti-intellectualism and staunch religious fundamentalism in his son. It didn't work. To Jamie, the world was too beautiful, and his mind too creative, to ever be locked into fear and racism.

My family, in contrast, was extremely excited about our wedding. As the summer months drifted into the wondrous fall in DC, Jamie and I decided that our nuptials would take place in June. Our wedding was booked onboard a two-story yacht called *The Catalina*, which would take our guests through the Intracoastal Waterway for hours. I would be the first kid in our family to marry and Dad was thrilled. Just before Christmas, I asked Yael to be my best man. Ebony agreed to be in the wedding party and offered to give a speech that would reflect on our life around the world.

IN JANUARY, I certified at Manassas Tower. What did that mean? It meant that I earned my license to control airplanes at that tower without an instructor next to me and could now focus on moving elsewhere. Marilyn Martin, the chief of Manassas, and I had gotten along extremely well. Throughout my training there, she had helped me when I needed help; like Donnie, she had believed in me.

"Garon, where do you want to go now?" she asked me one day in her office.

"Marilyn, the only place I want to go is DCA."

"All right. Let me get you a meeting with Donnie," she said warmly.

I had worked hard. She knew it and I knew it. I will always be grateful to Marilyn for showing me the way in those early days. And while female air traffic controllers are far more common now, I imagined it must have been quite groundbreaking twenty years prior for any woman, much less a black woman like Marilyn, to carve out a career as an air traffic controller. After a stint in the Air Force, she joined the FAA in 1991, the year I had sat across the table from Mom and Dad in South Africa at five years old and guessed that Yael was a parachute.

"I was the only black person in my class at the academy," she once told me.

From the academy, Marilyn became a controller at LNS in Lancaster, Pennsylvania, and was the first black woman there. Years later she arrived at Manassas Tower and rose in the ranks to become the chief, the first black female chief. That was a lot of firsts, and I was sure she wasn't always treated with the dignity and respect she deserved. When trailblazers open doors for others, it speaks volumes about their personality. When Marilyn sat down at her first academy class in Oklahoma City in 1991, I'm sure she never imagined that there was a little Sri Lankan boy growing up in Africa who twenty years later she would be mentoring and helping to advance his career.

54

THE DREAM JOB

WASHINGTON MARKS SPRING BY THE blossoming of the cherry trees that line the tidal basin around the Jefferson Memorial. People come from all over the world to view the sea of rose and white flowers (a gift from Japan in 1912). It was during this time that Jamie and I, well established in our careers and financially able, decided to start the process to adopt a baby boy. I thought back on our conversation four years prior, eating guacamole at Oyamel. "Where are you with kids?" he had asked me. We had come up with a five-year plan at the time, but we'd been able to accomplish what we wanted sooner than that.

One afternoon, an angel walked into our home. Her name was Maureen Kenny. In her seventies, Maureen hunched a bit as she walked, carrying a caseload of papers under her arm. She had white hair, a great sense of humor, and spoke in a remarkably calming voice. We had chosen her as our social worker and she had visited us for months, helping us to compile child abuse clearances from every state we had ever lived, FBI clearances, character evaluations, professional recommendations, financial reports, and much more. We would work with her to complete our home study and then look to her for guidance as to which US-based adoption route to pursue.

In the meantime, we had wedding invitations to send out across the world. People were invited from the UK, Uzbekistan, Germany, Jordan, Canada, and of course the United States. First, Jamie and I would get married in a quiet ceremony in DC on the first week of June in front of the US Capitol Building, where it was legal. Marriage equality had not yet come to the entire country. Then we would invite all our friends to join us in Lauderdale. The plan was that Jamie's mom and my dad would marry us in ceremony on the top deck of the yacht as we cruised through the tropical paradise.

THE LAST WEEK of January, I arrived back where I had started three years before: at Washington Tower, in Donnie Simon's office.

"Garon, so great to see you. You've come a long way," he said with a smile.

"It's all thanks to you, Donnie. I'm very grateful."

"Marilyn said you wanted to meet with me about coming to DCA."

"Yes. Manassas has been great: I've worked really hard and learned a lot. But it's always been my dream to come work here at Washington Tower."

Donnie leaned back in his chair and ran his thumb along his chin.

"Have you considered ASo, Atlanta TRACON?" he asked.

"No, I haven't."

"I think you should consider the TRACON. I worked departure control, it's really interesting."

"I appreciate that. But I don't want to work departure. I love airports. The whole reason I got into air traffic after you met with me was because I love seeing airplanes every day."

"You know, that's a very common feeling among new controllers. Look, it doesn't have to be Atlanta, have you considered New York Approach?"

Why was Donnie trying to convince me to leave the area and go into departure control? I was surprised at this.

"No, I haven't considered New York either," I said with a slight sigh and a smile. "Donnie, I really want to stay here in DC, this is my city, and I want to work here at Washington Tower."

Donnie looked me over for a moment.

"Garon, you're young. This career has so many avenues. You're not locked into this city, are you? I thought you were single," he said.

Oh lord, here we go. I had always been out, but the one thing that is oftentimes difficult to navigate is whether employers are cool with gay employees. I had no idea where Donnie stood on this.

"Actually, I'm engaged," I said.

"Oh, you're engaged! Congratulations. And what do they do?"

This is where it gets tricky. Do you lie? Do you say *she* instead of *he*? Do you talk about the person abstractly and never mention gender? He had said *they*. I could continue with *they*. It's a situation gay people have had to navigate for generations. But I knew who I was, and I wasn't going to lie to hide in someone else's idea of how the world should be.

"He works for British Aerospace Engineering," I said.

Donnie had been moving things around his desk but immediately paused and looked directly at me.

"He?"

"Yes, he," I said confidently.

There was a long silence. It was the moment of truth. Had I just slotted myself at Manassas Tower for the remainder of my career?

Donnie sat back in his chair and his eyes studied my face.

"Garon, I'm so proud of you. I had no idea you were gay. I'm so proud of you for saying it."

It wasn't what I was expecting, and I smiled at Donnie in appreciation.

"So, you're really looking to make Washington Tower your new home then?"

"Yes. Definitely," I said, nodding.

Donnie sat quietly for a moment, then leaned forward in his chair. "You know what? Go up to the tower and make some friends," he said.

Three weeks later, I learned that I had been accepted onto the team of controllers at DCA. It was hard to wrap my head around. Three years before, I had sat in his office as he asked me: "Do you think you'd like to be an air traffic controller?" Donnie had made my dream to be a controller for Washington come true.

BY THIS POINT, Jamie and I had become very good friends with Matt and Anne Gialanella, the couple we had met on the eve of our engagement. They had a running joke with us that they were our most diverse friends because the two of them were a white, straight, southern couple from North Carolina. When they would arrive at parties at our home, they were surrounded by a rainbow of absolutely everything: various countries, sexualities, religions, colors, but no southern straight white couples. "Garon, we're diverse because we are so white," Matt had once said, and we all laughed hysterically.

We loved hanging out with them, often spending Sunday evenings at their condo near U Street. We even asked them to be a groomsman and *groomslady*, as we decided to call it, at our upcoming wedding. They reveled in hearing stories about Ashoh and wanted to meet her.

55

THE WEDDING

JAMIE'S MOM, DENICE, AND HER BOYFRIEND Sherman
had come to visit us in DC in April. The newest monument
to grace Washington was the MLK Memorial, a towering
white statue of Martin Luther King, Jr., on the northwest corner
of the Tidal Basin. We were all extremely excited to go see it for
the first time. It was deeply evocative, and as we toured the
memorial, I wondered why Ashoh and Grandpa had never been
able to see the simple beauty in his message. My favorite quote
has always been: "Darkness cannot drive out darkness; only
light can do that. Hate cannot drive out hate; only love can do
that." I learned those words long ago and each time I hear them,
they reverberate through my soul.

As we were walking away from the memorial, I asked Denice
if she had seen her grandson, Jason, lately.

"We went to lunch together recently. But he's getting older
now and he's with his friends more. You know how it goes," she
lamented.

"Yea. It's just those teenage years. He'll circle back," I tried to
assure her. "And anyway, you'll be busy with another one soon."

"What?" Denice said, stopping suddenly and staring at me
with a blank expression.

"You'll be busy with another grandson soon," I explained. "And he'll want to be around you all the time, I'm sure."

Denice appeared in shock. We both paused.

"Hang on. Did Jamie not tell you . . ." I asked, now looking between her and Jamie, who was well behind us, talking to Sherman.

"Tell me what?" Denice asked.

"That we're having a baby."

Denice was speechless.

"Jamie!" I yelled. "Come over here, buddy." Jamie and Sherman walked over to us.

"Did you not tell your mother that we're having a baby?" I asked him. Denice and Sherman stared at him.

"Well, no. Not yet, I mean. I wasn't going to say anything until we got a match," Jamie said.

"Well, they know now," I teased, looking at their surprised faces.

We had talked about telling our families a number of times. Ebony, Yael, and Dad absolutely knew. We had even sent a message to all our friends in DC, letting them know that we had started the paperwork process. I had incorrectly assumed that Jamie had told his mother. Denice, though shocked, was overjoyed. As we walked away from the MLK Memorial, she wanted to know everything. I looked up at Jamie.

"You should have told her," I said, nudging him. He just smiled his Jamie smile at me.

ON JUNE 8, 2012, Jamie and I (already legally wed in DC) stood at the stern of *The Catalina*. Surrounded by our family and close friends, we moved through the Intracoastal Waterway with the azure beauty of Lauderdale surrounding us. Denice and Dad married us as the fiery orange sun set to the west. Our six groomsmen wore khaki pants, pale-violet shirts, and new navy Adidas sneakers. Ebony and Anne, our two groomsladies, were knockouts in royal-blue dresses. And Jamie and I stood surrounded by all of them in white ties framed by beige chino suits and gray Adidas sneakers. As I stared into his eyes, I remembered the moment I saw Jamie at the gym in Columbia Heights, how we had both been too shy to say hi initially. I thought of our first non-date at Matchbox and later the Constitution. I remembered our evening walking through the moonlit pathway at The Elvetham, the first night I had ever truly slept beside him. We had come a long way. I glanced at our wedding party, honing in on Ebony and Yael as Dad first spoke about Jamie.

"I haven't had as much opportunity to see Garon and Jamie because I've been overseas much of the time. However, I've had the privilege of commuting with Jamie to work in Washington on several occasions. And yesterday we had a long walk back from the rehearsal. He strikes me as extremely honest, very smart, and he has a calmness about him that is a very good counterpoint to the frenetic energy that Garon exhibits."

Everyone began laughing because it was true. I'm definitely a higher energy level than Jamie.

I listened closely as Denice's sweet voice came over the speakers. "I first met Garon at the airport from behind Jamie as they came through the security gate. Garon was very engaging, genuinely interested in learning about our family, and extremely pleasant. He seemed especially amused at how our family were all still living in the same location while he and his family had traveled the world. Garon is a hardworking, talented, and ambitious person. But above all, he loves my son. I know Jamie has found in Garon a partner, a trusted friend, and a husband. When children find true love, parents find true joy. I believe they've made a wonderful choice," she said and began to cry.

"As you can see, there are two candles on both sides of us," Dad added.

"These candles commemorate the rich lives of two people who have died but are often in our thoughts. Jamie's grandfather, Jack Deschenes, and Garon's mother, Niki Wade. Please share with us a moment of silence," Denice requested.

I closed my eyes and envisioned Mom's smiling face as we drove through Amman together. She shrieked in laughter as I emulated her hands turning the steering wheel and pushed my feet in sync with hers as she pressed on the accelerator. "Garon, stop!" She laughed out loud. To this day, it remains one of my favorite memories of the two of us. I loved being able to make Mom laugh.

Then Ebony stepped up to the microphone. "When Garon asked me to talk about family today, I thought I would just read a poem or quote a great philosopher. But Garon said no poems and no philosophy. So I thought I would start with a quote from someone he will truly appreciate: Angelina Jolie." Everyone broke out in an amused laughter. It was true, I'd rather hear a quote from Ms. Jolie.

"Angelina once said about her adopted children that she was meant to find her family around the world. Garon and I used to joke that our parents were just like Angelina and Brad, just a bit less rich and famous, but on the same mission to find their family around the world. They found Garon and me in Sri Lanka and The Philippines respectively, and had Yael in South

Africa. And now Garon has found Jamie and his wonderful family from Upstate New York. And we are eagerly waiting to be there for them as they start the exciting process of finding their own family through the adoption process."

Neither Jamie nor I had any idea what Ebony, Denice, and Dad were going to say. The three of them did an exquisite job of demonstrating the love of two families joining together. Not everyone felt similarly, though. Jamie's father and his sister, Melissa, holding fast to their fundamentalist beliefs, declined to attend the wedding. And although I had tried my best to persuade them, Ashoh and Grandpa decided not to come. But as I looked out at our guests, it was evident there was an outpouring of love and a community of people who were cheering for us. We were surrounded by friends from near and far. Tina flew all the way from Tashkent, Uzbekistan, where she, Jay, and their sons, Jonny and Leo, were now living. She beamed with happiness throughout the entire ceremony. From North Carolina, New York, Louisiana, Seattle, Massachusetts, and, of course, Washington, people had traveled into tropical paradise to celebrate the merging of our two lives.

Jamie and I had prepared vows and we agreed he would go first. Over the years I had come to understand that Jamie didn't always communicate what he was feeling easily and so I was intrigued to hear what he would say.

"You made us work, as you make everything in our lives work. When I give you five reasons why something won't happen, you give me six why it will. You know what you want, you go after it, and you get it against everything and everyone telling you, you won't have it. Your ability to make decisions about really big matters in really short periods of times to this day astounds me. You are Mr. Social. Nothing makes your day brighter than a giant gathering of people. You have filled our life together with so many wonderful people. You are gentle beyond words. You forget the worst of your life and remember the best. You allow me to be who I am. You want to be a father and I know that our son will always be your first priority. Love. I hear you tell me this and show me this every day. If you've ever been truly unconditionally loved, then you know there's never a bad day in this life. You are my best friend."

I looked up at him and saw that serious boy who had glanced my way on the rowing machine. He had let me into his heart. If he had ever said those words to me while sitting quietly on the sofa in our home, I would have lain my head on his broad chest and held him for a long time. He was right, I am Mr. Social; and despite my outgoingness, I actually tend to become quite shy when speaking in front of people. He and I almost reverse roles in these situations, and I become the introvert.

I cleared my throat, walked up to the center, took a deep breath, and turned to him.

"Jamie, you know that when people ask me about you, the most honest thing I can say is you are my best person. It is truly my greatest privilege to stand here together across from you. It is impossible and I know it's not true, but ever since I met you that day at the gym in Columbia Heights, seriously I just felt like somehow you were made for me. So many nights when we are back in DC, we fall asleep at the same time holding hands. And I lie there for a second and think, How is it possible that I so early in my life found my best friend? I listen very closely when our friends describe you. They say you are patient, kind, a great cook, and so many people say you are quietly confident. I know that all those things are absolutely true, but there is one thing that they don't know that I do by virtue of being able to sit next to you every day. And that is that you are going to make the most amazing father to our son. And you have no idea how in love with you, that makes me. Thank you for your time and your patience, and your careful consideration, your travel, and your effort that has made you and I—and this—a viable option."

Denice stepped forward. "Garon, will you take my son, James Suriano, as your husband, to watch over and take care of in the best of times and in harder times, to respect, love, and build a life together?"

"I will."

"And, Jamie, will you take my son, Garon Wade, as your husband, to watch over and take care of in the best of times and in harder times, to respect, love, and build a life together?"

"I will."

"We now pronounce you married. You may kiss your husband," Dad and Denice said in unison.

Jamie and I kissed, and true to form after we kissed, I turned slightly away from our guests who were wildly applauding, and buried my face in his chest, wanting to have a private moment in the most public of ceremonies.

WE LEFT OUR WEDDING weekend and traveled back to Washington together. As we landed at DCA, Jamie turned to me in his seat.

"Can you believe you're going to be a controller at DCA now?" he asked.

I looked out the window at the many airplanes taxiing on the ground around us. Then I looked up to the tower.

"No. No, I really can't," I said. It had all come together.

56

WASHINGTON TOWER

"**S**OUTHWEST 1560, GO AROUND. Turn right heading 250, climb and maintain three thousand," Eric Cole, one of the best controllers at DCA, directed.

I watched as the American Boeing 737 preparing to takeoff from Runway 19 hadn't done so fast enough. Southwest, who had been cleared to land right behind it, wouldn't have the six thousand feet of required space between the two airplanes, and Eric made the excellent decision to climb Southwest back up into the sky. Go-arounds at DCA weren't something to be ashamed of. On the contrary, they needed to be executed extremely well because the operation was so high octane that every second mattered. In fact, new controllers weren't allowed to certify until they could demonstrate that they were comfortable making the call to send arriving traffic around in order to ensure the required space down the runway. I loved watching Eric work.

It was morning rush hour at DCA, and I counted thirty-eight jetliners being maneuvered by the ground controller. Some were arrivals waiting for gates to open. Some were departures waiting to takeoff for Boston, Chicago, San Francisco, Atlanta, New York, Seattle, and other destinations. While there may have been thirty-eight on the ground, there were another thirty arrivals in the sky, rolling into the airspace like suitcases on a conveyor belt. Only these jets were spaced four miles apart and moving at 170 knots toward the airport. This was Washington Tower.

"A little different than Manassas, huh?" a woman said to me.

I looked over. I couldn't believe it. It was Cindy. The same Cindy who had reluctantly given me the tour three years before. She smiled and was much friendlier this time.

"Yea, nothing like Manassas," I replied. "You know, we've met before."

"We have?" Cindy asked, studying my face.

"Yes. I came up here for a tour three years ago and you were the one who showed me around."

"Ahhhh, yes!" she said, remembering. "Weren't you ... weren't you a reporter?"

"I was, yes. A long time before." I laughed.

"Sorry if I wasn't so friendly to you. All they told me was that a reporter was coming up and to not tell you much at all." We both laughed this time.

I looked out the south windows to Gate 7, where Frontier was parked. It was where I had loaded baggage and dog crates and oyster skids onto the Frontier Airbuses during those cold winter months. I remembered myself, bundled in my jacket with my beanie on, staring up at the tower and wondering if I would ever be in that world. I picked up the binoculars and narrowed in on the men and women loading the aircraft that sat at the gate. I had such an appreciation for them and what they were doing. I promised myself that when I would eventually take things for granted up here, I would look down at Gate 7 and remember.

MAUREEN SAT IN HER office at Lutheran Social Services on Georgia Avenue, compiling the last pieces to our puzzle.

"Your home study is complete, guys. You can now take it to Adoption Makes Family," she said, handing me our documents. Adoption Makes Family was an agency based in nearby Maryland. We had explored all our options and decided on working with the agency's owner, Dr. Dean Kirschner. He worked slightly differently than the rest of the agencies in the area. While he did work with expectant birth mothers, Dean also marketed heavily to hospitals. When an expectant mother showed up to deliver without an adoption plan, and made the difficult decision to place her child for adoption, Dean was the hospital's go-to. We liked him right way, and he felt we'd be a good match for his agency as well.

"I want you guys to be ready. It can happen anytime," Dean told us. "I have called couples at three in the morning to tell them I'm with a baby who will be their child."

"We'll be ready," we promised.

"One more thing, guys. I will only call you when I have a baby," Dean said.

From that point forward, I involuntarily found myself waking up at 3 a.m., sleepily reaching down to the wooden floor below our bed, and checking my phone for missed calls.

57

ASHOH'S NANNY CONCERNS

IGH OFF THE NEWS, I decided to tell Ashoh.
"We've signed with an adoption agency," I told
her excitedly. "That means we could have a baby any
day now."

Then came her long signature pause.

"Well, who's going to take care of it?" she asked with great
concern.

"Who do you think? We are."

I could sense Ashoh tossing the idea around in her head.

"I mean, usually there's a mother," she said.

"Right. But in our situation, there's no mother."

Well, it's just that you both are men and work."

After getting over my slight annoyance, I could understand
why it was impossible for Ashoh to understand how two men
could take care of a baby. She had grown up during a time when
the full weight and responsibility of raising children fell on a
woman. She had taken care of Robby, Mom, and Mike. Even
when Grandpa was home, he had most likely expected her to
tend to the kids. The world had changed, but from her seat near
the kitchen window of 30 Bernice Drive, Ashoh hadn't seen it
evolve.

"We are both going to raise him and have the help of a nanny," I told her.

"Will it be a girl nanny?" Ashoh asked. I laughed. I'm sure that many years before, Ashoh had trouble understanding why Mom had hired Mr. Twan in Sri Lanka, and Suraj in Jordan. They had been proof that male housekeepers/nannies were every bit as good as their female counterparts. But even the stories of how much we loved them hadn't convinced her.

"Yes, a female nanny," I assured her.

"Well, that sounds nice," Ashoh said, relaxing.

58

AMERICAN 77

I STARED OUT THE TOWER windows to the north, studying the White House. Then my eyes shifted west to the Pentagon.

"It's hard to imagine American Airlines slamming into that on 9/11, huh?" the booming voice behind me said.

I looked over my shoulder. It was veteran controller Robert Connell, or Sonny Bob, as we all called him. With a bald head and a big mustache, Sonny Bob stood much taller than me. Every day he wore a blue lanyard with white writing that read *Jesus Loves Me*. He had been assigned to train me at DCA. The tower had gotten quite a laugh when Sonny Bob—deeply patriotic, quite conservative, and obviously a very religious man—had been paired with the super-liberal gay brown guy who had come to the United States by way of Africa and the Middle East. Normally I, too, would have doubted that we would end up in the same circles, but Sonny Bob and I actually had a great affinity for each other. What the other controllers didn't know is that he reminded me a lot of Ashoh and Grandpa in Louisiana.

"Were you up here on 9/11?" I asked him.

"I wasn't, but some of these other guys were," he said.

It made me deeply sad to even think about it. "What did the controllers see in the moments before?" I asked.

"American 77 took off from Dulles. Once they were hijacked, the transponder was turned off. We had heard what happened in New York, but no one knew it was an attack. The guys up here said they saw a target on radar coming toward us. Then they said they watched as the 757 went right past this window, swung a 180, and slammed into the Pentagon," Sonny Bob told me.

I felt sick to my stomach. Even writing about this now I have a lump in my throat remembering that conversation. I can't imagine what it would have been like to watch that happen. 9/11 was both the worst day and strangely an extremely proud day for the profession of air traffic control. Once the nation understood what was going on, the command came for controllers across the country to land 4,200 planes instantly. It had never been done before, and the men and women who worked that day showed how exceedingly well trained the controllers of the United States were. I continued to stare at the Pentagon. Sonny Bob's words echoed in my head.

"Where were you on 9/11?" he asked.

"I was in the Middle East," I said pensively. I remembered that afternoon in Amman, taking the bus home to Amy's house. We walked into their living room and watched it unfold on TV just as United 175 crashed into the South Tower. Just thirty-four minutes later, the controllers in the tower where I was now working would watch helplessly as American 77 exploded into the Pentagon.

Sonny Bob and I didn't talk for a couple moments. It was too difficult.

59

ASHOH'S NEW NEIGHBORS

I HELD A GLASS OF BORDEAUX in one hand and waved to the neighbors, who were making their way back home from work. I went to my phone's favorites and dialed Luling.

"Well, we finally got new neighbors," Ashoh told me, clearly excited at the new events of Bernice Drive.

"You did?" I was surprised. With the exception of our family moving in and out that one year, Ashoh's neighborhood rarely got new families.

"Yes. Well, Julie next door finally OD'd. And guess what?" Ashoh asked excitedly.

I wasn't passed the whole overdosing bit. "Ms. Julie overdosed?" I asked.

"Yes. I was sitting in the kitchen minding my own business when I heard the sirens. Eventually I went out to see what was happening."

That was a lie. Ashoh was not minding her own business. She was glued to her wooden shutters from the moment she heard those sirens, dropping the *TV Guide* on the kitchen table and bursting out those front doors to watch the drama unfold.

"They say she overdosed in the bathroom. I saw them taking her body away," Ashoh said with dramatic flair.

"That's terrible. I'm so sorry to hear that, Ashoh. Who moved in?"

"An *interracial* couple."

Interesting choice of words.

"Oh really?" I said, knowing I was going to get the full story any minute.

"Well, the wife is white and the husband is black and they even have a mulatto baby."

I put my hand on my forehead and downed the rest of my wine. A *mulatto* baby. I let out a long sigh.

"Well, do you like them?" I asked.

"They actually seem quite nice," Ashoh said, an element of surprise ringing in her voice.

"Why do you sound surprised?"

"Well, Garon, because I've never had . . . you know."

"No, I don't know."

"I've never had interracial neighbors before."

Ms. Julie had been abusing drugs next door for decades. Unfortunately, she had finally died. But in Ashoh's world, her white drug-addicted neighbor who she never really liked felt a safer bet than a nice husband and wife who happened to be different colors and had a biracial child. I decided to let it go.

"Well, Ashoh, I'm glad you like your new neighbors. And I miss you. How's Grandpa?"

I rarely talked to Grandpa, as I knew he hated talking on the phone. Occasionally he'd make an effort and say, "Hey, Rambo," in the background, but mostly I just told Ashoh to tell him I said hello.

"He's just in his chair with the dogs," Ashoh said. I laughed. I knew he was watching Lifetime in his La-Z-Boy.

"I love you, Ashoh," I said and hung up the phone.

60

MATTEO

O N SATURDAY, NOVEMBER 3, 2012, Jamie and I had just
finished eating at The Coupe, a favorite brunch spot of
ours one block up from where we lived in Columbia
Heights. Once back in our bedroom upstairs, Jamie continued to
pull winter clothes out of his closet and fold them neatly in line on
the bed. He was packing for his annual trip to the UK for work. It
never ceased to amaze me the level of organization that Jamie
went through to pack. When I packed, I rolled clothes, instead of
folding, in order to allow for more room. Then I tossed them in my
luggage. He, however, had a carefully thought-out system. I stood
near the edge of the bed talking to him as he folded his shirts,
always a little sad when he would leave for work trips. I was happy
that he had the opportunity to travel as often as he did, though; I
knew he loved crossing the Atlantic.

As we were talking about what he would be doing in the UK,
my phone started ringing. I walked over to see who was calling.
There on the screen flashed *Dean Kirschner.* My heart stopped
for a moment. I gasped and looked at Jamie.

"It's Dean!" I yelled, showing him the phone. It had only
been three weeks since we'd first met with him. Jamie rushed
over.

"Hi, Dean," we said eagerly on speakerphone.

"Hi, boys, what are you dooooiiiiing?" he said with a knowing and almost teasing tone.

I looked at Jamie and did a combination of pointing at his suitcase and then a line across my mouth to convey *Do not say anything about traveling!*

"We're good. We just finished brunch," I said. Jamie was on the edge of his seat.

"Okay. Do you want to know where I am?" Dean continued.

"Yes! Dean, just tell us!" I yelled out. He laughed.

"Okay, okay. I'm sitting here holding your son. He was born this morning at 5:23 a.m. I'm at Howard County Hospital in Maryland with him now. Are you both ready to be parents?" Dean asked, knowing that we were about to lose our minds.

And we did. Jamie and I jumped up and down in our bedroom, our faces wild with excitement. It's hard to explain the exhilaration you feel in that moment. There's something so special about that very first moment, when you go from being a couple to becoming parents. It's instantly life-changing.

"*Yes!* Yes, we're ready!" My mind started racing.

"Is he okay?" Jamie asked.

"He's doing great. The birth mother didn't want to keep him and so she asked the hospital to call an adoption agency and they called me. I spoke to his birth mother and she's very clear about wanting to place him with a family," he said. "Do you want to know more about him?"

It was all so much to even begin to process. Of course we did.

"So, the birth mom is white and she says she thinks the father is black. They aren't a couple. They met at a nightclub in Louisville, Kentucky, while she was on vacation, and they had a one-night-stand."

Kentucky? I'd never thought about Kentucky in my entire life.

"Okay, I'm going to send you pictures of him right now," he continued.

I pressed the Home button and jumped into my texts.

Ding. Ding, my phone sounded. Jamie and I hovered over my screen.

In the first photo, Dean had him cradled in his arms, but it was hard to see his face. The second photo, however, was a closeup, and as soon as I saw his face I thought, *That's our son.* He had an olive complexion and a disgruntled expression, seemingly annoyed at his early morning arrival into this world. He had been born well before we'd gotten up that morning. We had taken showers, gotten ready, had an entire brunch, and sauntered slowly through our morning. Unknowingly, our son had been born and was moving through his first hours in this world.

"So, what do you think?" Dean asked with the same teasing tone.

"He's so cute, we love him!" Jamie said. "Oh, thank you, Dean, thank you so much!"

Suddenly the doorbell rang and I handed the phone to Jamie and raced downstairs to tell whoever it was that we wouldn't be able to talk right now. I flung open the door and there was Ebony.

"Guess what!" Ebony yelled excitedly.

"What?" I said, trying to mask my excitement of our news and listen attentively to hers.

"I just found out I passed the bar exam!" Ebony said jubilantly.

I froze. Fuck. This was her *big* news. She had been working her ass off at law school for the past three years.

"Congratulations!" I blurted out. "Listen, I'm really happy for you. And I really don't want to take away this moment, but guess what?" I didn't even wait for her to answer. "We just found out we have a son!"

Ebony's face went from being excited to even more wide-eyed and astonished.

"*Really?*" she asked, clearly not expecting any of this.

"Yes! The director of the adoption agency just called. In fact, Jamie's still on the phone with him upstairs right now, so I have to go. I'm really excited for you too, though." I turned to run upstairs. "Wait, can you just wait here?" I asked, turning back around. Then I took off up the stairs.

I had one hundred percent stolen Ebony's thunder. She stood there dumbfounded, but I could tell she was also excited.

Upstairs, Jamie and Dean were still going over details.

"You guys should plan to come get him tomorrow. The hospital wants to keep him here tonight but start getting things ready. Since he was born in Maryland, you'll need to move to a hotel in Maryland for a week or two. I'll be in touch later with more details," Dean said, ending the call.

Jamie and I looked at each other and hugged each other tight. We had a baby.

"Ebony is here," I told Jamie. We rushed downstairs together.

"Can you believe it?" I asked Ebony. "He was born at five something this morning and he's at Howard County Hospital. Here's a picture," I said, pulling out my phone. "Oh, Jamie, Ebony passed the bar exam."

"Congratulations!" Jamie said earnestly, trying to comprehend all that was happening simultaneously. Jamie and Ebony had, for years, shared a significant love of the study of law. They talked about it often over dinner. They ganged up on me when I had a differing opinion about a case.

"Thanks, guys. Okay, your news is bigger than mine," Ebony said, acknowledging the obvious.

"No, it's not!" I lied.

"Yes, it is." she insisted, knowing I was lying. "Text me the pictures of him," Ebony said. "Congratulations, I'm really happy for you guys. I'm going to be an aunt! Let me know what they say," she said, then left.

Jamie and I turned to each other and then back to the screen to stare at the photo of our baby. Over the past months while lying in bed together at night, we had read through more than five-hundred names, virtually never liking the same one. But two weeks before, we had finally agreed on a name we both absolutely loved.

"Oh my god, we have a son. Matteo," I said.

"Matteo," Jamie repeated.

61

ASHOH'S COLOR WHEEL

JAMIE CANCELLED HIS TRIP to the UK. We called Denice and Sherman in Massachusetts to relay the exciting news. Then we called Dad, who was now on an assignment in Astana, Kazakhstan. He was so proud to become a grandfather. Then Yael, who was still in Austin. Instantly, the realization that I couldn't call Mom hit me. She would have reveled in this moment. Her first grandchild. It hurt and I was profoundly sad.

"I want to call Ashoh," I told Jamie.

"Absolutely, you should call her," he affirmed, knowing that this was the call I was making in place of being able to call Mom.

I dialed Louisiana.

"Well, hey there!" Ashoh said.

"Hey, Ashoh, it's me."

"How are you doing?"

"We have some big news. Are you ready?"

"Big news? Well, sure. What is it, Garon?"

"We just found out that we have a son. He was born this morning!"

While she may have come to terms with the idea of two men raising a baby, Ashoh never imagined it happening so soon. Frankly, neither did I. I still couldn't believe it had only been three weeks since we had decided to work with Dean at Adoption Makes Family.

"A baby? Now?"

"Yes, we just got the call from the adoption agency about an hour ago."

Silence. It was expected.

"Well, Garon, that's exciting! What's his name?"

"It's Matteo."

"Mattel?"

"No, it's Matteo."

"Well, I can't say that. Is it Matt . . . el?"

"No, it's . . . it's not Mattel, Ashoh. It's Matteo. Say 'Matay.'"

"Matay."

"Now say 'O.'"

"O."

"You got it," I told her. Say it again.

"Mattel," Ashoh said.

"Okay, well, you'll get it eventually, Ashoh."

I hadn't imagined that the name *Matteo* would be hard for anyone to say.

"Now what is he?" she asked.

"What is he?"

"Yes. What is he? What color is he? Is he white, black, what?"

I paused. Like so many times before, I wasn't expecting this question. Though, in hindsight, knowing Ashoh, of course I should have.

"The director of the adoption agency said his mother is white and his father is black," I said, realizing that of course this is how she would contextualize the birth of our son, just as she had with her new neighbors.

Ashoh thought quietly on the phone. "Well, are you going to raise him white or black?"

I pulled the phone away from my face and stared at it. *What. The. Fuck.*

"Ashoh, I'm going to have to call you back in a bit, okay?"

"Congratulations, honey," she said.

THAT NIGHT, JAMIE fell asleep easily in our bedroom. Not able to sleep, I went into our guest room. We had positioned the queen-sized bed against the wall because there was a large window there that overlooked the hustle and bustle of 11th Street. I often lay in the bed, staring out at the city street down below, people-watching. I lay with my face pressed against the window, the cold November air meeting my nose against the pane.

I knew that this was the last evening of my life where I would be responsible for only myself. The dreams I had as a young boy as I walked the sandy streets of The Gambia or wandered through Wadi Rum in Jordan, of one day becoming a father, had come true.

62

LEARNING THE ROPES

THE VALETS AT THE HOTEL in Maryland we checked into, tall older black gentlemen with exceptionally welcoming smiles, seemed baffled at the amount of luggage we had. We helped them load a mobile crib with a bassinet, tubs of formula, jumbo boxes of diapers, and more onto the trolley. I could see the questions in their eyes, but they of course were absolutely professional. Once in our room, we spent the next hours unpacking, having lunch, and staring at the phone, waiting for it to ring.

I sat at a desk in my black jeans, black shirt, swinging my legs back and forth.

"Are you just dying?" Jamie asked with a smile. He was, and still is, the embodiment of patience. I, on the other hand, am not.

Around 4 p.m., my phone rang and I lunged at it.

"Hey, boys! Matteo and I are in the car driving slowly from the hospital," Dean announced. "He's doing great. You can start driving to the adoption agency. We will meet you there."

An hour later, we pulled up in front of Adoption Makes Family.

"You ready?" I asked Jamie.

"Ready," he said.

We opened the door to the agency and made our way into the waiting room, expecting to see Dean and Matteo, but it was silent. Instead, we were met by Caren, his administrative assistant.

"They're not here yet. Please have a seat over there and they'll be here soon," she said cordially.

Jamie and I sat on a brown leather sofa and waited. And waited. And waited some more.

Finally, we heard the roar of an engine approach the building and stop. A car door opened, then closed. Then another opened, closed, and then a baby's cry filled the winter air outside.

Jamie and I turned to each other.

"He's here!" Jamie said.

Dean flung open the door with a giant smile on his face, and there in his arms, crying, was our little boy.

"Who wants to hold him first?" Dean asked, positioning him in front of us.

Before Jamie could answer, not realizing how nervous I had become, I pointed to Jamie and said, "Him!"

Jamie laughed and Dean placed Matteo into Jamie's big arms. I had always imagined what the first moment meeting our child would be like. I had watched videos of other parents with their children for the first time, and oftentimes it included tears of happiness. I felt terrified. *What if I hold him wrong? How do I support his neck?* I hadn't thought through these questions before.

I leaned over, put my head on Jamie's shoulder, and gazed at Matteo. I started to relax and soon Jamie put Matteo in my arms. How had the world brought this little man into our lives?

Dean let the three of us spend our first moments together.

In short order, what I like to call Baby Boot Camp began.

"All right, Dads. Let's go into my office and I'm going to teach you guys how to feed, burp, hold, and change him," Dean said, laughing. He had done this so many times before.

For the next four hours, we hung out in Dean's spacious office, with him showing us how to correctly support Matteo's neck and hold him in various ways. Feeding him and changing his diaper felt easy. Burping him, on the other hand, that was new; and Jamie and I took turns burping him properly, looking at each other for reassurance. By the end of the fourth hour, we had gotten the hang of it. I remembered how gingerly Mom had held Yael once they returned from the hospital in South Africa. Ebony and I had only been allowed to hold him while sitting on the blue sofa in the living room. I remembered caressing his thin blond hair and being told "Be careful with his soft spot." I sat in the leather chair cradling Matteo as he slept, falling in love with him instantly. It's amazing the instantaneous love a parent experiences for a child. Was this how Mom and Dad had felt the first day they saw me at the Jayamani Center in Sri Lanka? Matteo and I had such different adoption stories. I looked out Dean's office window. The light of day had faded into darkness.

"It's time for you guys to get him back to the hotel. I'm going to teach you how to secure the car seat and how the carrier clicks in and out," Dean said. I honestly didn't know what we would have done had Dean not been so generous with his time.

Jamie ran outside to start the engine and warm up the car. Soon I brought Matteo out and Dean showed us how to secure the car seat properly. Once Matteo was inside the car, there were long hugs. We could never thank Dean enough.

"Remember, Dads. By Maryland law, his birth mother has

thirty days during which she can change her mind and take him back," Dean impressed upon us.

I climbed into the backseat and slid in next to Matteo. As we pulled out of the driveway, snow began to fall around us.

"His first night and it's snowing," Jamie said blissfully.

I stared at Matteo, whose eyes were barely open but were peering back at me slightly.

"Hi, baby boy, I promise we will love you forever," I said.

"Is he okay?" Jamie kept asking. I could tell he was nervous, so was I. And he was driving at what felt like two miles an hour.

"He's great. Hey, I want to play 'Cherish' for him. It'll be his first song," I said.

I knew Jamie would agree; after all, it was Madonna. I picked up my iPhone and searched through *The Immaculate Collection*.

I had been eight years old in the back of Baboucarr's Jeep when, after walking Yael home from French pre-school, I had wondered what it would be like to be a father someday. As the intro to "Cherish" rose through the car, I could hear Baboucarr's deep voice singing along. I held Matteo's tiny hands in mine. Thousands of miles away from the shores of Africa, I wanted Matteo's first song to be a reminder of the incredible journey I had taken to get to him.

An hour later, we pulled up to the Residence Inn and the valets kindly opened our doors. They stared in amazement. I would have liked to explain, but we were hyper-focused on getting Matteo safely out of the car seat and into the hotel. We, two guys, had arrived hours earlier with enough luggage to move in for a month, and now we were coming through the doors with a newborn baby. I would have loved to hear what was discussed after the sliding glass doors shut.

Once in the hotel room, we placed a sleeping Matteo on a big blanket on the carpeted floor and set up our computer near him. Denice had run over to her sister's house in Rotterdam and they were all standing by to get their first glimpse of Matteo by camera. When the cameras came on, Denice stood there in her robe, proudly gleaming at her new grandson. I was happy I had told her of our plans to have a baby at the MLK Memorial that spring day. It had all happened so fast.

Around 10 p.m., Ebony walked into our hotel room, knelt down next to Matteo, and began to cry. I was floored. Ebony almost never cries. Even that morning in Amman when Dad sat the three of us in the living room to tell us Mom had died, Ebony hadn't cried.

She looked up at me, tears loosely running down her face. "I really wish Mom was here," she said. It had been what I'd been feeling, but to hear Ebony say it and, more, to see her cry for one of the first times in my life, my heart broke.

"I wish she was here too," I said, trying to steady my voice as my eyes moved between her and Matteo.

Later that night Jamie and I put Matteo into his bassinet and both climbed into bed. Two minutes later upon hearing the slightest sound, we were both back up, hovering over him and making sure he was okay. I am positive this must be what first-time parents, the world over, experience the very first night.

63

OBAMA'S RE-ELECTION

T HE NEXT MORNING, THE SNOW had disappeared and the bright sun came gliding through the red curtains of our hotel room, welcoming Matteo to his new life. We changed his diaper, took turns giving him a pre-made bottle of formula, awkwardly burped him, checked his diaper again, and carefully put on his onesie. Then Jamie and I took him in his carrier downstairs to breakfast. Sitting at breakfast, the three of us, it felt surreal. I looked across at Jamie, who was looking down at Matteo, beaming.

"Shit! It's election day," I said, realizing the date. Jamie knew how important voting was to me, to both of us. Jamie, far more organized than me, had voted early.

"You have to make a trip back to the house anyway today to get the rest of the things. Maybe you can vote while you're there?" Jamie suggested.

By law, because Matteo was born in Maryland, he was not allowed to cross state lines until Maryland cleared him to leave and the District of Columbia cleared him in. It is a kidnapping protection regulation that I was very glad was in existence. Jamie stayed with Matteo in Bethesda and I drove back to 11th Street. Over the afternoon hours I made my way to The Children's Place and bought Matteo a new wardrobe. Then I arrived at a school near our home that was also our voting precinct.

Shivering, I stood outside in line, waiting for my turn to vote. I reminded myself that I was lucky and should be grateful to live in a country where democracy exists. After all, I had watched as a child as South Africa struggled to give their citizens equality, witnessed Yahya Jammeh's insurgency take over The Gambia, and had a front-row seat to various Middle Eastern countries pretending to have freedom of speech and press while clearly they didn't. And yes, the United States had its problems; but overall, democracy was in action and there was, unquestionably, freedom of speech.

I was proud to live in a majority black city that was re-electing the nation's first black president. I thought of Barack Obama's story from a different angle as well. He was the first biracial president, born to a white mother, a black Kenyan father, and raised exclusively by his mother's side of the family. He had grown up mainly in Hawaii, and briefly in Indonesia with an Asian stepfather. Later, he went from that life to Columbia and Harvard.

Since I had lived in Hawaii, grown up internationally, and had been raised with white parents, I'd often wondered what his concept of race was growing up. And I wondered how he felt carrying the emblem of "The First Black President" when he himself was not raised in a culture around black people. Perhaps by the time he had married Michelle Obama, and had their beautiful girls, Malia and Sasha, his identity over time had shifted, now seeing black people so reflected in his immediate family, the people he no doubt loves the most.

Still standing in line, I thought further about it. What if people in Sri Lanka poured their faith into me around some extremely significant, emblematic issue, when at my core I had very little identity tied to Sri Lanka. I just very much looked the part. And yet, when I considered Barack Obama, I thought he was a figure who transcended race, certainly for me. I knew as many white friends in my life who loved him and what he represented as I did black friends. And in the end, that is largely why he has, and always will be, such a transformative leader.

New to DC and irresponsibly not having registered myself at Ebony's address, I had been so disappointed at not having been able to vote for him in 2008. Nothing was going to prevent me from voting for Barack Obama this time. On the contrary, I was even more determined to make sure my vote counted, both for myself and my biracial son. One day I would tell Matteo how the very first full day he was with us, I went back to DC to vote for Barack Obama. I would make sure he knew what Barack Obama meant not only to the United States but to the world. I thought of South Africa and Nelson Mandela. He had that global appeal as well.

I stepped up to my voting machine. I thought of Dad, who had canvassed vigorously for Obama in 2008, and Mom, who I knew would have loved him. Then I thought of Jamie holding Matteo in our hotel room and said quietly to myself, "This is for you, Matteo." I proudly voted for Barack Obama, then walked out into the icy November air.

That night, after our first family dinner, Jamie was rightfully exhausted and wanted to get some rest. I kissed him goodnight, taking Matteo in my arms.

"I know he's only three days old, but I want to stay up and hold him while I watch Obama get re-elected tonight," I said. Jamie smiled, knowing exactly who he'd married. It's hard to grow up around the world, with the awareness of injustice and inequality, and not feel deeply tied to politics.

I sat holding Matteo for hours as we watched the election results roll in from across the country. Just after 11 p.m., he and I watched as Wolf Blitzer announced, "CNN projects that Barack Obama will be re-elected president of the United States. He will remain in the White House for another four years because we project he will carry the state of Ohio. By carrying Ohio, he wins re-election. The president of the United States defeats Mitt Romney... They're excited in Chicago, they're excited in Times Square in New York, they're watching all over the world right now. The president of the United States has been re-elected."

People from across the United States celebrated another four years of a family who so many of us had come to love. I kissed Matteo repeatedly and told him I hoped for a much better future for him as a black man in this country. I remembered back to 2008, when I had sat at Ebony's house on 11th Street watching the results pour in by myself. And how when they announced his win, I had sprinted through the streets of Washington to join her, and the hours of partying and dancing along U Street that followed. I remembered Jamie and I calling each other as soon as he had landed in Indiana and how thrilled we were. On any other night I would have been at a big election party, drinking champagne and celebrating. But tonight I sat in our quiet hotel room, holding my newborn son, smiling through tears at the Obama win, and I was completely at peace.

I was sure that in Luling, Ashoh was having a funeral.

64

THE CALL

TEN DAYS AFTER THAT SNOWY evening when we had first met Matteo, we had finally settled into what I can only characterize as parenthood by trial and error. We had both gotten fast at changing diapers and making bottles. Burping still felt strange, and I turned over my right shoulder to look at our son after every couple whacks on the back. Still not permitted by Maryland to move back into DC, we were starting to consider the Residence Inn home, becoming very friendly with a number of the staff at breakfast and, of course, the valets. And while we still had twenty days to wait until his birth mother's window to change her mind closed, there was no halfway to love this little boy. We had completely fallen for him.

One morning as we were in our hotel room playing with Matteo, the phone rang.

"Hi, Dean," I said, hoping it was the news allowing us to move back to Columbia Heights.

"Hi, boys. The birth mother just called," Dean said.

Jamie and I turned to each other with blank expressions. My heart plummeted.

"When I saw her name come up on my caller ID, I froze."

I looked at Matteo in my arms.

"But, guess what? She said, 'Dean, I'm calling because I wanted to make sure that the child went to a family who will love him. I'm just worried that no one will want him because he's biracial.'"

Jamie and I took a collective giant sigh of relief.

"Anytime any birth mother has ever called me this soon after, it's because they've changed their mind and want the child back," Dean added.

"Did she say anything else? Did she want to know what family he went to?" I asked.

"No. Here's what I told her. I said, 'You have no idea how happy the family is. They are over the moon!' If only she knew that he went to an interracial family and how much you guys love him. But I couldn't tell her that because, remember, she doesn't want to know," Dean said.

We thanked Dean for calling and hung up. Jamie and I looked to each other and then to Matteo. I felt horrible that his birth mother was worried that no one would want him because he was biracial. How, in 2012, in a cosmopolitan area just outside DC, was someone worried that a biracial child wouldn't be accepted? As a country, the United States had just re-elected a biracial president to the White House. It saddened me that this white woman had to endure the very difficult decision to place her child for adoption. Then, clearly, she had sat at home for days worrying that no one wanted him because he was of color. Obama's re-election win had felt like significant progress, but perhaps we had not come as far as I had imagined. I wished she had known who we were. That her child now had a brown Sri Lankan-American father and a white Italian-American father. That while he also had white grandparents, he had an Asian aunt and a white uncle born in Africa.

On the other hand, her call gave us and Dean an exceedingly high level of confidence that she would not call again and take Matteo back. Now we just had to wait for our lawyers to make a good-faith effort to advertise and search for Matteo's birth father. Adoption isn't easy.

65

FINESSE

DCA IS BUILT ON A RELATIVELY small manmade island in the Potomac River and moves about one thousand airplanes a day. To put it in perspective, you can turn the airport on its side and it will fit between two of the runways at Washington's international airport, Washington Dulles (IAD). What does that mean? Well, Dulles works just about the same amount of airplanes with triple or more the space. If you are a controller at DCA, moving these airplanes from runways to gates, and from gates to runways, you are weaving these airplanes in and out of one another in a way that I can only describe as a giant, high-speed game of chess.

It is not uncommon during the morning departure-and-arrival rush at DCA to look out the window and see forty-two airplanes in parallel lines trying to cross three active runways to get where they need to go. You have to memorize which ones are departures and which are arrivals, and it is entirely possible for even the most seasoned controllers to, as we say in air traffic control, *go down the shitter,* or lose your mental map of where each aircraft is and needs to be. While this all happens to us at one point or another, we are extremely well trained to climb out of it and piece it all back together in seconds. That is what makes an air traffic controller. This ability to pull a lost picture back together in seconds, keeping thousands of lives safe while working at hundreds of miles an hour.

After my hours of training and moving hundreds of airplanes, I would eventually take a break and sit back, watching others work. DCA is home to about thirty controllers—thirty men and women who move all the air traffic in and out of the capital of the United States—and I was extremely proud to be one of them. There were a number of excellent controllers there. Connie Thompson Jr. was one: a black guy about my height from Maryland, with an upbeat personality and who, strangely enough, was formerly the assistant to Supreme Court Justice John Paul Stevens. He controlled airplanes expertly and with such a tranquil ability. I watched Connie work often and learned as much as I could from his decision making and timing. He, too, had earned his degree in political science before arriving in air traffic control, something that was rare. We talked often about American politics while staring at The White House from two-hundred-plus feet in the air.

But by far my personal favorite to watch was a five-foot-three black woman who stood out because of her impeccable style. Her modest nature often made her the quieter person in the tower. Her name was Shanora Washington, and she had come to Washington Tower from Philadelphia Approach Control. She had it all. She moved airplanes in the air and on the ground, spitting out rapid-fire instructions with style, grace, and acute accuracy. Other controllers were able to control fast and with accuracy, but she added an extra layer of class to the way in which she controlled. As she spoke to each pilot, she was polite but extremely commanding. She was decisive but gentle in a way that made the pilots enjoy being controlled by her. It was that little bit of finesse that attracted me to her. When Shanora controlled, it was like watching the synchronicity of a conductor move an orchestra to exquisite perfection.

"Can I sit next to you, watch you work, and ask some questions?" I asked her one evening.

"Of course you can," Shanora said as she cleared the area in front of her.

"Are you going to roll United with the time to Chicago first, or launch the Embraer off of Runway one-five since there are three helicopters coming up the river at the same altitude?" I asked.

"I'm going to roll United to hit the slot time into Chicago, have the helicopters expedite up the river, and then launch the Embraer off Runway one-five behind them," she said confidently.

I watched her plan play out perfectly. Learning how to create plans on the fly that protect hundreds of lives in real time is what makes air traffic controllers unique.

"I see your Delta 737 coming down the river five miles out, descending out of fifteen hundred. Can you slow him there to get a departure out?" I asked.

"I can't slow him now because look behind him. That JetBlue Airbus is four miles behind him with a thirty-knot overtake. I'll lose my spacing there if I reduce Delta to their final approach speed, so I'm going to have to forfeit the departure, land both Delta and JetBlue, and then clear American for takeoff."

Shanora seamlessly switched to instructing the Delta pilots: "Delta 1253, plan minimal time on the runway for traffic close in behind you tonight."

Without batting an eye, she gave me thoughtful, intelligent, well-communicated answers while also moving helicopters effortlessly around airplanes. In a male-dominated profession, it was clear to me that Shanora Washington was a virtuoso. I wanted to be as great a controller as she was. And I made it my mission to be.

AFTER TWO WEEKS in Maryland, we got word from Dean that we were permitted by both Maryland and DC to return to our home in Columbia Heights with Matteo.

At 6 p.m. each evening, with a glass of Tempranillo in one hand and Matteo snuggled in my lap, we sat on our front steps, as I had always loved, and watched the city wind down. Friends who lived around the neighborhood would stop by and ask to hold Matteo. After cradling him in their arms and asking thoughtful questions about our adoption process, they continued on into El Chucho, the tequila bar three doors down, or Redrocks, the pizza place two doors in the other direction. Jamie, Matteo, and I settled nicely into what now felt more like a home than ever before. In the back of my mind, however, I knew our lawyers were still searching for his birth father, and we hoped nothing would come of that. Next year, we would be able to finalize Matteo's adoption.

A month later, I was at the tower when I learned there had been a horrific shooting at Sandy Hook Elementary School in Newtown, Connecticut. *At an elementary school?* Once on break, I made my way to the nearest TV and watched as the news coverage unfolded. Had the United States really reached a point where elementary students were now being murdered in their own classrooms? I felt like throwing up. For years the debate over gun regulation had gone round and round, with few changes made. I watched in horror as video of FBI agents escorting crying children across parking lots flashed across the screen. The images instantly transported me back to The Gambia. I remembered how terrified I had been at eight years old to have Yahya Jammeh's machine gun pointed at me outside the butcher shop.

I didn't want to imagine what these children went through in their last moments in their classrooms. Aside from giving instructions to pilots, I spoke very little for the rest of the day. Later, I watched as President Obama wiped away tears through his press conference in Newtown, saying, "The majority of those who died today were children. Beautiful little kids between the ages of five and ten years old. They had their entire lives ahead of them, birthdays, graduations, weddings, kids of their own."

I knew I worked alongside quite a few people who were steadfast National Rifle Association (NRA) supporters. I never understood it. I often wondered, Had they ever had a gun pointed at them? I doubted it. Because if they had, as I had, they would know exactly how powerless, how terrifying, how horrific it feels. I imagine they wouldn't want to continue to support an organization that allows for money to be fueled into furthering the prevalence of guns, with very little regulation. Naturally, I thought of Matteo and wondered what world we were raising him in. I hoped that Sandy Hook would be the start of massive gun regulation. I was wrong.

66

ARE YOU SPANISH OR ITALIAN?

O N CHRISTMAS EVE, I FOUND MYSELF once again at Jamie's grandmother's home. This year, instead of me, Matteo was the new brown person. Barbara and Denice and her three sisters fawned over the latest addition to their family. I don't think any of them ever expected Jamie to have a baby. Barbara and I sat more comfortably together on the sofa now than we had two years prior. I made sure not to mention anything about her medical history.

"Garon, would you like some wine?" Barbara asked thoughtfully.

"Absolutely. Thanks so much, Barbara," I said, smiling and making a beeline for the kitchen. This time I had prepared by bringing over my own bottles of Malbec. Denice had promised to drink some with me later. I looked over next to the microwave. A box of Franzia sat well positioned, waiting for its first attendant.

I returned to the living room with my glass of wine and resumed my seat on the sofa. I noticed out of the corner of my eye that once in a while one of the aunts would walk into a bedroom on the first floor and wave one of the cousins in. Jamie slid onto the sofa beside me. Denice was proudly carrying

Matteo around the house she had grown up in.

"What's the deal with Aunt Jayne waving Samantha into that bedroom over there?" I asked him.

Jamie laughed. "So that's the room where, if one of the aunts buys an *extra* gift for one of the cousins, and they don't want *another* cousin to feel bad, they quietly give it to them in there."

"Okay. But, I mean, everyone can see that. It's not that secretive," I said, trying hard to understand why it was all a secret to begin with.

"Remember, Garon, *everything* on this side of the family is a big secret. You *have* to give everyone the exact same number of presents. And if you decide to give someone one more, then you have to give it to them secretly in that room," he said, rolling his eyes. "It's been this way since I was a kid."

"Interesting," I said, sipping my Malbec. It was an early truth I learned about Denice's side of the family: as long as it wasn't talked about, it wasn't happening.

Later in the week, Denice and Sherman wanted to take us to one of their favorite Italian places in Rotterdam. With Matteo in his carrier sleeping under the table, we devoured a wonderful assortment of lasagna, rigatoni, and capellini dishes. I continued asking more questions about Jamie's childhood in this tiny town, still amazed that he had spent his first eighteen years in Rotterdam.

"So you guys had the same high-school teachers?" I asked, imagining how strange that would have been to think of one of my teachers at ACS Amman teaching Mom or Dad when they were younger.

"Oh yes. We both had Mr. Zentz for chemistry," said Denice.

"And we both had Mr. Oppedisano for computer science," said Jamie.

380

"I think back when I had him, he was my math teacher. Garon, we also both worked at Glenn Sanders Mansion," added Denice.

"What's that?" I asked.

"It's an old mansion that sits on the Mohawk River with a bar, restaurant, and banquet hall," Jamie said. "I worked there when I was sixteen. Mom worked in the restaurant at night after finishing her two other day jobs."

"I worked there one season so I would have enough Christmas money," Denice said.

"Christmas money?" I asked.

"Yes, I worked there to be able to make enough money to buy Jamie and Melissa Christmas presents."

My heart sank. I imagined Mom or Dad having to work extra jobs to be able to buy us Christmas gifts. Jamie and I had grown up in *completely* different worlds. While I was hanging out at opulent ambassadors' residences at sixteen, Jamie was working as a busser in banquet halls. All across the world, we always had enough, more than enough. Denice's impressive work ethic and hustle to make ends meet endeared her to me far more than any ambassador I had ever spent time with.

Once dinner was complete, and after playfully fighting over the check, we all got up to leave. Jamie, carrying the diaper bag, walked slightly ahead with Denice and Sherman, and I held Matteo in his carrier. Just as we were stepping away from the table, two men and a woman who had been sitting beside us waved in my direction.

"Excuse me," one of the guys said. He was every bit the Italian guy from New York, who one would cast in a film. Accent and everything.

I looked behind me. *Is he talking to me?*

"Yes?" I said, still unsure if it was me he was waving at.

"We got a question for you," he said.

"Okay, sure. What's up?" I said. Jamie was now standing at the front of the restaurant, looking in our direction with a perplexed look on his face.

"Where are you from?" he asked. The three of them leaned forward, awaiting my response.

"Oh. I was adopted from Sri Lanka," I said, understanding that they hadn't seen someone who looked like me before and were politely curious.

"Are you Spanish or Italian?" he asked, palms facing upward, gesturing forward.

I stared at them blankly. Maybe he hadn't heard me.

"I'm from *Sri Lanka*," I repeated, thinking that maybe the adoption part threw them off.

"Yea. But are you Spanish or Italian?" he asked again. The three of them stared in my direction intently.

I had no idea what to say, still standing there, holding Matteo in his carrier.

"I. Um. I'm. So, I was born in Sri Lanka, so I'm not Spanish or Italian," I said with a slight smile, trying to lighten the situation.

The three of them just stared back at me in silence, seeming to be gravely confused by my answer.

"Okay, it was nice talking to you guys. I hope you have a great dinner," I offered and then turned with Matteo to walk out.

When I got to the front door, Jamie had a concerned look on his face.

"What was that about?" he asked, taking Matteo.

"They wanted to know if I was Spanish or Italian," I said.

Jamie laughed knowingly. "What did you say?"

"I told them I was adopted from Sri Lanka, but I don't think they knew where that was.

"Trust me, they didn't," Jamie said, amused.

"Spanish or Italian, huh? Are those the only two options here?" I asked with a grin.

Jamie laughed. "Yes. And by the way, when they say Spanish, they mean Puerto Rican."

I looked at him quizzically. I still had a lot to learn about this small American town.

BACK IN WASHINGTON, where I could be more than just Spanish or Italian, my social life had quickly exploded.

I met three controllers whom I became extremely close with. There was Angela Hudson, a feisty girl from a small town in Indiana who loved airplanes as much as I did and was the life of any party. Angela was the daughter of a pastor. Growing up, she hadn't been allowed to cut her hair, use makeup, or wear anything but dresses. Now, living life in the big city, she was making up for lost time. I loved being around her. One night after getting out of the tower late, five of us went out to Carmine's, an Italian eatery in Gallery Place. Angela and I had three too many drinks. At the time, she was single and our waiter was a tall, handsome Central American guy with midnight-black hair.

"Where are you from?" Angela asked our waiter in an attempt to flirt.

"I'm from Panama," he replied professionally.

Angela turned to the table. "That's so cool, guys, he's Pomeranian."

I turned to the waiter, who looked confused, and awkwardly thanked him for his patience. Then I reached across the table to grasp Angela's hand and said, "Girl, Pomeranian is a dog. He's *Panamanian.*"

We all erupted in laughter. So did Angela. That was one of the things I loved about her most. She could always laugh at herself. And she was a damn good controller.

Patrick Barnes arrived at Washington Tower far differently than everyone else. In his mid-twenties he had been diagnosed with a rare form of cancer and received treatment at the National Institutes of Health. Patrick's doctors had initially told him he had a twenty percent chance of living. But he made it. Once recovered, instead of returning to his stable but boring desk job, he decided to go on the unknown journey to become an air traffic controller. Patrick and I logged endless miles walking the main terminal at DCA. We talked about our lives before the tower. When he would recount his days playing college football, I would tell him that I had no idea what he was talking about. When I would tell him of being chased by an elephant in South Africa or riding across the Syrian desert, Patrick would say, "Garon, I bet this is all a lie and you really just grew up in Ohio." Being with Patrick reminded me of my friendship so many years before with JJ and Saleem.

And finally there was Sherene Sumner. Sherene had been a controller at the Pentagon before leaving the military to join the civilian service. She had been raised in Jamaica, and oftentimes we would reminisce about living on the island at the same time, though we didn't know each other then, of course. When Sherene got annoyed at pilots not following her instructions quickly, her Jamaican patois would come out. I'd stand next to her controlling, laughing hysterically as soon as I heard, "American 573, tun left nah." The very first time I had ever spoken with Sherene, she was sitting in a chair in our lounge casually staring my way.

"Why did you want to come to Washington Tower?" I asked her.

Without missing a beat, she looked over at me and confidently said, "Because I want to be a big-girl controller."

I liked her right way.

67

THE 57TH INAUGURATION

HEY. DOM HAS AN EXTRA TICKET *to the inauguration. Wanna come with us?* It was a text from Ebony.

I texted back right away. *Are you kidding? Yea! That's so nice of him.*

Dom, as we called him, or Dominic Lowell, was a good friend of Ebony. He worked for Democracy Alliance, an organization whose mission is to advance the progressive movement in American politics. I was very grateful for his kindness, and on January 21, 2013, I stood next to Ebony, Dom, and a number of their friends in the frigid air on the National Mall, facing the US Capitol Building. A lively and robust celebration was underway. Jamie had offered to stay home with Matteo so I could go. It was a wonderful continuation of our evening in November when I had held Matteo in my arms and watched as Obama had been re-elected.

To both Ebony and me, Washington had, over many years, very quietly become our new home. Not home in the sense of a place where one lives, but home in the sense of a place where we belonged. All the countries we had moved to and from around the world as kids had a special place in our hearts. But after leaving high school and college, we were, in essence, homeless. There was no family home to go back to in the summers where we had once grown up. DC, with its cutthroat ambition, had oddly found its way into our hearts.

"Ladies and gentlemen, please welcome Kelly Clarkson," the announcer's voice boomed over the mall.

"Kelly Clarkson?" I said to Ebony. "Wasn't she on *American Idol?*"

"Yea. She has an amazing voice," Ebony said. At the time, I wasn't familiar.

Kelly Clarkson walked up to the microphone wearing a brilliant purple scarf that contrasted with her blond locks, and within seconds her arresting soulful voice rang out. Chills moved up my back as I looked in all directions at the people around me. Everyone was completely transfixed by this woman's incomparable version of "My Country Tis of Thee." It's not hyperbolic to say that her voice flowed with an exquisite, controlled force from the Capitol Building to Lincoln, and then floated above Washington. It resounded in the hearts of the sea of people who, like me, filled with emotion. To this day, it remains one of my favorite live performances.

Later, when Obama took the oath of office, with Michelle Obama and their daughters by his side, I looked forward to what the next four years might bring personally, professionally, and for the country. I also worried that we, the world, would be faced with horrible acts of terrorism and discord. I wondered where we would all be standing at the end of the Obama Administration.

"Dom wants to know if you want to come to a party?" Ebony said, leaning over to me. I was always up for a party. But I also thought of Jamie and Matteo at home and wondered if Jamie needed a break. As we filed out of the mall, I called Jamie and asked him how he was doing.

"Go have fun. It's freezing outside and we're just hanging out here in the warmth," he said. I thanked Jamie and followed our crew as we walked gleefully through the throngs of people, many headed indoors for warm drinks, alcohol, or both. After much walking and shivering, we found our event on F Street between 14th and 15th. I looked up: it was the W Hotel. A long line had formed on F Street that led into a security checkpoint. We joined the end of the line and felt grateful that soon enough we would be in the warmth of the W's lobby.

"So, are we just going to the lobby bar, or is it a party in one of the hotel ballrooms?" I asked Ebony.

"I'm not sure. I think it might be in one of the ballrooms," she said.

I imagined a ballroom with a number of large flat-screen TVs. We would be able to watch the customary walk the president makes from the Capitol Building, down Pennsylvania Avenue, leading directly to the White House, also known as the inaugural parade. Every four years, masses of people line the streets, braving DC's freezing January weather to get a glimpse of the motorcade. At some point the president gets out of the limo and walks a portion of the way, which is always the most exciting part. I was imagining how this might all play out when suddenly Ebony grabbed my arm.

"Garon, look who is standing directly in front of us in this line!" Ebony whispered excitedly. Anyone who knows me knows that I am not the best person to do this with, which is why I was surprised Ebony would even try this with me. Once, on a very crowded train, Jamie had turned to me and said, "Garon, don't say a word, but look at that guy's foot behind us." Instinctively, I whirled around and urgently and in full voice said, "Who's foot? Where?" My eyes landed on the man sitting directly behind me who had elephantiasis of his foot. I felt a deep sense of shame as my eyes met his and everyone else around us was now looking as well. I whipped back around to see a bright-red Jamie clutching his face and pretending not to know me. But, back to the W security line.

I peered into the lofty black trench coat of the five-foot-one woman standing in front of us. She wore big glasses and was staring into her phone, texting.

"Who is it?" I whispered back.

"It's America Ferrera!" Ebony whisper-yelled at me. I would love to tell you that I'm not one to get starstruck, but the truth is, regrettably, I do. It's not really even a choice.

"Are you fucking kidding me?" I whisper-yelled back. I took one step to the side to view her profile. "Oh my god, it *is* America Ferrera!" I said, knocking myself into Ebony's shoulder.

"Okay, shut up," Ebony said back in the exact way that older sisters tell their younger brothers. I couldn't believe we were standing in line behind actor America Ferrera. I had watched all four seasons of *Ugly Betty* numerous times. As I was convincing myself not to be super excited and that I was a mature person who respected other people's privacy, suddenly it was as if the Hollywood gods forced their powers upon me. I looked up from America's trench coat and whisking out of the lobby doors, walking directly toward us, was journalist Gayle King laughing alongside New Jersey Senator Cory Booker.

"Ebony, it's Gayle King and Cory Booker," I said, pinching her arm. The wonderful thing about being in these situations with Ebony is that while she, too, wants to pretend that she is a mature person who is not starstruck, she absolutely, without question, gets as starstruck as me. It makes the entire debacle even more fun. Our eyes followed Gayle and Cory as they walked right past us, assumedly on their way to another inauguration party.

As I turned back around to see America Ferrera, Ebony slammed her leg into me.

"Look to my left!" she said.

"My left?" I asked, looking left and right, already losing control.

"No, idiot, *my* left," she said.

I looked to the left and there standing against the side of the W nonchalantly in a white trench coat and brown glasses was Rosario Dawson. I was done. She looked radiant. Ebony and I, both now screaming internally with excitement, stopped talking and focused on breathing ourselves back into being normal, rational, mature adults. By the time we had gathered ourselves, America Ferrera had been called forward by security to walk through the metal detector. We followed, and soon enough we were in the warmth of the W lobby.

It was packed with people with red cheeks and equally bright noses who were reveling in their warmer surroundings. I followed Ebony and her friends into an elevator. We stopped at a number of floors, people got in, people got out, and then finally we were ushered out and down a long hallway. *I guess we're not going to a ballroom*, I thought. As we reached the end of the hallway, the door swung open and we were invited in.

I took me about five seconds to understand where we were. A luxury corner suite with magnificent vistas of Pennsylvania Avenue and the inaugural parade down below ran one length of the room. On the other side, 15th Street, which runs parallel to the South Lawn of the White House, bordered us. My eyes moved around the grand suite. In the corner was an enormous flat-screen TV reflecting what I could see very closely out the window. Off my right, the living room flowed into a white linen bedroom, where a few people were quietly sitting on the edge of the bed drinking champagne. Waiters moved around the room offering more champagne and light food to celebrate. It had been kind of Dom to invite me to the inauguration. But to also extend this invitation into this suite, which offered undoubtedly one of the best views in Washington of the inaugural parade—that was exceptional.

Ebony and I thanked the waiter who handed us two glasses of champagne and then made our way to the giant windows overlooking Penn Avenue. We had arrived just in time. Joe Biden and his wife, Dr. Jill Biden, were walking just below us, waving to the crowds lining the streets. The vice-president ran up at times to the edge of the crowd to shake hands with young children. I shifted my gaze from them, up to the TV, and back out the frosty window to the Bidens.

I looked over at Ebony. We were thousands of miles away from that remote beach on the west coast of Africa where we had boogie boarded each Saturday night, smashing into the waves as Lionel Richie's voice rose in the air over the Gambian shore. We drank Fanta, nestled close to Mom, Dad, and Yael, and watched as the orange sun brought the tiny African country into darkness. I'm not sure in those days that we could have ever guessed we would be standing together in Washington above an American president's inauguration. I missed those days in The Gambia as much as I enjoyed this moment. And I knew I would always remember it.

68

ASHOH'S BIG DECISION

"HOW'S THE BABY?" ASHOH ASKED, still apparently unable to pronounce *Matteo*.

"He's great, Ashoh. He's three months old now and we take turns waking up with him throughout the night."

"Lord, I bet he keeps y'all busy."

"Do you remember when Mom, Uncle Robby, and Uncle Mike were that small?" I asked.

"Heavens, yes! Oh, I was so tired, Garon," she said with a laugh.

I thought this was as good a time as any to tell her the reason I called.

"Hey, Ashoh."

"Yea?"

"Listen, I know that when I asked you before if Jamie and I could come for Christmas you said you didn't think it was such a good idea. But we are coming down to Louisiana with Matteo. We're coming down with Ebony and Dad and Yael to spend some time there. So, if you want to see us, then we are going to be there. If you don't want to see us, then that's fine, but you need to decide."

The expected pause came and went.

"Come on down," she said.

"Come down?" I said, surprised. I had prepared myself for a disappointing answer. "I'll be there with Jamie and Matteo."

"Yes. All three of y'all come down and see us. I think that'll be fine," she said. "I'll tell Grandpa."

I had expected this to be a much more difficult conversation. It had been two years since she'd told me I couldn't come, and it had hurt.

"I can't wait to see the baby, Garon."

"And I can't wait for Matteo to meet you, Ashoh."

I wondered what had changed.

69
NOT HUSBAND AND WIFE

BONY AND I RAN WITH MATTEO through the Baltimore airport. I always tried to fly out of DCA since I had a parking space right by the tower and because it was so much closer to home. However, the only flights we had been able to find that matched our schedules were out of BWI. Jamie was working in Fort Walton Beach and would meet us in Charlotte to connect onto New Orleans together. Our train and bus that took us up to Baltimore had taken much longer than anticipated, and here we were, scrambling through the airport, desperately trying to make our flight. As we approached the TSA agent, I cradled Matteo in my one arm, had the diaper bag on my shoulder, and rolled my carry-on to a quick stop.

"Do you have the tickets?" I asked Ebony, who was standing there, waiting for me to pull them out.

"Shit!" she said, starting to rifle through her red carry-on. The security agent waited patiently.

"C'mon, Ebony, I'm carrying everything. Can you just keep track of the tickets? We're going to miss our flight."

Ebony pulled out three tickets, along with our IDs, and handed them to the agent. He scanned our tickets and glanced between our IDs and our faces. "Hey, you need to be more patient with her. She gave you the best gift. The gift of a new life," he said, pointing at Matteo, whose head was snuggled up against my chest.

Ebony and I looked at each other in complete disgust. "No, man, she's my sister."

"Oh!" he said, his face flushing bright red as he swiftly handed back our tickets and waved us through.

Once on the other side of security, Ebony and I looked at each other again and snickered.

"That's so disgusting that people think we're together," she said. "Ughh."

"Yea, ugh. I could obviously do so much better than you."

"Shut up, Garon!" she said, laughing, and we continued racing toward our gate.

The final boarding call was announced just as we arrived at our gate completely out of breath. As we boarded, Ebony glanced through the tickets and I tried to hustle toward our seats, feeling badly that all the other passengers were already seated, ready and waiting to go.

"We're not seated together," she said.

"That's fine. Let's just get to our seats. It's not that long of a flight." Matteo would be sitting on my lap since he was under two years of age and I would connect with Ebony again once we landed in Charlotte.

Suddenly a flight attendant approached us. "Where are you all seated?"

"Oh, we're in two different seats. It's totally fine," I assured her.

She put her hand against her chest. "Oh my, look at this adorable little baby. No, I can't do this, I'm going to fix this." Then she turned to the entire cabin and in a loud voice said,

"Would anyone be willing to give up two seats together so that this adorable young family with their baby boy can sit together?"

Ebony and I quickly looked at each other, knowing that we couldn't show the slightest disgust as everyone stared onward at us. We needed to play the role being bestowed on us: a happily married couple with their child.

"Not a problem at all," a woman and her husband said, climbing into the aisle.

"Oh, you're so generous," the flight attendant announced and then turned to us. "I couldn't let such a cute family like you three be separated from each other."

"Thank you so much," I said with a gracious smile. Around us, other passengers were smiling as I handed Matteo off to Ebony and climbed into my seat. Then she passed him back to me. Once all buckled in, I looked over at my sister.

"Why does everyone think we're a couple?" she whisper-asked, mirroring my thoughts. "So a Filipina and a Sri Lankan magically had a black and white baby?"

"It's a progressive new world. They probably think we adopted him. I mean, he is actually adopted," I whisper-replied.

Once we got to Charlotte, and still with a tight connection, we power-walked to the neighboring concourse to catch our flight to New Orleans. Jamie texted me to let me know he was already onboard.

(Me) *We're not seated together. Do you want Matteo to sit on your lap, or my lap?*

(Jamie) *He can sit on my lap for this flight. I'm sure you'd like a break anyway.*

Perfect. I would take the offer. As we arrived at the New Orleans departure area, we boarded our flight and I handed

Matteo off to Jamie. I hadn't seen him for a number of days and it was always a pleasure to see his handsome smiling face. Then Ebony and I, who were actually seated together, took our seats and, once airborne and well on our way, ordered two gin and tonics.

"Cheers," she said, touching her drink to mine. It had been many years since the two of us had traveled together. As children, we had flown all over the world side by side with Mom and Dad and Yael. It felt great.

"I still love flying as much as I did as a kid," Ebony said.

"Me too. I still get that rush. I wonder if it's because we flew so much as kids that it continues to hold that sense of adventure for us?" I asked.

"For sure. Imagine how many flights we took around the globe. Mom and Dad always made it so fun, like there was a great new world waiting for us on the other side."

"Yea, I miss them together." I closed my eyes for a moment and saw Mom and Dad seated. They handed us little gifts that they had picked out to keep us entertained as we flew from Africa or the Middle East into Europe on one of our many adventurous summer vacations.

"You guys ready to fly?" Dad would ask excitedly.

"Are you comfortable, honey?" Mom would say.

And onward we would go, to start our holiday in Luxembourg, Andorra, or the former Czechoslovakia.

Those were the days.

I CLIMBED OUT of the rental car and, cradling Matteo in my arms, stepped onto the same red-brick walkway that I had sprinted up each summer, barely able to contain my excitement at the prospect of seeing Ashoh and Grandpa. The thick Louisiana humidity had given life to crawling green moss that sprung from the cracks in the brick pathway. The sun's rays baked the pavement and heat rose around the liriope that I had run my hands through as a kid. As we neared the yellow door, I heard Ashoh's voice.

"They're here! Garon's here with the baby!" she yelled through the house in exactly the same way she had always yelled, "Niki and the kids are here!"

As the door swung open, I watched as Ashoh's hazel eyes filled with tears. Her daughter's first grandchild stared back at her as she gently took his hand in hers and studied his face.

"What a precious little baby," she said as I gave her a hug and a kiss on the cheek. Behind her, Grandpa was standing in the doorway to the kitchen.

"Hey, Rambo," he said with a big smile.

"Hi, Grandpa," I said, still holding Matteo and putting my other arm around him. I was far taller than him now.

"I see we have a little man here," he said, looking at Matteo.

"Say hi, Matteo, this is your great-grandfather," I whispered, kissing Matteo's cheek.

I looked behind me as Ebony was hugging Ashoh and making her way over to Grandpa.

Jamie approached the door, rolling our bags.

"Guys, this is . . ." I started.

"Well, you must be Jamie. Lord, Garon, he's so tall," Ashoh said, laughing as Jamie leaned down to hug her and she tried to reach up and embrace him.

I watched as he made his way to Grandpa. Moment of truth.

"Hey, Jamie, I'm Petie," Grandpa said, still smiling and shaking his hand. Well, that didn't seem strange at all. In fact,

Grandpa seemed extremely relaxed and happy to meet Jamie.

Once we put our bags down, we all piled into the kitchen and sat around the same oval table where I had learned how to peel boiled seafood.

"Jamie, is this your first time to Louisiana?" Ashoh asked.

"No, I've been here before," he said as Matteo climbed onto his lap. "I worked for the Red Cross briefly, and after Hurricane Katrina I was helping out here."

"What part of Louisiana did you go to?"

"I was only in Baton Rouge. It's really nice to see another part of Louisiana, and especially to be here in Luling since Garon has told me so much about it over the years."

"Oh, Jamie. I used to count down the days until they would come flying back here with their mama and daddy from Africa and all over the world," Ashoh said.

"Coming to Louisiana was always the highlight of our summers," Ebony added.

"And how are you, Grandpa?" I asked. He was standing up against the door to the adjoining garage, with an unlit cigarette in one hand and a beer in the other, just as he had in all those years before.

"Well, I'm still married to your Ashoh, so I can't say I'm doing that well," he said, straight-faced.

"Oh hush, Petie!" Ashoh said. "Jamie, he likes to pretend he doesn't like me, but he couldn't live without me." We all laughed. I was glad after so many years that they still had their schtick down. Jamie smiled and I could tell he was reliving all the stories I had ever told him of Ashoh and Grandpa, now able to hear their southern accents and see their faces.

"And look at that precious baby. Isn't he the cutest, Ebony?" Ashoh cooed. By this time, Matteo had wiggled into his aunt's lap and was pushing her long black hair between his fingers.

"He and I are best friends," Ebony said. "A couple times a week on my way home from work, I stop by their house and we sit on the porch together," she said, pulling Matteo closer to her.

"That's so nice that y'all live on the same street," Ashoh said.

"Yea, remember when we lived at 1co Bernice, Ashoh?" I said. "I loved living down the street from you."

"Lord, Jamie, Garon ran me ragged that year. He would come over here and try to challenge me on just about everything. He about drove me crazy. I was always hollerin' at him," Ashoh said, laughing.

"She's been hollerin' at me for sixty-somethin' years," Grandpa said slyly from the corner.

"I holler at you because you deserve it, Petie," Ashoh shot back. They should have had their own show. Suddenly a car pulled up out front.

"Oh look! Your daddy's here with little Yael," Ashoh announced, peering through her front kitchen window onto Bernice Drive.

Dad had flown in from Europe to spend some time down the bayou with cousins on his side of the family. Yael had driven over from Austin, where he was still living after college, had spent a couple days with Dad, and then the two of them had driven here to Luling.

Grandpa followed Ashoh to the door to greet Dad and Yael. Soon we were all crammed around the kitchen table, hugging each other, and within seconds Dad swooped over to pick up Matteo. I watched carefully as he lifted up his grandson for the very first time. He has always adored babies and I could see the love in his eyes as he held Matteo, making funny faces at him. Since Matteo's birth in November, Dad had only seen him via a camera from

Europe. I was surprised that given all the countries we'd lived in, and with our home base in DC and his in Europe, that Dad was meeting his grandson for the very first time in his native Louisiana. There was something serendipitous about that.

"It's great to see you," I said, holding Yael's hand. I had seen him months before when he had flown to Washington to spend Thanksgiving with us.

"You too, bro. I love that we're all back here at Ashoh and Grandpa's together."

"Where do y'all want to go eat?" Ashoh asked.

"Spahrs!" Ebony and Yael said in unison.

"Yea, let's go to Spahrs," I added.

WE TOOK OVER a long table at Spahr's, our favorite restaurant near Luling, where twenty-one years before Mom had taught me that in America people say *napkins* instead of *serviettes*. It looked much the same, with its floor-to-ceiling windows overlooking the bayou out back. Parents with their children stood close to the edge of the marshy water hoping for an alligator sighting.

"I'm so happy to see you," Dad said from across the table.

"Yea, it's really cool to all be together here in Louisiana." I hadn't seen him for eight months, since our wedding in Fort Lauderdale, and he looked well. "Are you still doing laps in the Mediterranean throughout the week?"

"Sure am. I swim about two miles a day. Well, when the weather's warm. It's been chilly lately."

Grandpa was sitting next to Jamie and Dad. Ashoh and I were closer to Ebony and Yael. I played with Matteo, hoping to give Jamie and Grandpa a chance to talk. From everything Ashoh had said during our phone conversation that day, I imagined that Grandpa would be more standoffish or reserved with Jamie, but he wasn't at all. In fact, it seemed to me that it was the opposite. Grandpa was exceedingly comfortable talking to my husband, and I wondered if Ashoh had projected her own fears upon him for years. The waitress came over to our table and lined it with fried catfish, shrimp po-boys, gumbo, red beans and rice, and crawfish etouffee.

"Well, it's sure nice to be sitting here in Louisiana with all of you," Ashoh said. "Let's eat."

Jamie and Grandpa were lost in conversation. I dug into my catfish and fries and kissed Matteo's head. "Matteo, guess what? When I was small, Grandma Niki and Grandpa would bring us here in the summers. Sometimes we'd play outside while we waited for the food to come and watch the staff feed leftovers to the gators." He was too young to understand me, but I told him nonetheless. Then out of the corner of my eye I saw a sight I had never expected to see. Grandpa was cutting his catfish into smaller pieces and placing them on Jamie's plate.

"Here, Jamie, try some of mine," he said. Jamie glanced down at me and I nodded lovingly at him. I knew from a lifetime of hanging out with Grandpa that this was Grandpa's way of showing Jamie love. Aside from his jokes, he was a quieter man. And while he never would have come outright and said, "I love you" to anyone, when Grandpa shared his food with you, or his alcohol, that was his way of showing that he very much cared for you. With the simple act of sharing his catfish, he had indicated to Jamie that he liked him, was glad he was here, and had accepted him into our family. It meant the world to me, and I was sure now more than ever that Ashoh had been the one who'd been afraid of feeling uncomfortable and had pawned it all off on Grandpa.

The next morning, I gave Jamie a tour of the garage. "This is where I used to smash beer cans with Grandpa. Look, the hammer and bucket are still here." I turned to face the refrigerator. The Coors Women had been replaced by Budweiser Ladies, equally happy and high on life in tiny bikinis. "These are his girls." Jamie laughed, remembering. "Grandpa used to tell me I needed to find me a girl that looked like this. Instead, I chose you. By the way, Grandpa sharing his catfish with you last night means that he likes you."

"Oh yea?" Jamie said, clearly delighted.

"Absolutely. And I don't think he was ever uncomfortable with the idea of you coming to Luling. I think it was Ashoh all along. I'm just glad she came around."

Yael walked outside.

"Hey, Yael, want to walk with us down to the old house. I want to show Jamie."

"Yea! Let me grab my shoes and tell Ebony and Dad."

With Matteo in Jamie's arms, the six of us strolled down Bernice Drive. The same moist air and smell of lush St. Augustine wafted around us as the wind flowed off the Mississippi River. It was as if time stood still in Luling. Everything looked exactly as I remembered it. While I had visited once or twice in college, it had been six years since I'd walked down the street where I used to race my pink bike through the neighborhood and play cops and robbers with my friends.

We continued walking until the end of the next block.

"And here it is," Yael said. "100 Bernice Drive."

"This is it, Jamie. The one year we lived in Louisiana, this is where we lived," I said, looking up at the red-brick home still with the same decorative blue shutters.

"Dad, do you remember how in fall, you, me, and Mom would rake leaves in that big backyard together?"

"Yes. Your mother took such good care of our gardens all over the world, wherever we went," Dad said pensively.

"And when we first got Jazzbee as a puppy, she would run so fast around the backyard and dunk her entire head into her big green water bowl," Yael reminded us.

"I totally remember that! Wow, I haven't thought about her as a puppy for so long," I said. Jazzbee had died several years before and we all cherished the years of joy our little apricot poodle from Louisiana had brought us.

"Do you guys remember when Mom gathered the three of us one day after school and told us quite seriously that Heather, next door, was playing outside when a man stopped in his truck, opened the door, pulled open his trench coat, and flashed her?" Ebony asked.

"Yea! And we were like, Mom—what does *flashing* mean?" I added.

"And Mom said, it means some stranger showed her his penis, and immediately we all broke into laughter and she got so mad!" Ebony recounted.

Yael broke into laughter. "Oh yea!"

"We weren't even laughing at Heather. We were just so dumb and immature that imagining someone showing someone else their penis felt hilarious," I explained to Jamie, who was soaking it all in.

Dad stood on the street shaking his head at the three of us. "There's something wrong with you guys."

I looked at Jamie and Matteo and felt grateful that the two of them were finally standing on Bernice Drive with me. I pointed to the downstairs living room. "Jamie, that right there is where

Dad and Mom told us we were not going to be moving to Uganda but instead to Jordan."

"A lot of good memories here over just one short year, guys," Dad said. "Your mother would be proud of all three of you."

WE ALL SAT together in Ashoh and Grandpa's living room after dinner.

"Jamie, can I hold the baby again?" Ashoh asked.

"Sure," Jamie said, placing Matteo softly in Ashoh's arms. I moved onto the beige carpet of the living room and took a picture of the two of them together. Ashoh held her daughter's first grandchild as the cherrywood grandfather clock struck eight, sounding rich tones throughout her home.

"Now, how do you say the baby's name again?" she asked, gazing into his eyes.

"It's Matteo," I said slowly.

"Ma-tay-o," Ashoh repeated.

"I'll just call him Ramb-o," Grandpa said, smiling at me.

70

BOSTON

WITH SONNY BOB WATCHING BEHIND ME, I was training on Local Control in the tower. Local Control is the position that is responsible for landing and departing all airplanes. When working it, you are making hundreds of decisions based on a multitude of factors. At DCA, you are what is called "locking and loading the runways," or putting airplanes in position on three runways, calling exit points for arrival traffic to vacate the runway, and then clearing for takeoff while landing arrivals on those runways seconds out behind, timing it all in your head. It is a wonderfully synchronized dance in which you are directly responsible for thousands of lives an hour. If you give a wrong instruction, you better be ready to have backup plans B and C come into play in seconds.

It was April 2013 and I was departing an American Airlines Boeing 737 on Runway 19 and landing a United Airbus close in behind when one of the other controllers came bounding up the stairs.

"There was just a bombing at the Boston Marathon," he said.

"What!" I said quickly while watching American's wheels leave the ground just as United's nose came across the runway threshold.

I looked forward to the next controller relieving me so I could race down to the TV and see what had happened. I also knew that in very short order all traffic to Boston Logan would stop. "American 845, contact Potomac Departure, good day," I said, switching American over to the next controller, a departure controller, who would begin to climb them higher into the sky.

A phone rang, the supervisor answered, and then promptly hung up.

"Ground, stop Boston departures," he said loudly.

"Stop Boston departures," I repeated. In air traffic, when a command like that is called out, the controllers on various positions around the tower repeat it to verify that each of us has acknowledged it and will start making adjustments to the traffic in our control.

I reached out to a JetBlue Airbus departure that was just leaving Ground Control's frequency and joining my Local Control frequency for departure instructions.

"Good afternoon, JetBlue 250, Washington Tower, there is a situation unfolding in Boston. Logan is now ground stopped until further notice. Pull into the block and I'll have further instructions for you momentarily," I said.

Later, when I was relieved by another controller, I raced back downstairs to the lounge; violent scenes unfolded in front of the group of us who had gathered near the TV. Paramedics rushed bloodied bodies on stretchers into ambulances, and strangers made makeshift tourniquets to help slow the bleeding of those badly injured. Mayhem filled the area near the finish line of the Boston Marathon. I looked behind me out the lounge window at the White House and the Pentagon, knowing well that those buildings were both on high alert now. In the hours to come, lives would be ruined and families would be devastated, as parents of the deceased would be contacted. Spring was in full swing in DC, but it felt more like a cold dark day in the nation's capital as another American city had been so viciously attacked.

"GARON, YOU ARE working Obama today," Eric Cole, now a supervisor, told me as I came back up from lunch one day.

It would be my first time lifting Marine One. As I sat down in front of my radar screen, I thought about the many former American presidents who had been carried from the South Lawn of the White House to Andrews Air Force Base in these helicopters. I had also seen the famous green-and-white helicopters in films and TV shows as long as I could remember. One of my favorite films as a child was *The American President*, with Annette Bening and Michael Douglas, and I watched it repeatedly in the Middle East.

When the time came, and in communications that I cannot detail here, I spoke with the pilots of Marine One once President Obama was onboard, giving the information required to allow them to safely lift and proceed across the Potomac River. Then I gave instructions to all the other helicopters that were moving around Washington's airspace, to ensure they remained the required distance away from the president. As Marine One moved beyond the tower window, I felt a great sense of veneration. Once through my airspace, I transferred control of Marine One to Andrews Tower. Then I sat, leaning back in my chair.

How had this happened? How could a boy, abandoned on the steps of a hospital in Sri Lanka during a war, one day find himself in this position? It was improbable, feeling close to impossible. I had been given so much by so many people willing to take a chance on me.

71

A LOT TO CELEBRATE

DENICE STOOD TALL IN HER daffodil-yellow dress in DC Superior Court as Judge Dalton announced the finalization of Matteo's adoption. The proud grandma looked on as close friends and family hugged and celebrated the legalizing of love that we already knew existed in our family of three. Earlier, Dad had expressed his disappointment at not being able to attend due to a busy work schedule in Europe, and Yael had done the same, having to stay in Austin because of school. Ebony, who had become a lawyer and had practiced in the very court where we were standing, stepped away from her professional role and for that day was every bit the proud aunt, thrilled to have her nephew's permanence in our family recognized. Jamie's father was, once again, absent. Prior to Matteo's arrival, he had written Jamie a letter, telling him that he was not on the path God had for him and that marrying his "friend" and having a child were attempts to satisfy his own desires, but would ultimately end in his unhappiness. In his eyes, gay people weren't good enough to raise children. Jamie had made the very difficult decision to cut ties with him permanently. Jamie's sister, Melissa, on the other hand, had started to come around. Seeing Matteo with us over Christmas at Denice's house had planted a seed of doubt in her aforementioned fundamentalist opposition to two men building a life together.

Following the ceremony, Jamie and I thought it would be appropriate to reserve an area at Oyamel, the Mexican restaurant where five years before he had turned to me shortly after we'd returned from London and asked, "So where are you with kids?" I had laughed nervously that day, unsure of how we would find our way to having a child. But we had found it. Through nine months of trial-and-error parenting and trying our best to divide parental responsibilities equally, Matteo had blossomed into a healthy, social, energetic infant who crawled around the wooden floors of our row house and brought an immense amount of joy to our life. In playing with Matteo, I had learned to be more patient, and Jamie had learned to make decisions faster. No more sleeping in on the weekends and lazy long brunches at some of DC's best eateries. Our life seemed to move quicker now; and while brunches still existed, they were less relaxing and marked by a series of baby interruptions, which, frankly, we enjoyed. And then there was sex. Gone were the days of spontaneous sex at varying hours of the day. Raising a baby meant sex had to be scheduled; and given the intoxicating sexual chemistry that had continued between Jamie and I for years, neither of us wanted to miss out.

"Hey, we probably have about an hour to an hour and a half during his naptime. Want to have sex right after I put him down?"

"Sure. I'll finish cleaning up the living room while you put him down, and then I'll meet you upstairs."

It had all become our new reality and I wouldn't have traded it for anything.

At Oyamel, the waiter decorated our table with salt-rimmed margaritas and creamy guacamole. Ebony held Matteo tight, and Matt and Anne laughed beside so many of our other wonderful friends as we all celebrated Matteo officially becoming a Suriano-Wade.

"JETBLUE 560, TRAFFIC landing Runway one-five, traffic is three out for your runway, Runway one-niner, line up and wait, be ready to roll," I said and listened for the JetBlue pilot to readback correctly.

"Air Wisconsin 1134, turn right on taxiway Mike, hold short of Runway one-niner for departing traffic."

It had been an extremely busy morning with the departure-and-arrival rush at the tower. My supervisor was plugged in next to me. We were on what is called a "check ride," or the final evaluation of your performance. I looked to my right. The ground controller was talking nonstop to thirty-eight airplanes, bringing them to me as fast as she could. To *her* right, the helicopter controller was busy moving helicopters up and down the river around my stream of arrival jetliners.

"My helicopter has your American in sight, maintaining visual," the helicopter controller yelled over to me.

"American 585, helicopter traffic eleven o'clock, two miles, two hundred feet, northwest-bound, has you in sight, maintaining visual separation," I told my American flight four miles from the runway edge.

By 11 a.m., with thousands of passengers safely in the air and others safely on the ground, I fully certified at DCA, earning my license to work autonomously at Washington Tower. After a year of training on one of the most complex air traffic operations in the United States, I was finally a permanent member of Washington's control team. I looked behind me. Sonny Bob rested against the back counter with a smile across his face. The Jesus-loving, conservative bald guy with a mustache, who ministered at prisons in his off time, had taught me an immeasurable amount.

"Congratulations, Garon," he said, extending his hand.

"It's all thanks to you. Thank you so much, Sonny," I said, hugging him.

Then I walked quietly to the windows facing south along the Potomac River and looked down at Gate 7. Ramp agents were hustling to load bags onto an Airbus. It had all come true.

ON FEBRUARY 1, 2014, *The Boston Globe* published an op-ed piece written by Megan Foley, Virginia and Larry's daughter. It was hard to imagine that twelve years before, I had stood on Virginia's doorstep in Amman, hugging her on the night of her husband's murder by al-Qaeda operatives. The opinion piece was extremely well written and argued to not allow for the death penalty for the suspects of the Boston Marathon bombing. Megan wrote:

> *I didn't know beforehand what I know now. I didn't know that executing killers doesn't bring an ounce of peace to the families of victims. I didn't know that what makes a victim of terrorism feel better is to have a chance to connect, understand, and explain. I never got to tell my father's killers that my dad had spent his life trying to help people who didn't have medical care or clean water. . . . Just like the victims of the Boston*

bombing haven't been able to tell Boston Marathon bombing suspect Dzhokhar Tsarnaev who their loved ones were, and why the world is worse off without them and not better.... As we learned from Dr. Martin Luther King Jr., back when my father first committed his life to service: Hate cannot drive out hate. Only love can do that.

She had used the words of Dr. King that I had found so endlessly inspiring. It was a rational plea for human dignity and a chance at reconciliation. I was not surprised at all that this was the writing of the daughter of the woman, Virginia Foley, who had comforted me after Mom's death in Jordan.

72

DC POWER

I LEAPT UP THE TOWER STAIRS and breathlessly entered the tower cab. "Guys! Guess who just walked right past me in the terminal with his security detail?"

The guessing game of who any of us had spotted while on break was long and varied: Reese Witherspoon, Valerie Jarrett, Justin Bieber, Madeleine Albright, T.I., Ruth Bader Ginsburg, Hillary Clinton, Prince William (yes, he was actually flying commercial to New York), and Diane Sawyer to name a few. Each sighting brought with it the speculation of which aircraft they were boarding. So it was never a surprise when a new face joined the list.

"Who?" the controllers said in unison as they each continued issuing instructions to their respective aircraft.

"Ban Ki-moon!" I announced, eagerly awaiting the same jealous look that I'd had when I realized I'd missed Ruth Bader Ginsburg.

"Who's that?" they asked with blank stares. Maybe they hadn't heard me correctly.

"Ban Ki-moon," I repeated again slowly.

Nothing.

"Guys, he's the Secretary-General of the United Nations!" A

number of my friends shrugged their shoulders and continued working airplanes. I hadn't gotten the reaction I wanted, but I was still excited to have seen the distinguished Korean diplomat who had led the UN since 2007. Angela smiled at me knowingly, rolled her eyes, and continued controlling her helicopters. She was right, I should have known that I would be alone in this one. My friend Kristin Wagner, an American who I had attended ACS Amman with, and who had largely grown up between Jordan and Egypt, had said something to me that has always resonated.

"Garon, I think when American parents make the decision to raise their kids overseas, they know the experience will fundamentally change them, but they don't know exactly how."

For me, growing up around the world cultivated this eternal need to constantly know what was going on within the international arena. Even when I tried to take a break from it all, I found myself tuning in to find out what I had missed at the World Economic Forum, G-20 meetings, the UN Security Council, and so on. I loved that I got to work in Washington, the great political epicenter, but not have to be *in* politics. Air traffic control was separate from the domestic and international policy world, which allowed me to read, watch, and think about the international political spectrum at my leisure, instead of as a work obligation. I valued that.

Angela had once said to me, "You know, I'm watching this show, *Game of Thrones*, and there are all these kingdoms. There's this character, Jon Snow, and as he's growing up he goes from one kingdom to another. Throughout the show he's restless. There's a part of him that feels as though he's a part of each of these kingdoms. Other people can't understand that. He belongs to the world. The whole world. It made me think about you. There's a part of you that has empathy for so many different parts of the world, ways of life, and individuals, because you've experienced so much of that. It's like the more diverse and different something is to you, the hungrier you are to learn about it."

It was a great read by one of my closest friends who had taken time to understand my past. Seeing Ban Ki-moon in the terminal had, for a split second, allowed my mind to travel back into the very international world I grew up in. When I arrived home that evening, I told Jamie of my big sighting.

"That's so cool, buddy," he said. As his job had continued taking him around the United States and abroad, he, too, had interesting encounters departing DCA. Jamie had once been seated next to Justice John Paul Stevens and upon seeing him struggle had taken the initiative to help him lift his luggage into the overhead compartment. Another time he was making his way to a gate when he passed Nancy Pelosi. We both loved sharing these uniquely DC stories with each other.

ON OCCASION WE would leave Matteo at home with our wonderful nanny, Veronica, while we snuck out for the evening. Matteo had blossomed into a highly social, loving, and active little two-year-old boy. I loved Veronica, a Salvadoran-American woman who had long, wavy black hair, was heavily tattooed, and spoke to Matteo exclusively in Spanish at our request. Even Denice—who, true to form, had initially zoned in on Veronica's breast tattoo and had mentally labeled her as *wild*—had quickly realized that Veronica was simply amazing.

It was my birthday and after our little boy was fast asleep, Jamie and I walked over to Meridian Pint, a restaurant across the street from our home. Remember Giovanni, the fourth-grade teacher at the Oyster-Adams Bilingual School whom we had met the same evening as Matt and Anne? Over time, he and I had ended up at many of the same get-togethers, had struck up a friendship, and realized we shared the same birthday: November 29.

"Giovanni. Want to have a joint birthday party at Meridian Pint this year?" I had suggested. "We have a lot of the same friends."

With his open heart and outgoing personality, Giovanni had immediately agreed. We took over much of the downstairs area of the restaurant and bar and spent the evening surrounded by all our good friends across the district. Food and libations flowed.

"Happy Birthday, Garon," Ebony said affectionately. "I can't believe you're almost thirty."

"I'm so glad you're here," I said, hugging her.

Matt and Anne drank late into the night with us, catching up and laughing as usual. I was turning twenty-nine and Giovanni was turning thirty-one. Two cakes were brought out at the same time and we blew our candles out simultaneously. It was a wonderful birthday and I thoroughly enjoyed sharing it with Giovanni.

"NO, WE'RE GOOD with one" was the answer Jamie and I gave when friends would ask us if we were planning on adopting more children. But as we saw how much Matteo loved to be around his best friend, Ella, and other kids, we had a change of heart. The never-ending joy I felt snuggling up with Matteo at night had made me realize I had the desire to adopt yet again.

"Do *you* want to do it again?" I asked Jamie one night as we lay in bed, hoping he'd say yes.

"I do," he said. "I do for us and I want Matteo to have a brother or sister to grow up with." We knew we could provide a loving home for another child out there. We spent a couple months compiling new child abuse clearances and police clearances. The second time around was slightly easier than the first. Our social worker, Maureen, did her usual stellar job of guiding us through the paperwork and felt absolutely comfortable recommending we be able to adopt another child. Months later with a new approved home study, we called up Dean at Adoption Makes Family.

"You boys ready to do it again?" he asked us.

"Yes! We can't wait to get a sibling for Matteo, Dean," I said.

"You guys know how it works. I'll call you when a birth mom wants to place her child," he said. We had told Dean that we didn't want to be picked in advance by a birth mom, instead wanting to wait for a situation similar to the way Matteo had come into our life. Our families were so happy, with the exception of Jamie's father of course. And this time when I told Ashoh, she didn't ask me who was going to raise the baby. It was progress.

73
TEL AVIV

EVERYONE HAS THAT ONE PERSON who is their funniest friend. And for me, that person is Adam. I'd even venture to say that for a lot of people, that person is Adam. One night at his home in DC, he had sat me down in the kitchen. He had invited me to come hang out with him and his twins in Israel for the summer, and with Jamie's agreement to play the role of two Dads while I was gone, I had found a week in my schedule to make it happen. Adam talked unbelievably fast and managed to make me laugh, no matter what he was saying.

"Garon, are you listening to me? My sister once had a friend who flew all the way to Tel Aviv from Colombia. They turned her away at Passport Control and she had to fly her ass all the way back to Bogota. We don't need that to be you," Adam said.

"Okay, so what should I do?" I asked earnestly.

"That's why we're having this conversation, we're brainstorming. She was Colombian. *Colombian*, Garon. And she got sent back. Look at you. You're *Sri Lankan*, lived in Jordan and fucking Africa, and who knows where else, and they're going to take one look at you and think you're Iraqi."

I laughed.

"Oh, you think it's funny now, but it's not going to be funny when you're sitting for twenty-four hours detained at the airport and I'm waiting for your ass outside," Adam continued. "So we have to think of what you're going to say."

"Why don't I just tell them the truth?" I suggested.

"The truth?"

"Yea. I'll tell them I was adopted from Sri Lanka, the whole spiel about living all over the world, and that I'm coming to visit you?"

Adam put down his drink and paused thoughtfully.

"Oh my god, that's it!" he said, standing up from the table.

"What's it?"

"That's it. Look, they're going to think you're a terrorist because of how you look, just deal with it. But you're going to tell the truth. They are going to ask you why you're in Israel and who you're coming to visit. And trust me, bitch, they're already going to know. You're going to give them my name and address, and then tell them that you and your husband are friends with me and my boyfriend, and our kids play together, and you are coming to Tel Aviv to hang out with me."

"Okay. You want me to say exactly that?"

"Yes. Because think about it. No terrorist, no matter how badly they want to blow some shit up, is going to say that they are gay. That would be beneath them. It's a great idea!" Adam said, gesturing wildly.

Adam seemed content with his plan for me, which I had come up with.

"Okay, so do you remember what I said about where I'm going to meet you? You're going to walk out and then there's a whole arrivals area . . ."

Adam liked to organize every little fucking thing. I was the more free-spirited one.

"Adam, it's not my first time traveling," I said, putting my arm around him. I loved him. Everyone did.

I had taken an Ambien on the eleven-hour nonstop flight from Philadelphia to Tel Aviv. It was, and still is, the best sleep I've ever had. The last forty minutes of the flight we were told no one was allowed to get out of their seats for security reasons. I made sure I remained seated. All around me Israeli passengers got up to access their overhead luggage while flight attendants reprimanded them.

"Relax! I'm getting my toothbrush," an older Israeli man yelled through the cabin. This guy was worried about getting his toothbrush and I was worried about getting into the country.

I thought of Matteo and Jamie. I had taken a couple of quick trips by myself over the years up to New York City and once out to Vegas, but this would be the longest away from the two of them by far. Thousands of miles away, I already missed them. But before Jamie and I had even gone down the road to starting a family, we agreed to travel as a family as often as we could; when it wasn't possible to all go together, we would work with our schedules to enable each other to take fun solo trips with friends. That would allow us to continue to explore the world whether together or separately. The year before, Jamie had been planning a trip to London for work.

"Richie is going to be in Denmark for two weeks and I was thinking to extend my trip and fly to Copenhagen to spend the weekend with him. What do you think?" Jamie had asked me over dinner.

"I think that's an excellent idea, Jamie. Do it. You and Richie will have a great time in Denmark."

It was important to both of us.

Our American Airbus 330 that had shot us across the globe began its descent into Tel Aviv. I had been a controller at DCA for a little over three years now, was well seasoned, and had even started training new controllers who had recently joined Washington Tower. It had become impossible when flying to not think about decisions other air traffic controllers were making for our flight. Were we at the correct altitude for the descent profile, or is there a chance we would be too high and not be able to shoot the approach? As we became established on the final, was the controller moving helicopter traffic around us and ensuring altitude separation or visual separation by the pilots? Even when I tried to stop thinking about it, I thought about it.

Our Airbus roared down the runway at Ben Gurion Airport. It had been ten years since I had last set foot in the Middle East and it was strange to be back and not in Jordan. The Israeli passengers all had a separate automated entry point, and I walked with the rest of the foreign nationals up to Passport Control. Approaching the area, I saw four or five different lines. I looked at the men and women working as customs agents and tried to discern which one of them would give me the least hard time. They all sat with stern faces, looking equally intimidating. I finally settled on a woman in her thirties, with brown hair tied back, for no other reason than a gut feeling. I tried to gauge the amount of time she was spending on each person. The woman before me had been questioned for about three minutes.

The agent called me forward with a serious nod.

"Hello, passport please," she said.

"Good afternoon, yes, here it is," I replied, handing it to her.

"Why are you here in Israel?"

"I'm here visiting my friend Adam."

"What's his address?"

I pulled out the piece of paper I had written Adam's address on. "Here it is."

"How do you know Adam?" she asked curtly. I could feel her eyes studying my face intently.

Here it goes, I thought.

"Adam and his boyfriend live near me and my husband in DC. We both have kids and our sons play together," I said confidently. I had rehearsed it a number of times on the approach into Tel Aviv.

Her severe eyes glanced between my eyes and my passport. Then, and very unexpectedly, she smiled and said, "Have a nice time in Israel." The truth had worked. I walked out into the International Arrivals area and looked for Adam. No Adam. Hmmm. *Maybe I should've listened to him when he was trying to tell me where to expect to meet him,* I thought. All of a sudden, I heard a high-piercing scream.

"Garon!" Everyone around us turned. There, running toward me—complete with Hello Kitty balloons in his hand for reasons I can't explain—was Adam.

He jumped on me. "I can't believe you're in Israel."

"Me either, man!" I said, kissing his cheek.

We rode from Ben Gurion to the Airbnb I had rented for the week in Dizengoff. While there were some cars moving alongside us as we left the airport and headed for the coast of the Mediterranean, for the most part Tel Aviv was quiet.

"Remember, today is Memorial Day. Not like American Memorial Day, where everyone eats hot dogs and burgers and has a big party in someone's pool. Here, everyone is truly in mourning for twenty-four hours for all the Israelis lost during conflict. The city is completely quiet. Everything is shut down.

We're in the last hours of it now. So go check into your Airbnb, shower up, and by sundown tonight be ready to party, Garon, because this city is going to come alive for Independence Day," Adam instructed me.

And he was right. By 9 p.m. Adam and I were dancing in the streets with his sister and her husband as the Israelis threw one of the best street parties I've ever been to. Celebrations started in bars and restaurants and spilled out into the road. People of every age were laughing and dancing all around us as we jumped from bar to bar exploring different sides of the city. I don't remember what time I climbed into bed the next morning, but I do remember feeling high on life and adventure.

Over the course of the week, Adam introduced me to his spirited world on this side of the Atlantic. Like Jamie, his boyfriend had to stay in DC to work, and Adam had flown with the twins and his nanny to Israel. His mother had us over to her home for a welcoming lunch, where I got to meet his gracious extended family and play with the twins, whom I saw weekly in Washington. In the evenings we hung out with Adam's friends, who were so kind to me. Together we soaked up Tel Aviv's dynamic gay nightlife.

Ebony wrote an email to check up on me.

Did you make it to Tel Aviv or what? I assume you're too busy partying.

She was right.

Tel Aviv is amazing. By the way, the men here are among some of the most handsome guys I've seen in the entire world. How are you?

She replied: *Aww. Jealous! I'm great.*

And they were. I've seen attractive men in every country I've ever visited, but the men of Tel Aviv were shockingly handsome. Often while walking around the city I would say, "Adam, this is ridiculous. Honestly, how good-looking can everyone be?"

"Bitch, I told you!" he'd say back. I wasn't surprised. Middle Eastern men were often quite good-looking, and for the first time, in a very long time, I remembered the boy I had fallen for during my years in Amman, Mohammed. I wondered where Mohammed was living now and what path life had taken him down.

Prior to arriving in Israel, I had no idea what to expect. It was my first time returning to the Middle East in a decade. I noticed as we would walk the streets of Tel Aviv, men and women held hands lovingly. Next to them, gay couples sat kissing each other on park benches throughout the city, and children played in green spaces thoughtfully built into the double-wide median that blended city and park life into one. I was in the Middle East, but this open culture of social acceptance stood in contrast to the rather socially conservative Arab world I had been accustomed to.

I also had assumed that every Israeli I met would, for obvious reasons, be extremely pro-Israeli government in terms of the long-standing conflict with Palestine. I was wrong. I met a young Israeli woman who spoke with vigor in support of Palestinians. I was assured there were others who shared her opinions. Later, walking by myself through Dizengoff, I wondered why I had arrived with that preconceived idea. As an American, I quite often oppose the foreign and domestic policy decisions that the US government makes. There was a left and a right to every issue at home; and here in Israel, it was no different.

On my last day in Tel Aviv, I went with Adam and his family

to his favorite beach. We sat along the Mediterranean eating rich, creamy hummus and cucumber and tomato salad that had been delivered onto the warm sand by charming waiters. Ahead of me, two Muslim women walked gingerly across the sand, covered head to toe in long, flowing black abayas. Two Israeli women walked past them in bikinis, all headed to the same cooling water's edge. The four of them were strangers, and never spoke, but to me it was an image captured in my mind forever. It reflects for me how I think the world should be: people who appear to live differently coexisting together in peace and acceptance. I'm not a big fan of the word *tolerance*. Tolerance means you put up with something. I prefer *acceptance*. Accept that something is different from your way of life and embrace it.

74

RAMBO

MY PHONE RANG AT 11TH STREET. It was Ebony. She and I usually texted so I sensed something was out of the ordinary.

"Garon, Grandpa died." I felt sick to my stomach. My mind began to race.

"What? What happened?"

"Ashoh said his health had started to deteriorate while you were in Tel Aviv and he stopped eating. They took him to the hospital and his doctors said he had end-stage liver cirrhosis. They moved him into an assisted living facility in Luling last week and he died earlier today. Ashoh says she can't believe how quickly it happened."

I felt a heaviness in my chest. "We have to get to Louisiana. I'll start packing."

I WATCHED the Catholic mass through a large rectangular glass window of a soundproof room. Ashoh's priest moved back and forth at the front of her church, his long robe flowing in his wake. Jamie had been unable to fly down with us because of work. Matteo and I had jumped on the first flight down to

Louisiana with Ebony. Yael once again drove over from Austin.

Matteo, now a bona fide toddler, charged up and down the quiet room behind me as the priest's words poured through the speakers. He munched on small orange goldfish crackers that I had brought for him. The room had nicely carpeted, slightly elevated rows of seating and not much else, save for two delicate glass bowls of holy water on either side of the room. I had never been to a full Catholic mass before and I felt as though I were trying to understand a performance in a different language. After a few minutes I tuned out the priest's words, looked through the glass window at Ebony and Yael who were sitting next to a heartbroken Ashoh and Uncle Mike, then closed my eyes and focused my thoughts on Grandpa.

He had taught me quiet love. Mom, Dad, and Ashoh had all been verbal about how they loved me. But Grandpa never said it, he only showed me. My mind flashed through moments of the two of us together.

"Here's a penny, Rambo," he'd say, pointing to the gumball machine that sat beside his La-Z-Boy.

"Garon, you want to watch a movie on Lifetime with me?" I'd park myself on the sofa across the living room from him. "Maybe that Ashoh of yours will make us some popcorn."

One evening at dinner when I was eight, he watched me struggling to crack open my crab legs. He grabbed the crab claw cracker and I watched carefully as he broke through the shell of his crab legs. He then pulled the meat out and placed it gently on my tray. "Now you're in business, Rambo."

It was how I'd known he'd accepted Jamie that evening at Spahr's, when he shared his catfish with him. It was his little way of saying *I love you*. With the mass near complete, I looked over at Matteo. Unaware of the melancholy nature of the day, he pushed his green car along with one hand and carried his gray stuffed elephant in the other.

"C'mon, buddy. It's time to go."

I picked him up and headed for the door. I grabbed the diaper bag and just as I was about to walk out, I stopped in my tracks. There, floating at the bottom of both bowls of holy water, were Matteo's goldfish crackers.

"Oh my god, Matteo," I said. I had no idea what to do. Should I scoop the fish out of the holy water? Surely this was frowned upon. Were people even allowed to touch holy water? What if I touched it and that was worse than even goldfish crackers floating in it? I glanced around for answers and with no sign from God or otherwise, I decided to leave the holy water with the goldfish floaters and get the hell out of there as fast as I could.

In south Louisiana, bodies are buried in above-ground tombs. Dig a couple feet underground and you'll reach water. Lifetime friends of Ashoh and Grandpa's lined up to pay their final respects to the man they all called Petie. I stood holding Matteo just behind Ashoh and Uncle Mike. I watched as they walked up to the casket and my eyes filled with tears. Ashoh and Grandpa had been married for sixty-seven years. The two of them had brought Mom into this world and I imagined Mom standing with her mother and brother now. I knew she would have been bawling alongside Ashoh and Uncle Mike, saying her final goodbye to her father, whom she loved. Ashoh placed her hand on the casket, then made the sign of the cross, blew Grandpa a final kiss, and walked away with her arm linked to that of her only remaining child.

When it was my turn, Matteo and I walked up to the outdoor tomb and approached the casket. I took a deep breath.

"I love you, Grandpa. Thanks for bringing Mom into this world and thank you for always making me laugh. I'm going to miss hanging out in the garage with you," I whispered. Then I swiveled Matteo from my hip to face his casket.

"C'mon, buddy. Let's say goodbye to Grandpa one last time." I took Matteo's tiny hand and placed his palm and fingers on the side of the coffin.

"I love you, Grandpa. Mom loves you," I said quietly. Then we walked away.

An hour later we arrived at Ormond Plantation for a lunch in honor of Grandpa. Constructed in the late 1780s, the estate had an expansive green lawn, thick white columns, and multiple buildings. The Louisiana Colonial–style mansion had been a place of work for slaves forced to pick indigo and, later, sugarcane. It was always surprising to me that people in the south held big life events at plantations: weddings, graduation celebrations, post-funeral lunches. I couldn't imagine choosing to get married at a place where people had been enslaved, but it was the southern way and down here no one seemed to think anything of it.

Ebony, Yael, Matteo, and I sat at the lunch with our cousins Jessica, Erin, and Ryan. Decades before at our home on Flint Road in South Africa, Ashoh had told us about their life in Louisiana. Over the years we had seen them every so often, but never nearly enough. In Jordan, so many of my Arab friends had grown up day in and day out with their cousins. They were like brothers and sisters really. A part of me wished we could have all grown up together. I would have liked to go to movies with them as kids, hang out at their house on the weekends as young teenagers, and go out to bars and restaurants with them in later years, but we had grown up an ocean away from each other. Still, no matter what corner of the world we found ourselves in, Mom had filled our head with stories of their life along the bayou and I had always had such strong affection for them. While we didn't have shared life experiences growing up, the six of us had the shared experience of having Ashoh and Grandpa as our grandparents, and that was enough to trade family stories for hours.

Matteo was well taken care of as Ebony paraded him around the room to Ashoh and Grandpa's friends, who passed him around from lap to lap. I scanned the room and there sitting at a nearby table was Mom's best childhood friend, Ms. Connie. I made my way over to her table.

"Garon! Come here, baby," she said in the way that only a southern woman can. "It's so good to see you. You're all grown up now."

"It's so good to see you, Ms. Connie," I said, giving her a big squeeze. The year we had lived on Bernice Drive, Mom would often take me to her home. She had two dogs and a potbelly pig that would dart out to the driveway attempting to bark with the dogs. I remembered that well.

"Look at that beautiful baby boy. I can't believe you're a father now," she said.

"Me either," I said, laughing. "I love him so much."

We talked for a while about Mom. "I still miss your mama," Ms. Connie said.

"Me too. I think about her all the time." She went on to recount stories of the two of them growing up together.

"Ms. Connie. I've always wanted to ask you something. Not too long before Mom died, she and I spent this amazing day together in Jordan when I was home sick from school. She took me out to lunch and we laughed so much that afternoon. Later, on the way home, she said, "You know, honey, when Ms. Connie and I were in college, we used to hang out at the gay bars because the men were the most handsome and the most fun.' I wished I had asked her more about that, but I never did. Can you tell me about that?"

"Oh, that's right!" Ms. Connie said, clapping her hands. "Oh baby. Me and your mama had some friends who were gay at USL and we went out to the gay bars in Lafayette with them one night. We had so much fun there, we just kept going back for more. And they really were the most handsome. Those were wonderful days with Niki."

It felt great to hear Ms. Connie tell stories about Mom. It had taken thirteen years, but I had finally been able to find out more about the conversation that Mom and I had that day in Amman.

The next morning at breakfast, with Matteo in my lap, I sat across from Ashoh.

"I'm gonna miss him so much, Garon," she said, bursting into tears.

"I know you are." I reached across the kitchen table to hold her hand "You two had so many wonderful years together. I'm going to miss him too."

Ebony and Yael sat down at the table to be with Ashoh, and with Matteo squirming all over the place I decided to take him outside. I led him by the hand out of the kitchen and through the garage on our way to the backyard. Matteo bounced ahead of me, eager to see if any more squirrels were chasing each other around the oak trees. I stood next to the fridge, where Grandpa's girls were still guarding it. I looked down near the door where the sledgehammer and white bucket rested.

"Thank you for everything," I whispered. Then I took a deep breath and inhaled the cigarette-smoked air of the garage. "I'll never forget you."

75

THE ARREST

BACK IN WASHINGTON, I HAD just finished the morning departure push on Ground Control. So many planes and so few gates available.

"Delta 718, turn right on foxtrot, right on kilo, hold short of your alley, your gate is not available," I said. "Bluestreak 3459, you're going the wrong way, sir, I need a hard left turn now onto november, for opposite direction traffic. Taxi november, hold short of delta, I'll have further in a moment. United 200, I need you to start your taxi, please. I have three arrivals waiting to get into those gates."

It was the kind of morning that when you get off Ground Control, you feel both exhausted and exhilarated.

"Anybody want anything from Starbucks?" I asked the controllers. I ran down the stairs and opened the big door that led into our circular hallway and lounge. My phone was sitting in its place on a ledge against the wall. Behind it, out the glass windows, the Pentagon gleamed in the sun's warmth.

I glanced at my phone to see what I might have missed and lit across my screen were *fourteen* new messages. Something had happened. I quickly started reading through them.

Did you see what happened to Giovanni?

434

I can't believe he got arrested

Have you heard from anyone, what happened?

They went on and on. I shuffled through them, not understanding what had happened, and then walked into our lounge, where a number of my colleagues were sitting watching the morning news. I almost dropped my phone when my eyes met the screen. Plastered across the TV was a mugshot of Giovanni. *DC Teacher Arrested on Pedophilia Charges,* the headline read.

"Oh my god, that's my friend," I unexpectedly said out loud. The controllers all turned to look at me.

I dashed out of the lounge and found the chair I most often sat in on my break. I read news article after news article. Right away, I texted Anne.

(me) *Did you hear? Giovanni got arrested on pedophilia charges? I don't believe it.*

(Anne) *What???*

She hadn't heard yet. I turned to *The Washington Post.*

A teacher at a DC public school was arrested Tuesday on a sex abuse charge. The arrest came after police received allegations of sexual abuse involving a juvenile at Oyster-Adams Bilingual School.

The rest of the day was a texting frenzy among our broad social circles in Washington. No one could believe it.

"There's no way Giovanni did this," I had told Jamie at our home that night. I thought of our joint birthday party and what a memorable evening it had been. "I bet one of the parents found out he's gay, didn't like it, and made this up."

I was wrong. It's amazing how our brains will try to rationalize things, trying to convince us otherwise when we can't allow ourselves to believe the truth.

On June 11, the local CBS affiliate reported:

> *Charging documents say the 31-year old teacher admitted to sending a photo of his private parts via Snapchat to the alleged 10-year-old male victim. He allegedly also asked the victim to send nude photos back but the boy did not. Pena also admitted to touching the victim's genitals over his pants inside a classroom at the school on more than one occasion, according to the documents ... Pena also allegedly told the boy he "wished they were the same age," and taught the boy about sperm and masturbation.*

It was almost too difficult to read. On Friday, September 4, 2015, Giovanni was sentenced to two and a half years in federal prison and ten years of supervised release to follow. Jamie and I, and the rest of our friends, had slowly come to accept the truth. It was a moment of realization for me.

"I just can't believe someone like him did it," I told Jamie. "I never would have expected him, ever."

"Garon, you're too naive sometimes. You expect the best out of people and are so shocked when things like this happen," Jamie said. "There is a lesson in this."

He was right. And it changed the way I thought about who I would allow Matteo to be around unsupervised. Before, I would have considered letting a number of friends babysit Matteo, had they asked. That list included Giovanni. Now, I knew that I wanted to limit the list to Denice, Ebony, or Veronica.

Every year on my birthday, on our birthday, whether I want to or not, I think of Giovanni.

76

HARD CONVERSATIONS

O N A CRISP OCTOBER EVENING there was a knock on our front door. Ebony was standing there, with her suitcase and a demure look on her face. I hugged her. She had called the day before and asked if it would be okay for her to move in with us. She had finally decided to break up with her boyfriend. He was a nice enough guy, but I never felt they were great together. I was glad that she had taken my talk to heart. So many times I had told her, "If you ever need to leave him, you can always come live with us." Matteo especially enjoyed having his Aunt Ebie around. Almost three years old now, he zoomed around the house giggling and reveling in being the center of our world. I loved the fact that in this life, I got the opportunity to be one of his fathers.

MANY NIGHTS WHEN I got out of DCA late, I would call Ashoh on my drive home.

"Tell me about Mom as a little girl," I asked her.

"Garon, your mama was a defiant little girl. A defiant grown-up too."

I laughed. It was true.

"When she was small, if she didn't want to do something, she wasn't about to do it. It landed us in all sorts of arguments," Ashoh told me.

"Will you tell me about the night you found out that she had died?" I asked gently.

It was a question that had taken me more than a decade to ask her. Even now, I could barely get the words out.

Her signature pause came. Only this time I knew it wasn't because she was contemplating if the whole family was gay, or if two men could really raise a baby. This time it came from a place of incessant pain. "Oh, Garon. I was sitting on the side of my bed and the phone rang. I picked it up and it was your daddy. I said, 'Well, hey, Steve, how you doing?' He said, 'Dorothy, I don't know how to tell you this, but Niki died.' I don't remember anything after that. I just dropped the phone and started screaming, 'Petie! Petie! Niki died.' He came running in. We cried all night."

Tears fell down my face as I passed the Washington Monument. I hated that Ashoh had lost two of her children. No one should have to go through that pain once, much less twice. And I still missed her daughter. Now a parent, I couldn't even begin to imagine losing Matteo. Even as I write this now, tears are welling in my eyes at the thought of a life without him.

THREE WEEKS LATER, Ebony and I carried her furniture down the beige metal stairs of her house on 11th and into a U-Haul truck that she had parked out front. We were both extremely sad. She had lived in that house since early 2008. I had showed up months later from Texas. It was where she and I had gotten to know each other as adults. It was where Jamie and I had spent so much time together in those early days. As we carried out her bookcase, tables, and chairs, these memories coursed through my mind. I knew that for the rest of our lives we would pass that home on the corner of 11th and Harvard and say, "Remember when?" Ebony moved to neighboring Mt. Pleasant just across 16th Street into an adorable one-bedroom condo. And it was here that so many of our weekends were spent all together as a family.

Back at home with Matteo and Jamie, the winter sky was fading into darkness outside our front window when I heard the phone ring.

"Jamie! It's Dean," I yelled. Jamie came catapulting into the kitchen.

"Hi, boys! It's me," Dean said with the same teasing tone we had heard three years before.

"Are you guys ready to have a daughter?"

A surge of adrenaline coursed through my body. Jamie and I smiled in delight at each other.

"I'm holding a beautiful little girl in my arms," Dean said. "She was born yesterday. I plan for her to go to the two of you," he said. My mind started racing. Where was she born? Was she okay? I thought of Matteo, who was playing loudly downstairs with his toys, unaware that he had just become a big brother.

"She was born on your birthday, Garon!" Jamie whispered excitedly. Another smile spread across my face and I shook my head in disbelief. We'd be able to share our birthdays together.

"Now, guys, this situation is a little different. The birth mom was not as sure about her choice but finally decided she did in fact want to place the baby for adoption. I want you to be excited, but I also want you to be realistic and remember that she has thirty days to change her mind," Dean said, snapping me back into reality. "I'll call you tomorrow when they discharge the baby and with more information."

Jamie and I hugged just as we had three years before. We agreed not to tell Matteo until we got further information in the morning. I ran down the stairs to see Matteo and as I turned the corner my eyes filled with tears. I knew how much both Yael and Ebony had meant to me in my life. Siblings, whether you get along with them easily or not, are a lifetime friendship. When big moments happen within the family, there's no need to give context, they instantly understand because of a lifetime of shared experiences. As much as Jamie and I wanted another child, we also wanted that lifetime relationship for Matteo. I knew he'd make a wonderful big brother because of his sensitive and caring nature.

I jumped in my car, raced over to pick up Ebony, and the three of us sat in our living room celebrating.

"We're going to name her Niki," I told Ebony. It was a beautiful tribute to Mom, who had together with Dad paved the way for so much of our life.

The next morning, Jamie and I woke up to a call from Dean.

"Boys, I have bad news." I held tightly to the bedframe. "The birth mother tested positive for three narcotics. She also changed her mind and wants to keep the baby girl. But because of the narcotics, they won't let her take the baby home. The little girl is being put into foster care. Because the mom wants her, there's no chance for adoption. She will just have to live in foster care until the birth mom can get clean and possibly later reunite with her daughter. I'm sorry, and I'll call you when another baby comes up."

We hung up the phone and looked at each other in sadness, sitting together in silence. This is the thing about adoption. That one call can change your life instantly. There's no nine months of gearing up. It's all packed into one explosive moment, and you live nine months of roller-coaster emotion in that exchange.

"It's okay, buddy, there'll be another baby," I said to Jamie, trying to reassure myself as much as him. "If she wanted to keep her baby, of course that's her right and she should. It's just sad that the little girl is now going into foster care and might end up living in the system forever."

"Right. And honestly, if you're doing three drugs while pregnant, chances are you aren't coming out of that life," Jamie said. I knew he felt as badly as I did for the little girl.

We agreed that we were happy we hadn't told Matteo. He was blissfully unaware of the change of events as he zoomed around the house with his stuffed elephant. Now, every year on my birthday, whether I want to or not, I think of both Giovanni and that little girl. Two drastically different situations. To this day, I still wonder if she's made it back into her mother's sober arms. I hope she has.

THE END OF the year came and went without a call. So did January and February. We had enjoyed such luck in getting Matteo, but I understood, that kind of good fortune doesn't usually happen twice. At times when I grew annoyed at the process, I reminded myself that I should just be grateful for Matteo and allow the second adoption to happen in the way that it would.

The cold air had started to leave the city as Washington moved slowly into its cherished spring. I looked forward to seeing the cherry blossoms from the tower high above. One afternoon on a break at DCA, I decided to call up Maureen to discuss the situation with her.

"I'm so sorry to hear you haven't been placed yet," she commiserated. "How's Matteo doing?"

"He's doing great. We talk about you when we tell him his adoption story. He knows all about you," I said. I could hear the happiness in Maureen's voice. Jamie and I had always wanted to have dinner with her, but since she had been our social worker for both home studies, would still need to be in court for finalization, and would continue with our post-adoption placement reports, we knew it would be a conflict of interest to socialize with her.

"You know, Garon. I know you guys are happy with Dean, but there's also this relatively new program between the United States and South Africa."

She had piqued my interest. "Maureen, I used to live in South Africa."

"I remember," she said knowingly. "The adoption agency that runs the program is called Spence-Chapin and they are in New York City. It's takes a year to get matched, but there's no birth parents changing minds, and South Africa is accepting of gay parents."

I thanked Maureen and walked back up into the tower, intrigued at the prospect of an adoption opportunity in Africa.

That evening Jamie and I looked over the South African adoption program being run out of Manhattan. Reading the words *South Africa* over and over transported me back to our home on Flint Road in Johannesburg. Some of the kids who were eligible for adoption were the same age as I had been when we lived there. I remembered Mom and Dad taking us by the hand after dinner and dancing in the living room to "Midnight Train to Georgia." I saw Ashoh at Lion Park, holding an oversized bottle of milk, as hungry lion cubs clamored around her. And I smiled thinking of Yael's arrival into our family.

After much discussion over a number of days and always one to take a risk, I turned to Jamie. "Let's just do it. I love Dean and I would have loved to be parents to that baby girl. We did domestic once and it was wonderful. But here's this great program internationally and it's in *South Africa*," I pleaded.

We emailed Dean, thanked him, and asked him to remove us from his pool of families, explaining our change of direction. As expected, he completely understood.

Jamie had worked in South Africa twice over the past years and loved it. I had even asked him to take some of Mom's ashes back. He spread them out in the bush for me. I imagined her at peace there, under the star-filled sky among giraffes and elephants, in a country she had so loved. I was glad that I had been able to get Jamie to feel the excitement of this new path. That's always how we've worked: I suggest, he hesitates, and then he gets as excited as I am—or even more so.

Two mornings later, I pushed him even farther outside of his comfort zone. Matteo had already gone for his day about the city with Veronica and Ella. I walked to the bottom of the stairs, to where he was working at our dining-room table.

"Jamie. Question."

He looked up at me, scanning my face.

"You know I have a number of weeks off coming up—at the end of March and through most of April."

"Yea?" he asked cautiously. I could see he was bracing himself for my suggestion.

"We weren't going to travel because we were waiting for a baby from Dean. But now that that's changed, I think we should take Matteo and go somewhere."

"Okay. Where should we go?"

I was pleasantly surprised that he was equally ready to travel.

"Let's go to South Africa," I said, smirking, knowing the resistance was coming.

Jamie stared at me with the same face he gives me each time I plant an impulsive idea in front of him.

"Garon. You want to plan, book, and travel to *South Africa* in three weeks?" he said, looking at his calendar.

"Yes."

"Now how exactly are we going to make that happen?"

77

RETURNING TO SOUTH AFRICA

J AMIE, MATTEO, AND I SAT onboard a Qatar Airways Boeing 777 destined for Johannesburg. We had used Air Miles, upgraded to business class, and it didn't disappoint. Matteo looked tiny is his big seat, especially as it transformed into his bed. As we soared across the Atlantic Ocean once more, I looked over adoringly at my two guys. Copious amounts of champagne were offered, to which I gladly obliged, and after a wonderful multicourse dinner, we were given pajamas to change into. When I emerged from the lavatory in my new Qatar pajamas, two flight attendants were at my seat.

"We are just putting down your mattress and preparing your bed for the evening, sir," one of the flight attendants said. With Jamie and Matteo already tucked in, I fell into my luxurious mattress and the champagne helped me fall into a deep sleep as we made our way across the world to our connecting stop, Doha. I woke up to the sound of clinking silverware. I looked over. Two flight attendants were serving Matteo oatmeal and a wide array of fruit. My little American boy was having breakfast over Iraq.

After a twelve-hour layover, oscillating between the airport hotel and Qatar's business-class lounge filled with endless culinary creations, the three of us boarded our Dreamliner to Johannesburg. As we flew down over Somalia, Tanzania, and Malawi, I stared down at the continent I had fallen in love with as a young boy. Crossing from Zimbabwe into South Africa, my heart began pounding faster. I had spent much of the flight trying to decide if I had the courage to go back to Flint Road, buzz the intercom of our old home, and ask if they would allow me into the garden.

We had hired a wonderful travel company out of London, Jacada Travel, to customize the two-week vacation through South Africa and later Mozambique. For the first two nights, I had asked to stay in Johannesburg, close to Flint Road. They had arranged our stay at The Residence, a luxuriant hotel in Houghton that occupied the grounds of the former Chinese Embassy.

As our seatbacks moved forward and we prepared to land, I gazed out my window. Our aircraft's wheels made contact with the runway in Johannesburg; tears flowed freely from my eyes. It had taken twenty-four years, but I had found my way back to South Africa, with my own little family in tow.

THAT EVENING WE sat on the balcony of our suite. Two chaises rested under the sky next to a whirling jacuzzi overlooking a tranquil garden and tennis courts.

"Matteo, come lie down next to me," I said.

He scurried over and jumped in the chaise. "Let's look up at the stars together, buddy. You know, Daddy grew up here until he was a couple years older than you."

"You did?" he asked in his tiny voice.

"Yes. Do you remember how I told you that Aunt Ebie, Uncle

Yael, and I all began growing up together in Africa? Well, this is where we lived."

"Daddy, did you ever see elephants here?"

"We saw lots of elephants here, buddy. And not just elephants. Lions. Rhino. Giraffe. Hippos."

"Wow!" Matteo gasped in wonderment.

"And soon, you will too. Dada and I are going to take you on a safari day after tomorrow, remember?"

"We are?" he asked with big eyes. "I hope we see lots of elephants."

Jamie joined us, and the three of us lay out, staring into the African night sky. I inhaled deeply and exhaled my gratefulness into the world.

The next morning, I woke to the sound of the phone ringing.

"Mr. Wade or Mr. Suriano. Good morning. Your driver has arrived," the front desk attendant said politely.

I looked at the time. Shit. It was 9 a.m. I looked over in bed. Jamie was gone, but Matteo was still snoozing.

"Thank you so much. Please apologize to him, we will be down as soon as we can." After twenty-six hours of travel, we had overslept. I scrambled around the room getting ready, woke up Matteo, and found Jamie, who was quietly writing in the garden downstairs.

"Jamie! Why didn't you wake us up?"

"Why? What time is it?" he asked.

"It's nine and our driver is downstairs."

"Shit!"

When we walked outside, a South African man, about my height and dressed impeccably in a black vested suit, stood ready to greet us. "Good morning, sir, I'm Sipho."

We apologized profusely for keeping Sipho waiting and

thanked him for coming. "I am your driver for the day and happy to take you anywhere. I understand you would like to go to Parkwood first," he said.

"Yes, please," I said, climbing into the SUV next to him and giving him the address.

As we rolled through the city and neared my old neighborhood, I felt Jamie's hand on my shoulder from behind me. "Are you ready, buddy?"

I was, I was nervous, and I was sure the people living there would say no. What a suspicious story. An American shows up at your gate, tells you they used to live there, and wants to get inside. I think most people would say no.

As we turned onto Flint Road, I spotted our home.

"Wow, there it is!" I said, pointing to show Jamie and Matteo. I hopped out of the car, took a deep breath, and pressed the intercom. *You came all this way, just ask so they can say no and get it over with.*

A woman's voice answered. "Yes, hello?" she said with an Afrikaans accent.

"Hi. My name is Garon, I'm from the United States. I know this is really strange, but I grew up in this house and I've always wanted to see it again. Is there any way you would consider letting me in the garden? If not, I totally understand."

There was an extremely long silence, similar to the pauses Ashoh often took during our phone conversations.

"Sure. Do you mind just coming back around 3 p.m.?"

My face lit up with excitement. "Yes! Oh, thank you so much. I'll be back at 3 p.m." I turned back toward the SUV. "She said yes!"

We spent the rest of the morning and early afternoon walking around Zoo Lake Park, an enormous green space with a lake anchoring its center. Jamie and I walked with Matteo as he pointed out various ducks that chased us, hoping for food.

"Matteo, when I was your age Grandma Niki and Grandpa used to walk us here on weekends. Aunt Ebie, Uncle Yael, and I used to feed bread to the ducks and run around the lake. Sometimes there was even a popsicle vendor who would tow his cart around and we'd buy some."

"Are there any popsicles now?"

"Sorry, buddy, I don't see any."

As I watched Matteo skip ahead of me, I remembered the five of us decades before walking the very same path. I was the same age as Matteo then, and I had felt the love and protection of our little family of five. Now, I hoped Matteo felt secure, loved, and protected in his little family of three.

At exactly 3 p.m., we returned to Flint Road. I buzzed the intercom again, and shortly after a white woman and her teenage daughter opened the door cautiously.

"Hi, I'm Garon. Thank you so much for allowing us to do this," I said. Once she saw my face and saw Jamie and Matteo, I could see she was at ease.

"No problem. Please come in," she said. I handed her a bottle of champagne to thank her.

Then I turned to face the front garden. Jamie smiled, watching me from the side as he held Matteo's hand. It was exactly as I had remembered, albeit a bit smaller because I was so much bigger now. I saw Dad teaching me how to ride my red BMX in the grass. He had counted down from three and then let go, encouraging me to pedal forward. My eyes followed the walkway to the front of the house. The den, its large French doors opening into the front courtyard, was still there. Mom had held those green-and-white addition and subtraction flashcards up for me in that TV room.

What's three plus four, Garon? she had asked while I stared at the flashcard in frustration.

"Would you like to come inside?" the woman offered, clearly seeing how enamored I was.

"Oh really? I would love that. Thank you," I said. We turned the corner from the foyer into the living room and in an instant it all came flooding back. I could see Mom calling me over with her arms outstretched to dance to "Crocodile Rock" after dinner . . . Ebony and I stood side by side at the edge of the blue sofa as Dad pulled Mom's waist close to his, and she gazed into his eyes as "Lady in Red" flowed gently through the air . . . the four of us opening our gifts around the tree on Christmas Eve, the kitchen . . . Mom and Dad sitting on one side of the table, asking us to guess what was in the room with us. We never did guess a baby.

We arrived at my bedroom.

"Jamie, my bed used to be right here and I would lie awake at night looking up at this ceiling with my right hand in the shape of an airplane. I would fly it back and forth above me until I fell asleep."

"And now you're a controller," he said, running his hand down my back.

And finally, the yellow-tiled bathroom. One evening Mom was giving me a warm bath. "Garon, I'm running to the kitchen, I'll be back in a second." She stepped the three feet around the corner to the kitchen, and in that time I reached for Dad's razor that he had forgotten on the corner of the nearby sink. I had always watched him shave in wonder. What was all that white foam that smelled so good across his face? And how did it disappear so quickly? I picked up the razor and in one swipe I dragged it across my lips. Instantly, I felt the shock of pain, dropped the razor into the water, and blood poured from my sliced lips. I wailed in pain, my screams sending Mom bolting into the bathroom. She stared at the crimson water and screamed, "Garon, what happened!" I can still see the fear in her eyes.

I didn't want to get in trouble. Holding my mouth, my hand filled with blood, I cried, "Nothing!"

"No, you have to tell me! You have to tell me!" she screamed in fear, yanking me up out of the water. "Did you use your father's razor?" she begged for an answer.

"No!" I cried.

"Then what did you do?" she said, the blood flowing off my chin pooling in her hand.

"I used Dad's razor!" I confessed through my sobs.

She wrapped me up and carried me to their bedroom down the hallway. I sat in Dad's arms that night with a bandage across my mouth. Now, being a parent, I can only imagine the fear and self-blame that Mom would have felt that night in that bathroom.

Going back to our home on Flint Road is one of the best things I've ever done in my life.

"I'm so happy I can finally see where you first grew up," Jamie said to me as Matteo bounced around the garden just like Ebony, Yael, and I once had.

"This is where it all started for me, buddy. All my firsts," I said, still envisioning our childhood.

As we climbed back into the SUV, Sipho sat waiting patiently. "Just one more moment, please, Sipho," I said. Jamie and Matteo climbed in. I reached in my pocket for the small bag I had brought with me. I stepped out next to the flower bed that lined the sidewalk. Then I reached into the bag and scattered Mom's ashes across the green leafy plants. Niki Wade could finally rest peacefully here in Africa, outside the first home where she and Dad had raised all three of their children together.

THE NEXT WEEK was spent in the northeastern corner of South Africa in Mpumalanga Province at the enchanting Thornybush Game Lodge. In the early mornings and late into the evenings, the three of us rode through the dramatic bushveld surrounded by the most marvelous creatures to walk this earth. A lone giraffe towered above us, stripping leaves off branches as it surveyed the landscape. A mother rhino and her calf slowly trotted beside our open-air jeep, keeping a watchful eye. A pride of lions lay snuggled together along the banks of a dried-out riverbed. The lionesses slept alongside each other some thirty feet away from us while the cubs tumbled about.

"Did you know that lions sleep close to twenty hours a day?" our guide said.

"Wow, I had no idea," Jamie replied.

"What are the lions doing?" Matteo said, perking up in his seat.

Without warning, one of the older lion cubs aggressively made a beeline for our car. He roared; the other lions lifted their heads at the edge of their den. Jamie and I instinctively put our arms around Matteo as the cub raced at us, stopping four feet from the car. Our guide stood up on the front seat and started waving his hands in a bold circular motion. He deepened his voice and yelled, "Stop! Stop! Back up!" To our surprise, the cub stopped and began backing up, moving its head from side to side in a way that almost resembled a dance. Our guide clapped loudly and deliberately a number of times, and soon the young lion retreated to the den.

"What was that?" I asked, shocked, never having experienced this before.

"That was a young male lion. Probably about two years old. He heard our deep voices when he was at the edge of the riverbed. Then he heard Matteo's high-pitched voice and tried to attack."

"Why?" Jamie asked.

"They are instinctively used to catching and killing the youngest prey in a herd. So, for example, if they are hunting impala, they will listen for the high-pitched voice of the youngest one and attack them."

Jamie and I looked at each other, stunned. All that from Matteo's little voice. We made sure he sat securely locked between us and tried our best to keep him quiet for the rest of the safari.

We reached a thick part of the bush where the driving path was bordered on either side by Acacia karroo, unusual and captivating trees, their branches filled with menacing lengthy white thorns. Out of nowhere, the treetops began to shake. Our guide threw the car in reverse.

"What's that?" Matteo asked.

"I'm not sure, buddy," I said, holding his hand.

Suddenly a majestic herd of female elephants and their calves came running from beyond the trees. Our guide put the car in drive and surged us ahead to an expanse near a watering hole, where we could safely get out of the way of the herd. We watched in awe as the mothers ran by us: a wall of gray kicking up a dust cloud. A lone male had been chasing the herd in hopes of mating. I remembered how glorious and otherworldly African elephants are.

Later that afternoon, while Jamie napped, Matteo and I jumped into the invigorating plunge pool on our wooden terrace that overlooked the thick bush.

"If we're quiet, Matteo, we might see some more animals," I said, holding my three-year-old in my lap as he not-so-quietly splashed water all around.

"Daddy, I have a question. Did you buy me at Target?" An unpreventable burst of laughter rose from my mouth.

"No, buddy," I said, bringing my eyes level with his, surprised at his question. "Remember your adoption story that we always tell you? About how you were born in a hospital in Maryland and then we adopted you in DC?

"Oh. I thought you bought me at Target," he said, giggling and pulling at my chest hair.

"Target does have a lot of things, doesn't it? But not kids, buddy. Dada and I *really* wanted to have a baby. So we signed up to work with an adoption agency in Maryland. Three weeks later, a woman gave birth to *you*. That was your birth mom and she couldn't take care of you. But she wanted to make sure that you could find a family that would love you forever. So the day she gave birth to you, the hospital called Dr. Dean, who ran the adoption agency. He chose for you to become our baby boy. Dr. Dean brought you from the hospital to Dada and me at the adoption agency. That's where we first met you. And guess what, Matteo?"

"What?"

"You are the *best* thing that ever happened to us."

"Oh," Matteo said, taking it all in. "Do you think we'll see more elephants?" *Hallmark moment over. Typical toddler*, I thought as I kissed him.

After a week of game drives, late-night candlelit dinners overlooking a large watering hole, and snuggling with Matteo in a queen bed draped regally in flowing white mosquito netting, it was time to leave the bush and head to Mozambique.

Jacada Travel had arranged for us to fly to Vilankulos, a small town on the coast of the Indian Ocean. As we got off our plane and rode through that rich red African soil, I was transported to Banjul. I saw Juju and me walking to a nearby village, where kids my age played soccer happily in the red dust. All they needed was a ball and four rocks. Life was beautifully simple.

When we reached the coast, a mid-sized motorboat was waiting for us. Three Australian couples joined us. Mozambican men carried our suitcases above their heads through the waves until they were placed securely upon the boat. A light rain began to fall, and the waves tossed the boat harder and harder. Jamie and I positioned Matteo in a life vest between us, holding on to him tightly. We were all destined for the Mozambican island of Bazaruto. I had imagined the island to be close, but after forty minutes I couldn't see land on either side anymore. Just as the rain began to subside, a distant coastline appeared along the horizon. As we came in closer, the sun re-emerged high in the sky, shining its rays on the African island and the cool turquoise waters that surrounded it. Standing knee-deep in the ocean was a woman holding a tray of champagne. Beyond her, local inhabitants of the island sang in what I can only describe as the warmest welcome I've had to an island anywhere in the world.

"James, Garon, and Matteo, welcome to the Anantara Bazaruto," she said as we climbed into the ocean, handing Jamie and me a drink. I carried Matteo on my hip through the aquamarine water.

Bazaruto was spectacular. In the mornings, we would walk down the beach, greeting the native children of the island. Seven-year-olds carried long sticks with string dangling off the end. They were heading off to fish in the ocean to catch dinner for their parents. Their younger brother and sisters, closer to Matteo's age, trailed in the surf behind them.

"Where are those kids going?" Matteo asked me.

"They're going fishing for the day, buddy, to bring dinner back for their families for later tonight."

"Can you imagine if we gave Matteo a stick and rope and told him to come back for dinner with fish?" Jamie whispered to me with a smile.

"He'd never make it out here," I chided back. "Neither would we."

By lunchtime each day, the ocean receded about a mile into itself. Second to Kilauea's lava flowing into the ocean before me in Hawaii, this was one of the coolest things I've ever seen. Matteo was able to run far into the seabed and play for hours with shells that had been buried earlier that day beneath water. Vibrant-colored wooden boats that belonged to the locals sat hundreds of feet out in the ocean, no longer surrounded by the sea. Beyond the hotel, there was plentiful tall grass, sloping sand dunes, and crocodiles. It was absolutely a magical island. One evening at dinner we were seated next to two older ladies who were visiting from Hermanus, a port city on the west coast of South Africa.

"Are you having a nice time?" I asked.

"I wouldn't come here again," one of the ladies said in her Afrikaans accent. "There's literally nothing to do. We thought there would be shopping."

I wondered who had sold them this vacation. How could

there be shopping on an island with no roads, no stores, and no people beyond the natives and the guests. Her friend, who was friendlier and seemed content with Bazaruto, asked me, "What brought you all the way to this part of Africa, from America?" She had kind eyes, white fluffy hair.

"I was adopted from Sri Lanka and when I was three I moved to South Africa. I left when I was almost seven. I've always wanted to find my way back," I told her.

She looked at me pensively. "Yes. I think once you come to Africa, you can't quite get it out of your blood, can you?" she said with a warm smile. Her words continue to resonate in my heart to this day.

THE FOURTEEN-HOUR FLIGHT from Doha to Washington was filled with Indian families; in particular, Indian mothers flying by themselves with their young babies. The flight had originated in Mumbai and we were one of the few families onboard connecting in from Johannesburg.

"I think I'm pretty much the only white guy on this flight," Jamie said to me.

"You are," I confirmed. This time, we were seated in economy and I could see much of the cabin.

Across from us a woman sat alone in a red saree with her infant on her lap. She reminded me of my former housekeeper and friend, Suraj, and his wife, Banu. Every couple of minutes I would see her glance over at the three of us. When I would look back, she would quickly divert her eyes. This went on for a while. Jamie and I played with Matteo and allowed him to lie on a blanket on the floor playing against the bulkhead; I could feel her eyes moving between the three of us. Had she ever seen a family like ours before? We tried to make small talk with her, but she didn't engage us further.

Seven hours into the flight, I read her face. She seemed visibly uncomfortable holding her young son on her lap. I had once held Matteo on my lap for two hours on a domestic flight and was more than ready to hand him off to Jamie once we arrived. I couldn't imagine doing it for fourteen hours, but perhaps the decision to not buy a seat for the baby had been made for financial reasons. That was understandable. After ten hours of flying, I saw the brilliant scarlet fabric swaying above me out of the corner of my eye. Jamie and I turned to the mother, who was now standing next to us.

"Please take care of my baby," she pleaded, adding slowly, "I need to use the restroom."

"Of course we will," Jamie said, taking her infant daughter into his arms and cradling her against his chest.

I considered it a compliment. The Indian mother, who had initially seemed unsure about the three of us, had left her baby daughter in our hands. Though, to be fair, after ten hours in her lap, she might have left her with just about any willing passenger. The three of us looked in earnest at the little girl. She had an abundance of charcoal-black curly hair. I wondered why her family was traveling to the United States. Five minutes past. No mother. Ten minutes. No mother. Fifteen minutes. No mother.

"She needed some time to herself," I whispered to Jamie.

"I can't even imagine," Jamie said, holding the sleeping baby closer to him. Jamie loved babies and I knew he was happy the mother had taken extra time. Twenty-five minutes later, she came back to our seats.

"Thank you very much," she said, smiling at all three of us.

"No problem," Jamie answered. "Please let us know if you need to get up again."

She carried that baby for another four hours, changing her occasionally on her lap. When we landed in Washington, we wished her well. I had greatly admired her patience and would remember it. As we stepped outside, Veronica was waiting for us and Matteo leapt into her arms.

BACK FROM SOUTH AFRICA, I called Luling. Ashoh was eager to hear all about our trip. She loved that we had gone back to Flint Road and she shared loving memories of her time in Johannesburg with us twenty-five years before.

"I just couldn't get used to your mama and daddy drivin' on the other side of the road!" Ashoh told me. "And I can't believe I left poor Grandpa for that long."

"How are you doing without Grandpa? I really miss him."

"Oh, Garon. The house is so quiet. I miss fussin' at him."

"I know. I'm so sorry, Ashoh."

"I have a lot of good memories though, Garon, a lot of good memories." I wished I could have reached out and wrapped her hand in mine.

"Guess what, Ashoh? Jamie and I are in a program now out of New York City to adopt a child from South Africa."

For the first time, Ashoh didn't pause.

"Wow. You're adopting from South Africa this time! Boy or girl?"

"We don't know. It could be either. Or both. We're approved for siblings as well."

"Oh heavens, Garon. Y'all are going to have your hands full if you get siblings," she said.

A lot had changed over the years. Ashoh had tossed away her fears of our marriage, understood that we could raise a child, and it appeared she was slowly starting to accept a changing world. I was proud of my grandmother.

78

THE SLED

AS THE SUMMER HEAT CREPT into the city, the mom of Matteo's friend Ella, Susan Lagana, came over for breakfast one morning. Susan was notably tall, with long blond hair. I had always found her extremely likable. She walked in holding a giant red sled.

"Here! I bought a couple of these for the girls and we got one for Matteo this winter," Susan said. I felt terrible, I hadn't had a chance to tell her.

"Thanks so much, Susan. You're so kind," I said, taking the sled. I had to tell her. "Listen, we have something to tell you, and you're not going to like it."

Susan's normally smiley and engaging face turned serious.

"We're moving to Lauderdale."

Her mouth dropped open and she stared at me, speechless.

"I'm so sorry, I just found out a few days ago. Fort Lauderdale Tower called me and told me I had been accepted onto their team. I wasn't expecting it to happen so soon."

Matteo and Ella were running back and forth behind us.

"Give. Me. The. Sled. Back," Susan said slowly. I burst into laughter. This is what I loved about her—her dry sense of humor could always make me laugh. Jamie and I had spent a number of evenings over the years at her home. Susan was one of my favorite people in DC and I would miss her greatly.

Over many years Jamie and I had talked about moving. It had never felt like the right time. But recently, right time or not, we were ready for a change. One night in deciding between Los Angeles, Phoenix, and Fort Lauderdale, I stopped and turned to Jamie.

"Why don't we just move to where we vacation? Let's go live by the beach in Lauderdale."

He easily agreed, though neither of us ever thought the acceptance from Fort Lauderdale Tower would come as quickly as it did.

The next few weeks were a whirlwind. Jamie and I had great luck selling our row house in DC, almost immediately. We then left Matteo in Veronica's capable hands, flew down to Fort Lauderdale for twenty-four hours, and toured twelve homes. We chose a mid-century-modern, single-level home, anchored by thirteen coconut trees on a gorgeous peninsula near the beach.

Once back in Washington we began weeks of goodbyes with friends who had become our family. It had been eight years since I had arrived in DC. I knew that yet another chapter of my life was ending. It was hardest, of course, to say goodbye to Ebony.

"I can't believe this is our last Sunday dinner together," she said as we sat on the blue sofa in the living room of her condo. "Sunday nights are going to be so sad without the three of you."

"I'm going to miss you, and our dinners, so much, Ebie. We promise we'll come back up to visit and now you'll always have a place to stay at the beach," I assured her.

"Actually, that's true. Don't come up here, I'll just keep

coming to see you," she joked. Ebony and I had forever kept our love of beaches alive since those Lionel Richie evenings boogie boarding at sunset in The Gambia.

I TALKED TO Marine One carrying President Obama for what I knew would be my last time. I stared out at the White House as the helicopter lifted off the South Lawn. I felt confident that in two short months Secretary Hillary Clinton would win the US presidency. I felt a sadness that I wouldn't be a part of the team of controllers who I believed would soon carry the first female president in Marine One each time. For four years I had held so much pride in talking to Marine One, knowing that Obama was onboard.

I would miss the team of supremely talented controllers at DCA. It felt monumental to have arrived at my dream job so early in my career. I had Marilyn and Donnie to thank for that. In those first months at Washington Tower, Shanora had taught me how to control with precision, class, and grace; and now after incorporating those qualities for four years in my own controlling, I intended to carry them for the rest of my career. And I would miss my three controller friends with whom I had grown so close.

"I never went to college, Garon, so these unbelievably fun years with you have felt like my college experience. Thank you for that," Angela said. I would miss sitting out on the tower catwalk with her during our breaks marveling at the reverse thrust of the jet engines, and our late DC nights hanging out in our favorite bars and restaurants all across the city we both so loved.

Patrick and I never tired of talking about our sons and air

traffic control. While Matteo was closing in on four years old, Patrick's son was already ten. He was way ahead of me in the world of parenting. Patrick had enjoyed Matteo's many weekend visits to the tower while I worked. Jamie would catch the yellow line into DCA with Matteo, buy him ice cream in the terminal, and the two of them would come up into the tower cab and watch airplanes roll in and out of Washington, next to me. Our little boy delighted in toying with the binoculars as the controllers moved all around him, often stopping to land a quick hug.

"I promise you, it goes by so fast, Garon. Enjoy these years with Matteo because before you know it, he'll be a teenager." I appreciated his perspective and I couldn't imagine my little boy as a teenager, no matter how hard I tried to envision it. I would miss seeing Patrick each day.

My walks with Sherene up and down DCA's main terminal checking out attractive passengers would no longer be my reality. "There's a really hot guy in line at Starbucks in Terminal C. Want to come check him out with me?" she would ask. We'd get in the elevator, make our way down to the terminal, and position ourselves in front of Starbucks. "I think he's gay," Sherene said.

I observed for a moment. "Trust me, he's straight. Follow his eyes. He just checked out the girl's ass in the blue dress two people ahead, who just ordered the venti skim chai latte with two extras shots of espresso. Have I taught you nothing?" Sometimes on summer days, Sherene and I would walk outside to the parking lot, lie down beside each other on the concrete to soak up even more warmth, and stare up at the tower together. "Can you believe we get to work here?" I'd ask.

"No. I can't believe they ever let the two of us in," she'd say, and we'd laugh until it was time to go back up into our office in the sky.

ON SEPTEMBER 11, 2016, Jamie, Matteo, and I left all that we had known and accomplished together in Washington and flew down the east coast to our new home: Fort Lauderdale. Each year for the past four years at DCA, every September 11, I stood alongside the other controllers and observed a moment of silence at 9:37 a.m., as we stopped all departures, faced the Pentagon, and remembered the lives lost on that devastating day. While I was leaving Washington Tower, I planned to continue this moment of observation throughout my entire career.

We broke out of the fluffy clouds and saw the turquoise water below, speed boats racing up and down the coastline, and we celebrated. I experienced what only controllers can, departing from the one airport you've worked at for years and, very literally, landing at your next job. It's a strange feeling.

The first night in Lauderdale, the three of us walked to the beach where years earlier I had proposed to Jamie. Matteo took off running down the sand and into the warm Atlantic surf.

"I can't believe we actually moved here," Jamie said, looking up at the swaying palm trees while holding my hand.

"Me either. I'm so happy to be living by the ocean again. It's been too long."

Our new chapter in a place that brought such peace had begun. Each morning as I woke up, sunlight gently seeped through the floor-to-ceiling windows of our house, ushering in a tranquility of warmth and happiness. The hustle and bustle of 11th Street in Columbia Heights was replaced by tropical plants that surrounded our home in vibrant purples, pinks, reds and oranges, along with the ever-present humidity that coated us in a sheen of moisture. The three of us bolted outside each day to meet the brief afternoon sun shower that gave a refreshing reprieve from the Florida heat. Hearing our footsteps, the dozens of tiny lizards who called our garden home went scattering under the yellow and green leafy plants, only to stare cautiously at us from below cover. And in the evenings the three of us walked around our neighborhood peninsula meeting new friendly faces, taking in the brilliant sunset, and watching yachts glide peacefully along the more than 160 miles of waterways that wove throughout this city known as The Venice of America. We had a new place to call home and I hoped adventure awaited us.

79
ASHOH'S VOTE

I KNEW ASHOH DIDN'T LIKE HILLARY, but I was curious to see what she had to say about Donald Trump. It was hard for me to understand how the Evangelical community of the United States supported a man who was clearly not religious and emboldened the racism of so many Americans. I felt he wasn't a Republican or a Democrat; he was an opportunist. Had it been preferable for him to run as a Democrat, I'm confident he would have done that. Anything, as long as he was able to feel powerful.

"Oh, I don't know what I'm going to do," Ashoh told me one evening as she was cracking open crab claws. "I don't like either of them."

That was encouraging. At least she didn't *like* Trump. I had braced myself for that very possibility. "He's terrible. And I still don't like *her*," she asserted. I knew from previous discussions how much she disliked Hillary Clinton.

"Does this mean you like Barack and Michelle more than them?" I asked jokingly.

"I like Michelle Obama's arms," Ashoh said. Well, that was progress. Over eight years she had gone from her racist watermelon-garden comment to praising the First Lady's arms.

Change really had come to America.

"So are you going to vote?" I asked.

"Garon, this may be the first election where I do not vote," Ashoh said.

With most people, I might have offered a number of reasons why they should still vote. But for Ashoh, the fact that she wasn't voting for Trump was good enough for me.

"Are you liking Florida?" she asked.

"Yes, and I still hope you'll come stay with us," I offered. "I'll arrange everything for you, Ashoh."

"I'll have to talk to my doctors about it, Garon. I want to come, but I can't get around now as easily as I used to," Ashoh said. "Is your house on one-level?"

"It is."

"How are Matteo and Jamie doing?" she asked.

"They're doing great, Ashoh. Thanks for asking. I love you."

"I love you too," she said.

80

FEDEX 910

I REALIZED OVER THE COURSE of my first weeks at Lauderdale Tower (FLL) that I needed to acclimate myself to new pilots' accents that I hadn't encountered at DCA. My time spent living around the world made understanding foreign accents quite easy, when face to face. When controlling, however, you can't see any of their faces and are forced to interpret each accent using only your hearing, to ensure each instruction issued is being read back correctly by the pilot. I trained my ear to understand accents from Venezuela, Colombia, Ecuador, Panama, Mexico, and Brazil, and enunciated carefully when issuing instructions, hoping they could understand me effectively as well.

On Friday, October 28, 2016, I was on Fort Lauderdale Ground Control, under the watchful eye of a Dominican-American controller who had been fully certified at Lauderdale for many years. I enjoyed that aspect of working so close to the Caribbean: many of my new tower friends were Americans of Cuban, Dominican, and Puerto Rican origin. We were moving departures toward the two parallel runways and arrivals to the gates. A FedEx MD-10 was two miles from landing and I was looking across the taxiways, making sure that I wasn't moving any departures on the north side of the airport that would block his eventual exit.

Another feature of working at Fort Lauderdale Tower that I thoroughly enjoyed was being able to control wide-body jets. Due to the relatively short runways at DCA, restricted by its position in the Potomac River, the largest commercial aircraft weren't able to land there and stop in time. Fort Lauderdale's longer runways could well accommodate 777s, A300s, 787s, MD-10s, and the like. I had the pleasant experience of controlling a Virgin Atlantic A340 that the Miami Dolphins had chartered to transport them to a game hosted in London and a Lufthansa Boeing 747 that had to divert from Miami to Lauderdale during a thunderstorm. Both were aircraft that I had always wanted to control but never had the opportunity to at DCA. There's a captivating grace to watching wide-body aircraft land. These colossal machines appear to be floating seconds from touchdown before making contact with the runway. I looked out the window as the giant FedEx was roaring down. Suddenly, out of the left corner of my eye I saw the expression of the local controller shift from relaxed to aghast.

"Oh shit, oh shit!" he muttered beneath his breath.

My eyes raced back out the tower windows to the runway and I realized that the runway was alight with fire. I worked quickly to diagnose the situation. It appeared that FedEx's left wing and engine were scraping against the runway, igniting an enormous fire that now ran the length of the north runway. The supervisor leapt out of his chair and along with the controller overseeing me they raced to pull the crash phone, a phone that once activated alerts the entire airport emergency response apparatus simultaneously.

"This is an Alert three, I repeat, Alert three, on Runway one-zero-left," the tower communicated to everyone. Alert three signifies that an aircraft has crashed at the airport.

To my left, the local controller began clearing the sky of arrivals that would no longer be able to land. "Southwest 2789, cancel approach clearance, climb and maintain two thousand. Maintain heading 095," the local controller instructed the next arrival just five miles from the runway. Southwest quickly complied and began climbing.

FedEx careened more than five thousand feet down the runway and then slid onto its left wing, exploding into a thick cloud of smoke. As emergency vehicles called my frequency racing toward the runway, I quickly granted permission for each of them to expedite to the engulfed aircraft.

From the tower, we could no longer see the FedEx MD-10 through the black cloud of smoke billowing into the air, the fire raging all around.

"I hope the pilots are jumping out," one of the controllers said.

Suddenly a secondary explosion detonated and the deep boom pulsed through the air over the airport, into the sky, and around the tower.

"Oh no!" I whispered quietly to myself, now imagining the FedEx had completely exploded, the pilots likely dead.

No longer able to see the aircraft, we watched the rescue as dozens of fire engines braved through the dark smoke to extinguish the inferno.

I had prepared for years for this, starting at the Academy in Oklahoma City, but somehow it's never real until it is real. We later found out that the captain and first officer evacuated the cockpit window via an escape rope, then landed on the tarmac and ran away from the exploding airplane. The National

Transportation Safety Board (NTSB) report that came out confirmed that the left main landing gear had collapsed on landing.

For years at DCA, I had worked countless emergencies. Once, I cleared an Alaska Airlines to Seattle for takeoff. As soon as they were airborne, the first officer yelled, "Smoke in the cockpit, smoke in the cockpit, requesting vectors for Dulles." Her voice was panic-stricken, and we moved quickly to coordinate effectively and get them a safe arrival at nearby Dulles. I had controlled multiple commercial aircraft with cracked windshields, minimal fuel, and even loss of one of the engines, but I had never seen a major jetliner crash upon landing. I drove home that evening feeling grateful that it had been a cargo jet, the pilots had escaped unharmed, and no passengers were onboard.

ONE OF THE TOUGHEST parts of leaving DC was separating from our amazing nanny, Veronica. I had seen her as a third parent, and we loved her as much as Matteo did. After an extensive search for nannies and days of interviews, one evening a sixty-year-old Colombian woman named Martha walked into our home. Martha was an interesting combination of being elegant and poised but also extremely modest. Initially I had a hard time believing she would want to spend her days jumping in and out of the pool and shuttling back and forth to the beach with Matteo, but she convinced us otherwise. Within ten minutes of interviewing her, we knew she was the right person for our family. We hired her days later and started to enjoy the added benefit of listening to her lovely Colombian accent ring through our home on a daily basis. We requested that she only speak to Matteo in Spanish, just as Veronica had, and within days we had two languages circulating throughout our home.

"Buenos días, mi amor!" Martha would say with great enthusiasm each morning as she opened our door and extended her arms toward Matteo. "¿Cómo estás?"

"Hola, Martha. Estoy bien," his little voice replied.

"Ay! Precioso! Divino. ¿Qué quieres hacer hoy?"

"Quiero ir a la playa." And off she would whisk him, as requested, for a fun day at the beach. In the evenings Matteo would tell us stories of seeing stingrays and swordfish. This little boy who had been born on a winter morning in Maryland and adopted from DC now spent his days running beneath lofty palm trees and wading out to the nearest sandbar.

81

ANY DAY NOW

*Congrats! Your dossier is on its way to South Africa.
So excited for your family . . . during this next phase
of your journey of waiting for a referral.*

T HE EMAIL WAS SENT FROM Samantha Moore, the director of international adoptions at Spence-Chapin in New York City. Moving down to the beach had required a bit more paperwork after leaving Washington, but we finally had gotten everything we needed. We were now fully ready to accept a referral: an announcement of a little girl or boy, or possibly siblings, that South African social workers would match with our family. We knew from this point forth, the phone could ring any day with news from the country I so adored.

I HAD TRIED to contact Suraj many times over the years. After I left Jordan, he and I would communicate back and forth multiple times a year with the email address I had set up for him. The summer after I had left Amman, Suraj and Banu had given birth to their adorable daughter, Archana. But now, for close to four years, I hadn't received any responses from him. I missed Suraj greatly and thought about him often. Maybe he had moved back to India. I hoped wherever he, Archana, and Banu were in this world, they were living a life full of happiness. He deserved that.

One morning after returning from the beach, I checked my Facebook messages.

Hi Garon. How are you? It's me, Suraj.

When I saw the message, I yelled his name out loud and immediately wrote back.

(Me) Suraj!! *How are you and Banu? How's Archana?*

(Suraj) *Banu is good and Archana is good. I am still in Jordan. I am now the driver for the Indian Ambassador.*

When I read that he was the driver to the ambassador, it brought me immense happiness. As a teenager I used to sit in the kitchen and Suraj would tell me that one day he hoped to stop cleaning homes and be someone's driver. I wanted that for him. To know that he had achieved it delighted me. He sent me pictures of the three of them. Little Archana was now a beautiful teenager. Banu and Suraj looked healthy and happy. In return, I sent him a picture of my right forearm where the sequence MQ (-X) S +c4R- F is tattooed.

You see that tattoo of S? That S is for Suraj. It's for you, I wrote him.

Wow! Thank you so much, Garon, he wrote back.

I had gotten it long ago one icy winter night in Washington, when I had wanted to pay tribute in ink to him and the love that he had brought to my shattered life in Jordan. He had arrived as my housekeeper, became my brother and then, under the worst of circumstances, an extra parent. It brought me an inordinate amount of joy to be in contact once again with Suraj and I promised myself I would never lose touch with him again. I've held tight to that promise. To this day, we still talk every two weeks. The MQ stood for *mosque*, reminding me of our first day in Amman when Mom climbed into bed with the three of us, encouraging us to listen to the devastatingly beautiful call to prayer.

(-X) was losing her, a catastrophe I never expected to happen. And +c4R-F represented my senior year at ACS Amman, 2004. I remembered how I would sit peacefully on the (R)oof of our home, gazing across the arid landscape at the skyline of Amman and trying to understand my place in the world. I would turn west to face the United States and try to imagine what my (F)uture would bring on the other side of the ocean.

Sometimes at night, I journey back to that rooftop in my mind and try to retrace the steps that have gotten me to where I am. I can still see my neighbors, the warm Bedouin family moving with their flock of sheep outside their tall beige tent in the valley. Just above them, yellow taxis fly by, racing down the airport highway, taking visitors to the heart of the city. Saleem's Mercedes turns off the highway and slowly winds up my broken roads to pick me up for a night of partying with JJ, Vassia, and all our other friends.

I look down at that tattoo and remember how young I felt and how badly I wanted to find my way. Never could I have imagined perched high above the hills of Amman what lay ahead.

82

RUN, HIDE, FIGHT

TWO MONTHS AFTER THE CRASH of FedEx 910, I had fully certified at Lauderdale Tower. My breaks were often spent soaking up the sunshine on the grounds outside the tower. After laughing with a colleague and stowing my phone downstairs, I made my way into the elevator that carried me back into the tower cab.

"Okay, active shooter in Terminal two. Multiple casualties. Got it," the supervisor said, holding the phone.

I looked at one of my colleagues and asked, "Is this real?" She nodded. They asked me to get on Local Control. I knew I was going to be in for the long haul. I looked out the window: we had a long line of departures making their way to the runway.

"Move all the departures that are waiting to taxi away from the gates," the supervisor told the ground controller. We have multiple phones in the tower and all of them started ringing at once. Within moments, the Broward County Sherriff's Department, Fort Lauderdale Police Department, the FBI, and FAA Security were all involved.

I plugged my headset into Local Control and relieved the controller who had been working. There were a line of airplanes sitting short of the runway, waiting patiently for departure instructions.

"Sir, we are ready for departure when you are," a WestJet flight told me politely. Canadian pilots. They are always polite and highly professional.

"Departures are stopped until further notice," I announced to the line of aircraft. I had learned years before that during a fluid security situation we aren't able to divulge everything we know for fear of compromising the situation. As in 9/11, there could be cockpits that have been compromised and now terrorists might be listening to the controllers to gain a picture of what's happening. The decision was made to stop any arrivals from landing. Every law enforcement and news helicopter in the area was hovering over the terminals. The controller behind me was moving them all in and out of the airspace.

Suddenly there were gasps in the tower. I stood up quickly, looked out the east window, and saw hundreds of passengers breaking free from the secure terminal doors. They ran in terror from the terminal and onto the runway to get as far away as possible.

"It must be terrible in there," someone said. I had a giant lump in my throat and I felt my heart beating faster. I picked up the binoculars and zoomed out the window. Before my eyes, families were hiding behind luggage carts, couples were holding hands running for fear of being shot, and parents held their children tight to their body as they scattered like a herd of impala running away from lionesses. It tore my heart open. How many people were dead? How many shooters were there? I had taken active shooter training at DCA and had always been prepared for it in Washington. It was such a high-profile airport, it almost seemed an inevitability. Often as I would walk down the main terminal with Patrick, Angela, and Sherene, I would look up at the balcony of the second floor. I would decide where I might run to protect myself in the event of a shooting. As I had learned in training: run, hide, fight. But never did I imagine I would find myself watching from the tower as an active shooter crisis unfolded in this peaceful city by the beach.

After two hours, another controller came up to relieve me and I went on break. I knew that Jamie would be worrying. I grabbed my phone once I was downstairs and had an endless line of missed calls and texts. I called Jamie.

"Hey, I don't know if you're watching the news, but I'm fine."

He started to cry quietly.

"Jamie, I'm fine. I'm fine, I promise. But it's horrible. Passengers broke out of the airport and are hiding all across the tarmac. I have no idea how many people are dead, but I am sick to my stomach watching it. What is the news saying?"

"Everyone's been calling and texting me the past couple hours. I was out with a friend and once I heard, I went straight home. So many people from Washington have messaged me. Ebony called as soon as she saw it on CNN. Everyone is watching the news and wants to know if you're okay."

"I'm okay. Honestly, we are fine in the tower," I promised him. I reminded him that the tower at Lauderdale, unlike DCA, sits across from the airport terminal, not within it.

"The news is reporting multiple people dead and more shot in the Delta terminal," Jamie added.

"I can't believe this actually happened in Lauderdale, Jamie. I was always mentally prepared for this shit in Washington, but not here."

"I know. I'm so relieved to hear from you. You have no idea

the thoughts that were running through my head when I didn't get a call from you."

"I'm sorry. You know we can't take our cellphones into the tower cab. I promise though, we are fine. Listen, I have to go back up and continue working this nightmare. I'm not going to be able to call you for another hour or so. I promise I'll call you when I'm on my way home."

"That's fine. Go help. I love you."

"I love you too."

I made my way back up to the tower. We all took turns controlling the helicopter traffic above the airport and assisting the pilots as best we could on the ground. Given the uncertainty of the security situation, planes were not allowed to move for more than six hours. At some point there was talk from security services of the potential that a bomb had been planted underneath the south runway and this was a coordinated terrorist attack. Cabins full of passengers who had landed right as the shooting was taking place, or preparing to depart, were now stuck on the taxiways indefinitely. Pilots told us their cabins had run out of water and in many cases lavatories onboard were reaching capacity. A number of aircraft communicated to us that passengers with small babies had completely exhausted their supply of diapers and formula as hour after hour passed. We coordinated between pilots and airport operations who did their level best to deliver these desperately needed items to cockpit windows. Passengers who had flown into Lauderdale to jump on long-awaited cruises were realizing they would no longer be sailing into the Caribbean as their cruise ships had left without them. Across the tarmac, the hundreds of people who had run for their lives were now huddled

---

together surrounded by security trying to protect and contain them. Hundreds, if not thousands, of bags lay strewn across the airport tarmac left behind in the mass panic. I put my binoculars to the side and monetarily thought of my time at the academy in Oklahoma City six years prior. My instructor, Roy Hillen, had told us to prepare for absolutely anything. He had been right.

By nightfall, police cars lined the entire perimeter of one of the country's busiest airports. From high above, it looked like the airport was surrounded by a nonstop string of blue and red Christmas lights. Later that night, I drove home in silence. When I got home, the three of us hugged longer than usual.

The next day, Friday, January 7, 2017, the *Washington Post* reported:

> *An Iraq War veteran who had complained that the government was forcing him to watch Islamic State videos pulled a gun from his checked bag and opened fire Friday afternoon at Fort Lauderdale's international airport, killing five people.... The alleged gunman, identified by authorities as 26-year-old Esteban Santiago of Anchorage, was apprehended.... Santiago, a U.S. citizen with ties to New Jersey and Puerto Rico, had picked up his bag from the carousel and gone to the bathroom to load his gun before returning to the baggage-claim area and firing at people.... Travelers are allowed to bring firearms with them to flights as long as the guns are unloaded, locked in a hard-sided container and in checked baggage, according to the Transportation*

Security Administration. Ammunition can be brought onto flights but also must be placed in checked baggage.

Once again, our nation's gun laws, or lack thereof, had failed us.

83

DOROTHY NELSON

ONE EVENING IN MAY, I got the message that I always dreaded would come someday.

Hi all,
I write with sad news. Ashoh is now in hospice care.
I'll be headed that way shortly to see if I can catch her
one more time.
Love,
Yael

I stared at the computer screen. I hadn't called Ashoh in weeks.

Ashoh—or Dorothy Nelson, as her friends in Louisiana knew her—died soon after. I never made it down to see her. As I write this, I have *deep* regret. I should have jumped on a flight to New Orleans the moment I heard. I didn't. I would have liked to hold her hand one more time and tell her that I loved her. I would have liked to thank her for coming to South Africa so many years before to help take care of us. I would have liked to tell her how grateful I was for her daughter who raised me. Love isn't always easy. A lot of times it's really messy. And we all make mistakes.

I didn't go to the funeral, but instead promised myself I'd find another time when I could be with Ashoh alone. A quiet and peaceful time when I could travel back to Louisiana without the crowds of people, sit by her tomb, and truly say goodbye to a woman whom I rarely saw eye to eye with but whom I loved so very much.

Ashoh was buried right next to Grandpa in St. Rose, just minutes away from their beloved Luling. When I found out she died, I lay down in my bed and closed my tear-soaked eyes. All I could hear in the quiet of the room were the words she had told me as we sat beside each other on the edge of her bed twenty years before: *I can still see his little hand waving me goodbye as he left that weekend.* I took a deep breath. Then I imagined Ashoh lying peacefully holding Uncle Robby in one arm and Mom in the other. She was finally with her children again.

NOW, WITHOUT EXCEPTION, each time I clear a plane for takeoff to Louisiana, my mind transports to Luling. The hot sun beams down on the rich St. Augustine lawns as the sound of mowers ring in the air. Nearby, Spanish moss hangs elegantly from distinctly formed bald cypress trees anchoring the marsh below. A gentle breeze flows off the Mississippi River and coasts down Bernice Drive.

I see the red-brick driveway leading up to the yellow door. Grandpa is drinking a Coors Light in the doorway of his garage. Ashoh leaves the kitchen, slowly walks into the garage in her pink floral muumuu, and makes her way to him.

"What you doin' out here?"

"I *was* trying to get some peace and quiet, Dorothy."

"Oh hush, Petie," she says as he smirks.

84

EMMANUEL

O N THE MORNING OF APRIL 17, 2019, I was getting my beard trimmed at my barber in Lauderdale. Jamie was on a business trip working at headquarters back in Washington, and Matteo, now six and a half years old, was in his kindergarten classroom. Samantha from the adoption agency in New York City sent us the following: *Do you have time to have a call this morning? I'm free any time between 10a.m. and 12p.m. noon.*

At 10:15 a.m. we jumped on a three-way call. I drove through my beachy town back home, listening on Bluetooth.

"Good morning, guys. We did receive a referral for your family this morning. You've been matched with a little boy!" Samantha said, her voice conveying great excitement.

I felt a crashing wave of happiness envelop my white Highlander. I could hear Jamie's elation through the screams. There was exhilaration on all sides of the call.

"His name is Emmanuel and he was born in Soweto," Samantha continued. I knew Soweto. We had visited the township on our last trip and I had learned much more about it when reading Trevor Noah's memoir, *Born a Crime*. He was born there as well.

"Emmanuel," I said his name out loud.

"He's living at Princess Alice Adoption Home in Westcliff, Johannesburg. His birth mother couldn't take care of him and he's been living at the orphanage since his birth in 2017."

Wow, two years. He's been on this earth for close to two years by himself. His orphanage was only ten minutes away from Flint Road. I could picture exactly where it was in the hilly upscale neighborhood of Westcliff. Jamie flew home later that night and we printed out pictures of Emmanuel that Samantha had sent us. He sat on the green-and-white-checkered floor of the orphanage with a serious look on his face. His skin was the same color as mine, and his prominent dark-brown eyes and full lips were the first features we noticed. He wore a yellow-blue-and-white-striped long-sleeve shirt. It was April and I knew winter was rolling into South Africa.

We waited to tell Matteo together. The next evening, we sat our first-born down at the table and told him we had some big news. He had been so patient for three years, talking with us each time South Africa extended the wait time to be matched. Just as I had once learned I had a little brother born in South Africa, now Matteo would as well.

"Can I tell all my friends at school now?" he asked, hoping we would say yes.

"Of course, buddy," Jamie said.

The next day I sat toward the back of his classroom as Matteo stood confidently before his classmates pointing at a picture of Emmanuel.

"This is my new little brother. He lives in South Africa. We are going to fly there soon to pick him up," he said slowly and thoughtfully.

From their squares on the multicolored carpet, Matteo's little classmates, with wondering eyes, stared up at the photograph of Emmanuel in a turquoise shirt, and breadcrumbs dusting his face, and smiled. I wondered what kind of questions they might be asking their parents at dinner tonight.

At the end of the week, we invited all our close friends over for a Matteo's Going to Be a Big Brother Party. They, too, had waited years to find out. Matteo, Jamie, and I launched the cannons into the sky above our backyard and it rained blue confetti over the palm trees and around all our friends, who cheered in happiness.

In the months that followed, I'd often lie awake at night, counting seven hours forward to figure out what time of day Emmanuel was moving through in his orphanage. Then I'd take an unusually long, deep breath and find comfort in knowing that I had taken a breath at the same time as my little boy. We wouldn't be able to get him until a South African judge was able to offer us a day in court to finalize. I wanted to call Ashoh, but I couldn't.

85

THE FIRST LADY

"GARON, WHAT ARE YOU GOING to say to Michelle Obama?" my colleagues Sharmaine and Denise asked me from across the tower. Those two were fun to work with and controlled planes excellently.

"I have no idea, girls. You know how starstruck I get," I replied as they laughed, knowing it was true.

I had read Michelle Obama's memoir, *Becoming*, on my way to Stockholm just before the holidays the previous December. Ebony had met a handsome Swedish guy named Marcus, and after they each crossed the Atlantic numerous times to visit each other, she had decided to leave Washington and settle in Stockholm. The memoir had kept me company much of my flight out of the States and into northern Europe. Even the Swedish flight attendant had stopped once or twice to check out the book. That Christmas, Jamie handed me a gift. I unwrapped the decorative red paper. It was Michelle Obama's memoir.

"I already read this," I said to him, laughing.

"Obviously I know that, Garon. Just open it."

I opened the book and inside there was a note: *Let's get together, say hi, and take a picture.*

"No!" I said, slamming the book closed in disbelief. Jamie laughed harder.

"Jamie, no. Are you serious?"

It was a momentous gift. He and I had always found ways to give each other experiences instead of material things. Years before in Washington, shortly after we met, I surprised him one evening by taking him to see Tina Turner perform from the fourth row. He had looked at me then and said, "How the hell did you get these seats?"

I ran my hand across the cover of Michelle's memoir, hugged Jamie, and said, "I used to think about her when I was working Marine One. I always wondered when she was in there with him."

Later that evening, Jamie and I stood in a line that weaved around what resembled a hotel ballroom. Looking around I noticed three distinct groupings of people: black families, gay and lesbian couples, and white mothers with their daughters. I'm not sure what I expected, but the consistency of the groupings amazed me. As the line inched forward to a curtained room, I enjoyed watching the faces of the people time and time again as they disappeared behind the curtain with giant smiles. Surely Michelle Obama was on the other side. Suddenly a family caught my eye. An elderly black husband and wife, probably in their eighties, walking with canes, were being helped along.

"Jamie. Look at that older couple over there. For me and you, we are so inspired by the Obamas and we loved that we lived in Washington during their time in the White House. But can you imagine what meeting her will mean to that couple over there? Can you imagine what injustice they lived through? Segregation. The bus boycotts," I said.

Jamie nodded in agreement as he watched them with me.

"Imagine what it must mean for them to meet the first black First Lady of the United States," I continued. "I mean, in their day, they probably couldn't even imagine a black president."

The moment hit me hard. The elderly couple, who were Ashoh's age, inched their way forward in the line. I wondered where they had been on both election nights, and how they felt the moment Obama won.

Twenty-five minutes had passed and Jamie and I were now next in line to enter the curtain. Next to us stood a Secret Service agent. The curtain opened and we were waved in. We turned the corner and there she stood: Michelle Obama. Tall. Radiant. Poised and extremely well versed in welcoming people. All the people in line felt such affinity for her, something I had also felt from the very first moments I saw her on the campaign trail in 2008. It was finally our turn. She said goodbye to the person ahead of us, then turned to Jamie and me. I walked toward her first with a shy smile and she opened her arms wide.

"It's so great to meet you," I said as I walked into her embrace.

"Oh, it's so wonderful to meet you too," she said, closing her eyes and pulling me close. It felt surreal. I turned around to introduce Jamie, but he was already on her left side.

"Hi, it's so nice to meet you!" Jamie exclaimed, his eyes beaming with happiness.

She's called the Hugger-in-Chief for a reason. Without being hyperbolic, that was one of the best hugs I've ever had. The three of us turned to face the photographer, who snapped away and after about five seconds Michelle turned to me.

"How was your day?" she asked.

This was my chance to ask her a question. I wanted to, and really I could have, but I felt the weight of the line of people staring at us with starry eyes, awaiting their turn, and I failed.

"It was great . . . thank you," I said with an enormous smile. My nose had started to sweat, I could tell.

Michelle looked at me. "Okaaay," she said and paused with a smile and her eyebrows raised. I stared into her eyes and knew instantly that she was inviting me to say what I wanted to. Again, I failed. Here I was, starstruck again.

"Have a great day," I told her, feeling completely elated and yet annoyed that I hadn't seized the opportunity. As Jamie and I turned to leave, we walked a couple steps forward and then turned back one more time. I doubted I'd ever be this close to Michelle Obama again and wanted to see her once more. She was still looking at us with her radiant smile and kind nature. I locked eyes with her again and then shook my head as if to say, *You are just incredible,* and turned for the final time. It was a wonderful moment and sadly it was ending. All of a sudden, one of her Secret Service agents came walking toward us.

"Hey, guys!" he said, extending his hand.

"Lucas?" We both exclaimed, completely surprised.

"How you guys doing? I had heard you moved down to Lauderdale," he said.

"Yea, we've lived here for two years now. How are you?" Jamie asked.

Now this was definitely awkward. We were having this conversation less than three feet from Michelle Obama, who was now looking at the situation and, I'm sure, trying to figure out how we knew Lucas.

"Hey, actually, come over here so we're not right in front of her," Lucas said. We followed.

"Great to see you, Lucas. Are you exclusively on her detail now?" I asked.

"Yes. Actually, I'm her head of security ever since they left the White House."

"Wow, that's wonderful. Since you must go to a lot of amazing places with her, what's your favorite?" I asked, now apparently feeling all the courage I should have had just moments ago when standing in front of, perhaps, the United States' greatest First Lady.

"Well, her and Barack are good friends with Richard Branson, and he has a private island, so we often go there," he said.

"That sounds fun," I replied.

He nodded. "I've got to get back, but great to see you guys," he said.

"Great to see you, Lucas," Jamie said, and we headed off in different directions.

We had met Lucas in Washington years before. It was a nice surprise to see him with Michelle Obama in Lauderdale.

The rest of the night was the big event: the book tour that had taken Michelle Obama across the United States, then over to Stockholm, Paris, Copenhagen, Oslo, and then back home. Once the doors opened, we made our way through the arena to our seats. Jamie and I were seated center, about ten rows back, and had a spectacular view of the evening. Around us, I observed the same types of groupings as I had earlier, only now among thousands of people.

The lights dimmed, and a wonderful lead-up video showed the years Michelle Obama had been in the White House, her travels around the world, her interaction with little girls on different continents, her appearance on "Carpool Karaoke," her daughters, and so much more. It was a welcomed break from the bullshit of the Trump Administration and an exciting ride down memory lane of the Obamas and Washington.

When Michelle walked out, the crowd couldn't get enough. Standing before them, the first black, and most educated, First Lady in the history of the United States. People had such a love for her, that was clear. But what struck me even more was how honest she was about her experiences. It definitely wasn't a chance for her to speak about how great her life was but, instead, to tell hard truths. She spoke transparently about white flight on the south side of Chicago where she grew up, not being enthusiastic about her husband running for president, and later, their marriage counseling. She came across not only as authentic but extremely relatable.

Driving home that evening, I thanked Jamie profusely for giving me this opportunity, this experience. I knew that it was a night we would speak about for years and years to come.

86

SWEDEN

I DRAPED THE NORWEGIAN AIRLINES blanket over Matteo, dimmed his cabin light, and kissed him on the cheek as he sunk back into his large gray leather seat.

"Love you, Daddy. When I wake up, will we be there?" he asked.

"When you wake up, we'll be very close. We can have breakfast together above Europe. Deal?"

"Deal."

I stroked Matteo's curly hair and stared at him as he drifted off to sleep, admiring how sensitive and intuitive he had become. The little baby boy who I had played "Cherish" for in the back seat of our Honda CR-V that snowy night in Maryland was now seven years old. For the first time I was taking him to Europe, and for the best of reasons. Ebony and Marcus were getting married in Stockholm and our family and close friends were descending upon Sweden to celebrate. Yael had flown in days before from his new home base in Wyoming, and Dad had made his way north from Italy. Jamie had been working in London the week before, so he had flown directly to Stockholm to spend more time with Dad, Yael, and Ebony, who were all eagerly awaiting our arrival. It was August, just four months

YOU'LL ALWAYS BE WHITE TO ME

since we had found out about Emmanuel, but still no word from the South African court inviting us to meet him and finalize the adoption. If nothing else, this multiyear adoption process had taught me patience.

There was something very special about Matteo and I taking an international flight, just the two of us. I stroked his head and gazed out Norwegian Airline's purple tinted window as we cruised across the Atlantic in a magnificent Boeing 787.

Hours later as we crossed into European airspace, I remembered my many childhood vacations spent exploring the continent. In Andorra, Ebony and I had begged Mom and Dad to allow us to swim in a nearby lake. Finally, they relented, watching us with Yael cradled in their arms as we dove into the freezing-cold water, raced out to a protruding gray rock, hustled back, and then shivered our way into the rental car. In Finland one year, Ebony, Yael, and I cautiously attempted snowboarding while eight-year-olds zoomed by us on their boards, completely uninhibited and clearly adept, unlike us. My mind flipped through times in Estonia, Germany, Cyprus, France, Belgium, Spain, and Luxembourg. But what stood out the most was that trip through Amsterdam, twenty-one years ago to the month, on our way to begin our new life in the Middle East. I laughed in my leather seat remembering Mom guiding us through the Red Light District and how I had imagined the expression on Ashoh's face had she been with us. I remembered the postcard of the two handsome guys having sex, which I had gravitated toward but couldn't quite identify why it had appealed to me. In some ways, it was hard to imagine two decades had passed.

Hours later, I kept my promise to Matteo as we savored delicious croissants together while sipping on juice and coffee.

"Is Grandma going to be there?" he asked.

"Sure she is, buddy. Do you know Grandma's in the air right behind us, flying from Boston? She's going to land three hours after us. I'm sure she can't wait to see you."

As our Dreamliner made contact with the runway at Arlanda Airport, I leaned over to Matteo.

"It means a lot to me to be sitting beside you on your very first trip to Europe. You know, Daddy spent a lot of time here during my summers when I was your age." Matteo studied my eyes.

Once through passport control, the Arlanda Express, a high-speed train, rocketed us into the heart of Stockholm. Handling all our bags, as Dad had done so many times before on our family trips, I trailed Matteo with my hands full as he skipped ahead. Yael, Jamie, and Dad were all waiting on the train platform. With Dad's arms outstretched, Matteo ran to him and fell into his giant embrace. I hugged Jamie and then made my way over to Yael, whom I hadn't seen in a while. I pulled him close to me and wrapped my arms around him. Then I pulled back and studied his face.

"Wow, you still look so much like Mom," I said. Yael's smirk grew into a bright smile. "I'm so happy to see you."

"I'm happy to see you too. Matteo got big."

"Yea, he did."

The sound of clapping rose from beyond us. It was Ebony hurrying down the train platform with a small Swedish flag and a blue-and-yellow noise maker.

"Hi, guys! Welcome to Sweden!" she said as Matteo bounded toward her. Jamie grabbed some of our luggage and Dad placed his arm around me.

"Hey, big guy, how you doing?"

YOU'LL ALWAYS BE WHITE TO ME

"I'm great, Dad. Happy to see all of you."

The six of us walked together farther into the city. It felt wonderful to be back on this side of the Atlantic together, as a family.

"IS IT SAFE to drink the water here?" Denice asked from the bathroom of our hotel room at the Sheraton. She had arrived on time and Matteo was thrilled to have his grandmother and his grandfather in the same city.

"This is Sweden. It's the first world of the first world. You can lick the floor here," I said from the bedroom as Jamie laughed and Denice gave me the "Oh, Garon, you're always kidding with me" face. She was right. Over the years I had lovingly teased Denice over a variety of issues. Once, she had thoughtfully bought Matteo a monogrammed brown sofa chair from Pottery Barn Kids. She had toiled for weeks over the decision to buy it and wanted the color and textured fabric to be absolutely perfect. The day it arrived, she texted:

(Denice) *Did his little chair arrive?*

(Me) *It did! We were going to call you tonight and still will. Thank you so much, you're so thoughtful. But why does the monogramming say "M-a-l-l-e-o" on it.*

Denice went into full meltdown mode, racing upstairs to her laptop to find her Pottery Barn confirmation and preparing to write a strongly worded email before Jamie made me call the whole thing off.

"Garon, you got me again. I'm going to have to get you one day," she promised on the phone later that evening.

That night after an extremely warm and welcoming family dinner at Marcus's parents' home, we all parted ways to return to our various accommodations. Once back at the Sheraton, Matteo and Denice climbed into one queen-sized bed, and Jamie and I in the other.

"Grandma, guess what?"

"What, honey?"

At Ebony's wedding I get to walk out with her."

"I can't wait to see you beside her in her wedding dress. You are going to be so handsome in your little shirt and tie."

The morning of the wedding my phone buzzed. A message from Ebony.

(Ebony) *Can you and Jamie come to the venue and help us set up before the wedding?*

(Me) *Sure!*

(Ebony) *Also, you may have trouble moving around the city because it's gay pride. There may be some street closures.*

(Me) *Who the fuck schedules their wedding on the same day as gay pride?;)*

(Ebony) *I KNOW! I didn't even realize until recently and now I feel terrible since half the people at this wedding are gay and the rest of us love them. We could have all partied together at pride today and had the wedding tomorrow.*

(Me) *Honestly, I'm not sure if I'm going to be able to make the wedding now that I know it's pride.*

(Ebony) *If you ditch my wedding for pride I will fucking kill you.*

(Me) *Just kidding. We'll be there. See you soon.*

With Matteo and Denice thrilled to have exclusive time together at the hotel, Jamie and I took the elevator down to the lobby. As soon as the doors opened, a cacophony of cheering rose through the air.

"What's that?" I asked, looking around.

"Look, the pride parade comes right outside the hotel," Jamie said excitedly, pointing out the revolving doors.

The modern Scandinavian-style lobby boasted elegant white tile and floor-to-ceiling glass. Guests stood near the dark wood-paneled columns of the lobby bar staring out the broad windows as a wave of rainbow color moved by.

"C'mon, let's go check it out just for a couple minutes!" I said.

Always the measured one, Jamie hesitated. "We have to go meet Ebony, though."

"It doesn't matter if we spend five minutes here watching. We'll just walk faster later," I reasoned.

The cool wind of the Swedish summer rippled through the crowds as Jamie and I moved among throngs of people. We walked up a bridge that arched over the parade route, giving us a better view.

"Look at that!" I said. For as far as the eye could see, people lined the parade route all around the city. Gay couples and their friends marked the occasion, taking pictures; elaborate parade floats rolled by with exhilarated people waving from atop. Restaurants and cafés along the route lined their outdoor terraces with pride flags that whipped in the wind. And straight couples pushed their children in strollers while they playfully waved the rainbow flag to the sound of Beyoncé's voice cascading through the air. It seemed that all of Stockholm—straight, gay, and everyone in between—had come out to celebrate love in this Scandinavian city.

"This is one of the biggest prides I've ever seen," Jamie said, taking it all in.

"I love that it's not just gay people, it's everyone. There are grandmas out here. I hope the US can get to this point one day."

Jamie nudged me. "C'mon, let's get going, buddy. You never

want to miss a party. Luckily, you'll get to party at the wedding late into tonight." I wrapped my arm around his waist and squeezed him tight.

Moments later, away from the pride celebration, I led Jamie up a hillside in Ebony's neighborhood in Sodermalm, where I had walked the year before. It then leveled onto a vast walkway that overlooked all of Stockholm. A mix of sleek modern yachts and older fishing boats weaved through the deep blue waters of the Baltic Sea, a different hue from the turquoise waterways of Lauderdale to which I had become accustomed. Jamie and I marveled at the view of Stockholm, built on a collection of fourteen islands, with bridges connecting each one to the other. The buildings of the city—in bright orange, white, yellow, red, and turquoise—splashed color across the dark waters. The beige and more muted tones added a soothing balance. I walked over to the nearest bakery and bought chocolate croissants and coffees for the two of us to savor as we continued our twenty-minute walk above the city.

Once at the venue, a two-story event space and seasonal restaurant with clean lines, white walls, and golden light, we opened the sizable wood doors.

"Hey! Thanks so much for coming," Ebony said.

"Hi, guys!" Marcus said. "We're going over a number of things with the manager, so would you mind helping your father put down the name cards? He has the seating chart."

Jamie and I dutifully walked over to Dad, who greeted us with that dazzling smile and seemed relieved to have some help.

"We got it, Dad," I said.

Once each table had guests' names anchored at each seat, I walked through the dining room to the foyer, where a number of black-framed photographs decorated the entryway. As soon as I saw her, I stopped, focused my eyes, and took a deep breath. In one, a picture of Mom and Ebony in Denmark, three months before I was adopted. They were dressed in white, swinging together on wooden swings suspended by blue rope along the banks of the very same Baltic Sea. It had been quite a while since I had seen this picture, and I was deeply moved that Ebony had decided to share this one among many. While Ebony didn't always share her feelings about missing Mom as openly as I did, I knew that she was heartbroken that she wasn't here. This was her way of including her and sharing her with all of us on this most special of days.

EBONY AND MARCUS stood across from each other on an elevated platform overlooking the Baltic Sea. Matteo and Linnea, Marcus's adorable niece, held white and red roses at their side. Ebony's olive skin and jet-black hair contrasted elegantly against her long-sleeve white dress with an ornate-lace front. But perhaps the most memorable aspect of the dress was that Marcus's mother had worn it on her wedding day many decades before. She had offered it to Ebony, who tried it on. Remarkably, it fit to perfection without a stitch of alteration needed, and Ebony adored it. While both of Marcus's parents stood at his side, Dad alone stood next to Ebony as he spoke.

"My wife and I had just completed the paperwork for an adoption. We had been married for about ten years then, but we couldn't have children at that point. So it took about four more months and the paperwork was matched with this little girl down in Cebu. We were informed on a Tuesday, flew to Cebu on a Friday, and were told we could take her back to Manila. Lying there in her crib, which was under the only ceiling fan in the orphanage, she was cute as a button, but my initial remark to Niki was, 'Don't you think her head is a little large for the rest of her body?'"

Everyone laughed. *Typical Dad comment,* I thought with a smirk. I glanced over at Yael, who was similarly amused.

"Niki shot me an exasperated look and said something like, 'Steve, all babies look that way.' My wife passed away in 2001 while we were living in the Middle East and I know if she were here today, she would be so proud of our daughter."

I watched as Ebony's eyes filled with tears. I was thankful to be wearing dark sunglasses, which hid my pain that in this most sacred of moments Mom wasn't standing beside Dad to bear witness to her only daughter's wedding day. I looked across at Yael, who clearly was awash in sadness. The officiant read their vows. As Ebony and Marcus kissed, a thunderous applause filled the venue. Our two families had been joined.

We drank Italian wine late into the night, we socialized with guests from China, Tanzania, Jordan, Italy, Poland, Germany, and beyond. Matteo and Linnea enjoyed chasing each other up and down the stairs. Around midnight, as I was laughing outside on the terrace with Denice and Jamie, one of Ebony's friends from DC came rushing over to me.

"Your sister's been looking for you. She's on the dance floor and wants you to come dance with her."

I made my way to the indoor dance floor, where Ebony, surrounded by her crew from Washington, had been completely overtaken by Madonna.

"You look amazing tonight. I'm really happy for you and Marcus," I said as we danced to "Vogue."

"Thanks. I can't believe we're all in Sweden together at my wedding. Who could've imagined this?"

"There were a lot of places you could have ended up, but true. I never imagined you living in Sweden."

After "Vogue," the DJ shifted to Justin Timberlake's "Can't Stop the Feeling," and I raced out to the terrace to grab Matteo.

"Buddy, come dance with me and Ebie. One of your favorite songs is on," I said, taking him by the hand. Once on the dance floor, Matteo, dressed in dark-blue dress pants, a white shirt and suspenders, and a light-blue bowtie, took both my hands and started shuffling his feet in step with mine. It was the first time I had truly danced with Matteo at an event, and somewhere outside of our living room in Lauderdale. His smile lit up the dance floor and I began to giggle at the sight of my little boy swaying his shoulders and moving his hips surrounded by Ebony's friends from around the world. For the first time, I understood why so many years ago on Flint Road, Mom had giggled with delight as I danced with her. Over the years I've danced with many people. But never have I enjoyed a dance as much as I did on this night with my son.

Two days later, Dad, Yael, Ebony, Jamie, Denice, Matteo, and I walked together through the cobblestone streets of the old town of Stockholm: Gamla Stan. The medieval streets, a tight maze of pathways lined by thirteenth-century buildings, were filled with unique eateries and bustling shops. The seven of us sat down at a long light-wooden table at Mårten Trotzig, a traditional Swedish restaurant that came highly recommended. Our table was lined with appetizing fried herring topped with shredded butter and raw lingonberries, baked cauliflower, and full-roasted reindeer with butter-fried green beans and potatoes.

I leaned over to Denice, who was eyeing the food somewhat skeptically.

"Try it all. I promise you, it'll be delicious. Last year when I was here, Marcus's parents offered me bear pâté."

"Bear!" Denice repeated in a shocked tone.

"Bear." I smiled. "It was pretty good. I'm glad I tried it."

I pushed Matteo's beet salad toward him, which I was pleased he had such an affinity for.

"A toast to Ebony," Dad said, lifting his glass of Chianti. "Thank you for having us to your new home in Sweden and congratulations on your wedding." A melodic clinking of glasses ensued.

"I've had the most wonderful time," Denice said, looking around the table. Spending her entire life in Rotterdam, I don't think Denice ever imagined one day she'd be at her son-in-law's sister's wedding weekend in Sweden.

Ebony beamed. "I hope you'll all come back over the summers. Well, winters too, but it gets freezing here. If you come in the summers, we'll take you down to Marcus's family's home on the archipelago. I love it there."

I knew at that moment, with Ashoh and Grandpa no longer with us, that this northern European country would now become the new meeting point for our family. Over the years we would build new memories here in Sweden, a new place in the world to call a second home. Even so, I would never allow those memories of 30 Bernice Drive to leave me.

87

BACK TO SOUTH AFRICA

FIVE MONTHS LATER, MY EYES opened to the Florida sun streaming through our bedroom and I had only one thought: *We are going back to Africa today.* True to form, Jamie was already up and getting things in order. He had urged me to pack the night before, and I had. I walked out of our bedroom and glanced at the neatly placed suitcases that lined the walls. Matteo and Denice were buzzing around the house. After nine months of waiting, we had found out that we were granted a court date in South Africa and were clear to come get Emmanuel. It was January 2020. From my very first conversation with our social worker, Maureen, about this international program, *this* adoption process had taken four years.

"We are going to Africa today!" I yelled through the house.

"I know. I just can't even believe it," Denice said. She had spent a portion of her sixty-plus years on this earth telling others: "Well, I just have no desire to go to Africa." Now here she was—with her son, her grandson, and her son-in-law— thrilled at the idea of going to pick up her newest grandson. I wondered how the experience would alter her perception of the world, and I reminded her that no one leaves Africa unchanged.

This was, by far, the farthest that Denice had ever traveled.

In the early afternoon, our Delta 757 touched down at Atlanta Hartsfield Jackson International Airport, the world's busiest airport. Matteo enjoyed the high-speed trains that took us from terminal to terminal, and I smiled at how my seven-year-old boy took it all in stride. He was completely unphased by all the hustle and bustle of passengers boarding the train, bound for destinations around the world. I wondered where they all might be going. Seoul? Yaoundé? Lisbon?

As we stepped into the international terminal, I felt the rush that I had come to know so well as a young boy. Ebony, Yael, and I would run the international terminals of the biggest airports in the world, checking out all the destinations. We would often say things like, "Imagine if we were going to Tehran," or "I wish we were going to Antananarivo." Nothing excited me more than the idea of exploring the world, and luckily that feeling has stayed with me from my childhood.

As we neared our gate, I held my breath, waiting for the sign that I had hoped to see for four years. There, at gate E26, were the words that I had long imagined:

"DAL 200. JOHANNESBURG, SA"

I was joyous, reading the sign over and over. My marveling was quickly interrupted.

"Now why is that one engine spinning, I wonder?" Denice asked out loud.

"Mom, stop worrying about everything, it's normal," Jamie told her.

"Hard to imagine that thing can stay in the air for that long," Denice followed up.

Denice was an extremely nervous flyer, this I knew. I had spent years bringing her up to both the Washington and Fort

Lauderdale towers to explain how it all worked. I had emphasized how much safer she was in an airplane than a car, but none of it seemed to resonate.

"It's a triple seven, Denice, it's been doing this for years," I teased her. Matteo cracked a smile, knowing his grandma's penchant for worry.

THIRTEEN HOURS ACROSS the North and South Atlantic and we were now nearing the coast of Africa. With breakfast finished, I went over to Matteo and Denice's seats to see if Denice would like to stay in the window seat for arrival or prefer to swap with me and sit with Jamie. Since this would be her first time seeing the African coast, I understood completely if she wanted to stay in her seat, but if she wasn't dying to sit at the window, I happily would. She graciously agreed to go sit next to her son. I moved Matteo into the window seat and plunked myself next to him.

There it was. The first sight of the African coastline: Namibia. My heart began to beat faster.

"Look, Matteo, we're over Africa now, that's Namibia. Guess what?"

"What?"

"Many years ago, when I was just a bit younger than you, Grandpa took me on a white-water rafting trip down the Orange River in Namibia."

"Was it fun?" Matteo asked.

"It was amazing, buddy. We raced through the rapids for three days. Maybe one day, you and I can do that together."

I had promised Dad that day in our yellow raft that I would always remember our trip together. I had never forgotten it.

As we crossed into Botswana, dirt roads weaved for miles through the barren landscape below. I remembered the day as a boy when I had gone back with Mom to the remote school she had taught at. Those Botswanan women had jumped all over her jubilantly, in disbelief that she had returned so many years later. And finally, as I glanced between our GPS point on Delta's world map and the ground below, we crossed from Botswana into South Africa. I leaned over to Matteo and whispered, "We made it, buddy."

Delta 200 touched down at O.R. Tambo International Airport after fifteen hours of flight. I wondered what our little guy, just two and a half years old, might be doing at his orphanage now in the late afternoon. Surely, he was unaware that his new family had landed and his entire life was about to change. Tonight would be his last night at his orphanage, the only place he had ever known.

Once clear of Passport Control, bags retrieved, we met our driver, Messina, a stocky middle-aged man with a kind-hearted smile, in the main terminal. Messina's car service had been arranged by our adoption agency and he was used to picking up families arriving to adopt. I opted to sit next to him upfront in his spacious white van. As we cruised from Tambo destined for Morningside, he shared his experiences of picking up other families and getting to know them throughout the stay. He also told us how he'd been happy to be selected to drive in Michelle Obama's motorcade when the former First Lady had made a special visit to the country. Messina was lovely. I looked back at Denice, who was soaking it all in. We came to a stop light—or *robot*, as the South Africans call them—just outside of Alex, a large township. Denice's eyes followed the many young South Africans now making their way back to the township after their day of work. I wondered what she was thinking

Soon our van came to a halt as we pulled up in front of a luxury condo building, Masingita Towers, the place we had booked for the next six weeks. We checked in and were taken up to our condo on the ninth floor. Upon walking in, our mouths dropped. Beyond the pearl-white dining room decorated with hints of light gold was a staggering balcony facing northwest. The orange sun gently melted into the horizon. It was an extraordinary welcome back to Africa.

"GOOD EVENING, my name is Thabani, I will be serving you tonight," he said, his rich, deep voice and charming African accent resounding.

Jamie and I gave each other a glance, then continued staring at him. I wondered if Denice found him as attractive as we both did. His black skin contrasted so beautifully with his smile, and that voice—I wanted him to read the telephone book to us over dinner.

"Thanks so much, nice to meet you," I offered back.

"Where are you joining us from?" he asked.

"We just arrived here from the United States," Jamie said. "We landed a couple of hours ago."

"America? Wow. Welcome to South Africa!" Thabani said, flashing his smile.

And with that, he set off a multicourse dinner that was absolutely exquisite. Bowl'd, the restaurant in Masingita Towers, was every bit as incredible as the reviews we had read. The expansive earth-tones dining room was bordered on one side by an outdoor argileh lounge and on the other by a refreshing pool that was home to inviting tables situated in the shallow end. A lush garden surrounded the pool. On the third side, an open kitchen was filled with smiling cooks moving rapidly. And finally, a golden-brown framed bar ran the length of the restaurant, serving up creative drinks that were being hustled from bar to table.

"Denice. It's your first night in Africa. How does it feel?" I asked. "Can you believe you're actually here?"

"No, I can't, actually," she said with a cute laugh. "It's hard to imagine. But I'm so happy I came."

In the distance I saw candles flickering in the dimming light of the restaurant. Thabani was headed in our direction with a slice of cake. I smiled at Jamie, who I knew had arranged it. As Thabani placed the slice in front of her, Matteo's eyes grew big.

"Happy Birthday, Grandma!" he said, transfixed on the little flames.

Denice was suitably surprised. She put on her glasses and took a moment to quietly stare at the candles.

"I know what she's wishing for!" Matteo yelled out.

"What, honey?" she asked him.

"You're wishing for another grandson," he exclaimed. Denice smiled at him lovingly. She put her arm around Matteo, made her wish, and blew out the candles.

We thanked Thabani. "Dinner was incredible," Jamie said. We had been up for close to thirty hours now since leaving Lauderdale and it was visible on each of our faces. We made our way upstairs to our condo. Jamie and I slept in one room and Matteo and Grandma in the other. We faded into darkness.

88

PRINCESS ALICE ADOPTION HOME

"ARE YOU READY TO BECOME a big brother?" I asked Matteo as we climbed out of the car.

"Yes," he said, nodding his head confidently.

"Your whole life is about to change, buddy," Jamie told him, grasping his hand.

"You'll forever have a little brother to go through life with," Denice said.

I looked over at Matteo. He was beaming with excitement.

Anna and Lungile, our social workers, led the way. Princess Alice Adoption Home sat in the hilly neighborhood of Westcliff, surrounded by lush plants. A red-brick pathway took us to a modest forest-green home with white trim and big wooden doors. Through our long four years of compiling paperwork and seeking government approvals, this is where our little boy had been living for two and a half of those years, since his birth.

We were put in a small playroom and asked politely to wait. I looked at Denice, Jamie, and Matteo. I thought back to the moment Dean had handed us Matteo as a newborn. Now Matteo was standing ready to receive his little brother. I heard the creak of the door. It slowly pushed open. I gasped upon seeing his face. High in Anna's arms, Emmanuel's extremely large, dark, intensely magnetic eyes that we had stared at in pictures day in and day out slowly scanned the room with hesitancy. He was dressed in a red cut-off shirt, blue shorts, and some cool leather boots. In each hand he carried a small bag of chips.

"Ema, say hello," Anna requested, smiling at him.

He was silent.

"Hi, Emmanuel!" I said, my voice breaking in disbelief that he was actually, finally, in front of us.

"Hi," Matteo added, standing right next to where I was sitting on a wide wooden bench.

Anna placed Emmanuel on the floor.

"Let's go give Matteo his pack of chips," she whispered to him. With Anna gently nudging him, Emmanuel walked up to Matteo.

"You guys have gifts for each other," I said, still unable to pull my eyes off of him.

As he gave Matteo a pack of chips, Matteo gave Emmanuel one of his stuffed animal elephants in return. In that moment, they became brothers.

"Thank you," Matteo said, ever polite.

I slid down the wooden bench, inching closer to Emmanuel. "Hi, buddy," I said in a soft voice. I gently took the chips from Matteo's hand. "What are these? Are these your favorite?" I asked.

No answer.

I slid closer to Emmanuel and put my hands out, palms facing him. He handed me his pack of chips.

"Do you want some chips?" I asked.

Still no answer.

I carefully opened his bag, pointed it toward him, and offered him some. Instead, he took the bag out of my hand and then stood there almost motionless, chips in one hand, elephant in the other, staring into the bag of chips, the only thing familiar in a moment that I'm sure completely overwhelmed him.

"Okay, I'm going to sit on the floor," I said with a laugh, realizing that he might be more comfortable if I were on his level. Matteo followed me onto the blue carpet. We plopped ourselves down next to Jamie, who was all smiles. As soon as he saw us sitting, Emmanuel turned away from us, faced a wall that was home to artwork created by himself and his friends, and proceeded to focus away from us.

"Can I grab some of those toys?" I asked Lungile, who was watching with a grin on her face from a chair nearby.

"Yes, I was just going to say that," Lungile said, motioning to the wall of balls and wooden toys behind Jamie.

I came back with two green balls.

"Bouncy balls!" Matteo shouted with a big smile.

"Emmanuel," I tried. "Here, Matteo, try to give that to him," I suggested, thinking that he might feel more comfortable connecting with Matteo first.

He continued to face away from us, nervously looking at the wall. I grabbed a box of toys and brought them down on the floor behind him. Nothing.

"That's Ema for you," Anna said with a laugh. We all chuckled. I loved that the moment was real. It was real life, not a movie. Here was this adorable little boy who had spent two and a half years living with his friends. Now he found himself standing in a room surrounded by four strangers, staring back at him with their hearts full of love. We had waited for him for four years. He had known us for less than four minutes.

"Let me fade away and see what happens," Anna said, leaving the room.

"Emmanuel," I heard Matteo's little voice pop up, trying hard to engage him. Still, he focused only on the wall.

Jamie got up, towering high above all of us, and walked over to Emmanuel, picked him up, and sat down in a chair. Emmanuel, still quiet and still holding his chips and elephant, seemed skeptical but content. We gave them some space and watched on as Emmanuel's eyes seemed to focus on our faces.

Jamie started to gently rub his back. He looked more relaxed now. I could see his face clearly. His eyes were the color of dark chocolate brownies. Piercing. Focused and knowing. His hair appeared a bit longer than in the pictures we'd seen, still curly and black. Matteo and I slowly made our way over to either side of Jamie and Emmanuel, and for the first time, our little family was four. Denice smiled, taking it all in from her chair across the room.

"Are you happy you came? I mean, to the orphanage and to see where he's been living?" I asked her.

"Yes, *so* happy," Denice replied. "He's so cute. I can't believe we're all here together." I was glad she had made the decision to join us.

"Hi, buddy. I'm Daddy. And this is Dada," I said, pointing to Jamie, who still had him protected in his big arms. "We've waited for so long for you." Matteo was over Jamie's shoulder. "This is your big brother, Matteo." Emmanuel's eyes followed my words from face to face.

Emmanuel glanced at the door a number of times, undoubtedly hearing the voices of his friends, who were all having lunch just down the hallway. Jamie walked him over to the window and Emmanuel pointed outside. "Do you want to go outside?" I asked. He began to whine.

I left the room and looked for Anna, who soon was making her way toward me.

"Anna, Emmanuel is pointing out the window. Can we take him out there?" I asked, expecting her to say yes.

"I think this is your cue to leave," she said with conviction.

"Leave? Leave the orphanage with him?" I asked. We had been here for less than an hour.

"Yes," Anna said.

Just as we stepped through the doorway we had first entered, a middle-aged woman with blond hair approached.

"Sorry, the Gogos want to sing a song to Ema. Is it okay? Can you come back?" she asked. I knew *Gogo* meant *grandmother* in Zulu.

"Of course!" I said, delighted that we would be able to see the Gogos: the women who had cared for him since the day he arrived at the orphanage.

We were led into a big nursery, and my mouth dropped. There, standing in front of us, was the *entire* orphanage. All of Emmanuel's little friends stood in a line waiting to bid him farewell. Ten or more Gogos and orphanage volunteers stood before us, and without any prelude, the most captivating African choir-like singing began. Accompanied by a rhythmic clapping, these resonant South African voices rose through the hallways of the orphanage. They continued singing and harmonizing as Jamie rocked Emmanuel from side to side, and Emmanuel's eyes moved around the room, taking it all in, his face full of wonder and amazement at the celebration of him.

I wondered how many times over the past two and a half years had Emmanuel stood where his friends now were, watching a family arrive and take one of their friends away forever. I looked down at the faces of his friends. There were so many stories here that I knew we'd never know. Soon, the song came to a close. As the last notes rang out, a cascade of Gogos and volunteers rushed to Emmanuel.

"We love you. We will miss you, Ema! Bye bye, Ema!" they all exclaimed, grabbing his face and planting kisses all over him. Emmanuel thoroughly enjoyed it. We were getting a window into the exceptionally affectionate life he had been living these almost three years while we longed to be with him. I looked across the room toward the wall and there was a tall white woman with longer reddish-brown hair bawling in the corner. She looked at me out of the corner of her eye, her eyes swollen and red, clearly happy for Emmanuel but trying to shield her sadness at his departure. I wondered what her connection to Emmanuel was, how long she had known him. I wanted to engage, but the moment completely didn't allow for it. Sometimes that's the way it is with adoption: your child has a past that, as their parent, you may never know about.

With Emmanuel safely in Jamie's arms, we stepped out of the front door once more, and I looked back at the orphanage. I wondered how Mom and Dad had felt years before when they had taken me out of the Jayamani Malnutrition Center in Sri Lanka. Had they felt this exuberance combined with a tinge of guilt; had it been as unexpected to them as it was to me now? We were taking Emmanuel away from everything he had ever known and putting him into our world.

On the car ride home, Emmanuel sat quietly in Jamie's lap, staring out the window at the passing cars. We had been told by our social workers at Spence-Chapin in New York City that the children of Princess Alice had mostly spent their life in the three rooms of the orphanage and a small backyard. They were not used to the vibrance of a city and had rarely seen cars, crowds, dogs, or experienced loud noises. Denice, Matteo, and I sat sardined in the backseat next to Jamie. We all stared over at

Emmanuel, who seemed to take it all in stride, his bold eyes moving from sound to sound as pedestrians ran across streets and motorcycles came to an abrupt stop.

Once at Masingita Towers, we took him to our ninth-floor condo and sat peacefully on the floor with him. Matteo brought over some Legos for his brother.

"Here, Emmanuel. We got these for you," he said.

But Emmanuel wasn't having it. We watched as his eyes filled with tears. Then he walked over to the front door, pointed outside, and began to cry. It was heart-wrenching. I absolutely, without a doubt, felt as if we had just kidnapped him. And as I stared into his water-filled eyes, I knew instantly that he was begging us to take him back to his family at the orphanage. Princess Alice was all he had ever known. The twenty or so other children who lived there were his brothers and sisters. He had spent the entirety of life so far with them. Jamie and I looked at each other with pain in our heart.

"Let's at least open the door and take him downstairs to the garden," I suggested. "I don't want him to feel trapped in here." Jamie agreed.

Moments later, the five of us sat in the full green grass surrounding the pool and restaurant. We felt lucky to have the garden all to ourselves. With Jamie's long legs outstretched, Emmanuel sat on his lap facing his chest and didn't utter a sound. His eyes followed his brother as Matteo raced back and forth across the lawn. I occasionally reached out to stroke Emmanuel's leg, but I could feel his discomfort in me doing so and I stopped. I was glad he had immediately bonded physically to Jamie. Denice and I hung back and watched the newest member of our family take his new world in.

At dinner we chose to order up from Bowl'd to continue a

quieter environment. Matteo stood at his brother's side.

"Here, Emmanuel. Try some butternut squash ravioli," he said, loading up Emmanuel's fork and feeding him for the very first time. We all held our breath as he took his first bite. He chewed it up, swallowed it easily, and then looked at Matteo for more. Matteo obliged.

"He likes butternut squash!" Matteo announced proudly.

Then Matteo and I took turns feeding Emmanuel butternut squash and black rice. With each bite he seemed to chew faster and eat ravenously.

"I'm so happy he's eating so much. Hungry little guy," Denice said lovingly.

While he never said a word, I could see in our little boy's eyes that over dinner he had relaxed slightly and seemed less scared and more observant. When we asked him a question, instead of saying no he would tilt his head gently onto his left shoulder to indicate his answer. It was immediately endearing. I wondered what his voice would sound like and I hoped in the coming days he would allow us to hear him. At bath time, Matteo leapt eagerly into the luxurious tub. Emmanuel looked at it in fright, anxiety building within him.

"Let's not worry about a bath for him today. He's been through a lot," Jamie said. I agreed completely.

That night, Emmanuel fell asleep between Jamie and me. We stared at our little South African boy, snoozing between two perfect strangers. He was indeed an incredibly brave person. I looked out the window at the city lights below and wondered where his birth mother was. I knew that she had been born here in 1993, the same year I lived in The Gambia. While I had sat in my second-grade classroom at the international school, a little girl had been born at the bottom of the continent. I could never have imagined that one day she would grow up and give birth to a little boy whom I would then raise. Would she be happy today, knowing that her baby boy had finally found a family? I hoped so. And with that, I fell asleep next to her son, who had somehow become our son.

89

THE FICUS TREES

THE NEXT AFTERNOON, EXACTLY TWENTY-FOUR HOURS after we had met Emmanuel, Anna and Lungile came back to Masingita Towers to see how we were all doing. To our surprise, Emmanuel wouldn't look at either of them. They tried to engage him, but he refused to interact. Instead, he clung to Jamie's chest, buried his face in his shirt, and began to cry. I was shocked. I had fully expected him to run to them as soon as they set foot in the condo.

"This is actually a great sign," Anna said. "He's bonded with you extremely quickly and he sees us and thinks we are going to take him back to the orphanage. He knows he doesn't want to go back there. The kids all have different reactions, but occasionally we do see this reaction and it's the best-case scenario."

The little boy who had pointed to the front door in a plea to go back twenty-four hours before now wanted nothing to do with them. I wondered what had gone on his head in such a short time to make him feel like life with strangers after one day was potentially better than his few years as part of a group at Princess Alice.

Over the next several days, the little boy who we had been

told was serious and quiet showed himself to be completely the opposite. One day as he was trying to decipher which toys were his and which were Matteo's, he pointed to a car on the ground and said, "Ema's," his tiny index finger pointed to his protruding belly. His voice was innocent, sweet, and came out with an adorable thick Zulu accent.

Ema. My mind raced back to the orphanage. Anna had walked into the room and said, "Ema, say hello," and we hadn't caught it. When he wouldn't look at us and instead found comfort in the artwork on the wall, she had said, "That's Ema for you." And when we had been blessed with the choir of Gogos' voices bidding him farewell, the first words of their emotive song were "Goodbye, Ema." How had we missed it?

"That's right, buddy. That's *Ema's*," I said. It was his tacit way of showing us that he had slowly become more comfortable with us, and he was telling us who he was. From that point forward, we called him Ema.

In the mornings, we would sit out on our balcony overlooking Johannesburg, drinking coffee. Ema would yell out, "Birdie!" as birds soared by our window to his new world. We told him how much we loved South Africa and how we had waited so long to be with him. Afternoons were spent by the pool, Matteo and I braving the freezing water. It was so frigid that once we jumped in, we both agreed we couldn't feel our legs after the first minute. Every pool time was accompanied by a virgin mojito for Matteo and a gin and tonic for me. The G&Ts were presented in large crystal glasses, stuffed with an assortment of berries soaked in the Western Cape's Inverroche Gin, a gin originally from Cape Town and made from fynbos botanicals. And perhaps the most charming aspect of the drinks were the kind hearts and smiles of the people preparing and serving them, whom we grew to love.

With black hair reaching just above her shoulders, gorgeous smooth dark skin, and a radiant smile, Lindiwe would always arrive with something pleasant to say. As tall as Jamie, handsome, with large eyes like Ema's but decidedly not South African in appearance, was Patrick, who waved from across the restaurant and kept a good eye on us. I later learned he was from the Democratic Republic of Congo. And Busi, an intellectual man in early forties who was working on completing his master's degree. Busi enjoyed talking with us, telling us how his sister had moved to Atlanta years ago, and asked us what the United States was like. And of course, Thabani, whom we'd see more often at dinners, but who raced around the dining room to say hi even if he wasn't our server. They all reminded me of the kind and heartfelt South African spirit that my housekeeper, Grace, had embodied as she spread butter across my cut knee. It was woven into my childhood. Now these four were making the world a better place, three decades later.

As Ema and Matteo made their way through the garden at lunch or through the restaurant at dinner, the staff very quickly took a liking to them. They would come over to give the boys high fives. Recognizing Ema as one of their own, they would often accompany their clasp of hands with "Hey, boy!" which always seemed to energize Ema. But outside of the waitstaff, others such as maintenance men or landscapers caused Ema some discomfort. He would hug us tight and with grave concern say in a half-whispered tone, "Uncle!" His eyes would follow them as they further manicured the gardens, fixated on their presence. I remembered Ebony and I being taught to call all our parents' male friends "Uncle" as a child, and so it wasn't foreign to me. But his whispering and hesitancy at the sight of these

"Uncles" was. We were later told that Ema and his friends at the orphanage had very rarely ever seen men. The only men who they came in contact with were repairmen, and so when one of these mysterious "Uncles" would surface, the kids would find it fascinating and run to say "Hello, Uncle" or hide behind the only world they knew while daring to whisper "Uncle" out loud at the man as he fixed a broken kitchen faucet or the like.

DO YOU REMEMBER Sally Bates? The Sally who in 1989 helped Mom get our story in the hands of journalists after Mom was told I couldn't take part in gymnastics class? In 2016 when Jamie, Matteo, and I had traveled back to South Africa, I had tried to find her. I googled her. I looked through social media. Nothing. I remember leaving South Africa that year and wishing I would have found her. Just months before we traveled this time, I came across a picture of her sons, Christopher and Jonathan. I decided to make one more attempt. This time I found Christopher, and he instantly connected me with her. I wrote her and her husband, Terry, immediately.

> *Sally and Terry, I hope this email finds you doing really well. I looked for you both years ago when my family and I came to South Africa for holiday. How are you both? I'm so happy to be in touch with you. I can remember your house well. I remember Mom used to bring us there often and you were always so gracious and warm to myself, Ebony, and Yael. I would love to come see you soon, as we will be coming to South Africa as we are adopting our 2.5 year old baby boy from Johannesburg.*

Within twenty-four hours I had heard back from Sally:

Dear Garon, We were delighted to get your email yesterday and look forward to seeing you again after all these years and meeting your family. Sorry you weren't able to track us down on your last visit! At first glance the attached picture will not mean much to you but these two ficus trees were given to me by your mother when you left Flint Road. She didn't want to give them to the people who bought the house and insisted that I should have them. They have moved with us twice and on our last move had to be repotted. I was so sorry to hear about your Mum. It was a huge shock when I read your Dad's letter.

Ficus trees? I raced down to the bottom of the email to see the attachment. Tears welled in my eyes. Mom had created flourishing gardens in our homes around the world. I stared at the picture of the two ficus trees. It was so hard to imagine that somehow as three decades had gone by, Sally had continually nurtured the trees Mom gave her, allowing them a long life.

And so, on a Saturday afternoon, seven months later, I opened the large gray double doors to our condo at Masingita Towers, and there stood Sally and Terry. Her eyes scanned my face and mine hers.

"Right, hello!" Sally said in her mixed English and South African accent.

"So great to see you," I said, hugging them both. We were all so much older now and they looked at me the same way I look at Tina and Jay's sons each time, unable to believe that they have now transformed into adults. We spent the evening down at Bowl'd retracing old times. I asked about South Africa in the 1990s after we'd left, the turn of apartheid, and the return of Mandela. They asked of Dad and how it had been in the aftermath of Mom's death. The suggestion was made that Ema try ostrich.

"Ostrich?" I asked.

"Yes, ostrich, it's quite good," they said. "It's actually an extremely lean meat, very healthy," they offered.

And so we ordered Ema a plate of ostrich. He devoured it, his little hands shoveling piece after piece into his mouth. Matteo, the family vegetarian, stared at him in disgust. Denice, Jamie, and I all tried ostrich as well. It was absolutely divine.

The next day, Sunday, Sally and Terry invited us to their house for Braii. Braii is the equivalent to being invited over for a barbeque in the United States. The five of us arrived at their retirement community on the outskirts of the city. It was a relaxing and well-designed village of individual homes with walking paths winding through restful gardens that housed a community center and a restaurant. As we stepped out of the car and into their home to greet them once more, I felt a swirling in my stomach. I was excited and yet nervous to see the ficus trees. In all my planning of returning to South Africa, it never crossed my mind that I would get to see trees that Mom had once planted.

They invited us out into the back garden and there in giant pots framing the edge of their terra-cotta patio were two strong, healthy ficus trees standing almost six feet tall. I walked over quietly and touched one of the leaves. Its glossy texture slid between my fingers. Then my hands followed onto its branches and I rolled my finger over the trunk. Mom planted these so many years ago here in Africa and they were still living today. I knew Ashoh would have loved this story of her little girl planting trees around the world and having them live on for decades.

They felt like a metaphor for Ebony, Yael, and I. She had taught us so many things, even how to live without her, and we had managed. To cross the world three decades later and to find them unexpectedly, it gave me a warmth and a reminder of what is possible in this world. A world that often feels so big, and yet is so connected. Still now, I think of those two ficus trees on Sally and Terry's patio. I think I always will.

90

HOME

"I HAVE REVIEWED YOUR FILE and everything is in order," the magistrate stated in her black robe. "I am now able to finalize the adoption of Emmanuel. You both now understand that you are fully responsible for Emmanuel's safety and well-being?"

"Yes," Jamie and I said in unison.

"And are you willing and able to care for Emmanuel for the rest of his life as his parents?"

"Yes," we said, smiles creeping across our faces.

"Wonderful. By the power invested in me by the Government of South Africa, I now finalize this adoption. I've asked that his last name be conferred to yours. Please take care of him and bring him back to his country one day so he will know where he came from," the magistrate said, looking warmly at Jamie and me.

"We absolutely will," I said. I looked over at Ema, sitting quietly in Jamie's lap.

The magistrate and social workers got up to leave.

"Wait. Is it possible to get a photo with you?" I asked the magistrate.

Our social workers looked uncomfortable at the suggestion

and glanced repeatedly between the magistrate and the three of us. Perhaps this wasn't customary in South African adoptions? For years I had looked at my own photos outside of the courthouse in Sri Lanka the day I was adopted. Mom in her baby-blue-and-white dress, holding me proudly, admiring her new son. Next to her stood the matron of the orphanage in a lavender-and-white saree. I've always wished Dad was in the picture too, but he, of course, was taking it. I wanted this moment captured forever for Ema.

"Sure," the magistrate said calmly.

We all lined up against the door of her chambers and the magistrate's assistant took the photo of us. I wondered if they knew that decades later Ema might be looking at the picture of them, very much the way I still reflect on mine today.

We called Dad later that evening at his home in Italy. He stared lovingly at his South African grandson through his screen. The choice he had made to encourage Mom to move to the bottom of Africa years before had set the path for all this. I was extraordinarily grateful to him.

Denice's time with us in South Africa had come to a close. I was so appreciative that she had traveled thousands of miles to see the country of Ema's birth and of my childhood. The four of us walked Denice downstairs to get into the car that was patiently waiting outside Masingita Towers.

"Thank you for this adventure," she said, hugging Jamie and me. "I'll never have another birthday present better than traveling here to South Africa with you guys to get little Ema."

She turned to her two grandsons.

"I love you, Matteo," she said, tearing up and holding Matteo tight. "I'm going to miss sleeping with you every night. I'll call you when I'm back home."

Then she knelt down to Ema. "Goodbye, Ema. Grandma has to catch a flight back to the United States. I'll see you there very soon, little guy. I can't wait to have you over to my house. I love you."

As Denice waved from the window of her car, I thought back to that spring day at the MLK Memorial in Washington. I had spilled the beans that afternoon surprising her with the news of a new grandson in the coming months. I doubt back then that she would have ever imagined herself at the southernmost point of Africa eight years later hugging a second grandson. Yet again, it reminded me how truly unpredictable life can be.

ON A SATURDAY morning after much anticipation and excitement, Ebony and Marcus touched down at O.R. Tambo International Airport. They had flown from Stockholm to London, and then transited the continent of Africa overnight, arriving into Johannesburg in the late morning.

"Ebony and Marcus just landed!" I yelled in the direction of the boys.

"Yay! Ebie's here!" Matteo shouted and Ema copied, as was becoming the norm. An hour or so later we rushed downstairs to the rectangular water feature that framed the entrance to Masingita Towers. Ebony and Marcus pulled up in their Uber. They got out of the car and smiles gave way to their sleepy faces as they hugged the boys, Jamie, and me.

"Welcome back to South Africa," I said to Ebony as I hugged her. "How does it feel?"

She looked around, "Strange actually, but I'm so happy to be here," Ebony said, grabbing Matteo's hand. Their eyes quickly found their way to Ema.

"Ema, this is Aunt Ebie and Uncle Marcus," I said.

"No! Don't want!" Ema shouted defiantly and tucked himself closer into Jamie.

Unaffected, Ebony and Marcus just waved at him and we helped them carry their bags to the elevator, up to the ninth floor, and into the condo, where they, too, marveled at the view. We had biltong, a South African jerky, and chilled glasses of South African white wine waiting for them.

EBONY HAD NOT been back to Africa for twenty-eight years and I could see the pain and wonder in her eyes as we drove back to Parkwood and turned onto Flint Road. We stepped outside the car and walked up to the house. I watched as Ebony's eyes instantly filled with tears. I knew what she was seeing.

I looked over at Matteo and Ema playing near the driveway. I remembered bouncing out of the house to climb into the silver Suzuki for school. That little Sri Lankan boy could never have imagined that one day, many decades later, a little South African boy would find safety in an orphanage just ten minutes away, and eventually become his son. I looked at Jamie, who was gazing up at the jacaranda trees that anchored the sidewalk out front. What a journey we had been on together over a decade. I had told him many years ago over our first non-date in Washington of this home; of this life in Africa that had crawled into my heart and never let go.

At night, once everyone else had gone to bed, Ebony and I stayed up, staring out at the star-filled night sky.

"I'm glad you came. How exciting to be back here together after all these years," I said. "I wish Yael could have been here with us."

"Me too. It feels amazing to be in South Africa again," Ebony said. Then she paused. "Garon, Mom would have been really happy, you know?"

"I know," I said, looking into her eyes.

"I've never been able to show Marcus any of our life before today," Ebony told me.

We sat together in silence.

JAMIE, MATTEO, EMA, and I boarded Delta 201 destined for the United States.

We sat in four seats, side by side. As the airplane taxied to the runway, I closed my eyes and imagined that day in South Africa in 1992, when my six-year-old self, with legs dangling off the edge of the seat and no idea what journey lay ahead for me, had turned to Mom and innocently said, "Mom, why are you crying?" I saw her face, felt her tears, and heard her voice. Then, with the roar of the engines, I opened my eyes and grasped Ema's hand in one and Matteo's hand in the other. As the plane started its takeoff roll, I looked down at my sons, tears welling in my eyes. I kissed Matteo's forehead and then leaned over to Ema. I ran my fingers along his and then leaned down to his little ear.

"I will bring you back to South Africa one day," I whispered. "I promise."

While I may never have answers about Sri Lanka, and why I was left on the steps of that hospital in 1985, I have been given an incredible gift. I will likely never know what happened to my birth mother. Maybe I was stolen from her. Maybe she's still looking for me. Or maybe she made the extremely difficult decision to leave me on those steps, hoping someone would give me a better life than she could. Whatever happened, she gave me a chance at life, at love, of home, and unknowingly set me on a global journey very few people could ever imagine.

If by some chance she is alive in this world and still lies awake at night thinking of me, I hope she has found peace. It is my hope that she has been loved well by others and found love in the eyes of perhaps other children. Most of all, I hope that somehow she knows that however I left her arms, I survived, I'm okay, and I am deeply grateful.

And as for Mom and Ashoh: I will forever carry those two in my heart as I continue to travel this world.

ACKNOWLEDGMENTS

To my English teachers at the international schools: Vanessa Sanyang, Janice Nauman, Joyce Kasim, Vicky Jalamdeh, Rebecca McDaniel, Molly Van Cleave, and Jay Kuhlmann, I have such affection for you. At an early age, you encouraged me to question language and taught me the connectivity that is derived from storytelling. It was a privilege to sit in your classrooms.

Thank you to my good friend, high-school acting buddy, and now ACS Amman English teacher (makes me so happy) Nadine Zeine, for being my fact-checker on Jordan. I've never forgotten our win in Lebanon, senior year. My sweet cousin Jessica Nelson: I'm appreciative of our many discussions and fact-checks on Luling, thank you.

Theo Padnos: I hope to meet you one day. (Read his memoir, *Blindfold*, the story of his captivity at the hands of al-Qaeda in Syria from 2012 to 2014.) I read your memoir while writing mine, and you inspired me beyond words with your courage, resilience, and affability. I've written a long note in my copy of *Blindfold* to my sons: *Matteo & Ema: I read this book in 2021 when you (M) were 8 and (E) 3. Very few people in the world have experienced what Theo Padnos did—and somehow he survived it. If ever there is a story of survival and resilience, it is this. I hope you both will read his account one day. I spent time in Syria with Grandma Niki and Grandpa, Ebony, and*

Yael, in the early 2000s . . . we can't visit now, but I hope in your lives, when safe, you will travel to Syria.

Nicole Tung: There are many extraordinary photojournalists in the world, but there is something especially distinct and enthralling about your work. As I wrote this memoir, during breaks I found myself walking over to your photographs of Iraq and Syria that proudly hang on the walls of our home and staring into them, drawing inspiration. Your bravery has given the world a window into these conflicts. These victims have faces, names, families, and dreams. Thank you for bringing them to us.

Yael, Dad, and Ebony: Thank you for fielding my many emails, calls, and texts in Wyoming, Italy, and Sweden when I wanted to verify certain dates and gain insight into conversations. We have seen a lot, lost a lot, loved a lot—together.

I am the luckiest guy around to have, as my editor, the exquisite Heather Sangster. Heather, when I first read about your career, I never imagined it possible that I would be granted the opportunity to work with you. Somehow, the stars aligned. You understood my writing immediately—its intersectionality of culture, love, race, and identity. Through our innumerable revisions you managed to always keep my voice. You shaped this memoir immeasurably. Now, I look forward to our friendship.

To my husband, the other father to our sons, and my best friend, Jamie: Thank you for taking this ride with me. We have so much more of this world to see together.

And finally, Mom: When I was growing up, you sat with me for countless hours forcing me to read my writing out loud. "Garon, read that again. What are you missing?" "Honey, what's a synonym you could use instead?" You made it clear that we needed to learn to speak thoughtfully and communicate effectively. I often felt you were sitting beside me as I wrote this memoir. Your grandsons talk about you often. They call you Grandma Niki and I smile each time your name leaves their lips. Sometimes they walk into our living room and talk to the silver urn holding your ashes. Matteo and Ema will carry your legacy forward.

LETTER TO NIKI

The following is the complete letter that Dad read to Mom, at her funeral in Luling, Louisiana, in April 2001:

My Dearest Niki,

I begin this letter, the saddest I will ever write, in a haze of tears as I gaze from the cabin of the plane that will carry you to America for the very last time. I'm thankful that no one is sitting next to me; it makes it easier to believe that you are still here with me, as you have been through so many other journeys. I will be your guide on this one as you have been mine so often over the three decades of our life together.

I left our house on the hill outside of Amman at 7:15 a.m. on this, a Tuesday morning. Jon Lindberg was with me, along with the driver and expediter from the Embassy. Asma, our neighbor, was just leaving with her kids, heading for school. They waved, subdued by sorrow, bidding both of us goodbye, though you were already at the airport, waiting for me.

As we drove away, Jon commented on how green the garden looked, that oasis you created in the desert, greener now for all the rain we've had so far this year. His comment and my thoughts of rain reminded me that it was raining just two days ago, on Palm Sunday, the morning that you left us all. I descended the wet steps of the hospital that morning with no hope left for your recovery and faced with the dreadful duty of having to tell the kids and your parents. Randa, who was with me at that time, lamented "The whole world is crying, crying for Niki, my best friend."

Our plane has just left the runway and the Spring-greened desert is falling away below.

Since then, of course, the world has indeed been weeping, through emails, phone calls, hugs and kisses, and other gestures of support from every corner of the globe. There would have been even more had I had the time to go through your old address books. Still the word spread fast and far. I speak of these and other events of the past two days so that you might have an extra measure of comfort, or maybe it's just for me.

Nani and Angie called three times from Chicago; Andy and Judy from Virginia; Nalin, Annette and the kids from Sri Lanka. Primrose and Sarath were still unaware of the tragedy when I left but I am sure that another email or call will come from Colombo soon. Fiona emailed from the tiny North Atlantic island of Isla, just about the time that Jonathan, who just happened to be in town, came over with an entourage from USAID, including Toni, Roy, Jamal and Jon.

As I mentioned earlier, Jon took me to the airport this morning but that was the easy part. He and others at the embassy, as well as many Jordanians, have worked miracles to get you on this plane so quickly and with dignity. Kim and others at the consular section helped Jon move a mountain of paperwork. Mouna and her husband Iskandar, who you never met, took time from his precious vacation to tap their contacts with the Royal Jordanian Airlines, both in Amman and in New York, to make it happen. And of course, Tupo, herself recently recovering from a personal loss, was ever present, and little Ryan did his part with prayer.

Ambassador Bill Burns took the time out of his busy schedule in Washington with King Abdullah, to personally call to express his sadness and that of Lisa and their children. A note also arrived later from the Office of Queen Rania.

Mark, our Peace Corps buddy from yesteryear, with whom we tromped the wilds of Moremi Game Reserve and many other spots in Africa, called from Indonesia along with his wife Jo.

Even people you didn't know but who knew of you, like Malith in Colombo and John Nittler and his team in Bolivia, called or emailed their sorrow. John and his team down there are saving miles and miles of tropical forest, something that you would have loved and respected. Jesse called from Tucson, and David called from New York and responded quickly in recent days to set up the Knowledge Pipeline, a non-profit to continue transferring knowledge to the poor in a way that you gave life to as a Peace Corps volunteer in Botswana in 1973.

Derek and Marcel called from Cairo as did Yomna (overflowing with tears) - Muhammad sent his love too. Howard and Maria, among our lifelong friends from our Philippine days, called from Tennessee and will be coming to Louisiana along with one or two of their kids. Nancy and Rodney and Dolly tuned in from down the Bayou, Tommy and Connie Mars from Boutte, and Robin and Gerhard from Colorado. Countless others from south Louisiana have called your parents or mine to express sympathy and to do whatever necessary to help.

I caught Ewag and Edith on their cell phone as they were crossing the Italian border, but the line was bad, and they called back later from Croatia, their holiday there with their son, Hannes, now in shambles at the sad news. Remember how we, two Americans and two Germans, hitchhiked across The Kalahari Desert and then, for good measure, polished off the Namib Desert, both in a few days, just to see the seals on the Atlantic coast of Southwest Africa. And remember our later vacations together in Eastern Bavaria, Czechoslovakia, and the south of France.

Sam Morris sent an email this morning from Palestine. He said that you were his favorite dinner partner and he thanked me profusely for "forcing" him to come to our house for last Thanksgiving's Dinner. You will recall that he was having a significant low period at that time. He was thankful for that last memorable opportunity to be with you.

I heard from Sam Pintz in Hawaii. He said that his wife, Stephany, "lost it" when she heard the news and is still trying to work up the courage to call back - I am sure she will. David emailed from the farm in Safford, Arizona sending love on behalf of Tanya, Ben and Jessica. Tanya is travelling and they will call later.

By the way, we just left the coast of Palestine, heading out over the blue Mediterranean. I thought I heard the pilot say that our route would take us over Turkey. Remember how our fondness for that place came about when I returned that morning loaded down with bread, honey and yoghurt at the end of our two-week trek across Pakistan, Afghanistan and Iran, all Muslim countries at the time in the midst of the 1975 Ramadan fasting period - boy, were we hungry.

Yesterday, Jim put out word of your passing to friends from our Jamaica days, and then called Pauline at the Jamaica Exporters' Association in Kingston. They are all devastated at the news.

Indeed, the last few days have witnessed an outpouring of love, of shock and disbelief, of sorrow and grief, of offers of support, of memories, of concern for me and the kids, of prayers and endless sentiments for you. It would embarrass you to know that you have been called a saint by more than one person. Others have said that you changed their lives, that you were a devoted mother and wife, that you were a great light in their lives and a cherished friend. You were described as 'my best friend' by many and said to be 'a woman whose religion was a compassion for all her fellow creatures.'

That last line was from Catherine, but the list of tributes continued from Randa, Chris, Pat, Hamed, Lamia, Louise, Lena, Karen, Madeira, Diana, Asma, John, Andy, Jim, Muhammad, Ali, the Burkhardt's, Dan, Joe, the entire Abdul-Jabbar clan, the Bataineh and Sharp families, Suraj and Molly, and many others swooped into provide support for the kids and me, bringing love, remembrances, food, and other types of support.

Abdo, Kelly, and Thomas came over to keep us all engaged. Sara, and JoJo came over for Ebony. Amy, Francis, the two Samers, Patricia, and Yasmine came over for Garon. And many others for Yael. All came in the hours leading up to our kids' departure a day ago for Louisiana, a trip that they decided they could do on their own while I waited for your paperwork to be cleared to enable this trip.

Of course, in Arab tradition, the entire office wanted to see us and express their condolences in person. Of course, they had already done so by email, including some who are no longer with the project, or even in the country, like Rihanna, who called from Toronto, and Tonya who emailed from Bahrain. Rest assured, all in the office miss you, and are praying for you and our family.

Likewise, the entire American Community School of Amman went into mourning, dazed and disbelieving as the announcement was made at the general assembly on Sunday morning. And the teachers rallied to produce homework and reading assignments, which I understand the kids are diligently pursuing as you would expect them to do.

Ebony, Garon and Yael, exhausted and teary eyed, flew ahead in the wee hours of Monday morning. They flew through Frankfurt, then on to Dulles International outside of Washington, three troopers who turned down offers from Randa, Chris and others to accompany them back to the states, preferring to handle it together. Chris commented to me yesterday how proud you were of their ability to cross the globe on their own.

At Dulles International, they were met by Peter, Dan and Heather from headquarters, who took them under their wing and out for a meal. Of course, everyone at Chemonics is, as per usual, rising to the occasion with every manner of expression of love and support, from Scott and Tony at the top, right on down. Andy, Judy and their daughter came out to the airport too and spent time with the kids before they flew on to New Orleans.

Of course, your mom and dad, and brother Mike, met them in New Orleans and have been keeping them in good spirits despite the severe pain of this situation. I am sure that waves of your old friends will turn the house upside down - you can picture that, can't you? I talked to your mom this morning before I left. She said the kids all seem to be holding up well.

Back home, in south Louisiana from Galliano to New Orleans, people are moving in all sorts of ways to support your parents, Mike and our children. The list of people providing food, hugs, kisses, remembrances, and every manner of assistance is too long to relate. And I am sure this will escalate after we arrive.

So, in short, my love, it has been an international response beyond imagination. It is just as you would have liked to have seen it - Americans, Jordanians, Palestinians, English, Polynesians, Peruvians, Sri Lankans, Filipinos, South Africans, Germans, Greeks, Canadians, Scots, Afghans, Indians, Egyptians, and many other nationalities, all coming together to aid a family in need, as you did so often. People from all walks of life, high and low, all races, creeds, and colors, confirming yet again your own special gift for touching all kinds in this world of ours. I know that this would especially make you feel good, and that you would want your parents, Mike, your grandmother, aunts, uncles, cousins, nieces and nephews to know that such could be possible and that such can, indeed be the way of the world. We'll all continue to work for that as you have all the days that I have known you.

We are over Europe now where so many of your friends live. Eventually I'll reach all of them with the news.

By the way, our dog, Jazzbee, is fine. Chris, Dan and Kelly are taking care of her while we travel. Suraj has the fish, the turtles and the rest of the house under close supervision. So, no need to worry - everyone is being fed.

Of course, I know that the main thing on your mind is the kids. They are working hard to handle this in their own individual ways, I'm sure. Again, friends and family have been great in helping with this but most important has been the solid foundation you laid in their personalities. The tears will come and go, probably for a very long time, and so will the anger, but they will handle this like the champs that they are. So, do not worry about that.

We will do things differently now, I am sure. Take more time to say "I love you", not only because we feel the need to do that more often, but because it may be the only silver lining in all of this that we can see at the moment.

We're landing now in Schiphol airport, in Amsterdam. Remember that great Christmas season that started here in 1988, when, after flying in from Sri Lanka, we put our luggage in a locker there, and hopped on the train to France, not knowing where we'd end up, but feeling confident that we would like it. The only thing we planned for that side-trip, well to be more exact, that you planned, was that we brought along Christmas presents for Ebony and Garon. A couple of days later, as snow began to fall on Christmas Eve, we found a cozy little inn in the village of Clervaux, northern Luxembourg.

There we had a wonderful time making ornaments to decorate the makeshift Christmas tree we crafted from a branch of a real Christmas tree found near our hotel. We tied it to the window of our room and created ornaments from all sort of odds and ends to decorate it. Outside, beneath our window twenty Santa's dressed in red and white soon appeared out of the blue to sing Christmas carols in the courtyard. And later, after a long and wonderful dinner, the kids rushed back to the room on hearing the ringing of reindeer bells that you had packed along with the gifts which they found beneath the tree on arrival in the room. Thank you for that wonderful memory.

It is fitting that we should be coming back across the Atlantic via Amsterdam, since we also stopped there in 1998 in route to our new life in Jordan. It was brief, but fun, filled with great sights, sounds and laughter and, of course, you leave many friends in Holland too. It seems that no matter where we went, a Dutch person ended up as a friend. I recall your marveling at their linguistic skills, their mutual global interests, and their love of flowers.

By the way, when I boarded the plane, there were orchids sitting on my seat. I wedged them into the back of the seat in front of me, their purple and white petals, and dark green leaves, reminding me of how much you loved flowers, how beautiful you and your gentle nature were. Their petals are pointing in all the directions you took me in our life together, how you enriched me with exploration and adventure, with diversity and curiosity. Those benefits are evident in our children, in their ability to deal with every manner of person and problem, anywhere. Again, thank you for that.

I think now of one of your favorite family pastimes together, watching movies, and of one of our favorite films, <u>Parenthood</u>, which portrayed Steve Martin wrestling with the trials and tribulations of his family and life in general. I remember the gentle grandmother philosophizing about it all, recalling her first roller coaster ride, which must have occurred 70 years before. Even through all those years, she remembered being struck by how something like that could be at once so fun and exciting and at the same time, so terrifying. "The ups, the downs, the turns, the rushes of terror that following the slow, determined pulls uphill. Just like life itself," she said. "Some people like the merry-go-round," she added, "but that just goes round and round. I prefer the rollercoaster," she concluded as she walked off leaving Martin dumbfounded.

You also preferred the rollercoaster. Why else would you have taken me, and later the children, on the wild ride of the last 28 years. It was you who dragged me into the Peace Corps and began our life abroad. You thought of crossing the Great Okavango Swamp in a dugout canoe in 1974, 8 days of wonder in some of the wildest territories on the African continent. And I venture that you may well be the only "white" woman to have made that trip in that way or in any way.

It was you too who had us thumbing our way through Frelimo Guerilla territory down through central Mozambique on the very day the Portuguese freed that colony and the rest of their overseas holdings. It was you too who wanted to hitchhike a 1000+ miles across Southern and East Africa to Dar es Salaam to catch a ship to India rather than simply flying home after our Peace Corps assignment ended in Botswana in 1975.

Remember Mrs. Richardson, the English grandmother who befriended us on that ship, who had lived all her life in India, and was then just returning from her annual visit with her son and his family in England. She introduced us to the virtues of the Indian rail system, which would later carry us more than 7000 miles across the landscapes of northern India. It was there, while backpacking towards Mt. Everest, that you had your first brush with death - altitude sickness at 14,000 feet, just the two of us, surrounded by villagers who did not speak English.

Later, on the same trip, it was you who insisted that even though we were low on health, energy and money, that we go to Kashmir to rest on a houseboat on Dahl Lake. If you had not done that, we would have never discovered what would become our favorite spot on earth, nor would we have, over the span of the next 13 years, seen all of the children of Gulam Nebbi Rata grow into young adults, and have weddings and kids of their own.

It was you who took us on that final overland leg back to America - two weeks of buses, trains, and other people's cars from India through Pakistan, Iran, Turkey, Bulgaria, Yugoslavia, Austria and Germany, a trip that today can no longer be accomplished today without huge personal risk.

Remember the smiles on the faces of the motorists whizzing across the Austrian-German frontier when they came upon us, two skinny backpackers, standing beside an 8 Lane highway holding a sign which bravely read "New York". Remember the professor from the University of Berlin, who began laughing so hard when she saw the sign that she just had to stop and pick us up, even though her car was probably the smallest of them all and could barely fit our packs and us. When we finally squeezed in, she said that we had made her day. Of course, she had made ours too.

It was you too who, as an apprentice anthropologist, left me behind in Manila, to venture into an area of the Philippines so remote that it could only be accessed by helicopter, all because you wanted to study the habits of one of the most primitive tribes of hunters and gatherers left on earth, the gentle Agta people. It was there you had another brush with death and had to be Medivac'd out six weeks later with malaria, dengue or some such fever. But you made such a hit in the short six weeks you were there that an Agta woman name her newborn daughter after you. Who else, in just six weeks, would move someone to name their child after them?

And as each of our own children arrived, you did not retreat to the safety of North America. No, you kept us on the road, and instilled in Ebony, Garon, and Yael not only great memories but a wonderful appreciation of other people, rich and poor, around the globe. I remember Ebony, age 5, hobnobbing with the cook on our five-day trek around the Kathmandu Valley in Nepal, and Garon torturing one of the Sherpas who insisted on carrying him because we could not make enough time each day if Garon insisted on walking on his own. And remember how we lost the kids for a couple of hours that one day, only to later find them in the care of the Sherpas? And of course, Yael was just 14 days old in South Africa when he went on his first safari. You even got your mom to go on that one.

It was you who kept the kids calm as we went through the Indian invasion of Sri Lanka in 1986, and the rioting and looting that followed, which brought Army helicopter gunships so close to the roof of our house that our kids crawled beneath the bed and began to cry. You kept them cool-headed too during the coup d'état in the Gambia in 1994 while I was out scrounging food for us and the rest of the American community, even for the Ambassador's wife, who at the time had thirty Peace Corps volunteers at her house eating everything in sight. After all of that and more, how ironic it is that your final departure would come at the hands of one of the better medical practices in the developing world and through one of the simplest of its procedures.

So it was, over three decades, that you took me and the kids on that proverbial roller coaster across a huge swath of the world, managing risk after risk in pursuit of our greater potential:

- *To imagine the promise of a little girl from Cebu, Philippines, who because she seldom cried and consequently rarely got the handling necessary to develop muscle tone in her neck, was unable to hold up her head even though she was 5-months-old.*

You knew instinctively that she had potential to one day stun us all by independently reading her first sentence two-weeks before her 3rd birthday. Even then, you could envision her as a beautiful, accomplished 17-year old high school junior who last year, as her school's ambassador, led her team to the Model United Nations in The Hague, Holland, and addressed the opening assembly of 2000+ students assembled there from around the globe. Because of you, she felt sure that she had something in common with all of them.

- *You saw potential too in a malnourished Sri Lankan boy, barely a month old after having been left on the steps of a hospital. He would grow into our handsome 15-year-old Garon, multiple gold medal winner in international competitions in comic and dramatic duet acting among schools in the Eastern Mediterranean, a leader in student government, and though only a 9th grader, one of the most popular kids in the entire American school.*

- *You also took the risk at the advanced age of 43 to carry and endure the pain of delivery of our youngest, Yael, ten years old, leading scorer on his Little League soccer team, accomplished set drummer and confidant of all the boys, and I might add all the girls, in his 4th grade class, a distinction that according to his teacher no one else can claim.*

All three, now displaying a dignity, grace and confidence beyond their years, travelling a third of the way around the globe by themselves, while simultaneously dealing, each in their own way, with the tragedy of your parting.

We are now airborne again, leaving Amsterdam for New York, and as I gaze from the window out at the blue Atlantic, it is a glorious day, bright sky above patches of cloud. I am surprised at the traffic I see out there, at least four other jets at various altitudes, and several ships and boats all heading in different directions. People going places, doing things that some might say with sadness that Niki can no longer do, going to places that she can no longer go to, having impacts that she can no longer have. I would reply that shall not be the case:

- *You will forever be in the lives of your grandmother, your parents and brother, and my parents and extended family, your sons and daughter, your aunt and uncles, cousins, nieces and nephews, and the friends from your life here in Louisiana and around the planet.*

- *You will continue to travel, for Ebony, Garon, Yael and I will sprinkle your ashes all around the world where you will continue to contribute to the constant renewal of life for all time, starting with the rivers and bayous of your beloved Louisiana and then on to places where we have already been or you have wanted to see since the day you were born.*

- *Through our kids and theirs and their futures, you will forever enrich and enjoy life. I will be your reporter, filling you in on their graduations, their marriages, their sons and daughters, their successes and failures - their roller coasters. In each of those experiences you will have played and will continue to play, a part.*

We are now over the snowy hills of Eastern Canada, homing in on JFK. You and I have avoided JFK for years, but perhaps it is fitting to have you return to American soil via JFK, for it was from that airport 28 years ago to the week, that we first embarked abroad on the journey of a lifetime.

Your hair was longer then, your eyes never brighter, flaming with excitement. Remember how hours later, on the other side of the Atlantic, we all rushed to the windows to get our first glimpse of Africa and imagine our lives ahead. It was a heck of a ride, my love. Thank you for taking me along.

When we get home, we will have a ceremony in your honor, a celebration of life. I may read this letter if I can get through it. People will come and they will hear about a little girl from Luling, Louisiana who for some reason went out and touched the world; a woman barely 5 feet tall, but fearless, who became a giant in the lives of many. She did not have to do this; she probably did not intend to. She never sought an ounce of credit for what she did. She just did it, nonetheless.

She took grade schoolers in Botswana, deemed by other teachers to be mentally challenged, and she taught them to read. Years later, through her sex education classes, she saved lives in South Africa, then riddled with HIV and AIDS. Through her ever-present smile and gift for friendship, she changed the lives of adults and children alike in the cities, towns and remote jungles of the world. She showed the world by example the best that Americans, indeed that all human beings, can be. And she still found time to profoundly change the lives of three children and me.

For this, Niki, we thank you more than words can ever say. We apologize and ask your forgiveness for not telling you this enough when you were alive, for not saying I love you more, for not helping and hugging you more, and at least in my case, for being unable to do whatever it would have taken to prevent your death.

We will all face the future with you in our hearts. I promise to raise our children as you would have, though I know no one could quite do it as you would. I will resume vigorously the things you bugged me about constantly - eating right, getting exercise regularly, working less and spending more time at home. And yes, I will stop drinking coffee and start drinking tea. I will never stop loving you and what you represented. Thank you for letting me be part of your life.

All my love, Steve

SOCIAL MEDIA NOTE

For those of you who enjoyed *You'll Always Be White To Me* and would like to see photographs and videos of the many people in this memoir, please check out #YABWTM on Instagram.

Should you want to use the hashtag on your own social media, please feel free to use #YABWTM. I'd be delighted to see and hear from readers.

Finally, I'd be grateful for your review of the memoir on Amazon.

IG: @garwade

#YABWTM

#GaronWade

Made in the USA
Las Vegas, NV
28 September 2021